BARBARA CARDY founde
Buff" and "The Hot Sp
erotic anthologies. She lives with her husband and children
and a host of animals in a cosy cottage in the lush English
countryside.

Introduction

Barbara Cardy

It was an absolute thrill – in every sense – to put this book together and I sincerely thank everyone who took the time to send me their erotic confessions. I had to be ruthless to whittle it down to finally present you with this collection of well over 100 of them. Some will make you laugh, some will lift your brow, some you will find downright outrageous, but all unfailingly arousing.

I have deliberately not ordered them into categories to seduce you into each confession with an open mind, perhaps into genres previously overlooked.

Whatever your kink you will find it here from a good old-fashioned spanking to bondage, from solo to foursomes, from water sports to . . . well, I will leave that for you to find out. Let's just say that there are oodles of wonderful smutty themes!

WINDOW ON LUST

Sara, Sheffield

The story I'd like to tell you about took place on my honeymoon, and even though it all happened six years ago, I still get incredibly excited when I think about it now.

Because neither my husband, Mark, nor I have got much in the way of close family to speak of, we decided to go off to Las Vegas to get married, just the two of us. We planned on the full works, with an Elvis lookalike performing the ceremony and a couple of people pulled in off the street to be our witnesses. We booked into a suite in one of the plushest hotels on the Strip, so we could spend time in the casinos and take in one of the shows. Mark even suggested that we visit one of the lap-dancing clubs there, so we could really find out why the town was known as Sin City.

As it was, we had our moment of sweet sin without ever setting foot in a strip joint. Our suite was on the seventeenth floor of the hotel, and when we arrived we couldn't believe the view we had. It was night time, when the place really comes alive, and we stood looking out of the window, over the dazzling expanse of neon night below, and wondering what adventures we might be about to have.

The following afternoon, we got back to the bedroom after the wedding, giggly and high with excitement. Mark had ordered a bottle of champagne, which was waiting for us in an ice bucket, and he popped the cork as I stood admiring the view of Vegas, spread out so far below us.

"It's beautiful," I said, taking a glass of champagne from him as he came to stand behind me.

"And so are you, Mrs Smith," he said, pulling me into his arms and kissing me. "Especially with confetti in your hair."

His hands moved lower, caressing my breasts through my clothing. I could feel his cock starting to stiffen and press against my buttocks, and I knew how much he wanted me. I was getting horny for him, too, so I didn't object when he began to unzip the short cream lace dress I had worn for the ceremony, letting it fall to the ground so I stood there in my skimpy and ultra-sexy bridal lingerie.

My nipples peaked as he rolled them between his fingers, and I reached behind me to unzip his trousers and free his cock, then stroked the thick column of flesh to full hardness.

"Take me to bed, Mr Smith," I murmured.

"No, let's stay where we are," he said. "I've always wanted to fuck you up against a window and, after all, it's not like anyone can see us all the way up here, can they?"

It sounded like a deliciously kinky idea, and I didn't object as he shuffled me forwards until my palms were pressing against the triple glazing. I have a good head for heights, and I stood there, gazing down, as Mark stripped me out of my bra and panties, leaving me in nothing but my wispy flesh-coloured stockings, suspender belt and three-inch heels. His hands were all over my body, squeezing my breasts together before delving between my legs to play with my juicy pussy. My clit pulsed, eager for his attention, and when he began to gently bite my neck, I closed my eyes and gave in to the sensation. When I opened them again, I couldn't believe it – I was staring straight at a man who stood on a window-cleaning cradle, looking right at me.

"What the –?" I exclaimed, never expecting that someone would be riding up and down the side of the building. "Mark, stop it! We've got an audience."

To my disbelief, my brand-new husband just carried on with what he was doing. "Come on, Sara. The bloke obviously wants a show. Let's give him one."

He had to be joking, I thought, but no. One of Mark's hands went back to my tits while he used the other to frig me.

The window cleaner, who could only have been in his early twenties, with bleached-blond hair and a muscly body beneath the faded dungarees which appeared to be all he was wearing, just stood there with a sly smile on his face, enjoying the sight of me being so brazenly played with. The fact that I was practically naked while my husband was still in his wedding suit made the whole thing look that little bit more dirty, and despite my initial reluctance I suddenly found myself becoming really turned on at the thought of being fucked in front of this stranger.

I almost wished we could open the window between us, so our new friend could offer encouragement, or suggestions about what he'd like to see Mark do to me. Perhaps he could even reach inside, to pinch my hard nipple or even stroke my pussy and discover just how wet I was.

And then Mark was bending me forward, spreading my legs apart so he had better access to my cunt. Normally, he would spend a long time touching and teasing me, making sure I was ready to take his cock, but today we were in too much of a hurry for that and, anyway, the juices which were flooding my pussy showed I was more than ready.

As Mark's solid length began to slide into me, I saw that the window cleaner had got his own cock out and was stroking it as he watched us. It looked huge, with a red, swollen head which kept emerging from the tunnel formed by his fingers. I couldn't take my eyes off it and, as Mark began to plough into me with fast, fierce strokes, I snaked a finger down to my clit and began to rub myself, imagining what it would feel like to be filled by that monster.

All too soon, Mark's movements started to become jerkier, and I knew he was shooting his load inside me. I cried out and gave in to an orgasm so powerful it left my knees shaking as Mark sagged against my panting, sweating body. And then the window cleaner was coming, too, his white spunk spattering against the glass in tribute to us.

By the time Mark and I had recovered, the cradle had moved down to the next floor and the man was gone. We took the rest of the champagne into the bathroom and had a bath together, playing with each other under the water as we talked about the incredible experience we'd just had.

I don't know if there's anyone else who has had the first fuck of their married life in front of an audience, but if they have, I hope they enjoyed it just as much as we did.

ZIPPY'S FIRST DESCENT

Stephanie, Wiltshire

Just looking at the dress in the shop window made me feel horny. It still comes out with me on special dates, particularly if I think I may wish to allow the guy quick and easy access to my flesh. Made from a charcoal grey linen fabric, it has a long zip that runs all the way down the front. A small silver budgie ring hangs from below the V-neck, a budgie ring that begs to be pulled downwards. I even gave the dress a nickname, Zippy.

At the time I was teaching at a comprehensive school in a large market town. There was a fairly large group of us who liked to meet after work on a Friday for a drink, a good old gossip and some outrageous flirting. It was an ideal time to give Zippy her first outing. As I approached the pub entrance I lowered the budgie ring a few inches. A downward glance confirmed it was sufficiently low to let the men know I was wearing a push-'em-high bra. The man I ended up having sex with that evening was Ronan. He worked in the technology department and he spoke with a lovely gentle Irish accent. He was not the most muscular guy you would want between your legs, but he kept himself fit by playing squash and his skin was almost as soft as a teenage girl's. Needless to say I found him attractive and sometimes fantasized about him when there was no man in my bed to satisfy my needs.

This particular Friday I had caught Ronan looking down my cleavage and up my dress much more than usual. Not that I was complaining, you understand. During one conversation about women's knickers he even went as far as asking if I wore thongs to work. He was definitely getting frisky. I started to get interested in his interest in me.

"Of course," I replied as casually as I could muster. Everyone laughed loudly.

The topic of conversation eventually turned to prostitution. One thing led to another and us ladies enjoyed backing the men into a corner by forcing them to deny ever having paid for sex. A couple of them appeared to be lying, but Ronan's negative response seemed to be genuine. It was payback time.

"Why not?" I asked. "I bet you've happily bought women drinks in an attempt to get your hand down their knickers, what's the difference?"

He blushed and took a gulp of his beer.

I mirrored his action, smiled and looked into his eyes over the top of my glass.

As the clock approached the time when people usually started to drift away I noticed Ronan was only sipping his beer. Aye, aye, I thought, is he trying to be the last to leave? I slowed down my own consumption to ensure we were the last two sitting. It worked a treat.

"Can I get you a drink?" Ronan's soft voice betrayed a little nervousness.

I leaned forward and whispered, "Does this mean you're hoping to put your hand in my knickers?"

"I've always wanted to do that, but no, I'm just going to buy you a drink."

"Shame," I said, "but I'll have a pineapple juice anyway."

I think that was the moment I decided to take this as far as I could. I had no real plan but the little whore inside me wanted to continue down the "paying for sex" road. I shuffled my bum to raise the hem and expose a bit more thigh.

After Ronan got back I leaned forwards to take a sip of my drink, knowing his eyes would be able to see my tits bulging above my bra. "So how many drinks would you buy me to get a rummage up this dress?" I asked.

He gulped but then perked up and became noticeably braver. "Five," he said firmly and then grinned.

"Mmm . . ." Still leaning forwards I could just about see the crotch of his black trousers. I was unsure if the bulge was a natural fold or if he was stiffening up down there.

He leaned forwards so close my nostrils were almost overpowered by the smell of his freshly applied aftershave. "Do you want to do it?" he asked quietly.

Yearning to keep this going I got even bolder. "Let's say twenty pounds then. We could both stop at that large lay-by on the way home." My intention was to turn him on, but whatever effect it was having on him, it was definitely getting my juices flowing.

"Let's go one better," he whispered. "How about me getting a room at that new budget hotel by the motorway junction?"

I nodded and gulped down two large mouthfuls of my drink.

Ronan flipped open his mobile and tapped a few keys. "Enter your mobile number in there."

I took the phone and Ronan continued with his on-the-hoof plan. "You park up next to me and I'll go and see if they've got a room. If they have, I'll call you when I want you."

I didn't speak; I don't think I knew what to say. I just passed his phone back to him and then watched him get up to leave. It seemed like he was deliberately giving me enough time to back out if I wanted.

Twenty minutes later I was parked up in the hotel car park waiting for his call. I felt so nervous my stomach was threatening to call a halt to the proceedings. I also felt excited. In my fantasies I had often imagined walking through a swanky hotel lobby, catching a lift and gently tapping on a stranger's hotel room door. My make-believe client was always stinking rich and I always negotiated extra for anything more than a blow job. Somehow I also always ended up doing a striptease routine for the gentleman while he lay naked on the bed stroking his thick cock. This was not quite that dream scenario, but as I sat there, I definitely felt like a whore. It was time to apply some lipgloss; men like glistening lips.

My mobile rang. An unnamed mobile number appeared on the screen.

"Hello, Stephanie Escorts," I said cheerfully.

"How much for a fuck?" said a soft Irish voice.

The vulgarity heightened my excitement. "One hundred," I answered.

"How about anal?"

"Not with this girl, but I can give you the number of a tart who does." I hoped that negotiating over my arse was all part of the game, but I have to know a guy really well before I allow him to push it into my delicate back passage.

"Not to worry, room two-one-five." He hung up.

It was hard, very hard to walk through the small modern reception area without making guilty laden eye contact with the middle-aged woman at reception. Though to my credit, I did play the game; I courageously fought back the urge to raise my budgie ring up from the low position it had descended to back at the pub. I desperately tried to look like I knew where I was going. I was so pleased to see the lift sitting there with its doors open. As nonchalantly as I could, I stepped inside and pressed button two.

Ronan was sitting on a chair with five twenty-pound notes in a pile on the desk to his left.

"I like the dress," he said.

"I hope you like what's inside it more," I quipped as I leaned over to take the money.

His hand went straight up my dress and planted itself firmly on my crotch. This was not the way I usually liked sex, but then again, I had never got laid like this before. It felt scary and it felt exhilarating at the same time. As I stuffed the notes into my handbag I parted my legs a bit. The side of one finger pressed into my slit taking the thin strip of fabric with it. Now he knew I was not lying about wearing thongs for work; he also now knew how aroused I was. Suddenly two fingers hooked into the gusset and tugged them down to my ankles. He clearly felt he had bought the right to treat me badly. As long as he did not push it too far, that was fine with me. I had not gone there to be a good girl.

With my thong stretched out between my ankles his right hand went back between my legs and his left forefinger hooked itself through the budgie ring. He tugged it all the way down to my navel. Quickly he opened up the resulting long gash to expose my chest. He then started to take a bit more time. He gently caressed my pussy, occasionally moving up to stroke the carefully trimmed strip of pubic hair. I like to keep a neat but substantial bush above my slit. Ronan's fingers continued to caress and gently probe between my labia. His eyes drilled through my bra. I knew he wanted me to remove it but now we were moving into the stage where I took control. I made him wait; I wanted to be even wetter.

When I was sure his fingers would be almost dripping with my juices I unhooked my bra and pulled it under my tits. I dropped my eyes to check my nipples. I always like to know how I'm looking. They were nicely gorged. Ronan displayed his appreciation by slipping one finger deep inside me. While I was still standing there with my underwear displaced and my dress still on, he inserted a second finger and started to smoothly finger-fuck me. I indulged my client. Rarely did finger-fucking do much for me, I like to be fucked by cock, but I enjoyed the look of shear lust on Ronan's face. After all, he was paying, so if he wanted to squelch his fingers in and out of my hole, I had to let him.

I cajoled him into giving me what I love. "Why don't you bury your face in my wet pussy?"

"Get your kit off, lie on the bed and let me see it," he commanded.

I obeyed. Ronan leaned back in his chair and watched.

I shook my thong off my right foot.

Next I slipped Zippy off my shoulders and allowed her to slip down to the floor.

"Fucking hell, you look gorgeous!" exclaimed Ronan.

That was a little flattering, but then thankfully, sex does blur one's vision.

Leaning forwards I pointed my arms to the floor, my bra slid down and landed on my crumpled dress.

I almost kicked off my heels but decided to leave them on. This was a hotel, I didn't cherish the bedcover like I cherished my own. So I stepped over to the bed and climbed on board. As I rolled over onto my back and spread my legs like a good whore would, Ronan stood up and slowly undressed. His eyes locked onto my slit. I reached down and parted my lips a little to give him a glimpse of glistening pink I know men love. When I finally saw it, his cock was of typical length but it pointed higher than most and looked very solid. Despite his erection pulling them up, his balls still looked big. I momentarily thought about asking him to straddle my face and lower them into my mouth. How hard would he let me suck them?

In a flash his mouth was heading for my pussy.

"No fingers," I commanded as he nuzzled his head between my legs. He started slow and gentle in little circular motions around my clit. Only when I was even more aroused and my pussy was yearning to be mistreated did he start to firmly lick with the rough part of his tongue. Suddenly he started to alternate between delicately nibbling my labia and lapping at my juicy cunt. I hoisted my legs, took hold of my ankles and pulled them up towards my shoulders. His tongue responded to the invitation and pushed in as deep as a tongue can go. His nose ground into just the right spot.

It was now time to utter those two words every man loves to hear from a woman's mouth.

"Fuck me," I groaned.

He raised his head and stared at where his tongue had just been probing. I kept my ankles tight in my hands. I felt exposed, in my imagination he was looking all the way up my cunt.

As he climbed on top of me, I smelled that aftershave again. Then his cock pushed me open and drove in. It was just as hard and firm as it had looked. Ronan fucked me and he fucked me and he fucked me.

Once again I played the whore, or was it the real me? "Fuck me harder," I moaned loud enough to risk being heard in the next room. The thought of people listening to our humping added extra spice to the act. Straining to lift my head I watched Ronan's cock thrusting into me. He started to withdraw further. That is a sight I have always loved. His cock was driving into me; his shaft was dripping wet with my juices. I yearned to let go of my ankles so I could rub my bud, but I was a whore, I had to resist such urges.

"Slam me," I said, desperate for some extra stimulation. He looked confused.

"Bang into me. Bang hard against my pussy."

He got the message. The slapping of his balls against my arse was an unexpected bonus. Ronan was struggling to support himself. Eventually he solved the problem by grabbing hold of my shoulders. The weight of his body pushed my body into the mattress. He was getting rough. He was nailing me good and proper. I had no option but to drop my head back down and let my other senses take over. I closed my eyes and enjoyed every shove. I even enjoyed the pain of his nails digging into my shoulders.

The tension built and then the floodgates of orgasm opened.

"Fucking gorgeous," I shouted as the waves ripped through my lower body.

"Fucking gorgeous," Ronan groaned as he spurted his come deep inside me.

I could hold on to my ankles no longer so I let my legs drop down onto the bed with a thud.

"Shit, I was planning to come over your face," he laughed breathlessly.

"That would have been extra," I joked.

As I left the room I sensed Ronan expected me to give him back the money. Of course, I didn't, that would have spoilt the memory. If you are going to live out a fantasy, do it as close to the real thing as you dare.

LA VIEILLE FEMME

Brian, Stittsville

I'm a mid-twenties, single male with a healthy libido and a vigorous sex life. Until a few weeks ago, I exclusively fucked only young nubile women. Then an unexpected encounter changed my sexual preferences.

I was travelling on the TGV, the high-speed train, from Paris to Nice. After six months of intense work launching new internet software, I had a week's vacation and I intended to spend it inspecting the topless girls on the Riviera beaches. I looked forward to a week of hot sex.

The fragrance first alerted me to the woman. She checked the vacant seat opposite me then placed her shoulder bag on the table and tried to lift her heavy suitcase up to the luggage rack. At full stretch on her toes, she struggled with the case.

"Permit me," I murmured. Moving into the aisle behind the woman, I reached over her and pushed the suitcase onto the rack. Stretching up to reach the rack showed off her very provocative bottom and in the restricted space of the aisle I took the opportunity to rub myself firmly against it, feeling its ripe fullness through her skirt. The woman's reaction to my uninvited touch could have been very hostile, but, as she slipped into her seat, she gave me a quizzical smile.

"Thank you, Monsieur, you are too kind," she murmured.

The well-coiffed hair, impeccable make-up and manicured hands all signified an elegant woman. The scooped neckline of her top showed off generous breasts. I guessed her to be fortyish.

She took out a magazine.

"Madame travels to Nice?" I questioned innocently.

"No, Monsieur, to Lyons. I have been in Paris on business. And Monsieur?" she asked.

"I have a week's vacation in Nice."

"Alone?" she queried. When I nodded she smiled knowingly. "No doubt Monsieur hopes for some sexual encounters."

I was disconcerted by the directness of her observation, but replied truthfully. "Yes, Madame."

She opened her magazine and I began to read a technical report. I had trouble concentrating. The woman's perfume was seductive and I mused about her tempting rear. I glanced across at her. She was studying me, almost as if coming to some decision. Then she gave me a playful smile.

I felt her leg brush against mine then, very discreetly, her foot was placed on my seat, nestling between my thighs. Madame had slipped off her shoe and, beneath the small table separating us, had stealthily stretched her leg across the space between our seats. I looked at the woman. Her lips parted in unmistakable invitation and gently she nudged my crotch with her stockinged foot.

Our neighbouring passengers seemed to be dozing, so unobtrusively I stroked the sensuous arch of her instep and fondled the finely structured ankle. Beneath the table I stroked along her leg as far as I could reach, squeezing the well-toned calf. Furtively, through the sheer stockings, I massaged her manicured toes, separating and stretching them. Very deliberately, I pressed her foot against my crotch. With a knowing smile, Madame began to rub me. As her stimulation increased I pressed my burgeoning erection harder against her foot.

"Perhaps Monsieur would permit me to buy him coffee?"

I snapped back to reality, suddenly aware of my very obvious arousal. "I would be delighted, Madame," I replied.

She carefully withdrew her leg and slipped on her shoe. Sliding from her seat the woman proceeded towards the restaurant car. I followed.

Madame stopped outside the vacant *toilette* of the second car. She murmured, "I think this will do," then opened the door and stepped inside, pulling me after her. The *toilette* contained a toilet and a hand basin set in a vanity with a small mirror on the wall. The space was confined and we were squeezed together. Locking the door, Madame smiled at my bewildered expression.

"You appeared to appreciate my derrière, Monsieur, your foreplay with my foot was delightful and my foot massage has hardened your penis. So, Monsieur, are you willing to have sex with me . . . here, now? I am, of course, much older than you, *une vieille femme*, so if you find me too mature for your taste I shall understand."

I was stunned, disbelieving. I hesitated, but the woman boldly unbuckled my belt, unzipped me, slid her hand into my briefs and extracted my cock. Abandoning all caution I seized her ass, squeezing and kneading the soft flesh through her skirt.

"You are alluring, Madame, and I'd be delighted to fuck you. I hope I can perform to your satisfaction," I murmured.

She fondled my cock and smiled. "With such a fine penis, Monsieur, so big and strong, I'm sure you can. Think of me as the hors d'oeuvre for your week in Nice."

I pushed her against the door to grind my throbbing erection into the curve of her belly. Then, seizing her heavy breasts, I crushed the sumptuous mounds, feeling the pliant flesh through her top and bra. Madame played with my tumescent penis, caressing the shaft, fondling the glans with skilful fingers. In a frenzy, I pushed my hand up her skirt to probe between her legs. Madame gasped, pressing herself onto my fingers and I could feel the heat and dampness through her panties.

As we tore off our clothes, the fondling and groping in the confined space made us supremely horny. Stripped to her garter belt, stockings and high heels, the generous curves of Madame's voluptuous figure were fully displayed. She was sensuous and my hands roamed over her luscious body. I rolled her hardened nipples and then greedily sucked on them. Madame whimpered and responded by fondling my balls then began to pump my cock. When I probed between her legs and burrowed into her slit, she was already wet.

I turned her, spread her buttocks and jammed the hard ridge of my erection between them, grinding it into her rear. Holding her tight against my cock, I cupped her mons, stroking the luxuriant pubic hair, then probed lower to massage the hidden bud of her clitoris. Madame cried out and as her hips jerked under my touch the lush bottom rubbed my penis. The sensation was wonderful and I realized I was close to coming. But first I had to make Madame climax.

I sat her on the vanity and she had to hold on to the fixtures to steady herself. I put one of her legs over my shoulder and stretched the other along the vanity to spread her, so that by sitting on the toilet seat, I could study her private parts.

"Monsieur, you permit me no modesty," she protested.

I inspected the intricate folds and hollows and crevices, the distended inner lips and the wet, inviting orifice. The sexual aromas of the woman were intoxicating.

"None, Madame," I replied. "A woman as succulent as you has no need for modesty."

I caressed the soft thighs and above the tops of her stockings traced intricate patterns on the sensitive skin. Madame whimpered. I brushed my face into her thick pubic hair, breathing in the smell of her sexual heat, then opened her wide. Slowly I licked the shaved labia then sucked on the slippery inner lips, savouring the moist, pink flesh. When my tongue rimmed her orifice then pushed into her hole to lap the juices, Madame moaned. I drew back the hood to expose her clitoris. The little floret clamoured for attention and I wet the tip of my finger in her orifice before playing with the swollen bud, teasing it, rubbing it then squeezing it hard. Madame cried out and tried to close her legs. But I held them open and leaned forward to lick the hard little nub, caressing it with my tongue then sucking on it. The juices flooded out of her.

The flower between Madame's legs was now in extravagant bloom and its aromas filled the room. I began a rhythm, sucking at her orifice with my mouth, eating her inner lips, then using my tongue to play with her clitoris. She moaned in time to my stimulation and I increased the tempo and the intensity.

Her pelvis was rocking to my rhythm when slowly I inserted a finger into her vagina. Madame gasped and tried to seize my hand. But she could not retain her balance. I waited until she was steady again then eased two fingers into her. Madame cried out as I stretched the vagina, stirring parts deep inside her, exploring the moist walls of her passage to find her sensitive spot. When Madame gave a piercing shriek and her pelvis jerked off the vanity, I knew I had found it. I began to thrust my fingers rhythmically up her cunt. I alternated deep thrusts with stimulation of her G-spot and matched them to the tempo of my tongue on her clitoris. Madame's cries grew louder as her pelvis thrashed wildly, her bottom thumping on the vanity. Her climax was near.

"Put it in, Monsieur, put it in," Madame shrieked.

I stood up, raised her legs into the air, spread them as wide as possible and inserted my rock-hard penis into Madame's opening. She groaned as I pushed deep into her.

"No, no. I want to ride you," she breathed hoarsely.

She forced me down on to the toilet seat with my back against the wall. Then slipping down from the vanity she turned, presenting her luscious rear to me, straddled my thighs and positioned herself over my cock. Madame pushed its head into the mouth of her vagina and the juices flooding from her drenched us. I thought I would explode.

In one smooth downward motion, Madame impaled herself on my throbbing erection. Her cry filled the room. "Monsieur, you stretch me to the limit."

For several seconds she writhed on my cock then leaned forward to grip the edge of the vanity for support. I felt her thighs tighten as she lifted herself. Sliding up and down my rigid shaft, Madame began to ride. I seized her trim waist to lift her high on the up stroke then plunge her down hard to the root of my shaft so the full length of my swollen cock was thrust up her vagina.

After several slow, smooth strokes the tempo increased and Madame's ride grew wilder and more intense. Her bottom jiggled wildly to the rhythm and slapped against me as I drove her down into my lap. In the mirror I could see her breasts bouncing frantically. Her cries became a cacophony that filled the small space as the ride became frenzied. Up and down, faster and faster she rode until, in a final spasm, Madame climaxed. Her orgasm surged through her, consuming her in a paroxysm of wild convulsions.

Holding her above my lap, I plunged into her with all the power I had. My thrusts battered Madame's body, making the soft, ripe buttocks oscillate wildly. My furious assault drove her into a shrieking crescendo and Madame's cunt devoured my raging cock. Then, with a roar of release I exploded, erupting deep inside her, again and again and again. Like some feral animal we thrashed together in frenzied orgasm. I emptied myself into her.

Spent and gasping, we rested. Madame sat in my lap, my cock still clenched inside her. I fondled her breasts, stroking and squeezing them, playing with the swollen nipples.

"Monsieur was extremely fierce," she murmured.

"I hope I didn't hurt you, Madame."

"Oh no, Monsieur. But you took me with admirable penetration and made me come with great intensity. I had a delightful orgasm."

There was a knock on the door and a woman's voice said, "Have you finished?"

I now realized that the sounds of our lust must have been quite audible to anyone passing the *toilette*.

Madame said, "Oh, Monsieur, how embarrassing . . . to be discovered in flagrante delicto. We must leave at once. How disappointing, there's no time for post-coital play." She lifted herself off my cock and used the hand basin to wash off the juices splattered over her pussy and thighs. In the confined space I took every opportunity to again fondle her sensuous body as she dressed. Picking up her panties I said, "May I keep them, Madame, as a memento?"

"Oh no, Monsieur, it would not be respectable for a woman of my age to be without panties." Her reply was so incongruous that I burst into laughter.

To my surprise, Madame washed off my wet cock and, as I dressed quickly, said smilingly, "I hope it pleasures many ladies in Nice."

As we unlocked the door Madame observed, "The *toilette* will smell of our sex."

When we emerged several people were clustered around the door. They smiled and giggled and some even applauded. Madame blushed scarlet.

"Was it as good as it sounded?" one woman whispered.

Madame glanced slyly at me and murmured, "Oh yes, he performed outstandingly."

I too blushed.

Madame read her magazine, appearing serene and contented. I tried to concentrate on my report but it was difficult. Whenever I thought of our copulation, I became aroused again. As the train approached Lyons Madame slipped from her seat again and returned a few minutes later looking immaculately presented once more. When the train stopped I carried her case out to the platform.

She smiled at me. "I'm a happily married woman with a husband who keeps me fully supplied. But occasionally I enjoy harder, rougher sex. Then I want to be serviced by a young man with a big, aggressive penis. When you rubbed yourself against my derrière I thought you might be a suitable young man."

I was speechless. I had been seduced to service Madame's sexual needs. But after such fabulous sex, I had no complaints.

"Thank you, Monsieur, your performance exceeded my wildest expectations. I hope I was not too disappointing for you."

"On the contrary, Madame, you were a sensational fuck."

She blushed. "You flatter me, Monsieur." Extending her clenched fist, she whispered, "A gift, in remembrance."

I closed my hand to take her offering and she turned and walked away, pulling the case behind her. Aroused again by the view of Madame's provocative rear, I raised my hand to inhale the aromas from her panties.

I spent a memorable week in Nice. The topless girls were delectable and my cock performed valiantly. But, good though it was, the sex did not compare with my fornication with Madame.

I have Madame's panties before me now, a flimsy wisp of black diaphanous lace . . . feminine, revealing, sensuous. I fantasize the smell of her sex still lingers on them. Madame introduced me to the carnal pleasures of older women and I've fucked several more mature women since then. I revel in their softer, more voluptuous bodies and, although more demanding, I find their appetite for sex to be boundless. I'm becoming addicted to the erotic delights of *les vieilles femmes*.

SHARING MY WIFE THE BACK WAY

Martin, Hertfordshire

Not many men enjoy seeing their wives being screwed by another man – so I suppose I am a rarity, though I have to admit I do get something from this. Something I wouldn't have got unless I agreed to letting another man have her.

When I married Jeanne eleven years ago we were pretty much a standard, suburban couple. We had careers and more or less agreed we wouldn't have kids, though it soon emerged that we didn't have a choice as Jeanne couldn't conceive. Anyway, like a lot of couples we had plenty of sex in the first two years of our marriage but the frequency, and with it the intensity, fell away. When we did have sex it tended to be quick and simple. We were usually too tired and too stressed to do anything else.

After a few years I wanted to spice up our sex life though and I tried to persuade Jeanne to start wearing high heels and stockings when we had sex, but she was appalled at wearing shoes in bed so that more or less ended that idea. Jeanne also wasn't keen on stockings and her usual pale flesh-coloured tights weren't my idea of a turn-on. Sex, I should tell you, has to be in bed as far as my wife is concerned.

One day while surfing the net I came across a testimonial, if you can call it that, from a guy who had rejuvenated his sex life with anal intercourse. I was intrigued and the more I found out about it the more it appealed to me. Of course I reckoned Jeanne wouldn't be keen, but I had to try. And it was something we could do in bed. Introducing the subject however wasn't going to be easy, despite a mate of mine saying all he said to his partner was: "Fancy it up the bum?"

It worked for him but I was certain that wouldn't work for me. Then, while I was wondering how to raise the subject, Jeanne sprang a surprise on me. She said our relationship wasn't going anywhere and we needed to sit down and have a heart-to-heart. At first I thought she was going to tell me she wanted a divorce but it soon emerged she too wanted something "exciting" to happen in bed. Taking this as a cue I immediately blundered out my anal-intercourse desire and she stared at me as if I was crazy.

"I meant to say," she snapped, "I want another man." Once I got over the shock of that Jeanne added that while she loved me and didn't want our relationship to end, she did want to find out what it was like being fucked by another man.

It emerged that it wasn't just any man. One of her colleagues, Simon, had been making eyes at her at the office where she worked. He was a good few years younger than me and as he was in Jeanne's words "hot and ready", she quite liked the idea of seeing what he was like in bed.

For once I used my brain instead of refusing point-blank. I reasoned that she could just as easily have sex with Simon without me ever knowing and given her preference for sex under the sheets I said she had my permission to be screwed by him, but . . .

In fact, I had several buts, which I patiently listed. First of all, any sex had to be in our house and no more than once a month if it was to become a regular event between them. Second, I had to be there to make sure she was OK (I had no idea she wouldn't be anything but OK with this Simon, as he was hardly a stranger to her). Third, anything between her and Simon took place in our bed with me there.

"You want to be in bed when Simon has me?" Jeanne looked truly astonished. I think she was tempted to ask what kind of a pervert I was but I merely smiled, seeing the thought on her face but knowing she was unable to ask it given what she was wanting to do anyway.

I then added the final two more conditions, the first of which was she would have to wear stockings and high heels when he had her and last, but by no means least, I was to be allowed to screw her arse while he fucked her the usual way.

Jeanne looked thunderstruck. There was no doubt this matter she had raised with me wasn't a casual "I wonder if?" approach: she had very clear ideas that she wanted sex with Simon and had done for some time. Jeanne tends to let thoughts dwell for a while like that. I estimated that if she agreed to my conditions then it was a win-win situation. I didn't say that because she had to come to the thought herself.

It was one personality trait I had noted in my wife over the years we were together. When Jeanne says "no" straight out she means no, but whenever she is in doubt about anything she says she needs time on her own to think, and when she does that she usually comes round to the point of view I have. So when she said she needed time on her own to think, all I had to do was sit back and let her have that time. "As long as you want," I said.

It was a big decision for her, giving way to me on three things and though the underwear and heels in bed I could have easily surrendered if pressed I was keen to be in bed with them if only so I could go up her rear. I wasn't sure how I felt about another, much younger, man fucking my wife but I was sure I was willing to put up with it to gain the anal intercourse. And Simon having my wife once a month wouldn't be too bad.

This was a big thing for Jeanne to consider because she went to her mum's for a long weekend to think. I guessed, though I couldn't know, that she was no doubt seeking the advice of an old friend of hers as she came to a decision. I just hoped that Shelly wouldn't prove to be such a prude and be so horrified at any of what Jeanne told her that none of my plan would happen. I also figured she would call Simon up and test the idea with him. After all, if he wasn't happy with my conditions there was every chance it wouldn't happen.

I needn't have worried. Jeanne came home, dropped her suitcase in the hall and threw her arms around me. "Shelly and me went shopping, for some underwear I can wear in bed with you and Simon," she said as she hugged me. "And I have already spoken to Simon and he doesn't mind. In fact, he likes the idea a lot."

Then she paused. "But I have one request. If it's good, can we do it more than once a month?"

"We'll see," I said. "It depends how good you are between me and him."

It turned out to be very good between us. Simon is a good-looking twenty-two-year-old, and in a way I can see why Jeanne is attracted to him as he works out regularly. Jeanne's choice of underwear (or perhaps it was Shelly's influence) was perfect – a black lace suspender belt, charcoal stockings and black patent leather high heels – and I felt pretty aroused as I clambered into bed with them. I felt a little embarrassed at being naked with another man in the room but as he didn't seem to mind I resolved not to mind either.

Jeanne of course was in the middle and spent most of her time on her side facing Simon, alternating tender little pecks and longer, open-mouthed kisses with him having full access to all of her front. Jeanne's back was all mine and I carefully lubricated her back passage while she was in the throes of a particularly engaging French kiss and I soon had my finger replaced by my hard cock. I slid up into her bum just as Simon pushed his way into her from the front and I marvelled at both the way I felt his thick cock through the thin wall separating Jeanne's vagina and anal passage and the way my wife gasped. I really don't know if it was because of me in her rear or Simon in her front but she moaned like she had never done before as we fucked her simultaneously.

From my point of view at the back I missed kissing Jeanne and I suppose I was just a little jealous, but then I had what I wanted. It is slightly impersonal screwing someone from the back when their attention isn't on you, but I knew part of my wife's gasping and moaning was because of my cock in her rear. Simon was no doubt good, and I was too. I also tried to time my climax to match Simon's and though some practice is needed on that score I know we are going to get plenty of opportunity to try.

Once a month? More like twice a week at the moment, and Jeanne and I have even been shopping for more underwear for her to wear when she's sandwiched between me and Simon.

GETTING THE JOB

Kitty, Los Angeles

My name is Kitty Collins and I'm a "fantasy actress". That doesn't mean I work in porn. It means I'm one of those girls who do phone sex at the numbers you see in the back of the magazines. I'm really good at it, which is lucky since it doesn't look like I'm going to get too many other acting jobs in Hollywood.

Everything you think you know about Los Angeles is true, especially when it comes to the girls. They're all gorgeous, incredibly young and willing to do anything to anyone to get a part. I came out here when I was eighteen, but that made me almost too old already. And I was never beautiful; just cute. All my auditions were for the "comic relief" or the "best friend" or the "waitress who spills coffee" or something like that.

I've also got this voice. It's really deep. I like to call it husky and beg my agent to send me on auditions for sexy parts, but it doesn't work because, you know, cute. I've even had casting directors ask me if I'm really a man. That got me seriously pissed off.

The best gig I could get was a voice-over for an insurance company, which lasted long enough to get a SAG card, but after that, nothing. I wasn't making any money and I had to pay the rent. I know everyone waits tables eventually, but I am totally not waitress material, and all that left was finding something at the Beverly Center. Great place to look for celebrities, not so great for becoming one.

You can see where this is going. I'd always told myself I'd just give up the whole thing and go back to New Jersey before

I'd do anything as gross as being a hooker, but I knew a lot of girls who were working at the strip clubs, and somehow that didn't seem quite as bad, not like something I would actually do, just better than walking the streets.

My friend Morgan mentioned an opening at Hot Stuff. I was like "NO WAY!" until she pulled out a wad of bills and showed me how much she'd made that day in tips, so I asked if she'd call her boss and get me an audition. I told myself it was just for fun. Even if I were offered the job, I wouldn't actually take it. I just needed to prove that the gym membership wasn't a total waste of money; that I could still compete with the newest wave of silicon tits.

At least I could say I'd finally been on a stage in LA. I just hadn't planned on being nearly naked when it happened, smelling stale beer and bleach that barely covered up previous nights' puke. The walls around me were covered in red paint with zebra stripe stencils and the air vibrated with Bon Jovi singing "You Give Love a Bad Name".

I did my routine: dancing, swaying, strutting and performing unnatural acts with a pole, while desperately wishing that my personal trainer had been tougher about making me stretch and that I'd asked Morgan exactly how I was supposed to get my leg into that position.

She'd held my hand through the Brazilian and helped me pick out a G-string at Frederick's of Hollywood, but now I actually had to dance the dance. My sluttiest skirt and blouse were strewn about the stage and that G-string was the only thing between me and total nudity as I flaunted myself in front of an imaginary crowd of men, all of whom were dying to get their hands on me.

"That's enough. Get your clothes on and come down here."

It was better than "Don't call us, we'll call you," or so I thought until I found myself sitting at a small table waiting for a judgment from this kid who paid more attention to his cigarette than he did to me, even though my shirt was barely covering my tits. He let out two long streams of smoke through his nose like he was daring me to choke.

Jason Baron. He wasn't actually a kid, except I was old enough for twenty-two to seem pretty damn young. He definitely needed a shave and couldn't have gotten too much sleep before coming to see me. His hard grey eyes gave me the once-over, as if he hadn't been able to see enough when I was shaking my ass on the stage. Finally he shook his head and took a drink from the beer in front of him on the table.

"You're an actress, right?" His voice sounded like he'd spent the night yelling over the high-decibel speakers and smoking.

"Yeah."

"You can't act this stuff, you know. If you're up there thinking you're too good for it, they can tell. They'll either ignore you or try and drag you down to their level. Either way, I don't want you on my stage."

"Uh-huh," I muttered, trying not to show how much it hurt to be rejected for a job I didn't even want.

"Nice tits though. The body's good."

I actually considered thanking him.

"Have you thought about implants?"

Every time I didn't get a part.

"How old are you?"

"I'm legal."

"You were probably legal before I was born."

He started putting out the cigarette in an ashtray and then stopped. The eyes suddenly focused and narrowed. He'd just heard my voice and for once in my career, it wasn't the end of the interview.

"Have you ever done phone sex?"

I shook my head.

"You still want a job?"

"How's the pay?"

"Better than this. Make up a fantasy right now. You and me. Go!"

You can do this, I thought. Just like improv. class. Never mind the fact that he'd just seen me naked. I looked him up and down. He was wearing tight jeans and a black T-shirt. Wiry body, sexy lips. Kind of hot-looking once you got past the stubble and dark circles under his eyes. He could probably have any of the dancers whenever he wanted, so what kind of fantasy could be kinky enough? He still looked like a kid to me . . . a kid making out in a car.

"We're in a car," I started. "In the rain. Pouring rain. Pounding on the roof. Parked up in the Hollywood hills. The windows are already steamed up. I know the lights are out there, but they're blurry. Front seat's all the way back and you're on top of me and we're . . . um, necking, you know? Really hot and heavy. You've got your mouth on mine and you're just, just . . . devouring me. Mmmmmmm. Feels so good."

I thought I'd be embarrassed, saying that stuff out loud, making noises. I couldn't even understand why anyone would call those numbers. I thought it would be totally fake, but it didn't feel fake at all. It felt a little too real.

Jason was looking at me, mouth half open, cigarette stuck in mid-air. He gestured for me to go on.

"So . . . um . . . you're on top of me. I can feel your cock through your jeans, wanting to get out, wanting to get inside me. You've got your hands under my skirt, on my thighs. One hand in my panties. You slide a finger inside me, and I'm so wet. You can tell how much I want you."

I was panting now, feeling myself in the scene, right down to the sweat and the smell. My legs were starting to shake. I tried to pound a hand against the table to let out some of the tension, but I couldn't because Jason had grabbed my hand and was squeezing my fingers, his own hand trembling as he bit down on his lower lip and kept looking into my eyes.

"Oh my God . . . Please . . . I need more. Need you now. Please, put it in me. Please. I'm begging for it, but you keep teasing. More rain coming down. I'm breathing so hard I feel like I'm gonna pass out. You've got one finger all the way inside me. Oh my God. So close. I hear your zipper and you're moving up a little so you can . . . oh . . . oh . . . God! You push your cock into me. Oh God . . . so big . . . you're filling me up. I'm squirming under you. I hear the thundering outside. Thunder and lightning and, oh God . . . I'm screaming. You're pumping into me, deep, harder, please, please, I, oh, oh, so good. I'm coming . . ."

I couldn't take it any more and I didn't care if I got the job or what else happened. Jason was looking at me like one of us was crazy. I put my other hand between my legs, finding my own pussy so wet it was hard to get any traction. I needed to get three fingers inside just to feel anything. I noticed that Jason had reached down and opened his jeans. He was stroking himself, hard and fast. I kept talking, telling him how hard he was fucking me and how good it felt, until I saw his teeth clench and his nostrils flare and he finally had to close his eyes and that was when I pushed down hard around my fingers and clenched my muscles. Jason was grunting and groaning and still squeezing my hand so hard it should have hurt but all I could feel was the overload of pleasure hitting my cunt and making me scream so loudly I knew my throat was going to hurt for days.

I opened my eyes to find Jason staring at me, his face flushed and beads of sweat on his upper lip. He slowly released my hand, leaving me to massage it back into feeling, while he zipped himself up and lit another cigarette.

It was hard to tell if he'd actually been affected by my performance or whether this was just a typical day at the office. He reached into his jacket pocket and handed me a business card with an address on La Cienega.

He had to take a breath before he could speak.

"I think you're a natural."

BEDSIDE MANNERS

Steve, Bayswater

The first time I ever got to fuck a beautiful pair of tits happened when I was a medical student and, in a strange way, I owe it to the most boring professor I ever had, an old Scot with a voice that could have been used as a sedative.

"One of the more awkward jobs a doctor faces is asking clients about their sexual histories," he droned. "To make sure you know how to do this, your assignment for next week is to interview somebody and get his or her complete sexual history – everything they've ever done, and how, and with whom. Rather than inflict you on the general public in your current state of inexperience, I'm going to assign you each a partner from this class."

I suspect I turned pale when he paired me off with Suki, a petite but exquisite Singaporean girl who was so prim and proper that she'd been nicknamed China Doll. The idea of describing my (rather limited) sexual experiences to her was terrifying, and the only consolation was the thought that interviewing her shouldn't take more than a minute. We agreed to meet in her room in the girls' dorm wing the next morning, during a two-hour break in our timetable.

Her room looked as neat and tightly controlled as she did. We flipped a coin to see who had to speak first, and I lost. She sat there impassively as I recounted my adventures and misadventures, jotting down notes, and after twenty minutes I'd ground to a halt.

"Let's see if I have this right," she said, looking down at her notes. "No current lover, three partners over the past four years, cunnilingus with two, fellatio from one, no anal sex, condoms used every time?" I nodded and tried not to blush. "Before that, quite a lot of breast-fondling and masturbation?" Another nod. "OK," she said, sitting there primly. "I'm afraid I haven't had as many partners as you," she began. Surprise, surprise, I thought. "Only one," she continued, and gave me a detailed description of what she and her lover had done.

I managed to keep my composure until she started to talk about tit-fucking. I would have blushed if the blood hadn't rushed to my cock instead. I'd seen some boob sex in porn movies, but didn't know people did it in real life. Before I could stop myself, I asked, "Doesn't that hurt?"

"Not when we used a little lube," she said, with a slight smile.

"Do you come – I mean, have an –"

"Sometimes," she said. "Even when I didn't, I loved watching him ejaculate. It was something I'd never seen before; censorship is very strict in Singapore, and my family is even worse. David and I had to be very secretive, and I had to play the demure and dutiful daughter in public in case my parents ever found out."

"You certainly had *me* fooled," I blurted out.

Her smile became larger. "Unfortunately, David and I broke up months ago and, since then, the only thing I've had to hide is how often I masturbate. I have a good collection of magazines I can't take back home, and a vibrator, but I stopped using that because it interfered with the TV reception in the room next door." She looked down at her notes. "Do you have any condoms?"

"What? No, I . . ."

"Pity," she said, "because reminiscing like this is making me horny as hell – and I gather you're feeling the same way." I nodded, not trusting myself to speak. "We could suck each other off," she suggested, "or would you rather fuck my breasts?"

She removed her jacket and unbuttoned her blouse, then unfastened her bra. Her bare boobs looked enormous on her five-foot frame, and they were beautifully shaped, with long dark nipples – already swollen – surrounded by the tiny areolae.

A moment later, one was in my hand and the other in my mouth and I discovered that they tasted even better than they looked. She reached for my swollen cock, stroking it through my jeans, then began undressing me. She wiped a drop of pre-come off the eye of my cock, and tasted it, then slipped a finger into her pussy and then into my mouth. A minute later, we were both naked on her bed and she was straddling my face, almost drowning me in pussy juice. I watched as she played with her breasts and tugged on her nipples.

"Can you lick them?" I asked.

She grinned. "Make me come first," she said, "and I'll show you what I can do with them." She reached over to the night-stand and grabbed a bottle of lotion, and I wrapped my lips around her clit and sucked until she began gasping. She stuck her tongue out and pushed her boobs up to her chin, and managed to lick her nipples as I worked on giving her her second orgasm. Then she rubbed the lotion into her cleavage and climbed off me. "Sit," she commanded, and knelt between my legs, wrapping her breasts around the shaft of my cock and running her tongue around the glans.

As I'd told Suki, I'd never had unprotected sex before, had never felt so much wonderful woman flesh around my naked cock, and tit-fucking her felt better than I could have imagined. I tried to hold off, but soon my come was spurting out like a geyser, splashing onto her hair, face, chin, and tits.

She licked off as much as she could reach, then lay down on the floor and began slowly rubbing her clit and her breasts. "If you want to go and get some condoms," she said lazily, "we still have an hour before class."

I haven't seen Suki since we graduated, but I haven't lost my taste for tit-fucking and talking dirty. I always carry condoms, but when I meet women with big, soft, fuckable breasts, I sometimes pretend I've run out, and suggest alternative forms of safe sex.

TOP OF THE CHARTS

Nick, Costa Mesa

When I was a kid in high school, I used to indulge in what I thought were some rather risqué behaviours. What comes to mind immediately is masturbating in my backyard. Always after school, when no one was home, and always behind the closed gate, but it was enough to make me feel I was getting away with something.

It started with just unzipping but eventually escalated to taking my pants off and, finally, getting completely undressed. A porn magazine and a little hand cream got me going, but the real object of my activities was a cute little cheerleader I shared a class with.

Carol wasn't the most popular cheerleader on the squad. That was Rayanne, the perky, bubbly, effervescent nymph who got all the guys' dicks hard. Mine included. But I'm partial to a more ample physique. Besides, I didn't sit next to Rayanne in English. As a result, it wasn't Rayanne who'd lean over, periodically, and ask for help. Like, figuring out the differences between Elizabethan and Spenserian sonnets.

"Oh, Carol!" Sedaka sang.

Like anything, though, the backyard jerk-offs got old, and I moved on to more adult, and more tangible, pursuits. Some having nothing to do with sex.

I mention this because, a couple of years ago I received a letter announcing the thirtieth anniversary of my high school graduation. Which got me thinking of all the people I really wasn't all that interested in seeing again. I didn't much like them, frankly. That's why I'd never gone to any of the other

reunions. Then, one night I couldn't sleep, so I left my wife in
bed and went into the backyard for a smoke.

The night was cool. Cool for mid-June, anyway. A slight
breeze filtered under my shorts. That prompted me to recall
what a turn-on it had been to masturbate outside. Which
brought to mind Carol. My cock started to stir. The end result
was I walked over to the side of the house and pulled my pants
down. A few minutes of remembering her athletic legs disappearing under the little uniform skirt, and the way the mascot
laid his head so perfectly across her large, round breasts, and I
was releasing a healthy volume of ejaculate on the concrete.

The thrill might be gone for B.B. King, but it was certainly
back for me. I decided I should have trouble sleeping more
often.

I'd been engaging in my nocturnal emissions for a couple of
months when, one night, just as I was about to release, I was
startled by a noise. I stopped in mid-stroke, the urge to orgasm
suddenly suppressed, and got as quiet as I could. Although I
was certain my heartbeat could be heard across the street.

"Don't stop," a voice whispered from the other side of the
fence.

Shit! I grabbed my shorts and held them in front of my now
limp cock.

"Please, don't stop," the hushed voice said.

"Who is that? Sheila?" I kept my voice low.

My neighbour's head popped up above the fence. "Please?"

"Jesus! How long've you been watching?"

"You mean tonight?"

"Crap."

"You embarrassed?"

"Whaddya think?" I wanted to put my shorts back on but
that would have meant taking them away from my crotch.
Nowhere to run to, as Martha and the Vandellas so aptly put
it. What I really wanted was to melt into the wall.

"You have a nice cock."

"Yeah, thanks."

"I like watching you."

"Um, how long –"

"A few weeks. Does Lucy know you come out here like this?"

"No. Does Gavin know, I mean, does he –"

"No. Hold on. I'll come around."

"No! Wait!"

Too late. Her gate opened and closed quietly. A few seconds later, my gate opened and she padded over to me. It happened so fast, I was still holding my pants over my dick.

Sheila and Gavin were in their late twenties. Really eye-catching couple. Both very attractive and very friendly. We often exchanged pleasantries across the fence separating our driveways. When she came through the gate, it looked like all she was wearing was a long T-shirt.

"You shouldn't've come over."

"I had to. This way we can keep our voices down."

"No. You shouldn't be here at all."

"It's OK. Gavin is fast asleep. I assume Lucy is, too."

"Yeah, but that's not the point. I'm naked, and . . . and you're practically naked."

"I've been watching you all this time. I've seen all there is to see. Here, lemme take this off."

"Sheila, wait –"

In a flash, she had the shirt over her head. Her breasts were as gorgeous as I'd imagined them. Her freckles just visible by the light of the street lamp at the corner. In another second she'd stepped out of her panties. Unlike me, she made no attempt at modesty. Her pubic hair, neatly trimmed, drew my eyes to the shadowy space between her legs.

Suddenly The Archies started echoing in my head: "Sugar. Ah, honey, honey!"

"Come on, Nick. Lemme see."

I tried to think of a good argument but none came to me, except the embarrassment of being flaccid and small. She anticipated what I was thinking.

"Of all the things I've seen you do, the sexiest is when your cock starts out soft and you play with it until it's hard and standing up straight. I imagine it getting hard in my mouth."

"Christ, Sheila."

"You really want me to go?" She started to pick up her clothes.

"Yes. No! Wait a minute. It's just that you, I mean, you caught me, I was, you know, you took me by surprise."

"Sorry. I was doing some gardening this afternoon and I guess I didn't quite put everything away. I kicked a flowerpot. Usually, I keep really quiet. Then, when you go in, I make myself come before I go inside."

"You watch the whole thing?"

"Yeah. Can I touch you?"

"I don't . . . I mean, do you think that's a good idea?"

"I've been wanting to know what it feels like for so long. Please?"

"Yeah, I guess. I mean, why not?" The first touch of her hand was like a silk scarf around my cock. Her skin was at once cool and warm. I responded accordingly.

"I really like watching it grow like that. It's so thick and full."

"Me and Mrs, Mrs Jones". Fuck. Who sang that?

"Sheila. Oh, Christ. We shouldn't be doing this."

"Why not?"

"Because we're married."

"So? Married people get each other off like this all the time."

"Generally not with someone else's spouse."

"Want me to stop?"

"You can look at me and ask that?"

"So an erection means I can keep going?"

"You can take that as a yes."

She deftly slid her hand to the base of my cock until the tip rested halfway up her forearm. "I'm sure you'd be hard if anyone was stroking you."

"I'm sure I would."

"What if I was fat and ugly?"

"No woman's fat and ugly with my cock in her hand."

She put my hand between her legs and pressed it against her pussy. Her clit was so hard I had no trouble finding it. I inserted one finger and rubbed back and forth, feeling the nub roll against my joint. Her eyes closed for a few seconds.

"Sheila."

"Shut up."

"Sheila."

"Don't stop."

"Sheila!"

"Put anoth– Oh yeah! That's good."

"No kidding. This is a bad idea."

"I know."

"We could get in so much trouble."

"Wanna – hhuh! – stop?"

She had me, there. "We have to be very careful, and very quiet. Lucy's just on the other side of this wall."

"All right. God! OK. Let's set some guidelines."

"Like what?"

"Like no fucking."

"Including ass-fucking?"

"Fuck, oh, God! Yeah, dammit."

"What about oral?"

"I'll go down on you – fuck! – if you want, but you can't eat me."

"Why not?"

"I can't – fucking Christ! – 'cause I can't be quiet when I come that way."

"Keep your voice down."

"I'm trying. Shit! Don't stop."

"Hardly seems fair."

"Well – Jesus! – maybe when Gavin — oh, God! – goes out of town – fuck! Kiss me!"

She let go of my cock and wrapped her arms around my neck. Her orgasm was muffled in my mouth as her breath filled my lungs. Her hips bucked against my hand. She acted like she wanted to climb me.

Once she relaxed, and her body went limp, she took her lips from mine and laid her head on my shoulder. It took a few minutes for her breathing to return to normal.

"I've been wanting to feel that for weeks. Thank you."

"Maybe you should get dressed and go home now."

"Mmmm. What about you?"

"I'll be fine."

"But I want you to come. I wanna help."

"You've helped plenty. Believe me."

"But –"

"Next time. Now, get dressed."

I stroked myself while she put her clothes back on. Then she went down on her knees and kissed my cock. I spurted a little on her face but she opened her mouth in time to get most of it.

After that night we managed to get together at least once a week. More, if we could but, families being what they are, it wasn't always possible. Over time we worked out a signal to let her know when I'd be outside.

We never fucked. She liked sucking me off, and a few times I was able to sneak over to her house and eat her. She wasn't kidding. She's loud. But most of the time we just watched each other masturbate.

To paraphrase The Chiffons: "She's so fine."

Gavin and Sheila moved away earlier this year, so now poor Carol has to share time. "Memories, light the corners of my mind". I used to hate that song.

JOYS OF WATER SPORTS

Peter, London

I've always had a secret penchant for water sports. I used to play with myself, peeing and masturbating at the same time. The double flow of urine and semen gave me a deeply erotic thrill unmatched by the pleasure of simple masturbation. I especially enjoyed it when I found myself outdoors somewhere and had to go behind some tall bushes or into the edge of a forest. The cool fresh air on my exposed penis was always particularly exhilarating and pleasurable. There was something forbidden, something deeply secretive about playing with myself in the open like that. It also generated an air of danger, coupled with the fear of suddenly being discovered by someone and having to flee with my trousers open and my erect penis sticking out. It never did happen, of course, but the very thought of it sent shivers of additional excitement through my body.

My accompanying fantasies often involved women, although their roles tended to be quite nebulous since I had no direct experience in that field. I usually just pictured the women stripping off all their clothes and lying naked in front of me. I stood over them and sprayed their bodies with pee and come, particularly their breasts and the dark triangle I knew from pictures they had between their legs. But even with that limited knowledge, the fantasies made my activities much more exciting and my orgasms more powerful and more gratifying.

When I seriously started to date and sleep with women on a regular basis, my peeing fantasies receded into the background for a while, but before long they resurfaced again, stronger and more intense than ever before. My fantasies reached the point where I kept thinking I should broach the subject when I was with a woman, but I was always too afraid of being ridiculed or outright rejected, so nothing ever came of my intentions. In retrospect, it was just as well, because at that time I really didn't know anything about the topic and probably wouldn't have known what to do, even if one of them would have liked my idea and had wanted to participate.

Until Alicia came into my life. We met at a three-day science conference at the Convention Centre downtown. I walked into the lecture hall and found a vacant aisle seat not far from the back where I usually like to sit. I sat down on the chair, placed my briefcase on my lap, and found myself sitting next to a woman, probably about my age, perhaps a bit younger. I nodded in her direction and uttered a perfunctory, "Good morning."

She turned and smiled an engaging smile. "Good morning," she replied in a pleasant, melodious voice.

The lecture began and we both concentrated on the speaker and on our notepads. Yet I couldn't help glancing at her furtively every few moments. She was scribbling furiously in her notebook as if wanting to take in every word that was said, but I caught her looking at me several times and quickly averting her eyes before they met mine. There was something about her that attracted me to her, something between us that made us more than just chance acquaintances in a lecture hall.

When the coffee break came and we both rose, I turned to face her. "Peter," I introduced myself and held out my hand.

She smiled the same engaging smile. "Alicia," she replied. She put her hand into mine and I could feel the warmth of her body flow through mine.

We spent the coffee break together and chatted amicably about the lecture and the conference. By lunch time, we easily switched to more personal topics, beginning to reveal our lives and our personalities, our dreams and ambitions, our likes and dislikes. Over the next several meals, we continued what we had begun, getting to know each other more and more closely, opening up our inner selves, our togetherness. By the end of the conference, she invited me to her apartment.

We slept with each other several times over the ensuing weeks and grew more familiar and more intimate with each other. I felt that the time had come where I could reveal my fantasy to her without having to fear the repercussions. We had developed a sense of trust and mutual respect that made me think that even if she didn't like the idea, she wouldn't ridicule or reject me for it. I just couldn't decide on the perfect way and the perfect time to tell her about it.

We were sitting on her couch one evening, watching TV, when I decided I had been procrastinating long enough. I simply had to take the plunge and hope for the best.

"Have you ever heard of water sports?" I blurted out, waiting anxiously for her reaction.

She uttered a quick, amused laugh and turned to me with her pleasant smile. "Of course, I have," she replied to my great relief. "My girlfriend and I do it all the time. I've just never done it with a man before."

"I've never done it with anybody," I confessed sheepishly. "I've only fantasized about it."

"Time to make your fantasy a reality," she said lightly, confidently. "Would you like to give it a try?"

Would I! We quickly undressed and Alicia led me to the bathroom. She took a box out of the cupboard and opened it. I shuddered when I saw the collection of paraphernalia. This was certainly not a part of my fantasy.

"Just relax," she said in her quiet voice, sensing my apprehension. "I know exactly what I'm doing. You don't have to worry about a thing."

She reached into the box and took out a length of thin, plastic tubing, a small funnel, a tube of lubricant and a water glass. She had me stretch out on the floor and propped my head up with a pillow so I could watch. Then she put some of the lubricant on one end of the tubing, took my penis into her hand and expertly slid the tubing into the tiny hole. It didn't hurt at all. In fact, it was a rather pleasant and arousing sensation, being manipulated like that. She pushed the tubing all the way through my penis and into my bladder. Next, she put the funnel into the other end and handed it to me.

"Hold this," she said. She filled the glass full of lukewarm water, took the funnel from me, and slowly poured the water into the funnel.

I had never experienced anything like this. The warm water flowing through the tube and into my bladder was so arousing my penis grew harder and harder until I thought I would explode.

"There," she said when my bladder had been filled to bursting. "That wasn't that bad, was it now?"

"No," I admitted. "Not at all."

Alicia pulled the tubing out of me, washed it under the tap, and handed me the whole contraption. "Your turn," she said, stretching out on the floor and spreading her legs.

I knelt down between her legs, the tube with the funnel in my hand. I was shaking uncontrollably as I contemplated the wide-open pussy and my task at hand.

"Just relax," she said again in her soothing voice. "You'll be just fine."

I took a few deep breaths, steadied my hand, and touched the end of the tubing to her exposed pee hole. So far, so good. I put a bit of tentative pressure on the tube and it slid right into its receptacle. Alicia sighed contentedly. Encouraged by her reaction, I slid the tubing all the way in to her bladder and handed her the funnel end. I filled the glass with water and poured it slowly into the funnel and into her. She moaned as the water filled her bladder until I had emptied the whole glass.

Alicia rose from the floor and stretched out in the tub, spreading her legs and placing her feet on the edge. I climbed in after her and knelt down between her legs. She parted her labia with her fingers to expose her swollen clit. I let go of the pressure inside me and aimed the stream of pee and water at her pussy. She squealed with delight as the pale-yellow liquid splashed against her clit and ran down her pussy and over her inner thighs, down into the tub.

When the last few droplets had trickled down on her, she rose and had me stretch out in the tub. She squatted down over me, her pussy directly above my penis, and let go of her own pressure. It was an incredible sensation, feeling her pee hit my penis, run down my shaft and over my balls, and flow away between my legs.

As soon as she was done, she reached for her pussy and began massaging her clit. I stared at her with fascination. I had never seen a woman masturbate before. This was a real turn-on for me, and I quickly reached for my aching penis and began to stroke it slowly.

But Alicia pushed my hand away. "Wait," she said breath-lessly, fingering and rubbing her pussy more and more quickly and forcefully. She arched her back and screamed when her orgasm shook her body. She slowly relaxed again and then knelt down and took my penis into her hand, stroking it and rubbing it, until my come sprayed all over me and over her hands. She licked her splattered fingers, smacking her lips in obvious delight. We had completed our very first peeing game, much to both of our delight and satisfaction, and my fantasy had finally come true, even though in some rather unexpected ways.

A few days later, Alicia mentioned her girlfriend – Tina was her name – and that she had asked if she could join us.

"What do you think?" she asked, quite unnecessarily, I thought.

"Of course," I replied enthusiastically. "That would be great!"

Tina came to the apartment on the weekend. After the usual introductions and a few minutes of small talk, we undressed in the living room and headed for the bathroom. Tina took the box out of the cupboard and pulled out a large syringe with a small piece of soft tubing attached to the end. That certainly wasn't a part of my fantasy, either, but I didn't let it show this time. I trusted her to know what she was doing, just as I had trusted Alicia.

Tina filled the syringe at the sink while Alicia positioned herself on the floor. I watched with great interest as Tina inserted the end of the small tube and squeezed the water into her friend. Then they switched positions and Alicia did the same thing for Tina until they were both filled to bursting. The two climbed into the tub, one standing at each end, and motioned me to come and sit between them. As soon as I was in position, they both started peeing, directing their streams expertly with their fingers and spraying the contents of their bladders all over me and over themselves. Then they moved closer together and reached for each other's pussies, rubbing each other to simultaneous orgasms while I watched them from my vantage position below them.

"Your turn," Tina said when they were finished. "You can just lie down in the tub."

I did as I was told. Tina refilled the syringe, bent over the edge of the tub, and took my penis into her hand. She carefully inserted the lubricated tip of the tube and began to squeeze. It was a strange yet also very stimulating sensation, having a woman I hardly knew manipulate me like that, and then feeling the water flow into my penis and into my bladder until I was completely full.

Tina had me stand up at one end of the tub and the two knelt down in front of me, holding their breasts out for me. It didn't take me long to release the pressure and pee over their expectant bodies. They both cried out with pleasure when my stream splashed against their breasts and ran down over their bodies. True to my fantasy, I began masturbating while the last droplets still dribbled down on them. It didn't take me long to reach my own climax and spray my jism all over them.

After a communal shower and a thorough clean-up of the premises, we went into the bedroom and collapsed on the bed, satiated and content.

The whole thing was an incredible experience for me, and I was sure there would be many more to come.

TASTING HIM

Jessica, Los Angeles

We had been talking on the phone for weeks about how I was going to swallow his come when I saw him the next time. He knew I had never swallowed for anyone before, refusing to even allow a man to come near my lips. He was going to be the one to take this last shred of my virginity.

I had spent several hours wondering why after twenty-five years of saying no, I was finally willing to swallow Jeff's semen. I came to the conclusion that it was a combination of trust and lust for him. He had the ability to make it sound like the hottest sexual act on the planet. No pressure, the decision was to be mine alone, maybe that was the difference: he gave me the choice.

Last night I had finally gotten into town. When he picked me up at the airport, I climbed into his truck and kissed him deeply, tasting the beer on his tongue. "I want you, right now," I said, smiling up at him.

He laughed. "I guess that answers the question of should we stop for food on the way home? I'd screw you here in the airport parking lot, but the security guards would have a problem."

"No, I don't want food. I want your come in my stomach," I replied.

He sat up straighter in his seat and gripped the steering wheel tighter. I was satisfied to see his jeans suddenly look very uncomfortable. He shifted to relieve the pressure against his cock. I looked out the car window and smiled to myself.

We got to his house, left my bags in the truck, and headed straight for his bedroom. "Come here," he said as he stripped off his jeans and underwear in the same motion, and then sat at the end of the bed.

I kicked off my pumps, but didn't take time to undress. I wanted his cock in my mouth, and I wasn't waiting to get what I wanted.

He chuckled as I crossed the room, tying my hair into a haphazard ponytail, and dropped to my knees between his thighs. "Eager, are you? Let's see how much of my cock you can take down your throat."

In answer, I lowered my lips to his turgid dick, noticing the pre-come already glistening at the tip. His fingers wrapped into my hair, tightening in response as I slowly lowered my mouth down the length of his shaft, stopping only when he was fully in the back of my throat. I had felt a surge of panic when I realized he was so far back in my throat I could not comfortably breathe.

"Swallow me," he commanded.

He was so far back in my throat that my throat muscles were almost paralysed. Obediently I struggled to swallow, feeling the head of his cock slide deeper down my throat. I almost choked, my eyes tearing up from the pressure.

"Swallow again, come on, you can do it."

I managed to swallow again, fighting the urge to gag as his head slipped further down my throat. My mind registered the fact that I could not breathe like this, but, oh, it felt good to have him so far down my throat. I relaxed and tried to swallow again, frustrated that my throat refused to cooperate. His penis pulsed, cutting off any hope of air reaching my lungs.

Jeff pulled his hips back slightly as he used my hair to gently pull my head upwards, releasing the pressure against the back of my throat. I gasped around his dick for air for several seconds before beginning to move again, slowly up and down his hard shaft, using my tongue along the length of him, making gentle motions. His cock grew harder in my mouth as I swirled my tongue around his head, sucking down the pre-come that was pumping into my mouth in tiny spurts.

My pussy was drenched by now; I could feel my juices dripping through my saturated thong. I raised my shirt while I shifted my lower body until I was straddling his leg. Pressing down, I began to rub against his shin in rhythm with my mouth fucking his cock. He had helpfully pressed his leg against my clit so I could ride against him. I could feel my moisture starting to run down his leg as the room started to take on the musky smell of sex.

"You are a horny little slut, you like taking my dick in the back of your throat, don't you? Can you taste my pre-come? I'm going to come down your throat, and you are going to swallow it for me. Does it turn you on to think about having my come in your stomach?"

I nodded as I raised my mouth off his cock. I had to lick my lips to break the string of saliva that went from his shaft to my lips before I begged, "Fuck my mouth. Get yourself off down my throat."

He pulled me onto the bed beside him and arranged the pillows under my head. "Are you sure? I'm not going to be able to stop myself easily once I get started. I'm going to screw your mouth hard, Jessica, are you going to take it for me? I'm going to make your throat sore from pushing down it as far as you can take it. I'm going to come down the back of your throat."

I gazed up at him, mentally thinking that now was the time to find out what I was made of, and if I could, in fact, do what I had promised him and myself I would do. With a shiver, I nodded, replying, "Take my mouth. I want to feel how hard you get just before you shoot off in my mouth. I want you to come down my throat."

I closed my eyes as he straddled my face, feeling a moment of panic that I had asked for more than I was willing to give. A horrified thought crossed my mind: I barely know this man; I just gave him carte blanche to hump my mouth. What if he doesn't stop if I need him to stop?

I pushed that thought aside, took a deep breath and relaxed as he slid his very swollen dick home in my mouth. As he hit the back of my throat I gagged. He hesitated, pulling out slightly, and then, feeling my tongue and lips suckling on the head of his cock, started to again thrust his hips.

He was gentle at first, careful not to go so deep that he gagged me. I found a rhythm that matched his own: I took a breath when he pulled back, relaxed my throat when he pressed against the back of it, and then took a breath again when he pulled back. He'd hold his dick pressed firmly against the back of my throat for several seconds before pulling back, dilating my throat. Every time he slid home, he pressed his cock head a little deeper down my throat.

I suckled and licked his cock, relaxed now, all traces of doubt faded away. I wanted him to find his rhythm and spray his come in my mouth. My entire being focused on turning him on enough that he would come. I swirled my tongue around the end of his cock, dipping into the slit, gulping down the salt-tasting pre-come.

I heard his breathing change as his thrusts became faster, taking on a purposeful gait. As he shoved his dick down my throat, I could feel that it was getting harder, so thick now that I was nearly having trouble taking him in my mouth. I continued to use my tongue to lick around his shaft as he pushed it in and out of my open mouth, listening and feeling as his body became tenser.

My mind registered: He's going to come. He's going to come in your mouth. It was at this point I normally would panic and finish the man with a hand job or allow him to screw me. Instead of panic, I found acceptance wash over my brain as the thought went through my head: This is so hot!

"Jessica, I'm coming. I'm going to come in your mouth." It sounded like a question, maybe it was a warning, I didn't care which, I only knew that I wanted him to finish what he started. I wanted him to come down my throat; like he'd been promising he was going to do for weeks when we spoke on the phone.

I made a noise in my throat that must have passed for acceptance, maybe it was the fact that my lips and my tongue never stopped caressing his dick.

His breathing changed yet again as I felt his shaft grow even harder, taking on a life of its own, seeming to grow twice as long and twice as hard in seconds. His body began to shudder above mine; I could feel his legs shaking as, with one final thrust, he came deep inside my mouth. I felt him spurting come in my mouth, and I registered that I was swallowing for him, crossing over the very last threshold I had in place. He had become a first, taken my last hold on virginity. A virginity I had said no man would ever take.

I heard him talking to me, telling me I was a good girl, telling me that was so hot, thanking me, asking me if I was all right. My body was trembling as he moved from above me. I realized he was looking into my eyes, searching for something, but I couldn't quite understand what he was searching for.

I looked back at him from behind half-closed eyes. My brain couldn't focus for several seconds; I was still lost in the wonder of having swallowed for the first time. I was stunned from the feeling of having his dick battering the back of my throat, feeling him spurt in my mouth, of the salty sweet taste of his come that was even then covering my tongue. I just smiled and nodded at him, I was too contented to speak. I swallowed reflexively once more and winced at the slightly bruised feeling in my throat, then smiled up at him before drifting off to sleep.

ON THE BEACH

Sasha, Essex

I've always liked taking solitary walks even though I'm a sociable kind of girl, so on a particularly balmy summer evening I took a stroll along the beachfront near where I live on the Thames Estuary.

I walked briskly, enjoying the moonlight on the water, and came to a little bay area where the beach was much bigger than elsewhere. Walking around it I noticed two figures sitting some way from the pathway, near to the waterline and only just visible in the yellow wash of the street lights away on the roadside.

I smiled as I heard a wolf whistle, and realized that the figures were young lads when one of them called, "Hey, darlin'! Come and join us for a beer."

I chuckled at their front and on the spur of the moment decided to give them a surprise by accepting. "Is it lager? Hang on, I'll be right there," I called. I thought nothing of going over; they were both obviously a lot younger than me (I'm thirty-eight and they must have been in their teens), and I was not dressed at all provocatively, wearing a black U-neck T-shirt over a black cup bra and a black denim skirt that came to my lower thigh. It would be a bit of company on an evening when I'd nothing else to do, and knowing what young guys were like I could expect a bit of lively and funny chat.

I sauntered over and could see they hadn't expected me to, but they covered well and held up a small bottle of beer to me as I reached them.

"Cheers, boys," I said, settling down and taking a glug from my bottle. "I'm Sasha. You?"

"Martin," said the bigger boy. "And this is Geoff." He gestured to a plastic cool box on the sand and went on, "We've got plenty of beer. We could make an evening of it."

I smiled at him, aware that he wasn't as at ease as he was making out, but thought it showed a lot of self-assurance for a boy his age to maintain such an easy attitude with a woman my age.

"Probably will," I replied. "I like a nice beer on a warm evening. How'd you get it though? Aren't you a bit young to buy beer?"

Martin gave a deliberately worldly smile and answered, "We're not that young, y'know. I'm seventeen, and Geoff's sixteen. Anyway, beer is easy to get."

We carried on chatting, and they were good company. It was easy to get friendly with them and they quickly relaxed, and soon we were chatting away like we all knew each other well, they making the odd cheeky and flirty comment, me going along with it with good humour. We were chugging back beers, and after a while I started feeling just a bit tipsy. It was nice, relaxing, and the guys were sweet.

"Urrgh," I muttered, shifting my position to ease out my lower back. "You should have brought some seats, too."

"Martin," Geoff said, "where's your manners? The lady wants a seat."

"I can be a seat," he said, moving behind me and kneeling, then pulling me back by the shoulders until I was reclining against him.

I laughed and raised my beer bottle while complimenting him on being so comfortable. The natter continued, the drinking continued, and although the bottles were small the beer was affecting me, making me feel more and more relaxed so I hardly even noticed when Martin laid a hand on the crook of my neck, and occasionally stroked lightly up to my ear with his fingertips in an affectionate way. I was perfectly comfortable when the flirting became more brash and the subjects of conversation more intimate.

"So, I suppose you guys don't have girlfriends then," I said, "else you wouldn't be out boozing on the beach?"

"I did have," replied Martin. "And five others before her, but Geoff's only had two."

"Get out!" I scoffed. "You're both lovely boys but you're too young to've had that many girlfriends. I bet you've never kissed a girl properly in your lives!" I took another deep mouthful of beer and felt the tingle of alcohol, then recognized the sound of dented male pride as Martin said, "I can kiss all right. I've never had a complaint," and moved his hand from the side of my neck to underneath my chin, tilted my face up and, shifting round to the side of me, brought his mouth down onto mine. I was a bit startled, but realized that I'd probably bruised his ego a bit with my comment about girlfriends, and reckoned it'd be harmless enough to just let him snog me a little bit. Actually though, he was right – he could kiss all right. His lips flexed against mine and his tongue flicked against my mouth until, by reflex, my eyes closed and I opened my lips and let him kiss me properly, his tongue probing inside my mouth.

When he raised his lips from mine I made an appreciative noise, and said, "Mmmn, yes, you certainly managed that OK."

He bent forward to kiss me again and I moved to sit up and so stop him, but before I could he put his hand on my chest and restrained me, smothering anything I was going to say with another kiss. It was deep, and urgent, and maybe because he was so young and I figured nothing beyond this kiss would happen, or maybe because of the beer I had drunk, I let his hand keep me pressed against him while he took the kiss. I gave another little struggle when I felt his fingers begin to stroke downwards and slip into my cleavage, but I was still fully clothed and, being off-balance leaning back against him, my struggle was a weak one. I felt strange, being kissed so passionately by a boy so young, and still felt tingly from having had perhaps a bit too much beer.

I squirmed again as I felt his hand stroke over one of my tits and squeeze it through my T-shirt, and tried to speak to tell him no, but his mouth was pressed over mine and it just came out as a muffled squeaking sound. The hand moved back to the U-neck and slipped inside, pushing aside the bra and moving into contact with my nipple. I couldn't help myself; I felt it rise under the pressure of his fingers, and the tingling feeling centred around it as he stroked around in a circle, and my jaw eased its tension as I started to kiss him back. I relaxed back against him and let him do what he wanted.

He drew my T-shirt up until my chest was uncovered, and with one hand still stroking my boob the other reached behind me and undid my bra. My breasts were exposed and the cool evening air breezed across them. Martin's hands kneaded and stroked, pinched and squeezed, until my nipples hardened and rose to rigid points, and my back arched and my legs moved apart.

I was lost in the moment and jumped when I felt fingers on my inner thighs. I had forgotten about Geoff! He must have moved up to me while I was bent back in Martin's embrace, and he was now groping up my skirt. I couldn't let this happen! He was only sixteen years old! But Martin was holding me immobile, and I couldn't close my legs with Geoff's hands between them. Mortified at the situation I had allowed to develop, I felt the blood rush into my face as he reached my knickers and no doubt felt the wetness there. Martin had his hands over both of my tits now and they were aching from his attentions, and although I felt ashamed to be being felt up by a sixteen-year-old, I was undeniably turned on.

Geoff pulled my knickers to one side and pushed a finger inside me, and I knew things had gone too far to be stopped. I lay there, breasts bare and legs spread, while two boys less than half my age went at me.

Geoff continued to finger my cunt while Martin stopped kissing me to pull my T-shirt and bra all the way off.

"Fellas, fellas," I protested weakly, "you're gonna have to stop . . ." They both ignored me, young Geoff starting to move his fingers in and out of my by now sopping pussy and Martin laying me down and holding me with a hand on the base of my neck while bending to kiss my breasts. "Nooooo," I groaned, knowing that they would pay no notice, and when the hand at my neck lifted to lie without pressure over my lips, I stopped trying to speak.

After a while I felt Martin wave at Geoff to change positions and I opened my eyes briefly and watched little Geoff lower his mouth to nip on a tit with his teeth. I felt a warm breath on my snatch, then Martin's mouth closed over it and gave an almighty suck – the feeling was overwhelming! There was no resistance in me now as Martin flicked his tongue up and down my groove – I was simply a woman being sexed!

I didn't care when I felt Martin pull my knickers off, raise my skirt and pull my legs wide apart. The only sound I gave as he positioned himself and then took me was a deep grunt in the back of my throat. I sensed Geoff move away as Martin's weight pressed me to the sand and, through slitted eyes, I could see him kneeling beside me with his prick in his hand, rubbing himself. Martin was on top of me, holding my arms spread by the wrists as he pounded up and down on me with his cock reaching high into my fanny. Soon he tensed and gave a loud groan, and I could feel his prick jerking inside me with the force of his coming.

He pulled out and fell aside, and Geoff was upon me immediately, turning me over and raising me to my hands and knees, then plunging his knob straight into me. I could feel the cheeks of my bum quivering with each push forward as he fucked me, and could feel my tits swinging as he heaved back and forth. He was still going when Martin returned, moving in front of me and kissing me with his hands cupped under my boobs, the motion of Geoff's screwing moving them forwards and back so the nipples rubbed over Martin's fingers.

Then Martin straightened up and his cock was right in front of my face, semi-erect already. He grasped the hair at the back of my head and forced my face forwards until his prick was pressing against my lips, and I opened my mouth and took him inside. I sucked on his cock while Geoff carried on shafting me from behind, and when Geoff was finished Martin took his place.

Martin took longer this time, holding on to my shoulders to get harder thrusts, and as he gave me long regular strokes in and out I felt that warm sensation deep in my stomach that told me I was coming. Not caring that it was a young boy who was bringing me to orgasm I let go my inhibitions and thrust my butt back as he rode me until I came, then flopped forwards onto my front. He stayed in me and carried on humping me as I lay exhausted, until he came again.

I lay still for a little while between the two boys, until I got my breathing back under control. Then I pulled my clothes back into order and told them I had to go. They both seemed concerned that I was OK, and I told them I was fine, that I'd enjoyed what had happened and that it had felt great.

Little Geoff caught at my hand as I made to rise to my feet and gestured wordlessly at his groin. Looking down I saw that he was starting to come erect again, his slim cock lengthening. I knew what he wanted and realized that Martin had had two goes with me compared to Geoff's one. Anyway by now no reservations made any sense, so I knelt in front of him and closed my hand around his prick and started stroking back and forth. When he was fully stiff I started licking at his tip, then slid the blade of my tongue around the swell of his knob. As I felt trembles along his length, I plunged it deep into my mouth almost to my throat, and he shot a stream of spunk into my mouth.

I leaned back, spunk dribbling from my lips, and smiled up at him.

"Thank you," he said. "You're a really great lady. We're gonna be here again tomorrow night. We could get in some wine for you, if you'd like."

I smiled again and addressed both the boys as I explained that although they'd made me feel terrific I was far too old for them, and they should get to know some girls their own age. I kissed both of them on the lips, then walked back to the footpath and away.

I had been fucked thoroughly and felt very tired, and knew I'd fall asleep as soon as I got home and into bed. Then I'd get up in the morning and go to work. Then I'd have to make a decision about whether or not I fancied some wine . . .

HAND PUPPET

Angela, Los Angeles

I am not sure which of us brought up the idea of trying to fist him first. It seemed to be a mutual decision from the beginning, after he showed me the magazine pictures. After discussing it and finding myself aroused, I decided I wanted to try it as soon as possible. This being the case, we set a date for the following Friday.

I arrived at his house Friday, nervous but ready to play. He was waiting, freshly showered, still in his robe, his dark chest hair glistening from the dampness.

"I can't wait for you to do this to me. You are sure you still want to, aren't you? We don't have to, you know." The desire in his eyes told me he was going to be disappointed if I backed out.

I was still in disbelief that my hand was truly going to fit into his ass. What if I hurt him? I had stared, horrified and aroused, at the pictures in the magazine when he had shown me. In shock I had demanded, "Didn't that *hurt*?"

He had just smiled and said, "Hopefully only the right way." I wasn't about to back out of this now. I had to either call his bluff or find out if it really, truly could be done. The appealing thought of my whole hand up inside him, hurting him when it slid into him, making him come once it was in there, had kept me up late at night.

"No, I'm sure, I want to do this." My voice trembled with anticipation even as my pussy grew moist imagining my hand fully inside his ass.

"Thank you for trusting me in this. I know you are going to enjoy doing it. Shall I go and get the enema bag for you? I assume you want to give me one yourself?"

"Yes, bring it into the bedroom when you get it ready." I headed for the bedroom then turned and called out over the sound of the already running water, "Make sure you add lots of soap!"

"Yes, ma'am!" His answer made a shiver run up my spine. Being called "ma'am" was pretty new to me, having only recently realized that being dominant was almost as much fun as being submissive.

As I walked into the bedroom I saw what lay on the bed. He had left the fisting magazine there for me to look at. A convulsive shiver went through me, making my pussy begin to grow with a warm and swollen feeling. Hearing his footsteps stop behind me, I turned to face him.

He grinned, leaning down to kiss me. "Would you like me to help you undress or are you going to stay dressed? It's up to you, of course."

"Undress me." I turned and lifted my hair to reveal a row of small buttons down the back of my tight-fitting black spandex catsuit.

"Yes, ma'am. Let me hang this up first." He hung the full enema bag on the portable IV stand used just for this purpose then turned and walked over to assist me. His fingers made quick work of the buttons and soon he was pushing it down over my shoulders, past my hips, off my legs. Hooking his fingers in the thong I wore in place of panties, he slipped them off as well. His hands came up to caress my braless breasts only to find themselves pushed away.

"No, not yet. Take off your robe. It's time for your enema." I was trembling, on the edge from his fingers brushing against me as he had undressed me, afraid that if he touched my breasts I would come. I knew that by allowing my anticipation to build, my orgasm would be much stronger.

As he dropped his robe, it was evident he was very excited. His cock stood out from his body, rigid, oozing pre-come and pulsing so hard I could see it from a few feet away. Shuddering in delight, I motioned for him to get into position and reached for the lube. His head was resting on his arms, his tight round ass sticking up, his legs spread allowing me access to his cock and balls should I desire it.

The lube was cool as I squirted some onto my fingers, then I reached over and began to insert it into his twitching asshole. Parting his ass cheeks with my left hand, it dawned on me that he had shaved his cock, ass and balls for me. His usually furry skin was as smooth as glass. My nipples tightened at the thought of his cock and balls being lathered in shaving cream.

I slid my finger into his ass in one smooth fluid motion, feeling his ass tighten at first and then begin to relax for me. Grinning knowingly, I decided to torment him for a while. I took my time sliding my finger in and out, lubing his rosebud, watching it wink. Just by listening to his moans and feeling him squirm, I knew he was getting impatient.

Finally, I reached for the tube and slid the fat nozzle inside his ass. I turned on the flow, gently at first to give his body a chance to adjust. After he had taken a quarter of the bag, I opened the clamp all the way. When the water started flowing faster, I listened to him grunt as the cramps started, knowing he could take the full two quarts without my stopping the flow.

"Don't be a baby, you can take this! Did you already clean yourself out for me today?" I asked reaching over and lifting the bag off the hook.

"Yes, twice already, though I knew you would only do it again," he grunted.

"Fine, then I am only going to give you this one." I lifted the bag higher so that the last two pints rushed in, grinning wickedly when he groaned and tensed up.

"Oh God, take it easy!" he groaned, pleading with me, but I just smiled.

"Easy? This is easy! If you complain, I'll refill the bag and you can take that too. Do you want me to add more water to the bag?" His pained moans were making me hotter, even as I knew my refusal to be merciful was making him hotter as well. I reached out and began to stroke his ass and thighs.

"I need to use the john *now*," he insisted but I just stroked his ass and thighs telling him to behave and hold it for me. He was squirming now, his round ass twitching as he tried to find a comfortable position. Watching him twitch was almost too much for me and I reached between his spread legs to take his cock in my hands. Tormenting him was heaven, I reflected, then I began to jack him off, smiling as I felt his uncomfortable twitching ease and his cock harden still more. After a few minutes of teasing him, I was dying to try getting my hand up his asshole. Hastily removing the nozzle, I sent him to the bathroom.

While he was in the bathroom, I flipped through the magazine. My eyes widened in renewed disbelief at the pictures, my stomach fluttering at the thought of doing the same to him. Was my whole hand really going to fit inside his asshole? I still found it hard to believe but I was more than ready to try.

I jumped as the bathroom door opened and he came out, his entire attitude suddenly extremely submissive. The intensity of his submissiveness was frightening because it was usually I who was submissive to him. Wondering at this change in him, I stared at him for a few moments before realizing he was nervous.

Finally, he broke the silence. "I never realized how large your hands looked until now." He chuckled nervously as he continued, "I thought that it would be easier and safer if you used latex gloves. I put them over there on the nightstand for you along with the lube. I guess you want me on my hands and knees hugging a pillow like the man in the picture?"

I nodded and he climbed onto the bed.

After carefully putting on the latex gloves, I reached for the lube and smeared some on my first two fingers.

I massaged his rim, making his puckered hole spasm for me as he pushed his hips back towards me. Slipping my finger inside his warm ass, I began to fuck him, fast and furiously. It didn't take more than a minute or two before he was breathing fast, begging me to add a second finger. Obligingly, I slipped in the second, listening to him moan, feeling his hole close tightly on my fingers, gripping them. By this time he was whimpering for me to fuck him harder, and I had slipped in a third and started to fuck him with three fingers.

He shuddered as I added more lube, then slipped the tip of my fourth finger in and slowly, carefully, started to ease all four fingers into him. It was something I had never done before and

I was amazed they were fitting. His legs were tensed and I could tell that I was hurting him a little so I reached around and took his stiff cock in my hand to distract him from the pain.

As I eased my fingers in to the second knuckle, he groaned and tightened his hole around my fingers as he realized I had added my thumb. "No, wait, I don't think I can take all of your hand. Oh, damn, that hurts." I ignored his pleas to pull out, holding my hand still inside him, feeling him flex around me. It took every ounce of willpower I had to hold myself back as the pleasure of feeling his warm asshole encasing my fingers urged me to push all the way inside. My left hand continued to play with his cock, as I began to talk to him.

"Mmmm, do you feel my fingers? I'm almost inside you now, don't stop me, you know you want this. I know it hurts but you like it to hurt a little; do you feel how hard the pain is making you? I don't think your cock has ever been this hard and this big before. I'm going to make you my hand puppet, come on, now, open up for me. That's right, now take a few deep breaths for me. This isn't going to be comfortable for a minute or two, just think about how nice it's going to feel as soon as I'm inside you. You're so tight; you're never going to be this tight again. There, now, that's a good boy, deep breaths."

I started to slide my hand in further, continuing to massage his cock, gasping at how tight his asshole was around my fingers, doubting he would open far enough to get my hand in. Leaning over, I began to lick his ass cheeks, sliding my fingers in and out as my other hand continued to plunder his cock.

His asshole began to loosen up, his breathing came faster and he began to beg me to put my whole hand in him, to fist him, to make him my personal hand puppet.

"Take a deep breath for me," I said and, as he inhaled deeply, I nipped him sharply on the ass, sliding my hand in to the wrist, grinning as he let out a half sob, half howl.

"Bitch!" he hissed at me even as he pushed backwards further onto my wrist. His head was thrown back and I could see one tear trailing down his cheek, testifying to the fact that it had indeed hurt him to take my hand in his tight ass.

I shuddered excitedly, feeling my hand in his ass, curled tightly into a fist, grinning as I realized now why it was indeed called "fisting". Gently, I uncurled my fingers a bit and found that there was a second "anus" inside him. I shuddered again as he groaned.

"Easy, oh damn, I think that is my second sphincter. You have to go slowly with that one too, oh, man, your hand feels so large. Please, start fucking me with your hand, get me off."

I began to fuck him, easing my hand in and out, realizing that I finally knew what it felt like for a man to fuck another man, listening to him moan, feeling him spasm and shudder. His hand moved back to his dick and covered mine, showing me how he needed to be jacked off. I continued my assault on his ass, playing with his internal sphincter each time my fingers reached it. Finally, I was able to slip two fingers inside it and as I did, he came, jerking and crying out.

Just as he finished coming, I slipped my hand out of him, knowing that it was easier to do it while he was relaxed from an orgasm. Peeling off the gloves, I watched him, lying there limp on the bed, the pulse in his throat pounding, his mouth gasping for breath, eyes closed. It was some moments before he remembered I was there with him and he smiled up at me and started to sit up, thanking me, wincing at the soreness in his ass.

"I am going to remember this for a long while. I didn't realize I would feel so stretched afterwards," he said then leaned over to kiss me.

Afterwards, looking into his eyes, I realized that he was once again the dominant partner, forcing me to lower my eyes in proper submissive fashion but not before I mouthed the words "hand puppet" at him and winked.

His chuckle startled me as he said, "One day, little one, I will show you how it feels to have someone's hand fully inside you."

Once again, my mind jumped and I blurted out, "That's impossible! Isn't it?"

"Maybe, maybe not: you never know until you try. Let me know when you feel brave enough to trust me enough to allow me to try. In the meantime, come here and lie back on the bed."

Pulling me closer to him he whispered, "Go to sleep, little one, your body needs to rest after such an exciting night."

Agreeing, I curled up next to him, whispering, "Hand puppet," to him.

"Future hand puppet," he whispered back.

Before I could answer, I was asleep.

CLEANING DAY

Suzy, Baltimore

"We've got to get all the way back there," my husband had said, pointing.

The very back of our shed seemed so very far away. It was stuffed full of old furniture, paint cans, old clothes, the baby crib we hadn't needed in years. It was a beautiful shed full of crap. We wanted it to be neat and tidy. That didn't seem possible when I looked inside.

"Today?" I asked. It was hot and I was in no mood to burrow my way to the back of the shed. This was the sort of day built for a nice lawn chair, a cold beer and a trashy novel. Not full-on cleaning and organizing.

"Yes. Let's get it done with. OK? One fell swoop. Me and you. We'll get dirty and sweaty and then it will be done." Marshall gave me a little shove and I resisted the urge to swat at him the way I was swatting at the mosquitoes.

"There are better ways to get sweaty and dirty," I joked but stumbled forwards into the clutter and chaos. "Couldn't we have picked a better day to do this? It's so hot."

"The heat is good for you," my husband laughed and then started dragging the antique bed frame onto the lawn. I pushed as he pulled and soon it sat on the dry grass. We were both panting and we had just started.

I handed him boxes of baby clothes and a whole trash bag of shoes. The paint cans, a broken rake; I wheeled the wheelbarrow to the doorway and he removed it.

"See, isn't this good? We're working!" He grinned and I tried not to but I grinned back.

"Whatever."

"You're so stubborn."

"True," I said. The next box split wide open and a pile of clothes fell out. The item on top grabbed my attention and I did a double take. It was my "slut" dress from back in the day. I couldn't help myself. I started laughing.

I held it up when Marshall asked what was so funny.

"Oh yeah," he growled and before I could block him he stepped into the shed and pulled the door halfway closed. He yanked my shorts down and tugged my panties with them. "Out of those."

I made a lot of noise and carried on but his quick reaction was turning me on. I lifted my arms for him when he yanked my tank over my head. I had lost all shame. Sweat was running down my naked body from the heat of the day and the windowless shed. I let him slide the old black dress over my body. It hugged every curve, even the new ones, and fitted like a second skin.

"I like cleaning," my husband joked. "Remember this thing?"

I nodded but didn't say anything because his hand had wormed up under my dress and he pushed a finger into my pussy. I squirmed and sweat pooled between my breasts.

"When you wore this I would –" He stopped and turned me quickly.

I let out a shriek but loved the feel of his big hand on my hips. Pushing me forcefully. He put my arms up against the crib that stood on end and hiked the dress up, exposing my ass. I protested. Not much. He ignored me. Rubbed his free hand greedily over my bottom.

"I would do all kinds of things," he murmured under his breath. And then he sank to his knees and licked between my legs from behind. His tongue hot and seeking on my pussy. The tip of his tongue flicked my clit repeatedly and I grabbed the bars for support. I pushed back against him, trying to get his tongue more fully on my clit. I was soaked and the dress was hot. I didn't care.

He laughed as I wriggled against him. Then he stood and I heard his zipper in the quiet shed. Goosebumps sprang up my spine despite the heat and sweat.

"Oh, the things I would do to you," he grunted and pushed his cock against me. He ran it along the seam of my ass and then yanked my hips higher and thrust into me.

I sighed when he pushed all the way into me, fucking me hard. Just like we used to. When we were younger and crazier and horny all the time. His big fingers found my clit and started to stroke perfectly. He knew my body as well as his own after all this time.

"I love this dress," I yelled as his fingers found the exact rhythm I needed and I came long and hard. Marshall fucked me faster, harder. I rested my head against the old crib and pushed back against him to let him go deeper. Then his fingers were back and he played out one more perfect tune on my clit. He came with me this time with a growl.

He rested his forehead against the back of my neck. Both of us panting. Both of us laughing.

"See. Isn't cleaning fun, Suzy?"

I nodded and, after a moment, he withdrew and I stripped the hot, sweaty dress off. I got dressed and grabbed the next box while he went to get us cold drinks. I decided Marshall and I would have to clean more often. It really was worth all the effort.

HOTEL RENDEZVOUS

Jessica, Cleveland

As I stood in the lift waiting for the fifth floor I started to worry that I couldn't go through with this. It was a bit late to back out now, but I'd never been so nervous. I'd never done anything like this before.

I'd even had to go and buy something more appropriate to wear. The sort of clothing normally worn for this sort of "meeting" was not my usual attire.

I walked out of the lift and down the hall with knees that were trembling. Number 532 was about halfway down. I took a deep breath and knocked on the door.

He stood on the other side of the door looking me up and down. I'd opened my coat while I was waiting for him to open the door, so that he could see the corset top and skirt I had on and the black stiletto boots I'd bought specially that came over the knee.

The corset, although it certainly looked the part, was not too comfortable, but then, I supposed, it wouldn't be on for too long.

As I entered the room he asked if I would like something to drink. I asked for a glass of white wine and while he took my coat and put it away I gulped down half the glass in one go.

As he came back I smiled at him and said, "Hi, I'm Jessica, what would you like to do tonight?"

"How about I refill your glass to start with, then we could sit and get comfortable."

As I sat down on the corner of the bed I noticed the corset had pushed my breasts up even more. Normally I would have self-consciously realigned the top until I felt more comfortable, but that was not what this was about so tonight I changed the habit of a lifetime and left my breasts bulging out of the top. He seemed appreciative, I thought, by the way he looked at them as he handed me my glass.

He sat down next to me and brushed the hair off one side of my face. As he brought his hand back it wandered down and his thumb caressed over my left breast. My breathing had quickened and not only from nerves, I was actually finding this quite surprisingly exciting! I thought I would just be full of nerves and find it hard to fit into this role, but I was starting to enjoy it.

I turned myself more towards him and pushed my shoulders down and back, which made my breasts stand out even more. He put his hand on my hip and ran it up my body. As it got to the underside of my breast he pressed upwards and the breast popped out of the top of the corset, exposing my nipple. He looked me in the eye as he slowly took a mouthful of wine then bent down and sucked my nipple. As he swallowed, a bit of the wine escaped and ran down between my breasts. I inhaled sharply at the sensation of him sucking the nipple, already sensitive.

I pushed the other breast out of the top of the corset and moved his head over so that he could suck that too. I moaned slightly at the sensation. I was starting to feel totally wanton, this was sexy stuff; I was getting a real buzz from it. His hand had moved to my knee and was slowly making its way up my leg, which was parting of its own accord so that his hand had no opposition.

As he got to the top of my leg, his hand stopped and I wriggled impatiently. He laughed then kissed me deeply, his tongue filling my mouth. I stood up and moved round so I was standing in front of him. I unzipped my skirt and let it fall around my ankles. He looked at me standing there in my corset, stockings and boots, totally open to him as I'd worn no underwear, and he pulled me towards him.

My legs almost gave way as his tongue licked at my pussy. I clung to his shoulders while he kissed and licked my clit. I managed to get myself together enough to start to undress him.

I took off his top, which just slipped over his head, then knelt in front of him and undid his trousers. As I was doing this I was feeling his balls and cock, rubbing them through his clothes. I noticed his breathing had quickened and pulled off his trousers then boxers. I took hold of his cock with one hand and in the other had his balls. I slowly licked his cock and felt it jump in response. I took it as far in my mouth as I could then started to lick and suck it, all the time kneading his balls with my hands.

After a while he pulled me up and started to kiss me and he undid the corset. Once I was free he took both breasts in his hands and played with my nipples, then sucked and bit at them till I was moaning and more than ready to be fucked.

He turned us both around so I was stood against the bed then pushed me back onto it. He pushed my legs apart and went down on my pussy again. By now I was dripping and he slipped his finger into me. I groaned as my hips moved against him, wanting more than just his finger. He played with my pussy and clit for a while and I was starting to think I was going to come, but he moved up onto the bed and looked into my eyes as he thrust his cock into me.

I sighed and moaned at the same time; that was just what I wanted. He started to fuck me, slowly at first then faster and harder. My legs were wrapped around him; the feel of his hard cock thrusting in and out of me was pushing me towards the ultimate end. I could feel it building up and my breathing was getting more and more ragged. I realized I was digging my nails into his back and buttocks as I was clinging to him, but I couldn't let go. Then I was there, my whole body seemed to spasm and I felt a great release, and my pussy was just sort of pulsating with pleasure as he still kept thrusting. I don't know if I cried out or not, I didn't really notice anything except the sensations that were going through my body. Then he thrust harder and groaned. He thrust a few more times then started to slow down. After a few more gentle thrusts he stopped.

As I came out of the shower about half an hour later he was laid on the bed. "I think that went quite well," he said grinning at me. "What do you want to try next time?"

"I don't know just yet, let me get over this one first, though I have to admit it certainly spiced things up a bit, you were right there!"

"Well, I thought you made a very sexy prostitute," he said, laughing as I pulled a face at him.

"It does make it easier when you know the 'client' you're going to see is your boyfriend," I said as I lay on the bed beside him and took a sip of his wine. "Even so, I was still nervous as I was coming up here. I thought someone from the hotel might think I was a real prostitute and ask me to leave!"

GOOD BUDDIES

Larry, Hod Hasharon

I was almost fifteen when I first attended summer camp, but old snapshots from that period show a kid looking closer to twelve or thirteen. We'd just gone through a hard winter and my health, delicate at the best of times, had suffered accordingly. Imagine, if you will, a scrawny, undersized youth whose only signs of adolescence were a skin problem and compulsive masturbation.

Short on self-confidence but lavishly endowed with the cravings that gave my body no rest, I passed my days in furtive contemplation of the nubile teenage girls in my high school classes and my nights jerking off to lurid visions of Nancy Durbiner's pubic triangle, Sylvia Crage's dark-nippled breasts and Millicent Berko's resplendent rump. Of course, I had never seen these maidens in the altogether, but combining their faces with the bare tits, pussies and asses populating the semi-porno pages glimpsed over the shoulders of bolder boys fed the fantasies that brought me to climax after climax.

Picky about the charms of my virtual harem, I couldn't imagine myself enjoying the erotic favours of ladies less enthralling than Greek goddesses – big-bosomed beauties who thrust their pointy nipples in my mouth and their fingers up my rectum while they moaned their gratitude for the giant cock with which I reciprocated their attentions. The sad truth, however, was that only the women of my daydreams appreciated this supposedly awesome tool, of whose actual mediocrity I was only too well aware – barely five inches fully rampant if the tape measure lifted from my mother's sewing kit was to be believed.

It was this sad owner of post-pubescent shortcomings (a play on words the aptness of which was a source of much melancholy) who was sent off to Lake Kiniwaukie Camp for Young Adults in the Laurentian Mountains north of Montreal following a winter of antibiotics and thermometers. The theory was that the outdoor life would serve as a tonic and build up my strength. Due to a last-minute bout of stomach flu, however, I was the Johnny-come-lately of this rural arcadia.

I was not a happy camper during my first fortnight among the young adult nature lovers. As for me, I hated nature. I hated the mosquitoes and the sunburn I got my first day after forgetting to smear myself with sunscreen. I hated the hot cereal they forced me to eat at breakfast. I hated the smell of mildew that wafted from the mattress on my upper bunk. I especially hated the lack of privacy that forced me to whack off inside the concealing confines of an outhouse while my less inhibited tent mates joyously took part in circle jerks during siestas and after lights out.

What I hated most of all, however, was having to sit on the pebbly shore of Lake Kiniwaukie during the morning and afternoon swims while everyone else waded out into the chest-deep water. The trouble was that the buddy system was in effect, and all the other kids had paired off before my late arrival on the scene. No one was available to be my buddy.

"Let me be a third buddy with two others," I begged the swimming counsellor.

The hairy-chested whistle-bearer was adamant. "Sorry, son, the rule is one on one. Just be patient, I expect one or two to drop out in a couple of days and we'll be able to match you up."

Day after day, however, the camp population remained stable. A week went by, then two. I remained the only camper stranded on the beach. In the end, something snapped.

"The hell with it!" I muttered at last between gritted teeth, got to my feet and marched into the water. They would have to use force to get me out.

The counsellor's whistle shrilled, a long blast of fury. "You with the ribcage, out of the water!"

I stood my ground (or rather, water).

"Out, goddamn it! Out I say, or I'm coming in to get you and both of us will be sorry."

Though naturally timid, I ignored the threat, determined to make him sorrier than I if push came to shove. What was the worst that could happen? My parents would be called to remove me from the camp.

Arms akimbo, the counsellor studied me with evident reluctance to make good on his ultimatum. Finally he climbed down his tree.

"Muri," he called, "get in there and take care of that boy."

Muriel Slovak was the counsellor-in-training assigned lifeguard duty on the raft anchored twenty metres from shore. She was a tall, skinny beanpole of a girl with large feet and little frontage, universally known as 'the carpenter's dream' because she was as flat as a board. To compensate for her unlovely appearance, she was blessed with a disposition as sour as a crab apple.

"Aw, Jeez, Eddy, not with that squirt," she protested.

"Don't be a wise ass," he warned. "You're a C.I.T. on probation."

You didn't have to draw Muriel a picture. Without another word, she dived into the water and paddled to my side. From her superior height, she gave me a dirty look.

"You rotten little shrimp," she said, "get back to shore."

I crossed my arms to hide my nipples. "No way, Jose."

She plunged one hand below the surface. I felt a sharp nip below my left buttock. Ow! The bitch had pinched me, hard.

With the courage of a cornered rabbit, I returned the favour, not just with thumb and forefinger but the other three digits as well, grabbing and squeezing all I could of the bony butt beneath the lower edge of her bathing suit.

She didn't cry out, but turned very red. "That's enough, kid. Let go," she whispered.

"Say you're sorry," I demanded.

I must have been drunk with audacity. Her heinie felt very malleable in my hand. I pressed my palm against it and loosened my grip, then squeezed more gently. The sensation was very pleasant.

She sighed and I felt her hand navigate like a submarine to the small of my back. It slithered beneath the elastic waist of my bathing suit. A fingernail indented the top of the cleavage between my buttocks and then raced south along this track to the back of my scrotum. My mast rose instantly to take advantage of the impending fair weather.

It's hard for me to picture what we must have looked like to the casual observer, either in the water or on shore. To all intents and purposes, two kids – an older, taller girl and an apparently immature boy the top of whose head barely reached her shoulder – standing stiffly (and I use the term advisedly) side by side immersed above the navel. All the action was going on invisibly beneath the surface.

It took all my self-control to keep from gasping and my face expressionless as her fingers moved from back to front and began massaging the base of my engorged phallus. She frowned at me, as if still resentful of the imposition, but her thighs trembled with excitement, as my own questing fingertips homed in on her crotch, lightly brushed the thick, wiry pelt of her bearded groin, and pressed for admittance into the honeypot to which her spreading legs made me welcome.

Preeeeep! The swimming counsellor's whistle drilled through the hubbub of bathers. "Everybody out, everybody out. Fifteen minutes for showers."

"Oh, Christ!" I groaned. "It's impossible. I won't be able to for half an hour at least."

Imagine the jeers and laughter as the cantilevered front of my swimsuit emerged from the lake. No, I would drown myself first.

"Let me handle this," she murmured, and laboriously trudged ashore. A brief consultation with her boss followed. A small conspiratorial smile lifted the corners of her mouth as she headed back.

"It's OK," she reassured me, "I told him you can't swim, and I volunteered to teach you. I just got my instructor's badge and he promised me the first learner. We have an extra twenty minutes."

"But I can swim," I protested.

She gave me an evil grin. "Not in the free style I'm gonna show you. Float on your belly face down."

This was better than floating on my back and flaunting the pup tent at the front of my swimsuit to all the world. I did a dead man's prone spread-eagle, though below the waist I was anything but dead. The subaqueous protuberance between my legs, like the keel of a sailboat, was almost enough by itself to keep me stable in the water.

Muriel positioned herself at my side and placed both hands, palms up, under my abdomen in the classic pose of a swimming instructor encouraging the confidence of a novice still uncertain of his buoyancy in the water. The hand farthest from my head drifted in a southerly direction, as if inadvertently, until it encountered the waistband of my swimsuit. There, a pair of fingers found the drawstring and gently tugged the front of my trunks backwards until they popped free from and slid below my raging hard-on. Fortunately, my ass was still covered.

"Now I wonder what this can be?" she said, exploring blindly by touch. "Is it a log of driftwood?"

"Not exactly," I groaned, arching my back.

"Am I getting warm?" she asked, squeezing the shaft with exquisite pressure and pumping it ever so delicately up and down between its forty-five degree cant to my body and perpendicularity.

My voice was a hoarse croak. "Yes, warm."

"I'll bet it's a bonerfish."

I was too preoccupied with other matters to correct the misnomer.

"Warm, very warm," I moaned, and began to thrash in the water, compulsively imitating the frantic motions of a non-swimmer. Her fingers formed a cylinder and travelled slowly, lingeringly, up and down my piston. I couldn't restrain a yelp and a number of involuntary pelvic thrusts. From afar, it must have seemed that I was learning the rudiments of the butterfly stroke.

"Third guess," she said. "A water pipe."

"Hot! Hot!" I cried, and came in an orgasm so violent and explosive that, though its epicentre was somewhere behind my balls, I felt it from deep in my anus right up to the nape of my neck. The ejaculation seemed unending. I'd never experienced anything like it before, a fierce pleasure that threatened to tear my nerves apart.

Creamy-grey globules of semen popped to the surface of the water several inches in front of my head, so powerful had been the force that propelled them out the barrel of my prick like priapic projectiles.

"I should have known," Muriel said with a laugh, "A blow-gun."

The droplets of my jism gleamed like pearls in the sunlight. Muriel dispersed them among the sparkling wavelets with a sweep of her hand.

"You owe me one," she said, tidying me up with sisterly solicitude.

A gentleman always pays his debts. I made sure the rest of that summer, whenever opportunity offered, that mine were properly (you should pardon the expression) discharged.

SECRET MISTRESS

Lilith, Toronto

I have to get something off my chest and I can't tell anyone. When it first started, it was all in forbidden fun: a few secret encounters, a good orgasm and life as usual. No harm, no foul. Now, a year later and not long before the wedding, I feel I must confess. Of course, the first person I would want to tell is my best friend, but she is the last person that I can tell right now!

I met Jen at the advertising agency where we both work. She was the senior account director on the first project I was assigned to. Jen was nice to me from day one and took me under her wing. She taught me "the ropes" and gave me the inside scoop on the office politics.

One Friday afternoon, Jen told me her boyfriend was out of town and invited me back to her place for a "girls' night". I was positively delighted. You see, not only had I just started a new job, I also had just moved to the city and didn't really know anyone. The prospect of having a new friend to hang out with and develop some sort of social life was appealing so, of course, I accepted.

We had left a little early from work that day. Jen had some errands to run and I went to the gym. I pulled up in front of the Victorian brownstone at 7 p.m. as planned. I walked up the stairs and rang the bell. I was surprised to see a tall well-dressed man behind the door but no sign of Jen.

He must have noticed the look of confusion on my face because he promptly introduced himself. He was John, Jen's boyfriend, and his business trip had been cancelled. He proceeded to tell me that Jen had called to say she had a flat tyre and was running late. It was going to be at least an hour before the tow service came to help.

He invited me in and led me to the living room where he motioned for me to sit down while he poured me a drink. I watched him walk over to the bar and noted his pants hugged his perfectly formed bottom really well. I used the mirror over the bar to sneak a peak at his well-chiselled face; Jen had really caught herself a hottie! John smiled when he caught me looking at him and I was embarrassed. I may as well have been drooling!

We sat across from each other on the oversized sofa and sipped our martinis. The conversation was slightly subdued at first, but as the alcohol kicked in, the conversation flowed freely. We talked about John's job at a competing ad firm and how he and Jen had met.

One half-hour later and the start of a second martini, I thought that John's attentiveness towards me was a little calculated. It seemed as if he was flirting with me. That's when I realized that perhaps I should slow down on the alcohol. What was I thinking? Not only had I just met him, but also he was my co-worker's (hopefully soon to be my good friend) boyfriend! Jen never gave me any reason to believe that she and John were having problems so there was no way that John was flirting with me.

No sooner had I convinced myself that I was overreacting than John was sitting beside me on the couch. He was close, really close. So close that I could smell the scent of his aftershave coupled with the muskiness of a long hard day at work.

Before I could speak he was kissing me. His lips were soft and gentle as his tongue found mine. We sat there and kissed, passionately. Deliberately.

Without any words, his fingers found their way up my skirt to my increasingly wet mound. He skilfully pushed my panties aside and entered me with his fingers. I was swollen and soaked. With a primal grunt, John grabbed me and pulled me on top of him. He pulled my skirt up around my thighs, pushed my panties aside for the second time, and entered me. I let myself be driven up and down on John's throbbing cock as if on autopilot.

A few hard thrusts were all it took before my muscles tightened around his member and I rode the wave of a taboo orgasm. Feeling my pussy grip his cock must have pushed John to the edge, because he blew his sticky juice.

It all happened so fast. Fifteen minutes or so. We had just finished cleaning up and I was beginning to realize what I had done, when Jen walked in. I wondered if the smell of sex still lingered in the air.

She kissed John hello and waved at me, all the while apologizing for being so late.

Guilt was starting to sink in and I thought about leaving, but I was paranoid that it might look suspicious and that Jen would wonder why I bolted without having our "girls' night".

I decided it was best to stay. I did, however, accept the offer of what was now my third martini. John's presence began to make me very uncomfortable. The pheromones still hung in the air. John must have sensed it too because he excused himself and said something about a conference call with Japan and late-night work.

The fourth drink was finished and I barely remembered the third. I started to look at Jen in a different light. I had never been with a woman, but I couldn't help but find Jen attractive. Her five-foot frame, long brown hair and big blue eyes gave her an endearing impish quality.

I relaxed and talked to Jen as if she were an old friend. We sat side by side and giggled like schoolgirls. We shared secrets, most embarrassing tales and our goals for the future. We were having a great time when suddenly I got that familiar feeling that now *she* was flirting.

Jen ran her finger around the rim of her wine glass and looked at me lasciviously. She leaned in closer and, with the same stealthy skill as her boyfriend, Jen started to kiss me. Unlike John's soft gentle probing, Jen's kiss was full of lust and desire. Her tongue enveloped mine as she pulled me close. She stopped kissing me long enough to look at me coyly, brought her finger to her mouth and said, "Shh."

Jen kissed my neck and worked her way down to my breasts. She undid my buttons and exposed my black lacy push-up bra.

Jen's touch was hungry and her eyes drank me in. She wasted no time and yanked down my bra so she could suck on my nipples. I wanted to moan but I was scared that John would hear us.

Once she was satisfied that my nipples were hard enough to cut glass, Jen began to move down my body with a purpose. I was still wet from my previous encounter and I was scared that Jen would smell the sex emanating from between my legs.

If she noticed, she didn't care. Jen looked at me and smiled before she buried her face in my pussy.

I felt powerless. Lost in fear and paralysed by pleasure.

I threw my head back and enjoyed as Jen's tongue touched every fold and licked every inch of my swollen lips.

When she thrust herself into my quivering hole, I exploded in ecstasy. I had to grab the pillow and bite down on it to keep from making any noise. For the second time that night, I had a forbidden orgasm, and those were the most powerful kind.

Jen worked her way back up my body and kissed me again. Deeply and passionately. I tasted myself on her lips and it was hot.

I felt like I should return the favour. I mean, I'd gotten off twice already, well once officially, but I felt like I should do something for Jen.

I was nervous; as I said, I'd never been with a woman and the only pussy I'd touched was my own. While Jen kissed me, I timidly placed my hand up her skirt and on the inside of her thigh. I noticed that her panties were soggy and I was a little flattered that I had been the cause of that. Now it was my turn to push her underwear aside and find my way around. It was quite slippery and my finger slid inside her almost immediately. Jen grabbed my hand and showed me how to finger-fuck her. She found her rhythm and rode my hand like a pro. It wasn't long before Jen released all over my hand and down my arm. Her vaginal muscles tightened around my fingers like my cunt had held John's cock only a few hours before.

Feeling Jen come on my hand was exhilarating. I felt self-assured and even a little powerful.

Out of breath, Jen got up and pulled her skirt down. She kissed my cheek and sat back down on the couch.

The rest of the evening carried on as if nothing happened. We drank some more, we laughed some more and we talked a lot more. John eventually came out of his meeting and joined us. At first I thought they planned this but John didn't seem to have any clue what had happened between Jen and me, and Jen didn't know about John.

I was their secret.

This became an ongoing thing. Once a month or so, I'd get an email for a secret rendezvous with John or another "girls' night" invite when John was out of town.

Each and every time, there were barely any words spoken. When we were finished, we'd get dressed and return to our day, or carry on our "girlish gossiping" like nothing happened.

It was good. I got to enjoy the best of both worlds.

But now they are getting married and I have been asked to visit each of them in their quarters before the wedding. I wonder if they are going to tell me that these encounters can no longer carry on. Who knows, maybe they'll suggest the three of us get together sometime.

GETTING A HOT RECEPTION

Sophie, Darlington

If you'd ever told me that one day I would willingly let a man strip me and spank my arse, I would have said you were mad. I had never seen the attraction of a firm hand to bring me into line, or understood the pleasure in pain. But that was before my boss's wedding reception.

I had been working at the leisure centre for a little over a year, and almost as long as I had been there, I had been lusting over Gary, one of the pool area supervisors. He was gorgeous: well over six feet tall, with a lean, swimmer's body and a permanent growth of dark stubble on his chin. He was ten years younger than me, but we liked the same kind of music, and we would spend most of our lunchtimes talking about gigs we were planning to get tickets for or the latest songs we'd downloaded to our iPods. Even though we were always flirting with each other, I drooled over him from a distance because he had a serious girlfriend and that rendered him strictly off limits.

And then Derek, the centre's manager, announced that he was getting married. Only a handful of the people who worked there were going to be attending the actual ceremony, but the rest of us were invited to the evening do. I accepted without hesitation – after all, it would give me the chance to splash out on a new outfit and drink my favourite tipple, champagne – but I became even more keen to go after Gary's girlfriend left him for her driving instructor a couple of weeks before the event. When he told me about the split, I made plenty of suitably sympathetic noises, and I did genuinely feel sorry for him, because he'd had no idea that she had been cheating on him and he was too nice a bloke to deserve that kind of treatment. Inside, however, I was secretly excited about the fact I might now have a chance with him.

The reception was being held in a country hotel on the outskirts of town on a swelteringly hot evening in August. The taxi I had booked to take me there turned up a little early, so I was one of the first to arrive. I stood for a moment in the entrance hall, fluffing up my hair and checking that my lipstick wasn't smudged, just in case the first person I bumped into was Gary. Instead, I was greeted by a white-jacketed waiter who offered me a glass of pink champagne. I took it and made my way over to congratulate Derek and his new bride. When I decided it was time to mingle, my glass having been topped up a couple of times almost without me being aware of it, I realized that Gary was sitting at a table to one side of the dance floor. I almost couldn't believe the transformation in him. I was so used to seeing him in his work outfit of dark-blue polo shirt and tracksuit bottoms – which, admittedly, clung deliciously to his absolutely outstanding arse – but tonight he was formally dressed in a well-cut suit and black shirt. Unlike some of the other men there, he didn't look uncomfortable or strangely bulky out of his leisurewear. Instead, he had an air of assurance that was not only very horny but also a little bit dangerous. Just looking at him as he sat there, fingers toying with the stem of his champagne flute, made me think of stripping him out of that suit and doing all kinds of dirty things to him. I was imagining how it might feel to go down on his cock with a mouthful of champagne when I realized that he was watching me with an amused smirk on his face, almost as if he had read my mind. I blushed and smiled, feeling my pussy twitch with lust as he continued to gaze at me. I was about to go over and speak to him, even though I wasn't sure I could spit out a sentence at that moment without sounding like a lust-crazed idiot, and then Julia, one of the aerobics instructors, took my arm and insisted on dragging me onto the dance floor.

The covers band Derek had booked for the occasion were pretty good, belting out disco classics that were guaranteed to get people up and dancing, and I soon lost myself in the music. I didn't forget about Gary entirely, though; I kept glancing over to where he was sitting from time to time, and he always seemed to be watching me. So I began dancing more provocatively, grinding my hips and running my hands over my body as I moved. And then I flung one arm out, striking a pose, and hit something. I turned to realize that I had knocked a glass out of someone's hand and Gary – who I assumed had come over to dance with me – had only managed to avoid it splashing all over him by stepping smartly to one side.

"Now, that wasn't a very clever thing to do, was it, Sophie?" he said, grabbing hold of my wrist. I stammered an apology, but he continued, lowering his voice so that no one else around us could hear, "You're just a naughty little show-off, and I think you should be punished."

I didn't have a clue what he was intending to do, but the way he said "punished" made me start to grow wet between my legs. He began to lead me firmly away from the dance floor. "Where are you taking me?" I asked.

"We're going to my room. I booked it so I wouldn't have to drive home tonight." He smiled wickedly. "I could keep you there all night, if I wanted. After all, I doubt we'll be missed."

I glanced over my shoulder at my colleagues and Derek's friends as Gary hustled me away and realized he was right. They were all too busy drinking and dancing and having a good time to even notice us leaving. Within moments, we were heading up the stairs to Gary's room on the second floor. He didn't release his grip on my arm, and I started to feel giddy with anticipation and excitement. He was so much bigger and stronger than me, I knew that he could do whatever he wanted to me – or, rather, whatever I wanted him to do to me.

Gary appeared to have one of the nicest rooms in the hotel, with a bed that looked big enough for three people and a view out on to the golf course behind the hotel, but he didn't give me much of an opportunity to admire my surroundings. Instead, he sat down on his bed and calmly ordered me to get over his knees. This wasn't quite what I had been expecting, and I just stood there. "Do as you're told, or you'll only make it worse for yourself," he said, and when I still hesitated, he lost patience and hauled me bodily over his lap.

"OK, the joke's over," I said, wriggling to get free, but he was holding me securely and I couldn't move.

"Not till you've had the spanking you deserve," he replied. So that was what he'd meant by punishment, I realized giddily, as I felt him raising the hem of my new sage green dress up around my waist. When I'd first tried it on, loving the colour and the way the flimsy chiffon skimmed my curves, I'd had daydreams of Gary peeling me out of it, but not quite like this. It was so quiet in the room, away from the noise of the band and the party downstairs, and I found myself holding my breath as Gary gazed for a moment at my bum cheeks, just about covered by the black lacy knickers I was wearing. Then I felt his big hand come down on my upturned bottom. I gasped, partly in shock, partly in indignation – cute as he was, and as much as I fancied him, how *dare* he do this to me? I told him, as firmly as I could, to stop, but he just carried on as though he hadn't heard me, calmly alternating slaps on each cheek. They weren't particularly hard, but I felt each one, and I writhed on his lap, becoming aware as I did so that his cock was swelling and hardening beneath me.

After about a dozen spanks, he suddenly stopped. I thought that was it, and if so it hadn't been too bad. A little bit embarrassing, a little bit uncomfortable, but no worse than that.

And then I felt him reach for the waistband of my knickers. "No!" I squealed, deciding that things had gone quite far enough.

Gary ignored me, calmly continuing with what he was doing. "Let's see what that lovely little bottom of yours looks like, shall we?"

I was mortified at the way he was treating me, and yet the thought of being bared to him like this was making my pussy flood with juices. Surely this wasn't me, this person who was so incredibly turned on by being made to do as she was told, who suddenly wanted Gary to go further, to strip her naked, to make her get down before him in nothing but her heels and suck his cock? I didn't know how being spanked had brought me to this;

I only knew that it had, and I wanted more of this shameful, thrilling pleasure.

With one sharp tug, my panties were down round my knees and off.

"Beautiful," Gary murmured, stroking the tender flesh of my newly exposed bottom.

I wondered how it looked to him, blushing red from his slaps. I wanted him to order me to go and look at my reflection in the mirror, but he had other ideas. Almost immediately, he returned to the job of spanking me. Now there was nothing at all shielding me from the full force of his palm as it landed again and again. I kicked and squirmed on Gary's lap, begging him to have mercy, but it didn't have any effect on him. Occasionally, however, he would run his fingers down to my cleft, insinuating them between the damp, slippery folds of my pussy and distracting me from the burning sensations in my arse cheeks.

He seemed to delight in tormenting me like this, alternating between the rough slaps that were making my bum sting and the soft little rubs which were causing my clit to tingle and my body to move towards orgasm. I was still aware of the stiffness of his cock, pushing up at me through layers of clothing, and at that moment I would have given anything to feel him inside me. But Gary was in charge here; he was the one who decided if and when I came and whether or not I would be filled with his length.

And still the relentless spanking continued. I wanted him to stop, and yet I needed him to continue, grinding my body against the thick fabric of his trousers and the throbbing cock beneath them, trying to give myself that last, vital little bit of stimulation.

At last, he seemed to feel he had punished me enough, and his fingers suddenly plunged into my hole. With two fingers plunging in and out of my wetness and his thumb rubbing my clit, he swiftly had me moaning and thrashing around, no longer caring how humiliating it was to be lying, bottom bare and bright crimson, over his knees. My pleasure peaked sharply and I was coming, gasping and calling out how good it felt. Finally, I lay limp on Gary's lap.

"So have you learned your lesson, Sophie?" he asked.

"I think so," I replied. But, of course, I hadn't. I still seem to find ways of misbehaving which mean Gary has to punish me as a result, and I just can't get enough of the way he keeps me in line with a good, hard spanking. I hope I never do.

SHAMELESS

Steve, Australia

A guilty secret? OK, here goes. The first time I was in a threesome was with my wife, Chloe, and a young woman I'll call Jessie. I can't use her real name because last I heard she was calling herself a lesbian and denying that she'd ever been anything else. Which is a little strange, because when I first met her, she was nominally het. It took Chloe, oh, all of about five seconds to convert her to bi, and another woman about the same length of time to turn her again . . . but I'm getting ahead of myself.

Jessie was a co-ed of Chloe's, and she was one of those women whose body language and conversation are euphemistically described as "inappropriate", the sort who will casually describe the exact colour of her nipples to you in culinary terms, or stand close to you while massaging her breasts but slap your face if you interpret this as an invitation. Anyway, one night while I was away in the US, Chloe was feeling horny, so she called Jessie and asked her if she wanted to come around and have sex. Jessie was a little flustered, and replied, "I don't know what to say."

"Say yes," Chloe suggested, so Jessie said, "Yes," and drove over. As I said, about five seconds to change gender preferences. After that, they had sex a couple of times a week until I came back home and things went back to normal – well, normal for us, anyway.

I'd known since our first date that Chloe was bi – no problem, nearly all of my lovers have been either active or latent bi women – and that both of us had tried strict monogamy and decided that we didn't like it. We hadn't been together long before we started talking about threesomes and trying to choose a likely candidate from our friends. But that didn't prepare me for the time I came home from work early and saw two women sixty-nining on our futon, so tightly wrapped in each other like yin and yang, their thighs clamped over the other's ears, that they didn't even hear me walk in. In the near darkness, I couldn't tell who was who, where one began and the other ended, but it was a wonderful sight, as magical as the first time I saw Saturn's rings through a telescope or the first time I saw a woman I loved naked and wanting me. And the smell of sex was as thick as incense; you could have bottled it and sold it as an expensive perfume, or an aphrodisiac that actually worked.

I'm not sure how long I stood there and watched, with them oblivious to me, but it was long enough for my eyes to adjust to the dim light and recognize Jessie's dark blond hair at one end of this beauty with two backs, Chloe's auburn curls at the other. Minutes, certainly, before Chloe's face emerged; she smiled encouragingly, and I started undressing. Chloe changed position so that I could see more of Jessie, including her face and her breasts. Her nipples were the colour of musk candy, just as she'd described them, swollen and erect, though her areolae were so small and pale that they were hardly there at all. She opened her eyes a moment later, obviously surprised to find me there, but feeling much too good to be worried by anything. I knelt beside the bed, my lips millimetres from her nipple, and asked, "May I?"

She nodded, and I ran my tongue around the already-swollen nipple, then gently closed my lips around it and began sucking on her breast while Chloe continued licking her clit. Jessie just closed her eyes again and luxuriated; Chloe and I both pride ourselves on our technique, and maybe Jessie had been fantasizing about this too. I moved my head to Jessie's other breast and began sucking on that; it was firmer and a little larger than Chloe's, but the best thing about it was knowing that I was pleasing two women as well as myself, that Chloe was getting off on watching me feasting on this sweet white flesh.

I kissed my way down Jessie's belly until Chloe and I were almost cheek to cheek. She turned her head and gave me a quick kiss, her mouth wet and delicious. Then she moved aside, stroking Jessie's labia with her fingers while I began circling her clit with my tongue. Jessie looked at us, gave us a slow and slightly dazed smile, and closed her eyes again. I applied a little more pressure to her clit, a little suction with my lips, easing the pace along from languid to leisurely, watching and listening for her reaction. She remained silent, almost as though she were in a trance. I licked and sucked more vigorously, my beard rubbing against her cleft and her thighs; still not a sound. I continued until my neck was sore, and looked up uncertainly at Chloe, wondering whether I should stop. She shook her head slightly, and I resumed tongue-lashing Jessie's clit until suddenly she began shaking her head, flailing her arms about and drumming her heels on the bed. I moved my head out of harm's way and rubbed her clit with my thumb as she arched her back and writhed. It was like holding an earthquake in my hand, and I watched in awe as she subsided back into her trance. Chloe kissed me, then bent over and began sucking my cock. I lay down next to Jessie, sitting up against the bedhead, and Chloe straddled me; I kissed her lips, her neck, and sucked her breasts as we fucked. With Jessie's orgasm and afterglow as an aphrodisiac, a catalyst, we were so aroused, so intent, so overwhelmed by all the sex that had happened on that bed, so absorbed in each other and oblivious to anything else, that we barely noticed as Jessie opened her eyes and watched us, then climbed off the bed and staggered towards the shower. I don't know how often Chloe came, but we were still fucking when Jessie returned and began picking up her clothes, still fucking when she dressed and walked to the kitchen to put the kettle on. Even after I came, we just held on to each other, basking in the afterglow that filled the room.

I do feel slightly ashamed about our having lied to Jessie. You see, Chloe had told her I'd be home *late*, not early.

But my *real* guilty secret is that I'm sitting here at the office, reminiscing and writing erotica on the computer, while my boss thinks I'm working. *Please* don't send him a copy of this book!

THE IRISHMAN

Mariah, Bellvue

Two of my friends and I were drinking one night and got talking about the best cock we ever had. I would never have told them this if I hadn't been half smashed but they loved it.

Patrick was the most delicious man I'd ever known, pure porn. With black curly hair, blue eyes like jewels, big powerful arms, he was a burly beautiful Irishman.

His wife, my first cousin, had passed away after a two-year illness during which time I watched that man work himself to distraction doing everything he possibly could for the woman he loved.

I couldn't help but be aware that this was an extremely virile man who had not had sex in at least a year and a half. Sometimes I would see him looking at me in a way that was pure sexual hunger. But then he would quickly look away and I felt sorry for him that he was feeling unnecessary shame.

For weeks after she passed I saw that he was always being careful to keep his eyes off me and I was beginning to see that this man's suffering had gone on far too long. Something had to be done.

Sometimes he would drink too much and fall into his bed in a deep sleep. This particular night I slipped into his room, took out the handcuffs I'd bought that day and deftly cuffed his wrists to the rungs of the headboard.

Groggy, it dawned on him that he was tethered and he began to fight wildly until he saw me standing there in a white lacy little short thing that covered almost nothing.

Wide-eyed, he said, "Mariah, my God, what are you doing?"

"Patrick, please don't fight this," I said. "I'm doing something for you, something that's long overdue."

"What are you talking about? Let me loose!"

"Don't make this hard on yourself, baby," I said. "I'll let you loose when I'm finished."

He was wearing only boxer shorts and I could see that his cock was jammed up against the fly making a tent. The poor guy couldn't help it. He hadn't had sex in two years and was staring at a beautiful woman (if I do say so myself) wearing almost nothing. With the excitement of what I was doing, my nipples were turgid, my sex throbbing.

"Let me loose, Mariah, don't do this."

Gently I pulled down his shorts and it was interesting that he didn't kick at me. He could have, but being the old-world gentleman that he was he would never kick at a lady, even now.

His very large stiff cock was standing straight up and I could see that he was embarrassed.

"I can't – Elizabeth," he said, and it really sounded like he was on the verge of tears.

"Patrick, darling, Elizabeth loved you and you did everything for her you could do. She wouldn't want you to suffer like this."

"Please, Mariah, I can't," he whispered.

"You're not doing anything, sweetheart; I'm doing it, so you don't have anything at all to feel guilty about. You can't get free and you have no control over what I'm about to do, so you may as well just lie there and enjoy it."

The look on his face was excitement, and maybe a little fear, I'm not sure. "It's not your fault, baby," I said. "I'm the villain here."

I sat on the bed taking his beautiful rigid cock in both my hands, and bending down I sucked the full wine-coloured plum into my mouth.

With a loud gasp, almost a scream, he stiffened, his hips coming up off the bed. "No, baby, please," he moaned and I knew he was in ecstasy.

I continued to suck the plum, encircling it tightly with my tongue, now sliding my lips over the long shaft all the way down to the nest of dark hair, then back up and down again, a little faster, a little faster, my lips gripping it hard, my tongue circling, the suction powerful.

Now he was screaming, trying to pull away because he was about to come and was trying to keep from letting it erupt into my mouth.

No, you sweet, delicious man, you're not getting away, I thought, holding tight as he lost control. Hot semen was squirting in powerful spasms, his whole body was shuddering and he was groaning like he was dying. And I was still sucking it out, drinking it in, loving it. I love the taste of a clean, healthy man's come. There's nothing like it.

"Mariah, what have I done?" he murmured, like he had committed some horrible crime.

"You haven't done anything," I said. "I did it. Do you think you could have stopped me?" Even as I spoke I was fondling his cock and balls, caressing him. I lay down on top of him and rubbed my big breasts against his hairy chest, kissed his throat, his cheeks, the corners of his mouth, and his head turned, his open mouth seeking mine. His sweet mouth was so sensual and I opened it with my tongue, kissing him roughly.

He moaned and I clasped his cock, which had another powerful erection. "Patrick, sweetheart, I'm going to climb on top of you and fuck you, baby, so don't try to fight me because you can't stop me. I'm going to fuck the hell out of you and there's absolutely nothing you can do to keep it from happening."

The poor precious man was groaning, his hips pushing up at me. Climbing on top of him I straddled him and, opening my sex, I took his cock in my hands and placed it in the opening. Gently I slid down on his big long cock and it was so damn big it was hurting a little, but I was able to take in almost all of it.

I began to pump my hips up and down, slowly at first because it was so damn good I was very close to having an electrifying orgasm. But this was not for me; it was for him, and I was going to fuck him until I had drained him of every ounce of that stored up come. Now I was able to move faster, driving my sex down on that pulsating cock, pushing it deep into me, and Patrick was gasping, groaning, pushing up to meet me.

"Oh God, oh God," he whimpered, his body shuddering, jerking again, and I knew he was coming. He let out this loud gasp, stiffened, pushed into me, and I could feel him ejaculating, filling me up. With every electrifying spasm, he screamed, pushing into me until he finally went limp.

Somehow I knew there was still another orgasm in there. I got up and cleaned myself up a little while he lay there cuffed to the bed.

"I'm sorry," he whimpered, like he was ashamed for coming like that.

"You're going to be a lot sorrier, sweetheart, because I'm not through with you yet," I said, laughing.

I took out a slender phallic-shaped vibrator, plugged it in and went back to the bed. I greased it with petroleum jelly and laid it aside for the moment. Gently I began to massage his cock and balls again, kissing, sucking playfully at the head, then sucking more in earnest and after a while that beautiful cock was standing at attention again. Continuing to slide my lips down on his cock, I picked up the vibrator and began to gently insert it in his rectum. When he realized what I was doing he began to fight me, yelling for me to stop, and when he tried to push my hand away with his foot he inadvertently opened himself up and I went all the way into him. Flipping the switch, I turned it on.

"Aghhh," he screamed, and suddenly his cock stood straight up as hard as a wooden club.

"Oh shit, oh shit, oh shit," he was screaming, and his cock was squirting come into the air covering us both.

I was so damn turned on watching him shooting off like that. "Well, baby, I think I've pretty much drained you," I said. "I'm going to let you loose now and you can beat me up if you want to." I removed one cuff and then the other. "I hope you can forgive me," I said.

"Just a minute here, little girl, you're not going anywhere," he said. He was a very strong man and in a moment he had me cuffed to the bed. I was scared as hell, not knowing if he was mad or not, not knowing what he was up to.

With me lying there helpless those beautiful blue eyes were looking down into mine. "Now you're going to get your punishment for being a bad girl," he whispered. He kissed me hard on the mouth, then his lips brushed down my throat to my breasts, sucking hard on one nipple and then the other, pulling them, being rough, hurting me in the most delicious way.

"You thought you had drained me, honey, not even close," he murmured. Pushing my thighs open roughly, he buried his face in my sex. Seeking and finding my clitoris with his tongue, his lips and tongue sucked it so hard I screamed, the tingling spasms setting me on fire. But he was relentless, his tongue going deep in me, probing as he sucked, and I was coming so hard I felt I was dying. The shocks were radiating out from my sex in electric waves and I thought surely my heart would give out.

Weak and trembling I said, "Patrick, you can let me loose now."

With a devilish laugh he said, "Oh hell, no, little girl, not a chance. I'm just getting started. I'm going to fuck you till you cry, till you beg me to let you loose." As he said this he was mounting me and, shoving my legs apart with his knees, he went into me deep, hard, pumping in me like a flawless machine.

"I'm going to fuck you for every day of my life I did without," he said, grunting, slamming into me, stroking hard and fast, and I could feel a vaginal orgasm building in me to another volatile climax.

"That's a good start, baby," he murmured and then kissed me roughly, biting, pulling at my nipples. Everything this gorgeous Irishman was doing was driving me mad with desire.

"Let's see how you like this," he said, laughing.

When I saw he had the vibrator I screamed, "No," and tried to twist away from him, but he threw himself on me and held me down. Pulling my leg up, he pushed the thing all the way into me with me screaming for him to stop.

"Yeah, baby, I'm going to stop just like you did," he said, turning it on. Then, holding it in, he climbed on me and drove his rigid cock into me again. I was humiliated, trying to push the vibrator out, but he was holding it in, thrusting in me fast and deep, my whole insides vibrating.

"Hot damn, that feels good," he said, and when I stopped fighting and gave in to it, I never felt anything that felt so rapturous. I was moaning and groaning and wailing like a crazy person and he was fucking me like a wild man.

This time when I started coming it was a long protracted orgasm, and deep vibrating thrills were washing over me in waves that I thought were killing me. And somewhere in my dreamy, ecstatic state I felt him stiffen, drive into me, and he was gasping, pumping hot sperm, digging his fingers into my bottom, pulling me tightly to him like he was trying to drive that cock all the way to China. Finally he reached up, unlocked my cuffs and went limp on me as we drifted into a deep sleep.

There was more of the same when we woke up, but you get the picture.

P FOR PANTIES

Poulose, Boxboro

"*The degree and kind of one's sexuality reach up into the ultimate pinnacle of one's spirit*"– Nietzsche

I vividly remember the sowing of the seed that flowered into my obsession with panties. It happened one bright golden sunny spring morning in my backyard. The bell in the nearby church had just tolled the Angelus, and the shadow of the church steeple, cast by the setting sun, fell upon me. My younger sister had recently been toilet trained and I heard my mother ecstatically croon over her to a visiting aunt, "See how cute she looks in her panties!" No one had ever crooned over me like that and the incident struck me deeply. I was five and little to know that over the next twenty-five years I would be fascinated with panties, and that it would take Rose, Kurt and an unforgettable night with them before I would be rid of my obsession.

My obsession was triggered off many years later, when, at the local laundromat, I opened the door to the dryer and found in it a pair of white panties. Luminous in the reflected neon lights, it seemed magically alive, dancing and beckoning to me from the dim interior, mouth-wateringly perfect, white, soft, silky, scanty, petite and feminine. A few days later, I mail-ordered my first pair of panties and from this modest beginning gradually acquired a near perfect collection of panties and briefs.

Ten years later, one snowy winter, depressed by the early darkness, the snow and the cold, I visited the local Sears to buy some socks. I walked through the women's lingerie section and entered the men's area. Against the eye candy of lingerie in the women's section, the men's underwear looked like white burlap sacks. The bright neon lights and the deathly whiteness of the vests hanging around me matched the swirling snow outside. The store was cold – they seemed to have turned the heating off. My spirits sank deeper.

I found the socks section, bent down, rummaged through the bin and picked out half-a-dozen khaki socks. I straightened up when suddenly I saw hanging before me, against a layout of white vests, the most gorgeous pairs of men's briefs: one a shimmering gold and the other a metallic ruby red. Contrasting against the white background, they seemed to float in the air. Awestruck, in a trance, I walked to them and picked them up.

Quickly I buried them under the socks. They must have turned the heat up with a vengeance because I was now warm and sweating. I furtively glanced at the cashier as she rang it in. She had shoulder-length blond hair and a nice saucy look in her eye. I blanched, fearing the worst, but she caught my eye and smiled at me. I saw the flash of a jewel on her tongue.

She rang in the socks, and I braced myself as she picked up the ruby-red briefs.

"Mmm," said this angel, light rays flashing from her mouth as she spoke. "Are these for you? They suit your colour!"

I blushed and mumbled, "Yes."

To my surprise, she looked at me with frank enthusiasm and said, "I hung them out this morning. I really like them and thought they would brighten up the place on a snowy day like this. I bought a pair myself for my boyfriend, but he won't wear them – claims that they're sissy."

I nodded weakly, and mumbled, "I see." Quickly I signed the credit card slip.

As I was about to leave, she said, "If you need help trying them on, give me a call. My name is Rosalina, but my friends call me Rose. I work here most days."

Speechless, I left.

Spring came by and finally I summoned up the courage to call Sears and asked for Rose. In a surprisingly short time, I was connected to her. "Hi!" I stammered. "I don't know if you remember me – the guy who bought your briefs? You offered to help me try them on?"

To my delight she enthusiastically replied that yes, she did indeed remember me. She asked could she help me. Yes, of course she could. She asked if she could bring her boyfriend along. "Sure!" I said, not knowing what else to say. We agreed to meet at my apartment the evening of the following Saturday.

Time went by on leaden feet, but finally it was Saturday evening and a few minutes after eight, the doorbell rang. I opened it to find Rose and her boyfriend at the door.

"Hi!" she said. "Meet my boyfriend Kurt." Kurt was about my age and height, with shoulder-length brown hair, blue eyes and a somewhat sad, frozen look on his face. For some reason he looked familiar. I felt I had known him a long time ago. We shook hands and nervously I ushered them in.

We sat around the coffee table, drinking soda and making nervous small talk, until Rose asked suddenly, "So, shall we try them on?" I blushed and started to demur. "But that's why we came!" said Rose "I rarely get to see what I sell being worn by an actual customer, and this is a great opportunity for me." At this, I went into my bedroom and came out with the two briefs.

Kurt looked on impassively as I undressed and put on the red briefs. "Doesn't it look good on him?" said Rose to Kurt. Kurt said nothing. "Turn around," said Rose to me. I did. "Yes," said Rose. "It's just as I imagined." She then came close to me and wrapped one arm around me, beckoning to Kurt with the other.

Kurt came over and Rose wrapped her other arm around him. I put one arm around Rose and, since I felt it would be impolite to do otherwise, tentatively put the other around Kurt who did not seem to mind. The sight of Rose so happy and excited seemed to stir him. He leaned to her and kissed her. She reciprocated, then turned and kissed me. We stood there kissing Rose in turns. The kissing became more passionate and soon Kurt had a hand under her blouse and was softly moulding her right breast.

I knelt down between them, and gently removed Rose's shoes, stockings and then her skirt. I felt something against my ear, and turned to find that it was Kurt's cock, making a tent out of his pants. I tentatively tried to pull down his pants but he pushed me away. I turned to Rose, removed her panties and, as she and Kurt kissed above me, I nuzzled her cunt.

A few minutes later I rose and, in response to the question in their eyes, led them to my bedroom. I watched as Rose guided Kurt's throbbing cock into her waiting, anointed cunt. I moved up on the bed and placed my cock on Rose's lips. She smiled and started to suck on it, making muffled "mmph, mmph" noises as Kurt pumped her with his cock. Kurt looked woodenly at me, thrusting away like a machine. I leaned forwards and tried to kiss his left nipple, but he would not let me.

After about five minutes of hard pumping, Kurt groaned and came. Exhausted he fell on his side. Rose wasn't done though. She went on all fours and looked at me invitingly. I knelt behind her. Her asshole, surrounded by crinkles of gold skin radiating outwards, looked like a beautiful golden sunburst. Looking further down, I saw that she had been aptly named. The pink inner lips of her cunt were longer than its outer lips and had pushed past them. Like the petals of an open rose, they lay dewy and muskily fragrant before me. Reverentially I bowed down, stuck my tongue out and delicately, but firmly, rimmed her anus. She tasted sweet, with an almond-like bitter aftertaste.

I then put my cock into her and slowly started thrusting. I softly circled her ass hole with my thumb and, as I felt her relax, gently pushed it into her butt. Pressing down with my thumb I could feel my cock sliding in and out of her. She came within minutes. I followed soon after.

Rose then reached down and cupped her cunt with her right hand. She straightened up, her hands still between her crotch. Suddenly she took her hands away and held them out cupped between us. They were filled with liquid – her, Kurt's and my juices. The moment suddenly seemed sacred – Rose was the priestess; the cup of come the offering. Rose raised her hands to her mouth and drank some. She then offered it to Kurt. He looked at it closely but, with a strange look of guilt, turned away. She then offered it to me and, reverentially, I drank what was left.

"I need to pee!" said Rose, and got up. I noticed that Kurt's cock was erect again. A look of disappointment flashed across his face. Rose turned to me with an impish smile and asked, "Can you take care of him? He gets turned on when he hears me pee!"

Kurt blushed. Rose didn't close the bathroom door, and in the suddenly loud silence we heard the tinkle of her pee. Kurt's cock bobbed against his stomach. A tear of pre-come oozed from its eye.

Looking back, I realize that the unseen, though clearly heard, golden column of pee descending from Rose was the pole – the axis – around which all the events of that night pivoted. The sound of that shaft hitting the water was like a musical, wordless annunciation that birthed the remaining events of the night – sacred events that changed Rose, Kurt and me for ever.

Kurt looked at me and said, "You looked beautiful in those briefs!"

A strange feeling came over me, as if a weight I never knew I carried had been lifted from my shoulders. Kurt lay back on the bed, his cock sticking out. I bent down and delicately took his hooded rod into my mouth. He suddenly bucked upwards. I choked and had to move away to recover.

Kurt reached down and stroked the back of my head. I sucked his cock for a few minutes, and then moved up to his nipples. I sucked them lightly, then harder and flicked them with my tongue. Kurt groaned, but lay back unresisting. His eyes were shut. I reached up and kissed his cheek. He turned his face to me, lips slightly parted. I kissed him tentatively on his mouth. He reached up, cupped my face with his hands and started kissing me passionately. His tongue made its way into my mouth and, delicately, I sucked on it.

I looked up and saw that Rose was back in the room. She raised a finger to her lips, gesturing me to silence. I went back to working on Kurt. His asshole was a delicate pink and looked surprisingly tender and vulnerable. I outlined its rim with the pointed tip of my tongue. Kurt gasped. A few more circles around with my tongue tip, and then slowly and deliberately I started lapping at it with the flat of my tongue, feeling the circle opening with each lick. I felt him relax. I wet my thumb with spit and moved it in small circles against his asshole. He started to moan softly.

I felt someone move next to me and saw that Rose had found the Vaseline in my bathroom cabinet. Her eyes were tender as she stood next to me. I held my thumb out and smiled approvingly as she squeezed some Vaseline onto it. I lubricated Kurt's asshole and slowly pushed my thumb in. Kurt gasped. I moved my thumb in and out—slowly at first and then faster. I swivelled my hips towards Rose. She squeezed a bead of Vaseline onto my cock. Well greased, I placed it against Kurt's asshole and, with Rose watching closely in fascination, slowly pushed in.

Rose began passionately kissing Kurt saying, "You are so hot, sweetie, I love you!" over and over as I started thrusting in and out – slowly at first and, as he relaxed, faster. Kurt's eyes were closed; his face was a mask of pleasure. I smiled at Rose who flashed a radiant smile back.

I reached under Kurt's balls and with the flat of my thumb pressed his G-spot – the bulging root of the penis accessible from between asshole and balls. Suddenly, with a great groan, he came. I followed.

Afterwards, we sat around the table. "That was hot," said Rose. She was flushed and looked distracted. She asked if I had any other briefs like the ones she had sold me and soon I found myself telling them about my collection.

Rose wanted to see it, but Kurt looked bored. Hesitantly, I spread my collection on the kitchen table. Rose went through them one by one, asking me why I liked each one. She particularly liked a white cotton panty, with a rose motif on the waistband. "Can I wear this?" she asked me. I did not mind and agreed. I suddenly realized that at all times, even at the height of our fucking, Rose had never been completely naked. She had always been wearing or holding on to a piece of clothing – a bra or something.

Rose suddenly looked up still flushed and distracted. "I need you both now!" she said, her eyes glinting. She made Kurt lie down on his back, then straddled him, facing me at the foot of the bed. For a minute or so, Rose Jill-hammered Kurt, her slit slithering up and down his rigid, rock-hard tool, engulfing then releasing it from its furnace maw.

She then lubricated his cock with the Vaseline and, with her eyes focused steadily on me, slowly and deliberately slid down Kurt's cock, taking it up her ass. I stood at the foot of the bed, stroking my stiff cock and watching the scene before me. Rose closed her eyes. Her mouth was an "O" of pleasure. Squatting as she was on Kurt's cock, her cunt lips lazily pouted open, looking like a third eye, red, swollen, mysterious, a portal to infinite wisdom, winking sleepily at me with each thrust she made. She then lay back and I knelt between Kurt's marvellous, pillar-like thighs, cupped his full, heavy balls with my left hand, and gently parted Rose's pussy lips with my right. Slowly I inserted my cock into her. She started to moan. Her cunt was wet and slippery. The partition between it and her ass seemed as thin as gold leaf and I could feel Kurt's cock as if it were directly pressed against mine.

Rose seemed transformed. She threw off the bra she had been wearing and now for the first time that evening was completely naked. "Can you feel him?" she asked Kurt. "Can you feel him deep up inside my cunt?" Kurt nodded weakly. We began to move faster. Rose looked me in the eye. Her teeth were bared in a grimace; her eyes were narrowed slits. She started to make loud groaning noises. Her nipples, engorged and swollen, poked out like spikes. Kurt's eyes were shut, his face a mask of pleasure. United in Rose, we made a sacred and holy trinity.

Kurt's face was covered with sweat. I found the panties that Rose had been wearing lying next to me and used them to wipe his face. Rose was making loud, low-pitched and animal-like moans. I tried to kiss her, but she was lost in a world of pleasure and did not want to. Suddenly she opened her eyes. "Stop! Stop!" she shouted. "I need to pee again!"

But I was too far gone in my pleasure and kept thrusting. Suddenly there was a squirting noise and I felt a stinging sensation in my groin, as if it had been shot by a grease gun. A warm liquid spurted against me, around my balls and down the sides of my legs. Rose was coming, squirting out streams of fluid. In her wet, warm, welcoming secret, sacred, temple cunt, I had a wrenching orgasm.

I withdrew and watched a mix of my come and Rose's juices flow out of her cunt and onto Kurt's balls. "I thirst!" gasped Kurt. The panties were now drenched. I picked them up and offered them to Kurt to moisten his lips. He refused. I stiffened my thumb like a lance and jabbed the flat of it hard against his G-spot.

He came with a deep groan.

I woke up to the sound of eggs frying in the kitchen. Rays of morning sunshine flooded into the apartment. Kurt was at the stove, all showered and dressed. When he saw me, his face lit up. He flashed me a golden, liquid smile, came over and warmly kissed me on my lips.

"Care for some breakfast?" he asked.

I gathered my collection of panties from the kitchen table and threw them into the trash. Kurt looked at me quizzically, but seemed to understand. Rose joined us. She was completely naked, but seemed comfortable. Kurt and I toasted her with orange juice. Outside I heard a robin chirping and the sound of cars as people made their way to church to receive the sacraments. We had already received ours.

CONFESSIONS OF
A SEX THERAPIST

Pricilla, USA

It's not often you find people who truly enjoy the work they are paid to do. I am fortunate that I love my job. I am a sex therapist and I can hardly wait to get to work every morning.

On this particular day I had an all-day appointment in a wealthy part of town with a young man who had been in a deep coma since his car accident two months earlier. His doctors had sent him home with the dreary pronouncement that he could wake up at anytime, but probably never would.

In desperation his father came up with what I thought was a brilliant idea: to try to force him out of his coma with extreme and prolonged sexual arousal.

"Are you alone here today, Mr Templeton?" I asked as the young man's father led me up the stairs to his son's room.

"Pretty much, Pricilla," he said. "I dismissed his nurse for the day. Mrs Templeton is around here somewhere, but she's not at all happy with me over this idea of mine so we probably won't be seeing her."

"Good," I said. "We don't need any negativity."

"I must say, Miss Bellamy, you're not what I expected. I thought you'd look like a nurse."

"No," I said laughing. "I like to bring all the sexual attributes I possess into my work."

"Well, I hope you don't mind if I say your sexual attributes are quite abundant? This is Jeremy," he said when we entered the room.

The young man, as pale and lifeless as he was, was also quite beautiful with his dark curly hair and sensual lips. "He looks like you," I said. "I'll bet he has your blue eyes as well."

"Yes," he said. "Miss Bellamy, would you mind if I sit in on this? I want to watch for any changes."

"Of course," I said. "Pull up a chair next to me." I pulled down the sheet and took off Jeremy's pyjama bottoms. His flaccid penis looked like it would be quite large when erect.

I sat next to the bed, took his balls and penis in my hands and began to massage them. Leaning over him, I started to breathe hot air over them, bathing his genitals in the moist heat. "I do feel a slight hiccough in his cock," I whispered.

Mr Templeton sat near me, watching with keen interest.

"Nice rosy plum here," I said, sucking it into my mouth. Sucking gently, encircling the full rosy head with my tongue, I tugged at the shaft lightly. "I'm definitely getting a response here," I murmured, feeling the shaft beginning to stiffen a little.

When I looked up at Mr Templeton he looked flushed and seemed to be a little agitated. "Are you all right?" I asked.

"I don't know. I'm feeling a little strange. After Gladys went through the change she didn't have any interest in sex any more. After that my libido sort of went downhill, you know?"

"That's very sad, Rick. May I call you Rick?"

"Of course."

"You know, Rick, it's not healthy to be sexually deprived. Sex is a wonderful thing and it's every bit as important as food and drink and rest. It's vital to our very survival. I hate that so many people think of it as something dirty. How could anything that feels that wonderful be dirty? Unzip your pants."

"What?"

"I said unzip your pants. Don't be alarmed. I just want to see what we're dealing with here."

The poor man was beet red. "I'm too embarrassed," he murmured.

By now Jeremy had a pretty good erection going for himself. "Let me get this sweet boy set up and then I'll check you out," I said. Removing a slender phallic vibrator from my bag I greased it down and plugged it in. Lifting his leg I gently inserted the vibrator all the way into his rectum and flipped the switch. Jeremy let out an unconscious groan and his cock instantly stood straight up.

Rick was staring; I think he was a little shocked, his eyes wide.

Turning back to him I said, "Let's see what we have here." I unzipped his pants, while he sat there looking nervous, reached in and found that the cock was quite large and rigid. I had a little trouble getting it out of his pants since it refused to bend. Meanwhile the poor man was flushed and trembling.

"My goodness, look at that," I said. "Your organs haven't atrophied at all, Rick. That's one rock-hard erection you have there. When was the last time you had an orgasm?"

"It's been a while," he muttered.

"Don't you ever masturbate?"

"Not much. I guess since I don't have access to a willing woman I try not to let myself get stimulated often," he said.

"But you're very stimulated now," I said.

"Oh yeah," he said, a shudder running through his body.

I had been holding on to Jeremy's cock with one hand and I could feel it throbbing, his whole insides vibrating with that tool in his rectum.

"I don't want Jeremy to come yet," I said. "I want him to be aroused to the point of absolute sexual agony, his cock knotted in the pain of needing to ejaculate for a prolonged time forcing him to come up out of that coma." I had confidence it was working. Jeremy was moaning and groaning in his sleep and his hips had begun to push up to my hand. I was masturbating him a little but not too much. When he let out a loud groan and pushed up sharply I pulled my hand away to keep him from coming.

"That has to be misery," Rick said.

"I know," I said, "but it's necessary if this is going to work." As I talked to Rick I had my hand tightly around his cock and it was as stiff as a board. I bent down and sucked his fat plum into my mouth.

"Ahhh," he yelled, quivering all over. "Aghhh."

Now I was sucking hard, encircling it with my tongue, my lips sliding all the way down his long shaft to the nest of dark hair at the base. I was cupping his balls in my hand and they were firm, drawn tight up against his cock in extreme readiness.

"Oh my, oh dear," he was moaning. "Oh God, oh God, I'm coming! Oh God!" He was pushing his cock up in my mouth, his hips jerking, his whole body stiffening. With the first hot spasm I slipped my mouth off while jerking his foreskin up and down fiercely as his cock erupted like a spewing geyser again and again.

Seeing a cock erupt sperm like that and knowing the ecstasy the man is experiencing is an extremely stimulating thing to me and I get very aroused.

"That was a very healthy ejaculation, Rick," I said. "I'll bet you could do at least two more of those before I leave here today." The poor man looked like he was going to pass out.

"You just sit there and recover," I said, turning back to Jeremy. His cock was so stiff it looked like it was knotted in pain. He was still groaning and restless and now his eyelids were twitching. "I think we're going to get your son back, Rick," I said. "Let's see how he reacts to real intercourse." I slipped off my shoes and panties and climbed on top of him. "You may as well watch this, Rick. It will get you ready for your next orgasm."

I opened my sex, which was hot and wet, and placed Jeremy's cock in the opening. Then I slid down on it, burying it deep in me, and now I was the one groaning. The combination of that great cock and the vibration moving up the shaft was maddening, but I was trying not to come yet, wanting to save that for Rick. I began sliding up and down on Jeremy's cock and now his hips were pushing up to me, his eyes opening and sort of rolling around in his head. He was making noises like he was trying to say something, but he was not out of it yet, so I couldn't let him come.

I looked over at Rick and he was rock hard and ready. I slipped Jeremy's cock out of me and he let out an unconscious wail of protest. I lay down on the bed and pulled my skirt up. "Rick," I said, "get over here."

"Oh my," he said, quavering, and I thought he was going to faint.

"Get over here, it's therapy," I said. "Hurry." I was trembling and breathing hard with the urgency of my need.

Flushed, his cock standing straight out, he mounted me. He was so excited he was having trouble getting it in.

"That thing is so damn big," I said. "Let me try." Guiding it into me, I said, "Be careful, go in easy. That thing's a monster."

Carefully he was working it into me and I'd never been so filled up. If I hadn't been so ready it would have hurt badly. I was even having to open my thighs wider to give it more room. By the time he got it all the way into me he was panting, pumping hard and about to squirt. "Stop," I said. "Don't you dare come yet."

"Oh shit," he moaned, slowing down. Then he began to stroke in me again, and as tight as it was it was still moving in and out smoothly, in perfect tandem with my rising and falling hips and I felt a vaginal orgasm building in me.

"Keep that up, just like that, I'm about to blow," I said, my voice hoarse with passion. I was fiercely pushing up to meet his thrusts. "Oh shit, I'm coming," I muttered. I was exploding, cresting, one violent spasm after another, shooting electric shock waves out through my body. I think I was screaming, or maybe it was Rick because he was driving into me like a jackhammer. Then one deep plunge and he was erupting in me, his fingers buried in my bottom holding me tight into him as he emptied into me.

"Oh God, that was good," he said, his chest heaving.

"Hello, Mrs Templeton," I said, panting.

"Oh shit," Rick yelled, looking around. His wife had been standing there for no telling how long watching her husband enthusiastically driving his big cock into me, gasping and groaning as we fucked each other's brains out, exploding in volatile climaxes. "Don't look at me like that, Gladys. This is therapy. I need it for my health," Rick said.

"You bastard," she said, hardly able to speak.

"This bastard is going to be in weekly therapy from now on, Gladys," he said.

"I have to get back to Jeremy," I told him.

Jeremy's eyes were open, sort of glazed over, staring at his father and me, but I was sure he had not reached full consciousness yet. The vibrator was still doing its job and Jeremy's cock was standing erect. He was groaning and I was sure he had been stimulated by watching his dad fucking me.

"It's time for you to come out of it, kid," I said, climbing on him. I slid down on his cock and began fucking him fast, hard and deep. The old lady was really getting her eyes full. Jeremy suddenly grabbed my ass and was pushing up to me, meeting every thrust as I buried his cock in me again and again.

"He's coming out of it, Rick," I said. "Look at him."

"Oh yeah, oh yeah," Jeremy was now yelling. He threw me down on the bed and then was on top of me, driving into me like a wild bull. With the vibrator cord hanging out of his rectum he was pumping like mad. "Oh yeah, I'm coming," he yelled, burying his prod in me, his whole body shuddering, jerking with the intense spasms. "Oh baby, oh baby!"

Then he collapsed, rolling off me. As I removed the vibrator he was looking around wildly. "Where am I?" he muttered. "I wake up and I'm fucking this gorgeous woman."

"Hell of a way to wake up, isn't it, son?" Rick said grinning. "I can see that Jeremy's going to be all right now, but I'm not," Rick told me, glaring at his horrified wife. "I'm going to need therapy two, maybe three times a week from now on."

A WEEKEND WITH JOYCE

Antonia, Illinois

Joyce replaced the secretary where I worked when the last gal shipped off to a new army base with her husband. Joyce didn't seem to have many friends, and she and I just sort of hit it off. We started going to lunch together and eventually she invited me to dinner at her house.

Joyce was married, with a pre-teen son, and she and her husband owned three or four very successful florist shops. Their house was incredible. They had a built-in jacuzzi hot tub in their fenced-in backyard, a baby grand piano in their living room and it was at her house that I saw and heard my very first music on CDs.

One weekend, her husband and son were slated to go camping and fishing with some friends. Joyce told me that she was afraid to be in her big house alone. I thought she was kidding until I saw that she was ready to cry. Since I was single, I told her I would come and spend the weekend with her. We could do girly things, I told her, and drink some wine and just have a good time. She was thankful and we both started thinking it sounded like it could be a lot of fun, if we could think of enough things to keep ourselves occupied, anyway.

When the big weekend arrived and her husband and son had departed and I had arrived, we broke out the wine and listened to music and ate the dinner she had prepared for me and then we were pretty much bored. Since I lived pretty close by to her, I told her I was going to run home to get some videos for us to watch and I'd be back in a flash.

When I returned with the videos and another item I had picked up, I realized that she was pretty close to drunk and I didn't think that watching her get sick would be too much fun. I asked her if maybe we couldn't go sit in the hot tub for a while since it was something I didn't get to do very often.

We walked out back and she said, "We don't usually wear anything when we go in here," and she stripped naked and stepped inside the hot tub and settled back.

Not one to stand on ceremony myself, I stripped naked and joined her. We lounged in there for quite a while, enjoying the bubbles and the wonderful California night, and talked of inconsequential things.

Once we noticed that our fingertips looked like raisins, we decided it was time to exit the hot tub. She got a robe for herself and told me I could just wear her husband's robe, which I did.

By that time it seemed like she had sobered up a bit, and I was thankful.

"Let's see what videos you brought," she said.

"I thought that since it was just us girls we could watch a couple that were X-rated," I told her as I giggled and popped one into the VCR in her den. Then we sat back and watched naked men and women frolic on the big screen television she had.

I watched her from the corner of my eye. I could tell that she was getting excited by what she was seeing on the screen.

I had a sneaking suspicion about something at that point and finally asked her, "Have you ever seen an X-rated video before?"

She blushed and admitted that she had not.

I offered to turn it off, but she said, "No, I'm rather liking it, actually."

We watched mostly in silence, with the occasional remark about the size of certain parts of people, and I told her that well-endowed people seemed to be favoured in this type of movie.

We must have watched two or three movies, heavy with action of all types, including girl-on-girl, which I remarked upon. I said that they seemed to have a much better time with their own sex than with the men. She agreed with me.

Finally, we decided it was time for bed. I started off to her son's bedroom but she stopped me and said, "I have a king-sized bed. Why don't you just sleep in there with me? I'd feel safer."

"Sure," I said. "As long as you promise to not steal all the covers." We both laughed.

We were both naked when we got into bed: she on her side, me on her hubby's side.

I really *did* try to sleep, but she kept me awake with her tossing and turning and some really heavy sighs. Finally, I said to her, "Are you all right over there?"

"Not really."

"What's wrong then?" I asked.

"I'm horny."

Now, Joyce wasn't a model; she wasn't a leggy blonde. In fact she was about four inches shorter than me and a bit overweight. She *was* blond. A *real* blonde, I knew, from our time in the hot tub.

But I liked her. I liked her a *lot*.

"I can help you with that," I said. "Would you like that?"

There was silence for a moment, then she said, "Yes. I think so."

I slid on over nearer to her and put my right arm under her neck and held her close to me for a few minutes, whispering to her to relax her. As I did that, I rubbed her back and kissed her forehead then started exploring her body with my left hand. I heard her gasp when I fondled her breasts and her breathing increased when I moved down to suck on her hard nipples.

I stopped and asked, "Should I stop?" knowing full well she would say, "No."

I moved back up and kissed her gently and she kissed me back. I kissed her neck and moved back to her breasts and licked and kissed my way down to her pubic area. My hands never stopped roving and she never stopped gasping.

My tongue found its way around and it wasn't long before she was crying out and grabbing the covers and heaving her hips back and forth.

Afterwards she said, "Oh my goodness, that was wonderful. Thank you."

ed it was time for bed. I started off to her
she stopped me and said, "I have a king-
't you just sleep in there with me? I'd feel

As long as you promise to not steal all the
aughed.

ked when we got into bed: she on her side,
side.

o sleep, but she kept me awake with her
and some really heavy sighs. Finally, I said
l right over there?"

hen?" I asked.

't a model; she wasn't a leggy blonde. In fact
inches shorter than me and a bit overweight.
l blonde, I knew, from our time in the hot tub.
I liked her a *lot*.
with that," I said. "Would you like that?"
e for a moment, then she said, "Yes. I think

arer to her and put my right arm under her
lose to me for a few minutes, whispering to
I did that, I rubbed her back and kissed her
ed exploring her body with my left hand. I
en I fondled her breasts and her breathing
moved down to suck on her hard nipples.
ked, "Should I stop?" knowing full well she

p and kissed her gently and she kissed me
eck and moved back to her breasts and licked
down to her pubic area. My hands never
she never stopped gasping.
its way around and it wasn't long before she
grabbing the covers and heaving her hips

said, "Oh my goodness, that was wonderful.

sciousness yet. The vibrator was still doing its job and Jeremy's
cock was standing erect. He was groaning and I was sure he had
been stimulated by watching his dad fucking me.

"It's time for you to come out of it, kid," I said, climbing on
him. I slid down on his cock and began fucking him fast, hard
and deep. The old lady was really getting her eyes full. Jeremy
suddenly grabbed my ass and was pushing up to me, meeting
every thrust as I buried his cock in me again and again.

"He's coming out of it, Rick," I said. "Look at him."

"Oh yeah, oh yeah," Jeremy was now yelling. He threw me
down on the bed and then was on top of me, driving into me like
a wild bull. With the vibrator cord hanging out of his rectum he
was pumping like mad. "Oh yeah, I'm coming," he yelled,
burying his prod in me, his whole body shuddering, jerking
with the intense spasms. "Oh baby, oh baby!"

Then he collapsed, rolling off me. As I removed the vibrator
he was looking around wildly. "Where am I?" he muttered. "I
wake up and I'm fucking this gorgeous woman."

"Hell of a way to wake up, isn't it, son?" Rick said grinning.
"I can see that Jeremy's going to be all right now, but I'm not,"
Rick told me, glaring at his horrified wife. "I'm going to need
therapy two, maybe three times a week from now on."

A WEEKEND WITH JOYCE

Antonia, Illinois

Joyce replaced the secretary where I worked when the last gal shipped off to a new army base with her husband. Joyce didn't seem to have many friends, and she and I just sort of hit it off. We started going to lunch together and eventually she invited me to dinner at her house.

Joyce was married, with a pre-teen son, and she and her husband owned three or four very successful florist shops. Their house was incredible. They had a built-in jacuzzi hot tub in their fenced-in backyard, a baby grand piano in their living room and it was at her house that I saw and heard my very first music on CDs.

One weekend, her husband and son were slated to go camping and fishing with some friends. Joyce told me that she was afraid to be in her big house alone. I thought she was kidding until I saw that she was ready to cry. Since I was single, I told her I would come and spend the weekend with her. We could do girly things, I told her, and drink some wine and just have a good time. She was thankful and we both started thinking it sounded like it could be a lot of fun, if we could think of enough things to keep ourselves occupied, anyway.

When the big weekend arrived and her husband and son had departed and I had arrived, we broke out the wine and listened to music and ate the dinner she had prepared for me and then we were pretty much bored. Since I lived pretty close by to her, I told her I was going to run home to get some videos for us to watch and I'd be back in a flash.

When I returne
picked up, I realiz
didn't think that w
asked her if maybe
since it was somet

We walked out
anything when we
stepped inside the

Not one to stand
joined her. We lou
bubbles and the
inconsequential thi

Once we noticed
decided it was time
and told me I could

By that time it see
thankful.

"Let's see what

"I thought that s
couple that were X-
one into the VCR i
naked men and wor
had.

I watched her fro
was getting excited

I had a sneaking s
finally asked her,
before?"

She blushed and
I offered to turn it
actually."

We watched most
about the size of cert
endowed people see

We must have w
action of all types,
upon. I said that the
their own sex than v

Finally, we decid
son's bedroom but
sized bed. Why dor
safer."

"Sure," I said. "
covers." We both l

We were both na
me on her hubby's

I really *did* try
tossing and turning
to her, "Are you al

"Not really."

"What's wrong
"I'm horny."

Now, Joyce wasn
she was about four
She *was* blond. A re

But I liked her.

"I can help you
There was silenc
so."

I slid on over ne
neck and held her
her to relax her. As
forehead then start
heard her gasp wh
increased when I

I stopped and as
would say, "No."
I moved back
back. I kissed her
and kissed my wa
stopped roving an

My tongue foun
was crying out an
back and forth.

Afterwards she
Thank you."

"You're welcome," I told her as I moved back up to hold her in my arms again.

A few minutes later she said, "Can I tell you something?"

"Sure," I replied.

"That was the first orgasm that someone else ever gave me."

I backed up a bit and looked at her and said, "Tell me you are joking."

"I'm not," she admitted.

"But you've had orgasms before, right?"

"Only with my vibrator."

I could only say, "Wow. You've really been missing out, woman."

We lay there for some moments and then she said, "Would you like me to do that to you?"

"Only if you really want to," I replied.

"I think I'd like to try," she said.

For a novice, she was either pretty good or I was really ready or she had learned a lot by watching those videos.

We rested for a bit then she suggested we go sit in the hot tub again for a while. I agreed.

We sat out there for a bit sipping some more white wine and quietly talking, and then I moved over closer to her and started rubbing her clitoris under the bubbles. She laid her head back on the edge of the tub and let her body float in the water and I got her off once again.

"Let me try that on you," she said afterwards. We switched positions and this time there were no holds barred for her. She got her head underwater and her tongue went to town and when she came up for air I got up and sat on the edge of the hot tub and she continued until I had an orgasm.

We decided it really *was* time to get some sleep and the next day we pretty much spent in bed, getting up only to grab whatever was quick to eat. Of course, even a quick meal wasn't quick that weekend because we walked around naked the entire time. While I was tearing apart lettuce for our sandwiches she was on the floor in front of me, licking me and distracting me until I couldn't stand it any longer. The sandwiches were forgotten for a while as I helped her onto one of the kitchen counters.

When we got tired (or felt like we needed new ideas) we watched the videos yet again and ended up either in her bed or in the hot tub. She was like a woman on fire (and so was I) and we couldn't keep our hands off each other.

She took me out to dinner Saturday night and we said sexy things to each other and secretly groped each other while sitting in our booth and by the time we left the restaurant (with most of our food taken "to go") we couldn't wait to get naked with each other again.

When we got back to her house and were standing in her bedroom she stopped me and said, "Wait a minute. I want to undress you."

With the light from the patio coming through the windows in her bedroom I stood there as she slowly undressed me and laid me on her bed. All her clothes were still on at that point. Then she made love to me while she remained fully dressed. It remains one of the sexiest moments *ever* in my life.

She had lain next to me on the bed and I don't know that there was one inch of my body that remained untouched by her tongue or her fingers. My very skin was quivering from want and need.

She kissed my toes and made her way up, kissing the backs of my knees and running her tongue up the inside of my thighs. I wanted to scream for release, and I *did*, when it finally came.

After that I slowly undressed her and did the same to her (although I wasn't clothed), so I could feel *her* quiver and hear *her* moan.

We made love on her living room floor with the street lights shining in on us and where anyone who might want to peek in the windows could see us.

She lay on the piano bench for me while I knelt beside it and she had me actually lie *on top* of the piano for her.

We took a shower together and stayed in there giving each other orgasms until the water turned cold, then headed out to the hot tub to warm up again.

As we sat in the hot tub together that last time I said to her, "You do know that you will have to get my butt prints off the piano before your family gets home, right?" And we both laughed.

"I have a surprise for you," I told her finally. I had her lie on the bed and instructed her to keep her eyes closed and not peek until I told her it was all right to look. I went into the bathroom, then came out and said, "You can open your eyes now."

"What is *that*?" she said wide-eyed when she saw me.

"It's called a strap-on dildo," I told her. "My ex-husband got it for me as a joke and I picked it up when I got the videos. I was just going to *show* it to you, but I think I have a better idea now."

I slid up next to her on the bed and, whispering to her, I told her that I was going to make sure she was ready for me before I continued. I kissed her and licked her and sucked her sensitive spots until she was begging for release.

Then I straddled her and, while holding her legs closed with mine, rubbed the dildo across her clitoris until I could tell that she was close to climaxing.

There was no lubrication problem, of course. She was pretty ready for anything at that point. Moving my legs between hers to get her to open them, I then slowly inserted the dildo. Impatient and excited, she reached around, grabbed my ass and pulled me close to her and let out a sigh when the dildo was fully inside her.

I pulled back and slowly pumped the dildo. I watched her face and she, opening her eyes and looking at me, pulled my face close to hers to kiss me deeply.

I pumped a couple more of times but also did a little grinding motion with my pelvis, and she moaned.

I could tell by her breathing that she was starting to come, and I let her guide my actions. Her hands pushed and pulled me and she thrust her hips up to meet my motions and then finally, when I had worked up a fine glistening of sweat on my body, I heard her cry out, "OH MY GOD!"

I knew I had just given her the first vaginal orgasm she had ever had and that was a pretty good feeling.

We lay in bed, holding each other, and she told me that she wanted to try wearing the dildo and "doing" me. I fitted it onto her and let her take charge at that point.

She said she wanted to take me in the hot tub, so we went outside, and I assured her that I didn't care what the hot water might do to the harness; she could do whatever she wanted.

She knelt on the bottom of the hot tub and had me sit on the dildo and she was slow and she was loving and I had the idea that this was something she had often thought of, although she probably never thought her fantasy would be fulfilled by another *woman.*

After we dried off we lay in her big bed once more and caught a few hours of sleep while holding each other. Our "breakfast" that Sunday morning when we woke up was eaten in the sixty-nine position.

All good things must come to an end, and that weekend did, too. I left before her son and husband got home, reminding her that she had to clean the "butt prints" off the piano and we held each other and kissed before I grabbed my videos and dildo and left for my drive home.

The next day at work she told me that her husband had said, "What the heck did you two do all weekend? You look like you've hardly slept at all."

She said she had answered, "Oh, just girly things."

And I laughed and smiled because I realized she never suspected that I agreed to spend the weekend with her just so that I could seduce her.

SHE, HER MOTHER AND ME

Peter, Dorset

Do you remember the 1960s? I suspect that if you do, you won't want to admit to being that old! Or maybe you just go along with that saying, "If you can remember the sixties you didn't party hard enough!"

Some of it is a blur now but really that's only because most of the time not a lot happened to me worth remembering. But when I was twenty in 1969 that changed – with a bang!

I met this girl, her name was Susie and she was eighteen. She was a pretty girl, nice legs and great breasts. She dyed her hair peroxide blond, fashionable at the time, and overall she was quite a looker. It was winter so she wore this maxi coat which didn't give a lot away but, when it swung open, you would have sworn at first sight that she was wearing nothing below the waist, her ultra-micro miniskirt being just that, as short as she could get, and her long legs in flesh-coloured tights, or sometimes entirely bare, just an encouragement to fantasize.

She lived at home with her mother whom I met when I went round to pick up Susie for our first date. Her mother was nice, friendly and welcoming. I reckoned she had been quite a looker at Susie's age; still was, really. A far more curvy figure than Susie, she was at a guess late thirties. Her breasts were large and well shaped from what little I could see, and her bottom was full and lushly curved. Dark haired as Susie would have been without the peroxide bleach, her skin was smooth cream contrasting with dark eyes and scarlet lips.

Susie and I went to the pictures on that first date; we saw *The Virgin Soldiers*. Actually, I didn't pay much attention to the film; after it had started I held Susie's hand in her lap and soon felt her urging my fingers up her thigh and under that short piece of material she called a skirt and into her panties. Well, after that any film, no matter how good, was going to take second place. Luckily it was a weekday evening and the cinema wasn't crowded so we were alone in that row towards the back. Later, we went back to my car and parked down a local lovers' lane she knew and finished the job, so to speak.

She was never less than willing.

So it went on: normal boy–girl dating, heavy petting and, more often than not, boy–girl bonking.

After a few dates, I found I was going round to her house more frequently even when Susie herself wasn't there: still at work or out with girlfriends (she *said* and I *hoped*!). Thing was, as a woman on her own, Susie's mother managed well but some jobs she just couldn't do. Little day-to-day things like refixing a loose door on a kitchen cabinet, changing a high-up light bulb when the old one had got jammed in the socket, repairing some electrical appliance like a kettle with a blown element or a vacuum cleaner with a broken wire in the plug.

Susie's mother was always very grateful for my time and effort and I didn't mind.

Then one day Susie rang to say her mother was ill and asking to see me. I couldn't understand why particularly; I hadn't been due to go round that evening as I had work I needed to catch up on at home but I went anyway. Susie took me up to her mother's bedroom where she was lying down with just a dim table light to break the gloom. Susie said her mother had these spells of illness now and again, like a very bad migraine, and she was just getting over this one that had lasted two or three days. Then she left us alone.

I went over to the bed and said, "Hello," and "How are you feeling now?" – the usual stuff. Susie's mother hauled herself up onto the pillow and I smelled this attractive perfume, seemed fresh so I guessed she'd maybe just put it on. Well, she said she was a lot better but had wanted to see me to thank me again for the jobs I had done on her behalf as she had had a sudden morbid fear that she had been imposing on me and that

I wouldn't want to come again and she wanted to put that right. I said no, I was fine about these little jobs. I had no problem with helping her out.

As we spoke, the bedclothes slid down her chest and I saw that I was right about the size and voluptuousness of her breasts. Her nightie was really low cut and those torpedoes were just aimed right at me under the thin material.

I tried hard to look just at her face but I think I wasn't too successful.

She held my hand while we chatted and it seemed to me she was feeling a little better every minute. I got her some orange juice from the kitchen and, when I came back, I noticed that some buttons at the front of her nightdress that I could have sworn were secured earlier, had now mysteriously become undone. As she leaned forwards to sip the juice without either spilling it or choking, those pert boobs almost did an escapology act all of their own.

I began to feel feverish myself then.

After we finished chatting, I went back downstairs to Susie and I had her on the couch, on her back with her miniskirt up round her waist and panties off on the floor before she could draw breath. And I was in her, so hard and all, before she was really ready. But I just had to; I would have exploded otherwise.

And it wasn't Susie I was thinking of.

So, going back to what I was saying earlier. As we lay there, my fingers on her and in her, my lips to her nipples and my other hand caressing her soft, brunette hair, we heard the front door slam.

"Oh God," said Susie's mother, "Susie's back early. Better look respectable, lover!"

So that's my confession. It's one I was afraid I would have to make to Susie sometime but fortunately she never found out. It was every young man's dream: an experienced older woman to guide him and teach him and a younger girl, too! I never forgot what I learned then and I hope I've put it to good use since!

WILD URGES

Roxanne, Michigan

Sometimes my sexual urges seem to go into overdrive and I want to do something naughty. Usually I keep them under control because I don't want to do anything stupid. There are many times I have satisfied my urges by getting wild and completely uninhibited with my husband, Steve. Yet there are times when nothing seems to put out that fire and I just have to wait it out until the urge goes away.

This was one of those times. For days I was out-of-control horny. I pounced on Steve every chance I got. He loved it but started asking what had got into me. One night after we had wild sex, we were lying in bed. I tried to delicately explain the situation. I did not want him to freak out or get mad.

"I want to do something wild," I said to him.

"Wild how?" he asked.

"Sexy wild, I want to live out a fantasy," I told him.

He looked curious, but a little hesitant when he asked, "What fantasy?"

"I want to be with two men at the same time."

"What?" He looked upset. I knew it, I had gone too far. I shouldn't have told him.

"Honey, it's not that you aren't good enough. I have always been curious. You've been with two women in the past, I've had a threesome before with a guy and another woman, but I've never been with two men at the same time. It is just something I want to try." I tried to smooth things out but he stopped me.

"I'm not upset, just really surprised," he said. "I never thought you would say something like that. I don't know what to think right now. I don't know if I like the idea of sharing you with another man. I'll have to think about it."

"OK, babe. You think about it. I love you."

"I love you, too." Then he rolled over—and fell asleep.

I did not bring up the topic again and neither did he. I guessed he had made up his mind and I was not going to push the issue. I wished I had never even mentioned it to him.

That weekend I woke up late Saturday morning and Steve was gone. That's not unusual: I always slept in on Saturdays and Steve liked to get up early and go fishing. When I went into the kitchen to get some coffee there was an envelope on the kitchen island. I opened it. There was a hotel key card and a note from Steve that said to meet him at the hotel that night at 7 o'clock.

I was really curious. What is he up to? I wondered. I showered and got some things together to take to the hotel. I gave myself a quick manicure and pedicure and called the salon so I could get a touch up on my bikini wax. Whatever he had planned I wanted to look great. I also stopped at a lingerie store to pick out something really special to wear for the evening. Steve probably had something really romantic planned.

After carefully dressing in my sexy lace-up corset top, black thigh highs with lace tops, and black lace thong, I slid into a strapless black dress that hugged every curve and the slit showed the lace on the top of my thigh-high stockings. I stepped into my black heels and was out the door.

I found the hotel room and went inside. There was no one there. Sitting on a table were lit candles, wine and wine glasses. A note from Steve said to have some wine and get comfortable. A few minutes later the door opened and Steve walked in; to my surprise there was another man with him. I stood up.

"This is James from work," he said. "He'll be joining us tonight."

I didn't know what to say. I was in shock. He was actually going to go through with this.

"Hi, James," was all I could manage to say.

Steve walked over to me and kissed me passionately. "Isn't this what you wanted?"

"Yes, but I just wasn't expecting it," I replied. "After you didn't say anything more about it I figured it was not going to happen."

"Well, darling, after I thought about it, I decided I would pick out the guy. That would make it easier for me. I trust James and I think you'll like him."

He kissed me again and started unzipping my dress. I started to get nervous when my dress fell to the floor and I was standing there in my corset top and thong.

"Don't worry, babe, everything is going to be all right," Steve said as he led me over to the bed. "You look so beautiful," he said as he unlaced my corset and cupped my breasts in his hands. He kissed my neck and my shoulder then moved down to my breasts. I moaned as he took a nipple into his mouth and gently sucked on it. I opened my eyes and saw James watching us. Steve pulled off my thong and spread my legs. Then he backed away and got undressed. James also got undressed. When he pulled off his jeans and underwear I was shocked to see what a large erection he had. I looked at my husband and he too was rock hard.

I sat up on the edge of the bed. Both men stood in front of me. I took a penis in each hand, stroking the smooth shafts. I licked James from the bottom of his rod all the way to the top then took it into my mouth and began sucking. Then I moved over to Steve and did the same thing. After a few minutes of rotating back and forth they pushed me back onto the bed. I had four hands caressing every inch of my body. Their sensual kisses made my flesh burn with desire. James trailed kisses down to the wet folds between my legs and began to probe my flesh with his tongue. Steve moved up and placed his hard cock in front of my mouth while he watched James lick my pussy. I sucked hard on Steve enjoying every inch that slid down my throat.

I felt James move and turned to watch as he climbed on top of me. He positioned that massive cock at the entrance of my pussy then plunged it deep inside me. I lost hold on Steve's prick and it fell out of my mouth. I lay back as James thrust in and out of me. Steve crawled off the bed and sat down in a chair to watch James and me. Steve stroked himself while watching James fuck me. I wondered how he felt about watching another man do his wife. It looked like he was enjoying it. Then he stood up.

"It's my turn with my wife," he said.

James climbed off of me.

"Get on your hands and knees," Steve told me.

I rolled over and did what he said. He slammed his dick into my hot hole and started ramming me hard. It felt so good. James climbed on the bed in front of me and I started sucking his cock. My fantasy had come true. I was with two men at the same time. I was stuffed full of two big cocks. I began to shake and quiver. Steve reached around and rubbed my clit with his fingers. That sent me over the edge and I exploded. Once I stopped, Steve said that he wanted to watch me ride James.

James lay down and I climbed on top of him. Steve held on to my butt cheeks and spread me wide open. He wanted to watch every inch of James's shaft slide inside me. Steve leaned back on the bed and watched me ride James while he stroked himself with some lubricant. Our eyes locked and the feeling was so intense. He was enjoying this as much as I was.

Steve then crawled up behind me and teased my ass; pushing my cheeks apart he slowly pushed into my tight little hole. I never expected this. I was being double penetrated. Oh, my God! I was seeing stars and fireworks. I rode James hard, grinding my pussy on him as my husband shoved his huge cock inside my ass. Steve's cock felt bigger than usual.

The pleasure was so immense. I was sandwiched between two gorgeous, well-hung men who were screwing my brains out. I came over and over again, screaming so loud the whole hotel could probably hear me. James shushed me by pressing his full lips against mine and kissing me hard as he thrust deeper inside me. My husband kept ramming me from behind. Then I felt his cock tense and swell as he filled me with his heat. The sensation flooded me and sent me into another orgasm. As my body rocked and shook I felt James tense and he came.

The three of us lay there on the bed for a while revelling in the afterglow of very intense sex. Then we got up and took a shower together. Steve and James both washed me. It was so erotic; four soapy hands all over my body. Soon I felt hard cocks pressing against me. That led us to another round of wild sex. We ended up going three rounds that night and it didn't end there. Every once in a while when I get that urge to do something wild Steve gives James a call to come over for the evening. No one is ever left unsatisfied.

THE ULTIMATE DATE

Mandy, County Durham

One cold Sunday afternoon, Ian and I discussed the merits of internet dating. Over a bottle of Merlot and beef Wellington, I sat with my ex-boyfriend and planned my strategy for 2008. I hadn't dated for a few months, but wasn't desperate as I had many close friends like Ian with whom I enjoyed spending quality time. He suggested I try a site called plentyoffish.com so we fired up the laptop, and opened another bottle of rich red. I couldn't believe the number of eligible, fit and sexy men on the site. Together, we created my profile and downloaded some pictures. I was dubious at first, but Ian assured me that I would get far fewer messages without a decent photo. Actually, he wrote my description, which included words like: vivacious, bubbly, fun, sexy, tactile and adventurous. I suggested to him that the word "adventurous" might seem a little slutty, but he dismissed my observation telling me not to be such a prude.

A few days later, I checked my inbox to find I had thirteen messages, and alongside the messages were thumbnail pictures of the senders. Some had no picture, and Ian was right, I was reluctant to respond to those. One particular message caught my eye: it was from a girl! Curiosity got the better of me and I opened the message which read "Just thought I would drop you a line to say what an amazing smile you have, and if you feel like chatting, you can email me anytime, Jackie xxx." I clicked onto her profile page, and she too was looking for a man. I couldn't understand why she had emailed me, so I replied to her message: "Hi, Jackie, thanks for the compliment. It's nice that you took the time to write to me when all those nice men are looking for a date. I haven't been on the site for long, how about you?"

Immediately, I received a response: "Hi, hun, I just thought you might like to chat, who knows, we may become friends. I joined this site last year and have had a few dates, but nothing mind-blowing. There are a lot of strange men on here so be careful, and if you fancy meeting up for a drink, I will give you a few pointers."

I thought maybe she was chatting me up so I enquired in a very polite way about her sexual orientation. She explained that she had a fantasy about meeting a woman; she knew she was not a lesbian, but wanted to experience the "girly" thing. She certainly didn't mince her words; straight to the point, she suggested we meet. A little shocked at first, I can honestly say that I was a little excited too, and the more we spoke, the wetter I became between my thighs. I read an article in *Scarlet* magazine once which stated that inside every woman was the urge to fuck another woman. Most dismiss the very thought of it, and the more adventurous of us give it a go.

We met the following evening in town. She was obvious from the minute I stepped out of the taxi. Peroxide blond hair, poker straight. Smart jacket with bustier and black satin skirt with high-heeled boots. Her smile was unmistakable. We exchanged pleasantries as we headed for the gay sector of the town, that way, we both agreed that if we felt the urge to explore the "girly thing", we could do it without an audience.

Anybody passing might have thought we were two girls out on the town – attractive, sexy, looking for men maybe, but we knew different. In my head were new, exciting thoughts, and I liked that feeling.

As we ordered drinks, I looked at Jackie and she licked her lips and held her bottom lip between her teeth for a few seconds before her mouth broke into that amazing smile. Her teeth were white and framed by beautiful full lips painted with a pale rose gloss, complementing her tanned complexion. We were very similar in age, appearance, and attitude to life; we could be sisters.

The wine flowed, and so did the conversation. We received several fleeting glances from other customers in the pub, and I felt sexy. As we perched on bar stools, Jackie leaned forwards and whispered in my ear, "I feel like I would like to kiss you." As our eyes met, we felt no resistance as our lips met for our first prolonged snog. I must admit to feeling more than a little turned on at that point. Maybe it was the excitement of my first girly kiss, but I had never felt a twinge down below like that after kissing any man. As our lips parted, I could see her eyes widen and that smile appeared again. "God, that was good," she chirped. I couldn't speak so I just smiled and nodded.

After an hour, we knew a little more about each other. We both agreed that whatever happened that night had to be kept a secret. Neither of us wanted this little encounter made public. I had a lot of very close female friends who would act differently towards me should they discover I had had an encounter with another woman. Most of my male friends would definitely find it fascinating, and be so turned on by listening to every small detail, but they would never find out either.

We went to the toilet and, because it was a Wednesday night, the whole place was fairly quiet and the girls' room was empty. I couldn't wait any longer. We giggled as I dragged her into one of the cubicles. I held the back of her neck and kissed her passionately, grabbing one of her gorgeous breasts with my other hand. I can honestly say that I have never been as excited as I was at that precise moment; I wanted to taste her, feel her, and fuck her.

Not the ideal romantic setting, the toilets were clean at least, and I dropped to my knees and slid her satin skirt up to around her waist. She parted her legs, as I parted her transparent panties to reveal a freshly shaven pussy. The G-string pulled tight against her bottom as I slid my long thin tongue inside the plump slit and searched for that magical mound. Her clit was erect, and I flicked the end, tasting her sweet juices. She was soaking wet. She held my long hair and forced my face into her cunt, and I lapped it up. My hand clenched her plump buttock and my face was soaked in her slimy love juice as she began to orgasm into my mouth.

The external door squeaked as someone entered the toilets; we could hear them enter the cubicle next door. Her face was flushed as I climbed from my knees, and I could see she was still in ecstasy, and panting loudly, so I stuck my face against hers and kissed her, smearing her come all over her face. Her hand drifted down to find my wet pussy. Even through my jeans, I was dripping wet. Both her hands struggled to release the button and she slowly undid my zip. Quickly, she yanked my jeans down to my knees as the unsuspecting customer washed her hands. As the stranger made their exit, Jackie began to breathe again like a hungry animal. She lifted my top and sucked both breasts. She pushed both my nipples together and at one point had them both in her mouth at the same time – what a turn-on! She too dropped to her knees and found my clit first with her fingers, then with her gentle tongue. I didn't want to climax immediately; the feeling was amazing. I pushed her off and lifted her up to my face. We kissed passionately again as I fondled her breasts. She then gestured me to turn around and I put my hands against the wall. She kicked my legs apart and forced my head forwards as she sat on the toilet seat. From behind, she licked my hole and fingered me until I exploded into her face. The rush of blood to the top half of my body was something I had never felt before; the orgasm was so intense that I could barely control myself. I think I screamed, but I can't be sure.

As we pulled up our clothes, and opened the cubicle door, we saw a girl washing her hands at the smart chrome sink. She was smiling as she nodded once and simply said, "Hi," then left. We nearly wet ourselves with hysterical laughter. Having forgotten to use the facilities, we entered separate cubicles and both came back down to earth as we peed!

That was the first time I met Jackie, and we have met on a number of occasions since. None of my friends know about her, and vice versa. We both have steady boyfriends now. Neither of them are aware of our little encounters, but we try to meet up once a month for our girly fix. I will never make our relationship public, because half the excitement is that nobody knows (except you, of course). There's something about girl-on-girl action that really gets me going. That's not to say I don't still enjoy a big hard cock, but a little variety is the spice of life, believe me!

KOREAN OPPORTUNITY

Ken, Toronto

I won't name the club, but if you know San Francisco, you've probably seen it. I hadn't been there before, but I was in town with an evening to kill. We saw each other as soon as I walked in. "I like your hair," she crooned, walking behind me and stroking my ponytail as I was paying the cover.

"I like yours," I replied, smiling back at her. One of the many things I've always found attractive about Asian women is their silky black hair, especially when worn long. She was wearing a green dress that hinted at a petite but perfect body, and her face was lovely.

Her almond-shaped eyes lit up, and she reached for my hand. "You like me?" she asked. "You really like me?"

"Very much."

"My name's Kim. I'm from Korea. Like *kimchi*; you like *kimchi*?"

"I prefer *sashimi*."

She grinned at that, then shrugged off a shoulder strap to flash one of her small but beautiful breasts. Her nipple was already hard. "You want me to dance for you?"

"Sure."

"Hug me." I did, and she squirmed against me deliciously while the clerk stamped my free hand. Then she led me hurriedly along a corridor. "I have a room," she said. "You come to my room?"

"Room" was an exaggeration; it was a booth without a door, one of several around a stage where an attractive brunette was lap-dancing with a white-haired man. Kim led me into her booth. "Forty dollars," she said. "I dance for you, you can touch me, suck my breasts – you like my breasts?" she asked, as she peeled off her dress and stood before me, naked but for her pumps.

"I love your breasts," I said.

The booth was only dimly lit, so I couldn't see them as well as I would have liked, but that ceased to matter an instant later when one of them was filling my hand and the other in my mouth. They were small, but wonderfully round and firm and silky smooth, her nipples dark hard pearls. While I kissed and caressed them, Kim was busy undoing my clothing as well, expertly massaging my balls. When my shirt was on the bench and my jeans halfway down my thighs, she turned around to show me her gorgeous ass, which she slapped gently. It was as firm and as perfectly shaped as her breasts. "You like?"

"Very much," I said, continuing to fondle one breast while I reached down to caress her ass. My hand travelled down between her thighs to rub her pussy, then up between those lovely cheeks to tease her asshole.

"What's your name?" she asked.

"Ken."

"Ken? Where are you from?"

"Canada," I said. My hands explored her terrific tiny body while she kissed my neck and stroked my hard cock.

"You here on vacation?"

"Business."

"You don't look like a businessman," she said. "More like a traveller."

"I'm a writer."

"Wrrrrriter," she repeated, making an obvious effort to pronounce the "r" sound, and laughed. She turned around again to look at my face. "What do you like? What can I do for you?"

This wasn't the sort of sex I was used to. Even when the attraction is instantaneous and seduction unnecessary, I enjoy flirtation and foreplay, and like to make them last; small as Kim's body was, I would have loved to have spent another hour exploring and worshipping it with my mouth and hands . . . but despite the lack of privacy, she had me so turned on that waiting would have been difficult if not painful. I was still teasing her asshole with one finger; I applied a little more pressure, and asked, "How about this?"

"You like that?" She pushed back against me, rubbing her beautiful buttocks against my hard cock. "A hundred dollars."

"OK." Somehow I managed to get my wallet out of my jeans; she made the money disappear and produced a lubricated condom from out of the shadows, the neatest conjuring trick I'd ever seen. She pushed me into a sitting position on the bench, rolled the condom over my erection while caressing my balls and kissing my cheek, and then spun around, sat on my lap, and guided my cock into herself. She was tight, and hot, and I was astonished when I reached around her to stroke her thighs and discovered that I was firmly wedged in her pussy, not her ass.

She laughed. "Later," she promised, her muscles expertly squeezing my cock. "OK?"

"Wonderful," I moaned, as she squirmed against me – slowly, at first, then faster until I was on the verge of exploding – and then she clamped down for several seconds, making me come without ejaculating. My senses were still reeling when she relaxed, raised herself up off my lap, and then grabbed my cock and guided it into her asshole.

I felt the tip of my cock press slowly against her sphincter, then the wonderful sensation of the glans popping through into her anus. She gasped, then giggled again, and eased herself back into my lap, my shaft sliding easily into her depths. I'd thought her pussy was hot and tight, but this was the most intense feeling I could remember, and I wanted it to last for ever . . . until she started her special brand of lap-dancing again, taking control of the movement, and the feeling of pleasure became stronger and stronger, building towards a peak that I couldn't have postponed if I'd wanted to. The orgasm, when it hit me, was like an earthquake and a lightning bolt and a tsunami all in one.

When I could see and focus again, Kim was still sitting in my lap, looking over her shoulder at my face. "You like?" she asked.

"Yes."

"I like you." She peeled herself away from me somehow – I could have sworn we were fused together for ever, but obviously we weren't – then handed me a tissue, kissed me on the cheek and disappeared into the darkness.

I staggered out of the booth a few minutes later and into the auditorium, where I watched a few strippers until I was sure I was coordinated enough to walk back to my hotel.

Kim was waiting by the ticket booth as I left. "Hi!" she said. "Coming back tomorrow?"

ABOUT WET NURSING

Della, USA

When I was nursing my baby I was fortunate that I always had more than enough milk, so much in fact that I thought it would be a shame to let all that nourishing milk go to waste. I checked with a new-age midwife I knew to see if she might know of anyone who could use my wet-nursing services. She said she would check around and get back to me.

It was so long before I heard from her again that I thought she had forgotten about me. When she finally called she said she had been hesitant to contact me because of the unusual nature of this case.

It seemed there was a young man about twenty-four years old who'd had some kind of stomach surgery (she didn't know the details) and his father said he was having serious difficulty digesting ordinary food. The man was suffering pain and nausea almost every time he ate and because of this he was unable to get better. When he heard of me he thought that mother's milk might be just what he needed to soothe his stomach and nurture him until he got completely healed.

"You've got to be kidding," I said. "What does his mother have to say about this?"

"Della, he's a grown man, honey. His mother lives in some other state."

"Are you sure this isn't some kind of a joke?"

"I assure you, Della, that it's not. He insisted on meeting you before he decided to do it. You have an appointment with him this afternoon at two o'clock."

"Is his father going to be there?"

"Yes, but he said that when you get there he'll go upstairs and give you two some privacy."

When I rang the doorbell an older gentleman answered the door. "Oh yes, he's going to like you," he said, smiling. "My son said he couldn't bring himself to do this with some 'creepy-looking' woman.

"Jesse," the man yelled. "The lady is here. I'll be upstairs," he told me, and left.

When the young man appeared in the doorway I was stunned. He was barefoot, wearing baggy pyjamas and admittedly he looked frail, but he was absolutely beautiful. He had dark, curly hair and a slender build. Though he was pale, almost fragile looking, he had a face like an angel. When he saw me he smiled.

"Thank God you're pretty," he said.

"I'm glad you approve," I told him, smiling. "Would you like to start today? I hope you would because I'm so full that I'm soaking through my blouse. My breasts start to hurt when they get this full."

"I'm embarrassed," he said, staring at my damp blouse. "I'm not well and I really do want to do this but I'm so embarrassed."

"Come here, honey," I said to him, feeling so much maternal compassion. I wanted so much for this to work for him. In truth I couldn't wait to get that precious young man in my arms. "Let's do this on the couch. You lie down here facing me and I'm going to put my right leg over you to give you more room."

"That'll put me between your legs," he said blushing. "Are you sure that's all right with you?"

"Honey, it'll be just fine," I said, sitting down. "Come here and lie down." I held my arms out to him.

Obediently he stretched out on the couch facing me and I lifted my right leg up over him. "Now I've got you in a leg hold," I said laughing, "so don't give me any trouble." As I talked to him soothingly I unbuttoned my blouse and lifted my right breast out of my bra as if it were the most normal thing in the world.

The poor guy was flushed and trembling a little. I could see how nervous he was and I was doing everything I could to put him at ease.

"Your breasts are huge," he whispered, tracing a blue vein with his finger.

"That's right, baby, so you better be really hungry," I said, laughing as I gently brought his head down to rest on my bosom. "Don't be timid, take it in," I crooned.

Hesitantly he tenderly sucked the nipple into his mouth. "I don't want to hurt you," he murmured.

"Suck as hard as you want to, sweetheart, it doesn't hurt," I whispered in his ear. "It actually feels good to empty some of that milk out."

That was all the encouragement he needed. He was sucking that nipple like he was starved. "It's good," he whispered, "really rich." Slipping his right hand into my blouse he timidly whispered, "May I?"

"Of course you may, sweetheart," I said, and he clutched my other breast, kneading it with his fingers as he sucked.

It soon dawned on me that I was dealing with a problem I didn't have when I nursed babies. I should have anticipated this. As I watched him drink, watched his sweet throat muscles contract as he swallowed, watched this beautiful young man's forceful sucking on my nipple, I was becoming uncomfortably aroused. It was all I could do to keep from letting a groan escape my lips, to keep from squirming with the intense pleasure of it.

I glanced down and saw that he was having a problem as well. His rather large cock was rigid, poking against the fly of his pyjama bottoms. His eyes looked up at me from his nursing and he saw that I was staring mesmerized at the bulge in his pyjamas.

"Oh, I'm so sorry," he murmured, grabbing a blanket off the back of the couch. "This is so pleasurable I can't help but be stimulated by it. Just cover us and you won't have to look at it," he said.

Covering us both with the blanket I said, "Honey, please don't be embarrassed. I seem to be having the same problem myself."

"Are you saying you're aroused by me sucking your breasts?" he whispered.

"Well, yes, baby," I said. "I should have realized that would happen."

He began sucking violently and now I really did groan, feeling a heat rising in my sex, knowing that if he kept that up I was going to come, that there was no way I could stop it.

"Ma'am, please don't be upset with me, but I'm so worked up I'm about to spill," he whispered, grabbing at my nipple again.

"Jesse, can you see how easy it would be?" I whispered. By now the heat between my legs was like a fire overpowering any feeble thought of resistance. "You're right there," I murmured. "I'm wearing a skirt and my panties are loose. All you have to do is pull them aside and go into me."

At the thought of this possibility he was trembling violently. "What if Dad comes downstairs?" he whispered.

"Honey, we're well covered with this blanket. All he would see is you nursing." My voice was quavering with the urgency of my need. I slid down on the couch a little and opened my thighs wider.

He scooted up to me and, trembling with excitement, I reached under the blanket and took his engorged cock out and guided it into my open lips. I was so frenzied I was gasping.

He was shuddering and groaning as well. "You need to switch to the other breast now," I whispered, taking it out. Greedily he grabbed it into his mouth and I almost screamed as his thick cock went smoothly into me so deep I felt the pressure as it pushed against the top.

"Oh God," he whispered, "I don't think I can keep from coming."

"Just be really still for a moment, honey," I said, "because I'm about two strokes from an orgasm myself. Let's take this slow and easy. You've got more nursing to do yet."

After a while he was able to begin working inside me with strong, smooth and deep strokes as he nursed my throbbing breast. When we would get too close to orgasm he would slow down a little.

"Oh shit, this is unbelievable," he groaned.

"Shhhh, here comes your dad," I whispered.

He pushed deep into me and held it as he continued to nurse. I couldn't keep my sheath from biting down on him, convulsing.

His father poked his head in the door. "Is everything OK in here?" he said.

"Fine, Dad, go away," Jesse yelled. Grabbing the TV remote he turned the television on and turned the volume up. "Oh shit, ma'am, I don't think I can hold it any longer." He was moaning, driving hard into me.

"It's all right, baby," I murmured gasping and pushing into him. "I'm coming too." My orgasm was cresting in powerful spasms that enveloped me in continuous fiery waves.

Stroking fast and hard he stiffened, thrust deep into me and cried out, his come squirting into me again and again, hot and powerful. It was bathing us both. I held his head to my breast rocking us gently, my heart pounding.

"I hope this milk is what you need, sweetheart," I said. "I hope it makes you all well."

"If it doesn't I'll die happy," he said, biting teasingly at my nipple.

Jesse did get well. It took three months of nursing therapy and we stretched that into four. I let him come by as often as he needs to for a little tender loving care. He still has that fragile, angelic look about him that drives me mad.

STUDENT BAWDY

Jarrett, Lawrence

I felt Dean's foot on my foot. I looked up from my book, across the table at the guy. He slowly raised his pale-green eyes from the *Introductory Psychology* text he was supposedly studying and stared back at me, thick eyebrows lifting in question.

"Cut it out," I whispered, drawing disapproving glances from the other students studying at the long, polished table.

Dean bunched his eyebrows and shrugged his huge shoulders, went back to his textbook.

Ten seconds later, I felt his long, socked foot on my shin, my knee, sliding inside my thigh and landing in my open crotch. My *Basics of Commercial Law* book slammed down on the table, shaking the entire library.

Dean looked at me, anger on his face like the other students, the waddling-our-way librarian. Then a big, wide grin spread across the second-team basketball player's handsome mug, his teeth showing white as piano keys under his thick lips. The sixteen-inch foot attached to the forty-six-inch leg started rubbing my cock, getting the rise out of me intended.

The big guy can always do that to me – turn me on like a switch, no matter where we are or how close to finals. We shared the same dorm, and more and more often into our freshman year, the same room whenever we could manage it.

My face burned red, my body hotter, cock swelling hard under Dean's persistent, caressing foot until it was straining the bounds of my zipper.

"Time to check out?" he suggested, just as the librarian huffed up to our table.

I kept the thick law text glued to my groin as we hustled out of the hushed building and into the underground tunnel that connected the library to the science building and then the dorms. It was early April in Lawrence, and still as chilly as a professor's personality outside. But it was warm in the tunnel. And three-point-machine Dean made it even warmer.

We managed 100 feet or so before he shoved me into a blazingly white washroom, pulled me into a stall and bolted the door. Then, eyes shining with want, he took me by the hips and lifted me up and plopped me down feet first on the black toilet seat. He had my belt loose before I'd even gotten a good grip on his soft, inch-high hair.

"Big Daddy needs his meat," he growled, yanking my Dockers and Jockeys down.

My cock bounced out into the open and hung there, large and loaded, pointing straight at my college lover, shaft pulsing pink and cap shining purple. I'm a little guy vertically – barely up to the big man's nipples – but horizontally I'm cocking tall. Dean grabbed my prick and squeezed.

"Yes!" I groaned, shuddering with the erotic impact of the man's huge, warm mitt on my hard shaft.

I kept one hand on his head, the other on the top of the stall, as he stroked me, expertly pumped my throbbing length with his smooth hand. Then he bent at the knees and got his big mouth level with my big cock. He looked up at me, and snaked out his tongue, bumping the ultra-pink tip of it into my bloated hood, wet and warm. I groaned some more, trembling body tingling.

But he just gave me a taste, letting go of my dick and grabbing on to my furry balls, leaving me achingly bobbing in front of his face. He clenched my nut sac, making my knees buckle and my knuckles light up white in his black hair, on the bathroom stall, as I dangled and dangled in front of his open mouth, his hot, humid breath streaming over my straining prong.

Finally, he engulfed my hood with his lips.

"Jesus, yes! Suck my cock!" I implored, voice echoing in the empty washroom.

He sucked on my bulbous head, pulling my hood with his lips, cheeks billowing and nostrils flaring wide, long fingers juggling my balls. He moved his head forwards, taking more of my cock into the wet-hot cauldron of his mouth. I teetered on the toilet seat, legs shaking, Dean's soft, moist lips sliding down my pulsating shaft, consuming me. The man knew his way around a cock; he had me buried to the blond fur in his mouth and throat in a matter of sweating seconds.

I whimpered, staring down at him staring up at me, only my bushy pubes visible, tickling the man-eater's flat nose. My whole body started to vibrate, as the time ticked by in super slow motion, Dean holding me locked in his bulging mouth and throat, his hand crushing my balls, the pressure on my cock and sac incredible, outrageous – and mounting. Shivers of delight stung my skin and shot all through me. I felt the come rise up my shaft, the sealed-tight steam box of the man's gripping maw sending me over the edge.

I tried to ride it out, couldn't. I desperately tapped Dean's head, and he pulled back, releasing my pent-up prick in a gush of hot spit and pre-come.

"Almost a full minute," the sexual athlete gasped, grinning. "A new record."

He grasped my dripping dong and started stroking it again, mouthing it again. He swallowed me all the way down in a dizzying, headlong rush and then slowly pulled back up. Repeated it, sucking on my pulsating meat, deep-throating with glorious abandon.

I let go of the stall and clung to his head with both hands, pumping my hips, fucking the stud's oven-hot, ocean-wet mouth in rhythm to his powerful head bobs. "Eat my cock!" I screamed, churning his mouth.

Dean gripped my hips and held his head still, letting me fuck his mouth, throat-deep, snot bubbling out of his billowing nostrils, teary eyes on my eyes. I crammed the guy's kisser full of pistoning dick, faster and faster, my balls boiling and my body burning with approaching ecstasy.

"I'm coming!" I wailed, cock detonating, pulsing hot ecstasy into Dean's mouth, down his throat. I was jolted by blast after blast of orgasm, clinging to my lover and wildly churning his mouth, emptying every last ounce of myself inside of him. As he gulped it all down.

Then a buzzer sounded, signalling the end of classes. And almost instantaneously, guys started pouring into the washroom, the outside tunnel alive with students. I ducked my head down and yanked my spent cock out of Dean's mouth with a soggy pop, stuffed it back into my underwear and did up my pants. I jumped down off the toilet into Dean's arms.

He kissed me, lifting me off the tile to meet his hungry mouth. His heavy tongue burst through my lips and thrashed around inside my mouth, giving me a taste of what I'd given him.

"I th-think we better get back to the dorm," I garbled, chasing his tongue with mine.

He grinned and spun me around, smacked my ass and sent me stumbling out of the stall. "Time-out for now," he agreed.

As we were exiting the noisy washroom, I looked back and saw a plump, red-faced guy emerge from a stall. He was zipping up his fly, a big, satisfied smile on his mug, too.

MY LESBIAN SEX CONFESSION

Teresa, Stoke-on-Trent

It all happened over the August bank holiday in 1999. Claire and I had been bumping into each other and giving each other a good licking and fisting every now and again since the day that we'd left school. But sometime around May that year, ideas about fantasy role play and being the naughty little schoolgirl who was punished by the strict headmistress had started to creep into the conversation and the relationship had become more and more intense.

With one of us wearing our old school uniform and the other dressed in a sharp, stern skirt suit, we would act out our C.P. and teacher-fucking fantasies on each other over and over again. But the one thing we really wanted to do seemed impossible.

We both wanted to be schoolgirls again and to be punished and abused by a gorgeous blond teacher, just as we had wanted to be when we were at school and were being punished for our "disgusting and disgraceful behaviour".

Then finally, after much hard work on Claire's part, our fantasy would finally come true. Someone would be visiting us at her house over the long weekend.

Claire had been planning it for a month, but refused to say anything about who was visiting. In fact, I didn't even have a clue as to whether it was a man or a woman!

I tried to get her to tell me but she wouldn't crack. All I knew was that she was horny as hell at the thought of this person's visit and that she couldn't wait for the day to arrive. She grinned like a Cheshire cat whenever I mentioned it and when we fucked I swear her honey had never tasted sweeter.

Eventually, however, the big day came and I arrived in the afternoon with a bag of my school uniforms and *plenty* of knickers. I had packed some normal clothes as well but when Claire saw them she said that I shouldn't have bothered since we'd be schoolgirls all day long.

Taking me by the hand, Claire then took me upstairs and told me to change into my uniform. And eager to find out what was going to happen, I did so as fast as I could.

My pussy was dripping and my breath was quickening as I slipped into my lovely new, white cotton panties. And although I loved all this horny anticipation, it was almost a shame when they were ruined less than a minute after I put them on.

I was also watching Claire as she got changed into her pleated blue PE skirt, blouse, tie, white knee socks and black shoes.

My heart started to pound in my chest. It was really true. We were both going to be schoolgirls again.

Even while we were both stood side by side in front of the dressing table mirror putting our hair up in pigtails she refused to tell me what was happening. She just stood there grinning and telling me that 'You'll find out soon enough.'

I could see how hard her nipples were through the thin cotton of her blouse and that she was standing with her legs tightly crossed, squeezing her pussy with her thighs. She was obviously very excited about something, and it was getting closer and closer with every tick of the clock.

I pleaded with her to tell me, but she just started giggling like a twelve-year-old and led me back downstairs. And once we were there, we sat cuddled up together on the sofa staring at the clock and feeling so horny that we both felt like we wanted to explode.

Claire was finally starting to crack under the pressure, but all she would say was that the person would be here at seven o'clock and that if we weren't both behaving like good girls when she arrived that she would be very angry indeed.

At least I knew now that we were expecting a woman. But how long would I have to wait before I could lick her out?

Of course, knowing that we had to be good girls was like a red rag to a bull, because the only thing nicer than being naughty was being punished when we were caught.

Claire was the one who started it.

Licking her lips she put her hand between my thighs and started to stroke my pussy through my damp cotton knickers. Groaning with satisfaction, I reached out and caressed her firm ripe tits through the cloth of her blouse. And in less than a minute, we were hopelessly lost in each other's arms and fucking each other like a couple of bitches on heat.

By the time the clock struck seven we were both a total mess. And when someone finally knocked at the door we leaped to our feet with shock.

Rushing to the door, we did our best to smarten ourselves up and answered it as curtly as we could, standing side by side and smiling sweetly with our blouses unbuttoned, our knickers around our ankles and lipstick smeared everywhere that our mouths had been. And as soon as the door opened and I saw the face of our new teacher, I finally realized what Claire had been so horny about.

Standing angrily on the doorstep and towering over us in her four-inch stilettos was Claire's friend Paula, a woman who I would call Miss Johnson and worship until the day that I die.

She wore a stern, charcoal grey skirt suit with lapels so crisp you could cut your hand on them. Her shoulder-length hair was in a tight bun with not a single strand out of place, and her expression as she sized us up with her steely cold eyes, peering over her glasses, truly frightened me, but also excited me as well.

We curtseyed to her, lifting the hems of our tiny pleated skirts so that our moist shaven pussies were revealed. I remember that I didn't dare make eye contact. Even before she had said a word I was in a submissive and cowering state of mind because she was so domineering that she didn't even have to try.

Miss Johnson didn't even say hello. She was obviously disgusted with our appearance, which was just what we'd both wanted. And, tutting with repugnance, she held out her car keys and told us to run out and fetch her bags from the boot.

Twenty people must have seen us as we did what we were told. But having waited for months, we were both so horny that we honestly didn't care. So without a second thought, we both muttered, "Yes, miss," and curtseyed as we left.

After putting the bags upstairs in the room that Claire had prepared for her, we stood patiently in front of Miss Johnson in the lounge with our hands behind our backs waiting for her to punish us for our slovenly appearance after our little fuck on the settee.

We stood fidgeting with shame for what felt like a minute as she paced up and down before us, until finally she spoke.

As she lovingly straightened our ties and smoothed down our hair, she asked in a soothing voice what we had been up to.

I said we had been cleaning the house for her, but she was still curious as to how our lipstick had become so smeared and how our knickers had come off.

We were stood as we always had as schoolgirls – hands behind the back and feet apart – so of course we were totally exposed when she put her hands up our skirts and groped our juicy pussies. And although she knew what we'd been up to and how horny we must have been, I really think that she was shocked to feel just how juicy our pussies actually were.

Fuming and disgusted, she called us lesbian sluts and pulled us one at a time over her knee on the sofa and spanked our bottoms bright pink. And as Miss Johnson spanked me, I actually came so hard that I sprayed honey all over her hand.

Standing side by side again with tears welling in our eyes as we rubbed our sore bottoms better, she shoved her fingers up our cunts and asked repeatedly if we were slutty lesbians and if we enjoyed being fisted by her.

We did our best to deny it as we gasped and wailed, our knees trembling as we grabbed hold of her wrists for dear life, but being fucked so roughly by such a dominant and interrogatory figure eventually compelled us to talk.

I must have come twice before Claire finally gave in and confessed. I can tell you now though that when Miss Johnson had finished with us, her suit sleeves were soaked with come.

I was really quite sad that it had ended so soon. It was one of the deepest, most intense and most satisfying fucks I'd ever had. But although the fisting was over, the fucking had just begun.

For the rest of the day we took it in turns having our bums and pussies caned, strapped and paddled, being forced to kiss, suck each other's tits or lick one another out as we were punished.

She said that she was trying to "beat our perverse tendencies out of us" and it was exactly what we had been longing for.

The thing that I remember most is being forced to sit on Claire's old school-type desk with my legs apart as she bent over and touched her toes with her face buried in my pussy, licking me out as her backside was caned before we were made to swap over.

I think it must have been 3 a.m. before we finished. We'd come so much that we had stained the carpet and our arses and palms were red raw. And even then we were forced to assist Miss Johnson as she changed into her nightie and got into bed while we just cuddled up at her feet.

As soon as we were sure she had gone to sleep though, being careful not to wake her, we fucked each other stupid until the sun came up.

We were Miss Johnson's slaves all Saturday and Sunday. It was just like being on punishment back at boarding school, except for the relentless fucking, that is.

Reporting promptly at nine in our neat uniforms with perfect hair and make-up, we spent all day cooking, cleaning and doing any other menial task Miss Johnson could think of.

Of course, she would always stand behind us with a cane or a strap in her hand, ready to punish us for any slight misdeed, and we always did our best to make sure that she had plenty of reasons to punish us.

Only in the evenings did Miss Johnson relax and unwind. And taking off her knickers, she would force us to take turns licking out her pussy as she watched television or listened to music with one of us stood holding her drinks tray.

She stripped and bathed us together at the same time each night, paying close attention to our tits and pussies and turning a blind eye when we touched each other up. She would then towel us dry, slip us into the two long girlie white nighties she had brought especially to make us feel like schoolgirls, before brushing our hair and tucking us both up in Claire's double bed. Then she would get ready for bed herself and go to sleep in the guest room.

We were all far too horny to sleep however, so each night at about 3 a.m. she would perform a dorm check; and woe betide us if we'd been doing anything that we shouldn't.

Dressed in a sexy black nightie, dressing gown and slippers, she would quietly creep into our dorm, torch in hand, and reach up underneath our bedclothes to check the state of our pussies which were invariably dripping, having fucked each other stupid since "lights out".

We then pretended to be asleep when, throwing off the bedclothes, she knelt on the bed between us and slipped her fingers one by one up our juicy cunts.

"Wake up, darlings," she whispered. "Auntie Paula wants to talk to you."

I thought my look of shock and surprise was really rather well acted as I woke up to "suddenly" find my teacher on my bed with her fist inside my pussy, but Claire insisted that I hammed it up far too much.

Once we were awake, Miss Johnson proceeded to make sure that we wouldn't get up to any more "filthy behaviour" by making sure we had come at least five times so that we were either satisfied, or just too knackered to do anything when she left.

I can still vividly remember lying there on the bed when Miss Johnson sat on my face, her thighs holding me securely, and urged me to lick harder as I heard her hand slap against soft flesh and Claire whimper with pain and delight.

At the end of Sunday's dorm inspection, she gave us each a good hard fucking with the torch, slapping our arses and shouting at us to "take it like a woman" until we collapsed on the bed weeping tears of exhaustion and relief.

It was absolutely wonderful, but we knew that the next day would be her last day, so I think she was glad to put in the extra effort.

On the Monday morning we arrived promptly for inspection to find her stood with her car keys in her hand. She had decided that we were going to go out in the city centre for the day and there was nothing that we could do to change her mind.

Claire told me later that my jaw dropped so far that Miss Johnson could have fitted the car in it!

Going out in public in a tiny pleated skirt, white knickers and knee socks? She had to be joking! Then Miss Johnson said something about it being all right as it was a bank holiday so there were bound to be fewer people about. And the next thing I knew, Claire and I were in the back seat of the car being driven to the shopping centre in Newcastle under Lyme – a place that I've never been before or since.

For the rest of the day we were dragged around all the shops that were open. But while Miss Johnson was very relaxed, I spent most of the time pulling my skirt hem down as far as I could and feeling people's stares all over me.

It was obvious that Claire felt the same, but we were betting that Miss Johnson would have no problem making a scene, or perhaps even punishing us in public, so we decided to keep up the act.

Miss Johnson had it all worked out. If anyone asked, and a few did, she was a teacher from a boarding school near somewhere out of town and as a reward for our good conduct, she was taking us shopping.

It was the most humiliating experience of my life, but I just can't help getting wet thinking about it.

I was dripping like a tap then too, so when we stopped at the big kind of seating area surrounded by cafes and restaurants, I'm sure that I must have left a puddle on the plastic seat.

Miss Johnson had all the money, we didn't even have any pockets, so she went over and ordered a coffee and a garibaldi for herself and two Pepsis and sticky buns for us.

Having finished, with the icing from my bun all over my fingers, she took me by the hand and walked me to the toilet complaining about what a mess I was and how she couldn't take me anywhere for all to hear, before pushing me into a cubicle, pulling off my knickers, sitting me down on the toilet and giving me the deepest, most satisfying fist-fuck of my life.

Lifting her skirt to reveal that she didn't have any knickers on either, Miss Johnson then pushed my face into her cunt and ordered me to eat her out. The danger of getting caught made it so good you wouldn't believe it.

Having smartened back up, I was led back out and made to sit alone as she obliged Claire the same way. And then we walked back to the car park where Miss Johnson said her goodbyes.

She had packed her bags the night before. And only when she got in the car and started the engine did reality kick in.

She was going to drive off without us!

"How the fuck are we going to get home?" I screamed after her.

"Hitch-hike!" she replied. And that was the last word she ever said to me, because to this day, I haven't seen her since.

For the next hour, with no money, no mobile and no way of getting home, we both hung around the car park not knowing what the hell to do. And so when a nice older woman came and asked if we were all right, convinced that we were both lost little schoolgirls, we both played along and did our best not to touch each other's pussies as she kindly drove us home.

Despite being left in the car park like that, however, we were both still so horny when we got back to Claire's house that we spent the rest of the day in her bed reliving the whole experience. And even though I don't see Claire any more, I do think about this little incident quite often, and it always makes my pussy wet every time.

FIRST PERSON, SUBMISSIVE

Amanda, Ottawa

When did I know I was submissive? Actually, not until my mid-thirties. I didn't even realize there was a term for the way I was. It never seemed unusual to me to feel this way.

As a child I would save the plastic wrap from my sandwich at lunchtime for a windy day. I would let that wrap fly into the air and marvel as the wind shaped it, filled it full of air, tossed it high, then swept it low over the tarmac playground, then scraped it against the brick walls. Sometimes that wrap came back to me, but more often than not it soared free. The wind released it.

Do you remember those games you played as a child? Red light, green light? What Time Is It, Mr Wolf? They all revolved around the same principle. There was a commander and those who followed commands. I followed.

In the business world, I had to be a leader. Take charge. Make decisions. And I did so, every day for decades. But at night in the dark I read fantasy stories of women being told what to do in bed. I imagined letting go. I imagined flying through the wind. I yearned to fly, yearned to let go. I yearned for something I didn't understand.

So when did I learn there was something to this, something real? I never had orgasms all through my marriage. My husband did what many men did; perhaps some still do: lick and stick fingers inside the cunt for a few minutes. They call it foreplay. Then stuck his dick inside. That's what the real thing is, apparently. I just lay there mostly. He asked me if it was good for me, and of course it was. It was what I was taught was good for me. Mostly I thought of other things during sex. When he came, I cried out. Was I faking? I didn't know I was.

Did I masturbate? Yes. I zipped back to those stories. It wasn't intentional; my brain just took me there. I was on the floor at a masked man's feet. He told me what to do and I did it. Of course it was really me, telling myself what to do. But the thought of being told not to think, just to act, just to obey. Someone strong would be able to override my thoughts and fears. It freed me.

Flash forward to my mid-thirties. A lover wanted to engage in some soft-core BDSM. I wasn't sure what he meant, but he was very experienced. He pointed me towards some books and websites, and we discussed it. He was a gentle, intelligent man, very rational, very controlled and also very patient. He didn't rush me into anything I didn't want. When I was ready, he tied my arms and wrists with silk scarves, gently so as not to cut off circulation points or nerve endings. He put a blindfold around me. It felt good, incredibly so. I wasn't me. I was just a flying, floating being. This lover, he showed me. Commanded me. I respected him and trusted him. Wasn't like I could do that with any man. No, it took months before I was ready to give that trust to him, and I never gave it all the way. We were just casual lovers. But it awakened something in me.

He liked role play. We'd set up scenes ahead of time to try. His fantasy was to come to my door, to find me tied up and blindfolded, and then to use my mouth with his cock. The plan was set up carefully, ensuring that I was very comfortable with the idea. Neither one of us was supposed to talk and I wasn't supposed to peak, that was all part of the fantasy.

The day arrived. My telephone intercom rang and I saw him arrive through my apartment's security video camera. I un-locked the door and put a scarf around my eyes, then attached my legs to the table with two soft, silk scarves, then tied my hands, loosely because it's hard to work with one hand and with not that much time. It was fun, and kind of silly too. But it was also arousing. I remember lying there and slipping in to the fantasy. The door opened. My heartbeats quickened and I felt an adrenaline rush like I'd been running. I heard a set of footsteps, then a shushing of material as the stranger walked towards me. I smelled a mixture of cigarette smoke, fresh cold air and cologne. At first I wondered if this was really my lover. I didn't remember that cologne. My heart raced and my body tingled. My cunt was wet with excitement. This man was going to fuck my mouth, just use me.

I'd had fantasies like this all my life and now it was coming true. I was still a bit scared, then he reached down and stroked my cheek with his thumb. His hand felt familiar to me. He always did that during our lovemaking. It meant so much to me that he cared enough to reassure me, reminded me that this was all fantasy. I heard the sound of a zipper going down. My tits hardened as I felt the draught of his body moving over mine. He ran his hands over my breasts and I heard his unmistakable moan. My pulse quickened as I realized he was as turned on as me and I felt so good to be giving him his fantasy. I felt his warm cock rub over my face and along my body, then back up again, seeking my mouth. I held it there. When you can't see there are so many sensations you are suddenly awakened to. I never really noticed the texture of a cock before, how soft the head was, how much like a nipple. He pushed it in further.

Ahead of time, we'd talked about whether it would be OK to be a bit rough or whether I would prefer gentle. I told him that I didn't think I wanted rough when I was tied up and blind-folded, not without being held afterwards. So he was gentle. He respected my wishes. I felt sexy and tender all at once. He started to pump in and out of my mouth, and I was all mouth and he was all cock. Meditative. Sexy. Primal feelings coursed through me. My cunt tightened. All the motion made my blindfold, which was very loosely tied, turn up a bit, and I got a sneak peak of my lover. I closed my eyes, but smiled against his cock. The come started to seep out—hot and salty on my tongue. I heard his breathing grow heavier and smelled the musky scent of his balls. Soon he was coming and I received it, felt like my mouth was my cunt. I didn't orgasm, but felt so exhilarated and happy. I heard him zip up and felt a tissue rubbing against my face, wiping off his come. He told me it was amazing and we both laughed a bit. So much for our anonymity fantasy. But he couldn't help himself and that was both sexy and charming and loving all at once. He left then, and I untied myself and went to bed, using my vibe to reach orgasm while reliving every sensation. Later we chatted and he told me how ravishing and exuberant I looked and how wonderful I was for giving him this fantasy. I felt good, powerful and satisfied.

I learned through all this experimentation that sex can be wonderful and that submission was the thing that really turned me on. I read a bit, was too afraid to experiment with other lovers, kept this side of myself quiet, until he came along. The one. My Master.

Like me, his own path was not straightforward, but he can tell his own story. First he was my friend and confidant. I could tell him anything, everything. All about other lovers, my past, my ex, the orgasms I faked. He let me sit in his arms and cry. I'd missed out on so much in my life. I'd been asleep. I was his sleeping beauty. I tasted food, saw sunsets. I wrote poetry and songs. I was becoming me.

Then he was my lover. He was a good lover. Knew his way around a clit. Found my sweet spots. Kissed the nape of my neck until I had goosebumps all over my body. Then he kissed those too. Wanted to discover every inch of me.

He knew about my experiments with scarves and a blindfold. My favourite books to read at bedtime. What turned me on. This man knew me inside out. And what turned me on, turned him on. So we learned. Together. He read and asked questions. How could we set each other free?

Books and websites and chatting with people online taught us the safe, sane and consensual rules of BDSM. We started with what you'd expect. A starter kit from one of those sex shops. Cuffs made of Velcro, easy to get out of, but strong enough so that when attached to the bedposts, they could withstand my yanking on them as my lover tortured my little clit to stiffness, rolled my nipples between his dexterous finger and thumb, then pinched them hard, till I felt alive again. To erase the numbness. To make me come. So I pulled on those restraints as I surrendered myself to his will, and his will was to release me.

Afterwards, the questions began. What part did I like best? Were there things that made me uncomfortable? What else made me curious? Months went by with me being put in these restraints regularly and my lover exercising his control. He tickled me lightly with a feather, but that just made me squeal and I didn't like it, so he stopped. He placed ice cubes in his mouth then sucked my tits and my clit. So cold, then so hot. He thought I might enjoy wax, and it sounded good, but flames were scary to me, so he rigged up this effective method involving a mug warmer, a metal Turkish coffee cup and white kosher candles, plus a candy thermometer. He found out that white candles don't burn as hot as coloured ones and were therefore much safer. We'd moved up to chains; they were stronger and could handle the pressure of my pulling better. Plus they were cold against my skin, much more sensual and theatrical. They made me feel like I was truly bound. Stirred both our imaginations. So much of BDSM is theatre, role play, getting into the mood. I had panic snaps of course. All I had to do was pull, and the chains would release. From there it was so simple to unhook my velvet-lined oxblood leather cuffs.

Ah yes, the wax. He blindfolded me, let me feel the heat of the metal cup gently on my inner thighs, and up onto my breasts. My cunt juices flowed. I didn't know then what was going on. He surprised me, but not totally out of left field. We'd discussed it in one of our briefing sessions, and in a survey he had me fill out regularly to figure out my limits, which changed all the time. Finding a way to communicate with him was and is essential. It is my number one obligation and the way I serve him best: being open and honest at all times.

The wax: the drip down, down, down onto my breasts, around the nipples. Oh so hot, burning almost. God, I was alive and this man was putting me there. Exciting and dangerous feeling, although not really so. But it was the edge of something. The edge of real trust, mine of him. He could do this to me when I was all bound up, unable to resist, well, unless I really insisted. Vulnerable.

I felt him coming as the wax hardened on my skin. Heard him cry out. Felt the cold splashes of his orgasm all over my body.

Opened my mouth to drink the rain of come. The sky had opened, releasing us both. We were sticky and wet with it, with him.

He unbound me, washed me in warm water, then dipped his head down, put his tongue in to taste me. So tenderly he licked, then moved up to my lips so I could taste myself. We kissed as he caressed along my moist sex lips, immersing his fingers in plum juice. I was greedy to quench him and he wanted to taste every drop. His head moved down again. His breath so warm on my breasts, my stomach, my cunt. What I had done for him, he did for me. He found my vortex and swirled it, creating the storm of my passion for him once again until I shook and stopped, shook and stopped, shook and stopped, until this rhythm and the heat and his tongue all coalesced into an open, flowing orgasm.

Days and nights after that were magic. Busy with some daytime chore, we looked up at each other and smiled, knowingly. We had a secret no other person knew of. We had shared intimacy in its truest, most honest form. We knew everything there was to know about one another. Trust. Control. Release. Love. Knowledge. Peace. Joy. If there were seven deadly sins, these were seven happy blessings. And we had experienced them. This was the secret of life as far as we were concerned. Details are sharper when you're as exhilarated as we were and still are. It's like being constantly high. Euphoric.

Then a hotel visit to the city. High, sturdy bedposts, a four-poster bed. Made for bondage. And our first flogger, made by my lover out of rope from a hardware store and a rubbery bicycle handle. That first lash with the soft silky rope turned rough against my skin . . . What was that? Pain? Yes, slightly, but not more than a bit. Heat, yes some. Excitement. Tension. Surprise. What would he do? Strike harder? Could I handle it? Did he think I could? He did. And, oh. My cunt was wet. Those first whispered orders. "Hump the bed." I paused. The flogger struck again. This time harder. I humped. "Count the lashes." His voice had never seemed so urgent, so strong. So confident. I trusted him. He wouldn't hurt me, but he'd push me, beyond. He'd show me, beyond. He'd trust me to tell him what I could handle and what I couldn't. Then that first slip as the words rumbled and the bed creaked and my body softened and yielded to the beat of the whip and the rocking of my hips, the rhythm of his lashes on my skin, soft then hard, then soft then hard as I count and moan. I want to come. "Not yet," he whispered. "Tell me what you are."

What was I? I was his, I was nothing, I was this bed, I was this whip, I was this heat, this soft, this hard, this come, this . . . his and only his.

I am not who now, but what. I am a piece of plastic wrap floating, driven by the wind.

WIFE SANDWICH

Giselle, Scarborough

I can't believe I'm actually going to tell this story. I'm still pretty amazed that it happened at all. You see, my younger sister Rachel played soccer for her high school's team. I had finished my studies and entered the workforce by that time, but I would often attend her games to cheer her on and all that. Well, I actually did more reading than cheering, but the fact that I was sitting in the bleachers at all meant a lot to my little sister.

I noticed Steve at the first game I attended, partly because the sunlight was reflecting off of his bald head and partly because he was the only other person there who was sitting alone. Steve was the father of one of the girls on Rachel's team, which meant that I got to see him at every game. I'm generally shy and cautious around new people, but I took to Steve right away because he seemed rather shy as well. He was an intellectual sort with a toned physique, and I've always had a thing for older men who work out.

At first, Steve and I would discuss the books that we were reading. Eventually, our conversations became more intimate. Steve told me how lonely he felt in his marriage. Steve worked from home as a technical writer and was fairly deprived of human interaction for that reason. He told me that he had always looked forward to six o'clock, when his executive wife Helen arrived home from work. Over the past five years, though, Helen had been working later and later into the evenings and when she finally arrived home she was always too exhausted to pay him any attention. I felt very close to Steve because he had confided in me and it soon became apparent that an intense attraction was developing between the two of us.

At the end of each soccer game, Steve and I would go our separate ways, he with his daughter and I with my sister. One day, after our team had achieved a 4–1 victory, I wrote my address down on a scrap of paper and invited Steve to come over on Friday afternoon, since I did not have to work. He knew what the invitation implied. I remember Steve staring down at my address and saying that he would have to think about it. When Steve arrived on my doorstep that Friday at two o'clock, I was overjoyed. I really wasn't sure if he would come or not. I took the man straight into the bedroom, stripped off his clothes and rode his cock until he flipped me onto my back and pummelled me with penetrations. It was the most frenzied, passionate sex I had ever experienced. I'm now convinced that bookworms have the best sex!

Steve and I continued seeing each other every Friday afternoon. By the time he arrived at my house, we were already so hot for each other that we almost never remembered to lock the front door before heading to the bedroom . . . or living room, or kitchen or wherever. One Friday in May, two years into the relationship, Steve sat on my sofa while I devoured his hard cock. Suddenly, I heard the front door open and I just about had a heart attack. Who would just walk into my house unannounced? I froze, thinking it might be a family member or a friend of mine, but it was not. It was a stylish woman with short blondish hair and a professional demeanour. I had never seen her before. I had no idea who she was, but Steve certainly did: she was his wife.

He said: "Helen, what are you doing here?"

I was shocked! Steve had never told me that his wife was so lovely and curvaceous. I had thought that she was a dowdy old woman. Why had she come? This woman was going to kill me, I figured. I braced myself for a thrashing, and I was thoroughly confused when this Helen woman did not seem angry at all. She merely said, "I found this scrap of paper in your contacts book and I figured that it must be your girlfriend's address, since it was the only one I didn't recognize."

Steve could hardly deny what was going on. After all, he had literally been caught with his pants down. He quickly started telling Helen that he was sorry and that he never should have started this up, he was a terrible husband, that sort of thing. Much to my astonishment, Helen wouldn't hear it. She wasn't interested in his excuses. I was still sitting on the floor at this point, and Helen simply walked into my living room and sat down beside her husband on my sofa. I wasn't quite sure what to do, so I sat up on the coffee table so that I was at eye level with the pair.

"I've known about you two for ages. I'm not about to tear a strip off you, don't worry," Helen told us. She admitted that she was never home and that she and her husband barely spoke even when she was. Helen understood why Steve might look elsewhere for fulfilment. She then looked straight at me and said: "I've never been much good at all this sex stuff. Never had much time for it, really. Never thought it was important. But I can see that it's something my husband thinks is important, so I'm willing to give it another go." Steve apologized once again, but Helen told him not to be silly. Helen then looked over at me, sitting on my coffee table in my black satin dressing gown, and said in a thoroughly businesslike tone: "I came over here today for a reason. I'm guessing that Steve likes whatever it is that you do, so I want you to teach me how to do it. I'll pay you, if that's what Steve does."

I was taken aback at the thought of being paid for sex, but also a little bit titillated by it. I agreed to take Helen on as my student, even though I had no idea how to teach someone to be good in bed. Should I teach her theory or technique? I paced about the living room wondering how to begin when a thought occurred to me, which I shared with Helen: "The only way to have really incredible sex is to be a truly desirous partner. Steve and I have such great sex because we're so hot for each other. Half the fun of it, for me, is watching Steve get off on me getting off on him. Do you know what I mean?"

Helen just stared at me blankly. She had no idea what I was talking about, but Steve understood. He told his wife: "I would never want to make love with you if you didn't want it as well.

There's nothing sexy about that. The best part of it is in knowing that your partner is really aroused by what you're doing."

I asked Helen what turned her on and she was perplexed. She had been focusing on other aspects of her life for so many years that she had pushed sex into some hidden corner of her consciousness. It occurred to me that Helen didn't need to figure out how to give Steve pleasure, she needed to remember how to receive it. Steve and I conspired to help his wife remember how good sex can feel, and Helen was only too happy to go along with our idea. Our intention was to stimulate Helen generously until she begged Steve for more.

I ran to the bedroom to grab a vibrator and some lube. By the time I got back to the living room, Steve had already removed his wife's silk scarf and used it to cover her eyes. With Helen standing in front of my sofa, Steve and I removed her suit jacket and her pants. I ran my hands along her arms and down her breasts and her stomach over the top of her silky blouse, while Steve stimulated her legs and buttocks. I watched Steve rub his fingers gently against his wife's mound, stimulating her over the top of her sensible underwear. I slowly unbuttoned Helen's blouse, touching the skin underneath as I did so, until the diaphanous garment fell from her arms. When I unclasped Helen's bra, Steve removed her underwear. She was naked now, but for a gold chain with a diamond pendant, which she wore around her neck. I kissed that chain, at the side of Helen's neck, and that one simple act caused the woman's knees to buckle; she fell backwards onto the sofa, with me behind her.

As I ran my hands down Helen's full, naked breasts, I told Steve to start up the vibe. I cupped Helen's breasts while Steve slathered Helen's pussy lips with lube. He massaged his wife's lips with the wet stuff on his fingers until she started moaning softly. It was then that I squeezed Helen's large breasts together. The sight of that full cleavage was really turning me on, and I could feel my own nipples harden against Helen's back. Her husband then fired up the large cock-shaped vibe and sat up on the sofa beside the two of us. Steve placed the vibe lengthwise, facing downwards, against his wife's labia and she reacted very positively: Helen pushed her whole body up against the raging vibrator, which gave me a chance to get my legs into a more comfortable position. Steve started rubbing the vibe against Helen's clit as I squeezed the woman's ample breasts. Helen moaned louder. As she writhed against the vibe, Helen's buttocks inadvertently massaged my drooling pussy in a circular motion. I pinched the woman's nipples and she cried out. I told Steve to rub harder with the vibe. The harder he rubbed, the more Helen thrust against it, and the greater the sensation of Helen's fleshy ass against my own clit.

"I want you, Steve!" Helen suddenly cried out.

I smiled at Steve. It was working! Leaning back against my deep sofa with Helen still on top of me, I motioned to Steve to position himself before his wife. When I removed the silk scarf that veiled her eyes, Helen immediately grabbed her husband and kissed him wildly. Helen then seized Steve's hard cock, which had become delightfully familiar to me over the last two years. She pulled on it as Steve crept closer and closer to her body. I watched as Steve rammed his cock into Helen's pussy, feeling a momentary pang of jealousy which was erased by the pleasure of the pair's motion on top of me. I thought this might be a good time to duck out, but when I attempted to get out from under the couple, I found that I was stuck. I was getting absolutely trampled by the fornicating duo on top of me but, boy, did it feel good! Every time that Steve lunged forwards into his wife, the motion of her ass against my clit thrilled my senses, so I rubbed myself against the woman. I was getting more out of this than I ever would have imagined, so I decided to stay put.

With one hand remaining on Helen's breast, I sent the other hand down to mash my palm against the woman's clit. I could feel Steve's slippery cock diving between my fingers as he penetrated his wife. The unexpected action of my naughty hand caused both Helen and Steve to gasp, and Steve began thrusting with renewed intensity. The pressure on my clit was indescribable as the combined efforts of Steve and myself brought the revitalized woman to a loud and frenzied climax. Steve pulled out of his exhausted wife, but I kept him going by getting a tight grip on his warm, rigid cock and tugging until hot come shot out across Helen's ample breasts and down her curvaceous stomach. Helen laughed riotously: "Ah, my husband!" she said, leaning forwards to kiss his lips. By that time, though, Helen was absolutely crushing me and I had to get out from under her.

Helen told me that I was a great teacher, but I refused to take her money. I proclaimed Helen cured of her affliction and sent her home in her husband's care. I wouldn't have felt right about seeing Steve after that, but I still hear from the couple every so often. Helen was at the end of her tether with her job, so she took early retirement and the pair does a lot of travelling together now. I'll always think fondly of Helen and Steve. That was a pretty wild afternoon for a bookworm!

TRAVELLING NORTH

Sandra, London

I always travelled north when I wanted to satisfy my desire for sex of a certain kind. I just couldn't risk bumping into someone from my London office. Maybe a secretly filmed video of me in action is out there on a website somewhere, but it's almost impossible to guard against that.

It was early on a Tuesday evening when I was left standing outside the club in the cold wind. The onset of rain only added to my torment. The club never opened on a Tuesday but Doug had emailed a request for me to participate in a private session. Dress like a working-class girl going to a nightclub was the instruction. I knew Doug was inside, but this was all part of his game. I was wearing my long black coat, the one I always wore to cover my sex outfits when I travelled. It offered little protection and my whole body was frozen.

Finally I sensed a shadow passing across the peephole in the door.

The intercom crackled, "Take off the coat, I want to see if you meet our dress code."

I met the request and held my coat out at arm's length so it did not drag across the dirty wet pavement. Slowly I rotated round in a full circle. I was wearing quite standard cheap black four-inch heels, black fishnets supported by a suspender belt. A black satin G-string just about covered my shaven cunt. The specially shortened navy blue halter-neck dress was soaking up the rain like blotting paper. A curtain twitched in a first-floor flat across the road. Even at that distance, the voyeur would be able to see I was not wearing a bra. My long black hair must have been hanging in rat-tails. I wiped my cheek. The black deposit on my fingertips told me my mascara was running big time.

The door opened. I entered. There were no courteous offers of a stiff drink or even a cup of tea. Doug walked straight through to the dance floor area. I followed. Five men in white towelling robes were sitting at two small circular tables set out in the middle of it. Though I did not know their names, I recognized them from the regular Friday and Saturday night sessions. Doug's wife Jenny was sitting on a high chair in the shadows over by the bar. I dropped my coat on the floor and stepped up onto the spot-lit stage. Suddenly a wave of goose-bumps broke out across my freezing cold skin.

This was not the first time I had bent over the leather-padded bench that was waiting for me. Usually it lived in the bondage room upstairs.

"Popcorn," I issued my codeword.

I paused for a moment to allow the men to look at the bitch they were going to fuck. Most looked in their mid-forties, about ten years older than me. I enjoyed feeling their eyes upon me. The lust in their eyes helped to warm my skin. A little bit of tension hung in the air as if they didn't know what I was waiting for. Doug tugged the lapel on the jacket of his black designer suit. The penny dropped, the five men stood and slipped off their robes. I studied the five cocks that were standing up in anticipation.

As I bent over the bench Doug jumped onto the stage so he could fasten the restraints around my wrists. He did not attach the ankle straps. Nor did he apply a blindfold as I thought he might. My thighs pushed against the end of the bench. The bench was just low enough for me to spread my feet without the need to go up on tiptoe or take excessive weight on my stomach and chest.

After a few minutes I heard and felt a pair of scissors cutting up the back of my dress. They also snipped through the neck strap. Once I was unwrapped, a circumcised cock appeared to my right. Roughly the man pulled my dress from under me. The resulting friction stung my nipples as it went. I exhaled sharply through clenched teeth. The cock went out of view. Two more snips through the strings running over my hips, another yank, and my G-string was gone. The cock then loitered between my pussy lips before driving into me. There were no preliminary slow strokes. He thrust hard and fast, his hips slapping against by butt. In less than three minutes his come was inside me.

My cunt was not left without hard flesh for very long. This one was thicker. It stretched me as it penetrated. As it opened me up some of the first lot of come dribbled round my clit. Soon I could hear the rhythmic squelching of a cock getting sloppy seconds. It was equally impatient and soon added to the spunk I had already received.

With one limp member still inside me, another firm one appeared in front of my face. It was the longest of the five, comfortably eight inches in length. I opened my mouth invitingly. He took hold of my hair and pulled up my head. I did not raise my eyes to meet his. He tried to drive it in deep. Clenching my teeth around it I signalled my limits. With the rules established I started to milk it with my mouth, occasionally pausing to flick its helmet with my tongue.

One cock replaced another at the other end. It started to feel good, one cock fucking my dripping cunt, another nice long one in my mouth. That was what I had made the long journey for. Two hands grabbed my arse and pulled my small butt cheeks wide enough apart for it to hurt. In my mind he was drilling my anus with his eyes while he screwed my cunt with his cock. I was working hard to make the cock in my mouth come, but he was having none of it. Every time I had him close, he tugged my hair and withdrew. Another load went up my vagina. Another cock went limp with satisfaction.

The guy with the long dick manoeuvred round to the other end. Slowly he pushed all the way in. With the state my cunt was in, I hardly felt the early stages of entry. But when it got to the top, I definitely felt it hit home. Gently rocking in and out he started to knead my buttocks, partially opening my anus with his thumbs. I knew where we were heading. After withdrawing his cock he started using two fingers to smear the plentiful supply of come and juice from my cunt over my arse. He went way beyond the area that needed to be lubricated. He covered my arse with warm sticky come.

As I felt the head of his cock nestling between my butt cheeks, I relaxed in preparation. It forced its way in.

"Fucking hell," I groaned.

He slapped the side of my thigh with both hands. Clearly there was to be no dialogue.

Now we were getting there, now we were arse-fucking. The pulses of orgasm rippled through me, but I don't think the guy even noticed. He just slapped the sides of my chest as I groaned. The tallest of the five appeared in front of me. I found myself staring between his thighs. Lifting my head I saw his balls pulled up under a cock with a hand wrapped round it. A man shooting in my face while I open my mouth to try to catch some spunk is one of my favourite sex acts. It is the act that really satisfies my lust to be a sex object, even more so than a stranger pummelling my arse with his long cock. I hoped this guy had more than an average supply of spunk in those balls of his.

Long dick's hands were on my hips at the time, so I knew the two fingers that went to work on my clit were not his, but whose they were is still a mystery. The guy in front of me bent his knees to lower his cock down to my face. In anticipation of what I was about to receive, I came again, only this time much more violently. A convulsing cock exploded into my arse. My face was showered in spunk. I was forced to shut my eyes as at least six good spurts hit their target. With one hand still easing his cock down, he used the other to guide rivulets of come into my beckoning mouth. I like to swallow spunk; it makes me feel so submissive.

After cleaning myself up in the toilets, I went back out to collect my coat from the dance floor. I slipped it over my naked body and went outside to wait for my taxi. A taxi Doug had called to take me to the railway station; I needed to catch the last train back to London.

LAWN SERVICE

Roxanne, Flint

It was a very hot summer and I was suffering. I was hot and very horny. The heat always did that to me. I was bored and decided to mow my lawn before it turned into a jungle. Weeds and bugs had taken over my backyard. After mowing it the lawn looked worse than it had to start out with. I decided I needed to do something about the lawn before my big 4 July pool party.

I called to have my lawn fertilized and I was very happy to open the door and find a gorgeous dark-haired man with sparkling green eyes and nicely tanned skin. He was around my age, early thirties. When he lifted the lawn spreader from the back of his van, I could see his muscles rippling. I was getting wet just watching him move. He spoke to me in a sweet Southern drawl which just turned me on even more. I was such a sucker for an accent especially that of a good-looking country boy.

The day was extremely hot and humid. I wore a filmy little sundress with tiny spaghetti straps, no bra so my full breasts moved freely under the thin material. I walked around the yard with him, pointing out problem spots I wanted to make sure he took care of. I made sure to bend over often to give him a good view of my cleavage, which did not go unnoticed. At one point I got down on my hands and knees in the grass to point out a clump of strange weeds. I made sure to hike my dress up a little so he could get a good view of my thong. I turned around to get his reaction and found him staring at my tanned, firm behind. I could see the bulge of his erection in his khakis, a very large bulge.

I was glad he enjoyed the view. I decided I was going to enjoy watching this fine specimen of a man working in my yard. I sat down by the pool and watched him while he worked. He looked so hot and miserable pushing that big, heavy spreader around the yard. At one point he took off his uniform shirt and threw it on the hammock. I just stared at his tanned chest, chiselled with muscles and covered with sexy dark hair. Part of my yard had a slight hill and I could see his arm muscles strain and bulge as he pushed the spreader back up the hill. Sweat covered his skin making him glow like a bronze statue.

As he worked, I imagined those strong arms wrapped around me, that muscular chest pressed against me and that massive bulge buried inside me. I was getting very hot and it wasn't from the temperature outside. My thong was getting soaked and I could feel that aching need deep inside. I couldn't help myself and slid my hand under my dress. I moved my thong aside and slipped a finger into my already drenched pussy. The thong was getting in my way so I tore it off and threw it onto the patio. I pulled my dress up to my waist and spread my legs wide open. I had my eyes closed. I was so lost in my fantasy I did not hear him walk up to me.

He asked, "Is there anything else I can do for you today, ma'am?"

At that point I was so aroused it didn't matter that a complete stranger was standing in front of me while I had my fingers buried inside my pussy. My yard was surrounded by a tall privacy fence, plus there were not any neighbours close by. So I stood up facing him, slipped the straps of my dress off my shoulders and let it fall to the ground. I walked over to him and reached out to undo his pants. I undid the button and pulled the zipper down. I got on my knees and pulled a very large, stiff cock out of his pants.

I moaned and said, "Today is definitely my lucky day," and I started licking his shaft, circling my tongue all around it right up to the tip. When I reached the tip I wrapped my lips around him and sucked it in as far as I could. He was so large I couldn't fit the entire thing in my mouth, but I did my best. Moving my mouth back and forth, I sucked him hard as he thrust against me. I heard him moan and saw his knees shake. I stopped; he wasn't going to come yet. I told him to get undressed. He kicked off his shoes and slipped out of his khakis. I led him over to a large lounge chair.

"Lie down on that chair," I ordered him.

"Yes, ma'am," was all he said. He lay down on my lounge chair big enough for two.

I climbed onto the chair, moving in between his legs. My breasts brushed across him as I moved up, positioning myself above him, my hot, aching pussy pressed against his hard throbbing cock. I stared into his beautiful green eyes. I pressed my mouth against his and he eagerly kissed back. Passionate kisses just the way I liked: lots of lip, not too much tongue.

I reached down to guide him into me; I'd never had something that big inside of me before. I was so wet he slid in easily. I rode him hard, grinding my body against his, feeling his hips thrust, pushing deeper and deeper inside me. I came hard and fast exploding onto his massive cock.

"Lie down, ma'am. I want to taste you."

I did what he wanted and he spread my legs wide open then climbed between them. First he kissed my lips, trailed down my neck to my breasts and kissed them, then sucked my nipples, first gently, then harder. He gently nibbled at them with his teeth. Then he ran his tongue across them and starting moving down until his face was between my thighs. There he licked all around my outer lips, dipped his tongue in to taste me and then moved up to find my clit.

He was very skilled and knew just what to do. Soon I climaxed again. He licked up all the sweet nectar that flowed out of me, pushed my legs up and back and inserted his hard dick into me again. Those Southern boys really know how to please a woman. My pussy was still pulsating and I could tell it was driving him wild. He thrust into me hard and fast; I screamed so loud the neighbours probably thought someone was killing me. He hit places that had never been touched before. He was sweating and moaning, fucking me wildly. I knew he was getting close. He pulled out of me and shot a stream of semen across my breasts. Breathing heavily he collapsed beside me on the lounge.

"I hope that was satisfactory, ma'am."

"Oh God, yes, that was wonderful. By the way, my name is Roxanne."

"Well, Roxanne, my name is Rob and I think I'm hotter and sweatier now than I was to begin with. Do you mind if I take a dip in your pool?"

"No, I don't mind at all. I think I'm going to join you."

He stood up and dived into the pool. I grabbed a towel and quickly cleaned off the sticky stuff on my chest and jumped into the pool with him. That man really looked good wet. After he did a few laps in the pool he swam up behind me and wrapped his arms around my body. I could feel his erection pressing into my back. Wow, already hard again. Not only is this guy gorgeous and hung like a stallion, he has stamina too! I thought to myself.

He pressed me against the side of the pool and entered me from behind. The water splashed around us as he thrust his big shaft in and out of me. The cool water felt good against our naked bodies as the hot sun beat down on us. He told me to turn around and face him. My back was now pressed against the side of the pool and I wrapped my legs around him. His cock was angled to rub my clit and still hit all the right spots deep inside. I could feel the tingling sensation moving throughout my body as he pumped faster and harder into me. I felt the rush of hot semen flood inside me as I quivered and came with him.

We climbed out of the pool and I gave him a towel. I watched him dry off his gorgeous body, admiring every inch of him. I slipped my dress on and watched him gather up all of his lawn equipment. All I could think was that he could spread me anytime. He finished and packed his equipment back into the van. I never took my eyes off him.

He walked up to me and handed me the bill along with his business card. "I also do some handyman work on the side and during the winter. My cell number and home number are on the back of the card, you can call me anytime, for anything."

"Thank you, I will be calling you." And I did, every chance I could get.

BOTTOM MARKS

Jenni, London

A woman is changed for ever by the first proper spanking from her lover's hand.

Minds find it impossible to recall accurately the bright, sharp clarity of pain. Marks fade from buttocks within an hour or two, within a day or two.

But bodies remember. And for ever after, if you catch her unawares and trace your fingers gently up between the backs of her legs to that place where buttocks and thighs bisect then you will feel the tiniest shiver of apprehension, an involuntary tensing of muscles . . . no matter how delicate the caress.

At least that's how it was for Mark and me. We'd met in our second year at uni and for me at least it was love, or more correctly lust, at first sight. Mark played rugby for the college team and it was some end-of-season bash. I've been described as something of an English rose – tall at five feet seven, slim and blond – but at six foot two, Mark still towered over me. He was well built at fourteen stone, with dark-brown eyes, very short, light-brown hair and as fit as the proverbial butcher's dog.

We were introduced by a mutual friend and spent most of the evening talking. He turned out to be very much the "gentle giant" – intelligent, thoughtful, considerate and charming – and pretty much that was that.

"An item" for our final year, we were very much in love and really quite innocently discovering the joys of sex. One other thing I discovered was that I had quite a nasty green-eyed streak and got terribly jealous if Mark even so much as looked at another girl . . . or even if I caught a girl looking at him. Mark used to find this completely incomprehensible and, worse, I knew it was one of the few things that actually got under his skin: "I love you and I'll never give you a reason to mistrust me. But if you don't trust me, that's your problem, not mine," he used to tell me.

Both lucky enough to get good degrees, without having to work too hard for them, jobs up in London followed: Mark with a City firm and me with a public relations company in Knightsbridge. We've been sharing a flat together in Willesden for coming up to three years.

It was Shari, one of our old college friends, who invited us to a party, almost a reunion, one Saturday evening, at her house on the outskirts of West London, and we had both really looked forward to going. The party was great, the beer and wine flowed, and we both sort of circulated and chatted, catching up with old friends and gossip.

I'd noticed Mark spending an awful lot of time talking to Zoe – high heels, short skirt, gauzy blouse and too much make-up – who I vaguely remembered as being engaged to Tim. And then at around half past ten I realized they'd both gone missing.

I gave it about another quarter of an hour and then, quite discreetly, searched the house from top to bottom – bedrooms, bathroom, even the downstairs loo – but there was no sign of either of them.

It was a warm summer's evening, dusk had only just fallen, and I went outside and walked up and down and round the block for a while until I saw them, arm in arm, coming towards me from the opposite direction.

As we neared I could see she was somehow "mussed up". To this day I don't know what came over me or why I did it, but I just suddenly lost it.

I slapped Zoe hard, a stinging swipe that left a livid palm print on her cheek made all the more striking as her face went white with shock. "Keep your fuckin' hands off him, you slag! He's mine, d'you understand?" I snarled.

"Jenni, what on earth do you think you're doing? You don't understand . . ." Mark began.

"I don't care! I don't care! Just tell me you didn't fuck her, that's all. Tell me!" I'd grabbed hold of the front of Mark's shirt and was tearing at it so furiously that buttons popped and I felt a seam split.

"Tim's just dumped Zoe. The engagement's off. She's really upset and I was just giving her a shoulder to cry on."

"See! I knew it. Tim doesn't want her any more and now she's trying to get her hooks into you. Stay away from him." I aimed another blow in Zoe's direction.

Mark grabbed hold of my arm. "That's it. That's enough. Sorry about this, Zoe, just get yourself back inside. I'm taking Jenni back home," and with that he dragged me away, still kicking and screaming, into the car.

As we drove home I was still white and shaking with adrenaline, scarcely able to believe what I had just done, and beside me, in the driver's seat, Mark was also white-faced and ominously quiet.

When we got indoors he left me downstairs, pushed past me and went up to our bedroom. I followed him forlornly a few minutes later and found him packing, a suitcase open on our bed.

"What . . . What are you doing?" I began.

"What does it look like? I'm leaving you. I love you, you know I do. I really do. But I can't stand this jealousy and tonight was the last straw. I really do think you've got a problem and I don't know what to do any more."

"Where are you going to go?"

"Don't know. But I thought I might try Tim since he's on his own as well," he said with a bitter laugh.

That was when I lost it completely, when I realized that he was serious, that he meant it. I think I was actually hysterical – love can do that to you. I howled, I sobbed, I begged. I pulled at my own hair. I pummelled at Mark's broad chest with both my fists and all my strength until exhaustion forced me stop.

And that was when I threatened to kill myself . . . as soon as he walked out the door.

"You wouldn't, would you?"

I nodded dumbly and in pain: "I can't live without you."

"And I can't live with you like this."

There was a long, long silence which grew and grew between us until Mark broke it, speaking slowly and quietly, little more than a whisper: "OK, I'll give it just one more try. But you've got to change.

"What you did earlier was wrong, dreadfully wrong and unforgivable. I'm going to punish you. I'm going to spank your arse just like a naughty little girl, since you insist on behaving like one. I'm serious, this is something I should have done a long time ago. I want you to know what it feels like to be hurt, particularly by someone you love. So it's going to be a lot more than a couple of playful smacks.

"You've got to agree, of course. But if you don't then I'll simply carry on packing and leave. You can be quite sure of that."

And with that he put one finger under my chin and lifted up my tear-stained face until his calm gaze held my own. I nodded my agreement, not trusting myself to speak, still overwhelmed by events, shocked by what I had just heard and consented to.

Mark continued to stare impassively down at me until I felt compelled to speak: "OK. Yes. Do it now. Let's get this over with."

"No, not now. Not like this. It wouldn't be right. Let's make it next Friday evening. We've got nothing planned for the weekend and you won't have to worry about not being able to sit down at work," he said ominously. Of course he did. I know now that being made to wait, the anticipation and the apprehension, is at least as important as the punishment itself.

Looking back now I remember the week that followed only as a blur. I struggled through at work on autopilot. I was distracted, found concentrating difficult and caught myself drifting off into dark reveries – but no one else seemed to notice.

At home things were superficially normal. Mark was his usual kind and considerate self but there was an unspoken tension between us. We didn't have sex, which was unusual. Normally we'd make love at least two or three times a week. I even tried to seduce Mark, in fact none too subtly, and he very gently but firmly rebuffed me. This too, I know now, was also all part of the game.

On Friday we met up after work for a drink, not something we did every day but not entirely out of the ordinary. Mark suggested we ate out – at least in part, I think, to prolong the moment even further – I declined.

Once we got in I told Mark I was going to fix him something special: good steak, mushrooms and salad, one of his favourites; with a decent bottle of red wine . . . and more than a little Dutch courage for me. Normally I change as soon as I get in: T-shirt and jeans or jogging bottoms and trainers. But that night Mark insisted I stayed in my business outfit: charcoal two-piece – jacket and skirt cut just above the knee but with a sexy slit up one thigh – classic white cotton, fitted blouse and black court shoes, not stilettos – too tarty – but still with a decent heel.

After we'd eaten I cleared away and then we went and sat in the lounge, still each with a glass of wine, and Mark put some Bach on the stereo.

We sat in silence. I could feel myself becoming hot and breathless and my heart hammering within my chest. Eventually I had to give in: "Mark, please. Let's do it. Let's get it over with now."

"Yes," he replied, "I think you're just about ready."

He made me stand, removed my jacket and then unbuttoned my blouse down to my waist. Then he told me to take off my shoes and pulled down my knickers and tights. Sitting back down on the couch he motioned me across his lap, my head to his left, and used his tie to bind my hands and secure them around the arm of the couch – not too tightly, but more than enough to let me know I was helpless and unable to protect myself. Finally he eased my skirt up over my hips until I was naked from the waist down.

Then nothing. Two or three minutes passed and Mark had neither moved nor spoken. I was becoming increasingly uncomfortable and started to squirm in his lap. The gentle pressure of his left hand in the small of my back was a warning to be still and the fingertips of his right began to stroke and caress me.

They explored the flanks of my thighs, the rounded hills of my buttocks and the horizontal crease where they met. I felt him grab the cheeks of my arse, one in each hand, and begin to knead and pull at the flesh. Fingers dug in deep, pulling me apart and I knew he would be able to see the whorl of my anus. I blushed with embarrassment and, yes, a rising tide of passion as well. Unbidden my legs began to part, exposing myself in supplication, willing him to explore.

Mark's fingers transferred their attentions to my inner thighs, tickling and teasing the creamy skin. Moving upwards, they trailed through the curls of my pubic hair and began to probe at the swollen, tender flesh of my mound beneath. I found myself pushing back against those fingers and trying to grind my groin into his lap beneath me.

Under the lash of caresses I began to shiver uncontrollably, tiny spasms rippling up and down my body. I was wet and I knew he knew it too.

Again I was forced to break the spell: "I don't think this is supposed to happen, but you're actually making me incredibly randy."

"Yes, I know," he replied. "That's because we haven't really started yet."

And with that he brought his right hand crashing down on my arse. The blow was so sudden and completely unexpected I had no chance to prepare or brace myself. The impact knocked all the wind out of me, so there was no shriek in response, just a breathless gasp.

The shock was followed by a blaze of white-hot pain. My parents had never even smacked me as a child so nothing could have prepared me for this. Just one slap and it went beyond imagination. How could this be? How could I not have known?

Mark simply waited until I had recovered, got my breath back and stopped writhing, then he hit me again, on the other cheek. The shock was less unexpected, the pain every bit as bright, and this time I did yelp.

A shorter respite and he smacked me again, alternating left and right in a slowly increasing rhythm, blows on top of blows.

Incredibly the pain increased, nerves sending little messages of distress coursing round my body. Then the heat, building and radiating like a furnace. I knew without being able to see that my backside was glowing crimson.

And still that hand came down, all over my rosy cheeks and then the tops of my thighs as well. I was bathed in perspiration and began to cry, great racking sobs, as tears coursed down my face and dripped onto the floor.

Suddenly everything shifted with a wrench that was almost physical. Mark was still smacking me and it still hurt, God did it still hurt, but somehow the pain was distant, far away, almost as if it was happening to someone else. Mark's beating had lit a fire inside me that was warming, almost pleasant.

I began to *respond* to his rhythm, my body undulating across his lap, provocatively thrusting my bottom to meet the blows, almost inviting them. With a great wordless yell I actually think I climaxed or something very close to.

Mark stopped immediately, untied my hands, held me close until my sobbing stopped and then carried me upstairs to our bedroom.

He made me strip until I stood naked before him on legs still slightly wobbly and then laid me down on the bed. I remember wincing at the coolness of the quilt against my burning skin. He undressed and his prick was already rock hard and fiercely erect.

I came as soon as he shoved his prick inside me. My cunt was a well of hot oil into which his manhood plunged and I could feel the walls spasm, clenching and relaxing as I tried to suck his cock deeper and deeper inside me.

As soon as my orgasm subsided Mark withdrew. He rolled me over onto my stomach, lifted my hips and then took me doggy-style. Hypersensitive, the glowing cheeks of my arse responded to every thrust as he buttressed up against me.

Mark's cock swelled inside me. I could feel each fractional increase and knew he was only seconds away from his own release. So I increased my own tempo, pushing backwards to meet each thrust and hearing my own disembodied voice give a little gasp of pleasure/pain each time I did so.

Finally he came: I could feel that final swell and hardening of his prick that presages orgasm and then each separate squirt as he pumped his spunk into my womb. I don't recall whether I came again or not, but I think I must have passed out for a while because the next thing I remember was coming to, our bodies entwined.

That's about it really. Except to say that my bottom was so sore for a couple of days that sitting down was a real problem. That I promised myself that I had learned a real lesson and I was *never* but *never* going to let anyone do anything like that again to me, ever.

But that two or three months down the line I found myself actively thinking of ways that I could provoke Mark so he actually would do it again . . . just to see if it could possibly be as good and as bad as it was the first time . . . and it was.

These days both of us knows that if I want a good spanking all I have to do is ask . . . either literally or metaphorically.

And if we're out or at a party and I catch him giving a girl the eye he'll come up behind me and give me a playful pat, just a little pat, on the backside. But it's still enough to set my pulse racing and my pussy churning.

He can go off and flirt with any Tom, Dick or Harriet and I don't mind at all. I'm not the jealous type any more. Mark's cured me of that. And anyway I know it's me he's coming home to.

A woman is changed for ever by the first proper spanking from her lover's hand.

Minds find it impossible to accurately recall the bright, sharp clarity of pain. Marks fade from buttocks within an hour or two, within a day or two.

But bodies remember. And for ever after, if you catch her unawares and trace your fingers gently up between the backs of her legs to that place where buttocks and thighs bisect then you will feel the tiniest shiver of apprehension, an involuntary tensing of muscles . . . no matter how delicate the caress.

MOUNTAIN STREAM

Gerard, Halifax

My whole life I've been an indoors kind of guy. After the first wild, late-teenage years I even became the lights-off kind: a pasta tummy is better seen in the dark. Sex has never been an out-in-the-open activity. Except for this one time.

I had been visiting friends in Europe and was driving my hire car through the mountains. I was feeling on top of the world until the engine started to clank and the temperature gauge crept up to red. I pulled over on the side of the narrow road and got out. I'm not bad with engines but I wasn't going to mess with a hire car from another country. My mobile phone had almost no bars at all and I could not get a signal. I wasn't sure whether getting higher or lower would be the answer, but after walking up and down the road waving my phone above my head for a few minutes I decided to try up. Locking the car I set off up the mountain track and into the shade of the trees.

It was a gorgeous day. The sun was hot. The signal flickered in and out and, looking at my phone, I almost stumbled into a wide mountain stream. Looking up I saw I had almost disturbed a woman, standing in the water. She had her back to me and was oblivious to my presence. She had tumbling brunette hair and was wearing a floral print dress. The water came up to her calves which were shapely and honey-coloured. She was holding the hem of her dress out of the water, revealing the backs of her thighs. I stood and stared. The breeze blew her dress against her curves. I must have watched her wade for some time. My cock stirred in my jeans. Then she reached crossways for the hem of her dress and made as if to pull it over her head. I caught a glimpse of white cotton panties before I cleared my throat in alarm. I didn't want to be accused of peeping at her.

The girl turned in surprise but when she saw me she relaxed and smiled. For some reason I did not address her and she did not address me, she just waded over until she stood near my bank. Her face was oval and her eyes feline. She had a light dusting of freckles and a profusion of unruly curls. She was as full in the front as in the back and I saw her nipples harden through the dress's thin fabric. The girl was as natural and earthy as the woods around her. She gave me a look, a long, significant look that could mean only one thing, and I dropped my mobile on the grass at my feet.

Now, as I say, I am a lights-off kind of guy, so when this mountain lovely reached for my belt I was in no way comfortable. Panicked is more like it. Here we were in the dappled sunlight of a mountain glade, with the birdsong echoing and the water rushing. I looked around in concern but could see no one. She popped my fly and eased down the denim, causing me to sit awkwardly on the bank. No kiss. No introduction, just a soft hand on my tent pole. She parted the slit of my boxers and brought my penis into the world. Then she lowered her head and covered my cock with her mouth. I could not believe my luck. Was this a joke? A trick? Being sucked off on a mountain-side is quite an agoraphobic experience.

Her mouth was soft but she sucked hard, massaging the base with her fingers. Well, just as the up and down motion was bringing me to a crisis and I was wondering about the etiquette of coming in her mouth, she lifted up her head, licking her lips, and pulled her dress over her head. I saw she wore plain, three-in-a-pack white cotton pants and a wireless white bra. It made her look virginal, which she was clearly not. Her skin was that colour which has always known the sun, not tanned as such, but healthy and as rich as pine. I kicked my shoes onto the grass and peeled off my tangle of boxers and jeans. She was already clambering up the bank and across my lap. Her damp bra rubbed my mouth and I found a nipple through the material and sucked. It was ice cold and hard. My hand stroked her thigh and buttocks and dipped between her legs, rubbing against a springy mat of hair. I fingered gently and heard her moan into my fringe as a clit shape poked through the cloth. She pushed me onto my back and crawled along my body, stopping with her pussy over my face.

I knew what to do and taking her bottom in one hand I peeled aside the slippery strip of fabric with the other to reveal dark, curling hair and a slice of inviting pink. She moaned as I curled my tongue onto her cunt and I responded deep in my own throat. Her taste was wild and pungent, not the fresh-from-the-shower, Saturday night, premeditated pussy-eating taste but a feral, spice-and-sandalwood, musk-and-resin flavour. It scared and aroused me as I jabbed her large clitoris with my tongue, lapped at her labia and, forcing her bottom down, stretched my tongue up inside her vagina, all the time conscious of my absurd cock-stand waving in the breeze for all to see. When her hips started to pump I stopped and tried to sit up. Her pants came down and I eased off her bra, letting a pair of heavy, cool, creamy tits capped with dark nipples loll in my face. Utterly naked she straddled my mouth again. Backwards this time, lowering her deeply clefted bottom onto my nose. I gave her anus a tentative lick before eating her pussy once more. She knelt up, moaning softly, holding her breasts and rubbing the swollen tips. She fingered her clit and dew poured from her cunt. I found myself lapping and swallowing as I ate, listening to her sighs. Soon my tongue was fighting for purchase as she shoved two then three fingers up her slippery cunt, leaving me only juicy knuckles to lick.

Then she stood and pulled at my T-shirt. It was my turn to be totally naked. Again I looked for voyeurs, but we were alone. Nude as a babe she took my hand and stepped into the river. I followed. It was shocking, like ice, but only came up to my knees. She lowered herself into the stream and let the water touch her pussy, which she opened to its touch. Her middle finger twiddled her clit and her breasts rose and fell. I sat in the shivery water, gasping with cold and she climbed astride, lowering herself onto my cock. It is testament to her desirability that I stayed hard in that water, but I did. The icy fingers of the stream were replaced with the warm mouth of her cunt, with its secret supply of lubricant and she sank down with a sigh on my length.

We fucked in the water for nearly an hour, numbed by the mountain stream into a kind of Tantric anaesthesia by the cold, cold water. The pleasure rose and fell but never came. We fucked missionary on a mossy bank with her legs pointing at the treetops, we fucked woman-on-top in the shallows, the water splashing onto my face and in my eyes. The end came on all fours. She had got down on her knees in the soft sand and raised her exquisite, goose-fleshed arse to the sky, her legs apart. I mounted her, noticing the bijou perfection of her tiny, dark anus, and pushed into her cunt. As I thrust, the water lapped her nearly blue nipples and the sand ground into our knees, delightfully abrasive.

The orgasm was like a sunrise, breaking slowly with a feeling of water and sunlight and earth in it, me beginning first, and wild with abandon, licking my thumb and easing it into her anus. She made a surprised sound and then groaned, tightening her grip on my cock. We came together, yelling like apes, scattering the birds.

My clothes were damp but not too wet to wear. We dried on the grass in the sun, like Adam and Eve, the touch of the daylight lifting moisture from the skin indescribable. Before I left we had one more slow, languorous session of sixty-nine, which, after our sunbathe, seemed dreamlike and dazed. She licked just the tip of my cock, maddeningly, and I sucked on her long, deep-pink clitoris, as long as a woman's pinkie, as if it were a tiny dick. To my delight she ejaculated a fine spray when she came, sobbing with pleasure deep in her chest.

I dressed, waved goodbye and decided to follow the road to the nearest town to see if they had a working phone. We had not exchanged a word.

IN THE KITCHEN

Michelle, Oxford

When I first started going out with boys I was in my late teens, maybe seventeen. I had this boyfriend, Peter. He was all right, quite fit, nice enough, and we had a lot of innocent fun. He was my first and we tried all the vanilla things you try first of all: fumbling, nibbling, dry-humping on the bedroom floor, you know the kind of thing. Things changed when I met his family. We had a nice drink in their front room, all photo frames and books. When his dad served me my whisky and coke, his hand touched mine and I looked up into those brown eyes and – a spark. I must have blushed. I tend to blush up my neck – goodness knows what he thought. From that moment I could not take my eyes off him. I don't think anyone noticed. He was a history professor, interesting when he talked, with a deep voice. I noticed he had long fingers when he held his glass. There were hairs on the knuckles. He must have been twenty-five years older then me but I just stared and stared.

The next visit was a few days before Christmas. Peter and I had tried our first sixty-nine at my house three nights before and had found it a rather clumsy experience. Anyway, sex was on my mind when I walked into his parents' house and sat down. Within half an hour I was feeling fiddly and fidgety. His dad's voice sounded warm and treacly and I found myself self-consciously crossing my legs over and over. This crossing of the legs was the way I had discovered masturbation. I used to lie in bed at night squeezing my thighs together to capture the "warm glow" as I used to call it. Only later did I discover my trusty middle finger. Well, in the living room that night the crossing and uncrossing was having the same effect and a whole cloud of butterflies was gathering in my stomach. Blushing all over my neck I excused myself "to the loo" and locked the door. There I took down my wringing knickers and, I'm ashamed to say, lay on the floor with my shoes on the loo seat and wanked my little clit until I came. I didn't cry out, just panted and thrashed a little, thinking of Peter's father holding his glass of brandy to his lips. Pulling my wet panties back over my wet pussy was uncomfortable, but I was glad of the relief, however sticky, when I got back downstairs.

I had no intention of letting it happen again but a few weeks later, Peter's dad cleared his throat at dinner with a sound that sounded to me in my altered state like an aroused moan. I excused myself once more to the bathroom and, locking the door, diddled on the bath mat on my hands and knees with my knickers around my thighs and my arse in the air. It was a very good come.

My covert wanking became a regular thing. Every time we visited something would set me off. One time I was sure Peter's dad was looking up my skirt and I had to slip away and masturbate; another time he playfully hugged me in a welcome-to-the-family kind of way and I spent the evening squeezing my thighs to a mouth-watering peak before heading to the bathroom for a much needed flick off, my knickers stuffed into my mouth. You would think this secret life would have added a little spice to my love life with Peter but in truth, so far I had only come on my own. He was keen but inept, and the locations we tried for our first few tentative fucks (his car, my bedroom, his bedroom) lacked finesse. The parents' house situation got to be a habit and the normality of this habit finally caught me out.

We were at Peter's parents' place one afternoon in spring and his dad was wearing a sexy cotton shirt and chinos. I had offered to make a cup of tea, and was alone in the kitchen, putting tea bags in cups and filling the kettle, thinking about the man in the other room. Automatically my hand stole to my crotch as I leaned on the counter waiting for the kettle to boil. I pressed on my clit through my tights and let my mind wander. Before I really knew what I was doing I had my fingers in my knickers, stroking my clit from side to side. I didn't hear Peter's dad come in. I'd left him playing Scrabble. He had no reason to come in. He came up behind me and placed one of his large hands on my shoulder – the right, the same arm which was buried in my underwear. I knew it was him by the smell – aftershave and cigars, whisky on his breath. I turned, terrified, and he took me completely by surprise by kissing me fully on the mouth. I returned the kiss with enthusiasm, but was so clumsy I think I bit his lip.

To my shock and delight he turned me around again to face the counter and reached beneath my short floaty skirt to the waistband of my tights. Easing down both navy hose and lemon cotton knickers he exposed my bottom to the air. It was a small, tight, soft bottom in those days and I was proud of it. I could well imagine the expression on his face, faced with my pale, shapely peach. I heard the buckle on his belt jangle and the next thing I knew he was easing a very hard, very thick cock into my pussy from behind. Remember, I was seventeen, just starting out. I had never had sex in any way other than on my back, certainly not from behind and certainly not standing up. Not only was this completely new and more than a little pervy, he was *huge*. His cock smarted going in, despite my wetness, stretching me up and out, filling me deeper than I had ever been filled. I gasped and stumbled forwards, my breasts squashing against the counter. In response to the gasp he shushed me gently and covered my mouth with his hand, as softly as if he were brushing hair from my eyes. I groaned into the hand and eased my hips back onto his, forcing his thick cock deeper, the stinging pleasure of it bringing tears to my eyes. I wanted him to know how much I wanted this crazy, dangerous fuck to happen. He began to pull in and out, rocking slowly against me, chugging that big, middle-aged cock of his in a gentle rhythm. The sensation was indescribable, nothing like Peter's clumsy stabbing. He was much harder for one thing, and the sensation had an itchy, slippery friction which made my eyes roll back in my head. My hand stole once more to my tacky clit and I rubbed and rubbed, panting into his large, warm hand, breathing through my nose. My lover responded to my fingering by further nudging apart my thighs with his own and picking up the pace of his thrusts.

My orgasm wasn't long in coming. The expert pumping of my cunt from behind and the lightning-fast clit-flicking in front tipped me over. As he felt the tremors in my body, Peter's father reached under me with his other big strong arm and lifted me off the floor. One of my shoes fell off, I think. I gripped the marble countertop with my free hand, the black stone freezing cold on my throbbing nipples, and came, really, really hard. It was ten times the climax I'd ever had with my hand and, jerking on his amazing dick, I bit hard into his fingers until I tasted bone, just to keep from howling in ecstasy. He came too with a small grunt, deep inside me, squirting at least four times, his come hot and prodigious. He pulled out of my raw vagina with a slurp and kissed me on the bum. He then deliberately broke a glass, right in front of me, picking up the shattered pieces as an explanation of the blood dripping from the passionate bite on his hand. How he explained the tooth marks I never found out. He will have had them for years. I hauled up my sticky knot of knickers and tights and returned, a little breathless and pink, to the game of Scrabble. I couldn't look Peter in the eye and we never made love again; in fact, I finished with him a week later. I never forgot the stolen minutes bent over the counter by a real man, gasping senselessly into his big, strong, whisky-scented hand.

SKIRT

Anna, USA

Brandon bought me the silly little skirt. It wasn't something I would have picked out for myself but he was so happy with his choice, I took it happily and thanked him. It hit me mid-thigh and had flirty little pleats. Green and blue plaid very much like the uniform skirts I had to wear in school. Not my idea of sexy but I kept that to myself.

On the phone one day, Brandon said, "Will you wear the skirt for me?"

At first I was at a loss. What skirt? Then I remembered the lonely little schoolgirl skirt hanging in my closet. I laughed but said I would and hung up.

I wore the skirt for the rest of the day. I topped it off with a plain white T-shirt and some flip-flops. Plain white panties were underneath. I thought that was a nice touch.

When Brandon got home, he took me in. He smiled and then kissed me and thanked me. "Can you bring me a beer on the deck? I'm beat." Then he wandered outside leaving me confused. Why was I wearing the skirt if he was beat?

I played along. I brought him a beer and found him in one of the deckchairs. Tie pulled loose, sleeves rolled up, newspaper in his lap.

"Your beer," I said and waited. What was this?

"Sir."

"What?" Now I was really confused. Maybe the heat had gotten to my husband. It was a very warm day.

"Your beer, *sir*," Brandon corrected me.

I went from confused to angry to somewhat turned on. Apparently, the heat was getting to me too.

"Sir?"

"Say it," my husband commanded.

"Here's your beer, *sir*." I really had to force the words past my lips. I view myself in all ways as Brandon's equal. He does too.

"Are you giving me a hard time?" His eyes were harsh but I saw the familiar humorous twinkle buried under the intense stare.

"I . . . I . . ." I was flustered but turned on. I decided to go with it. "No, sir."

"I think you are and that skirt is too short. Turn around, young lady."

I turned on my heels so fast I had to grab the deck railing for support. I waited and tried to breathe. It was suddenly hard to draw air.

Brandon's hand slid up the inside of my thigh. His touch so light I felt goosebumps break out on my skin. Then he flipped up the back of my skirt and exposed my bottom and panties. I waited.

I felt his familiar hands on the white cotton panties. He smoothed his palms over the fabric and then I heard a crack before I felt the pain. I yelped and grabbed harder at the railing. He was spanking me!

"Six swats for being difficult."

He alternated smacks on my bottom until it was tingling and hot. I could feel how wet my panties had become. My breath wouldn't come. I was surprised and thrilled at the same time. I had no idea that Brandon had this in mind when he bought the skirt. If I had known, I might have worn it ages ago.

I heard him stand and felt my nipples peak beneath my T-shirt. He stood close behind me and pulled my panties down with a tug. When they hit the deck he growled in my ear, "Kick them off."

I did. I kicked them to the side and tried not to push back against him. I knew by the sound of his voice he would be hard and ready. Brandon pushed his fingers into me and they slid in with ease.

"You're so bad. Look how wet you are from being bad."
Then he flipped up the back of my skirt and I felt the soft breeze
on my naked ass. "Lean forwards," he commanded and I did. I
pressed my belly against the railing and felt my pussy open to
him.

Brandon's zipper sounded loud to me and made the wetness
between my thighs worse. I felt his cock probe at me and
glanced around through the various trees that shaded our deck.
The thought that someone could be watching this display made
me even wetter. Then he slid into me and I forgot all about the
neighbours. His big hands pulled at my waist and forced me
back against him. He drove into me hard and fast. Pushing
deeply as I clutched the railing.

"Rub your clit, bad girl," he growled and I obeyed. Caught
up in the fantasy and the moment and his command over me.

I rubbed circles with my fingers. My clit so swollen and
sensitive I knew it wouldn't take much. I held on tight to the
deck railing as he fucked me harder. Brandon made that sound
he always makes right before he came. I rubbed my clit a little
harder. Suddenly it was very important that we come together.
That would make this scenario that much better for me.

"Next time I ask for a beer you give it to me properly," my
husband grunted and then he smacked my bottom hard again. I
yelped from the sudden pain but then my orgasm was flowing
through me. He spanked my other cheek as I continued to
come. Rubbing my clit and moaning. Hanging over the deck rail
praying that no one was watching. Or maybe praying they were.

Brandon pulled me back tight. "Baby," he sighed and emptied into me.

We stood frozen for a moment before getting ourselves
together. I sighed, my body loose from the orgasm and tingly
from the excitement of it all.

"Want another beer?" I asked and then giggled.

"Sure, babe. And get one for yourself." He winked and
settled back in the deck chair.

"Yes, *sir*," I trilled over my shoulder as I went into the house.
I smoothed my hands over my new favourite skirt.

TIME FOR A CHANGE

Richard, Melbourne

I have a confession to make. Last week I came home early and caught my wife having sex with the guy next door. It was her high-pitch laugh that made me look across the road. They were at his house, in the lounge room with the curtains open, fucking their brains out. I was speechless, couldn't believe my eyes. Every instinct told me to go over there, knock down the door and smash the guy in the face but as I watched something happened, something I'd never tell any of my mates.

I snuck over to the window and peeked in. I've seen plenty of pornos but never actually seen a couple having sex, live that is, and I was intrigued. Watching Brad's arse fucking her rhythmically had me wondering what it would be like to have sex with another guy. Just watching his cheeks clench and contract had me wanting to grab hold of them, to rub my hands over his skin, pull apart his cheeks and run my cock up and down his hole.

I was shocked I could think of something like that at a time when I should have been furious. I'm not gay or anything, never even thought about it, honestly. I don't have any gay tendencies, really I don't.

I moved away from the window, tried to get a hold on my feelings, but I wanted to see more: more of Brad, his thighs, the muscles in his calves and more importantly his cock. I sidled back to the window. They'd changed positions. He was lying on his back and she was riding him, her hot cunt sliding up and down his shaft.

I wished they were closer, that I could see better as I could only catch glimpses of his shaft, slippery and wet as she rose before slamming herself back down on him, impaling herself, grinding into him while his fingers squeezed her flesh.

My cock was throbbing, wanting some sort of release. I couldn't very well pull it out and jerk off there in the front garden. Anyway the more I watched the greater the desire so I snuck off, didn't confront them and headed off into the city. I was confused, didn't know what I was thinking and why. There wasn't anyone I could talk to; I'm married after all. What could I say to someone? They'd be more shocked about me than finding out my wife was cheating on me.

I knew where a gay bar was and thought I'd go and check it out, you know, just to get the feel of the place, see if I could maybe get some answers to the questions running through my brain.

I was surprised it was so packed. There were guys everywhere. Drinking, dancing and just sitting around talking. I was nervous and felt self-conscious so I moved over to the edge of the bar, perched myself on a stool and ordered a drink. Before the drink arrived this guy came over, started some small talk. He didn't look gay to me so we started chatting. His name was Frank. Next thing you know we've downed half-a-dozen beers and we're getting on like a house on fire.

Anyway I had to take a piss and asked him where the toilets were. He said he had to go too so we made our way through the crowd. It was bizarre. I think three guys groped my arse and I'm sure one was lunging for my cock before he got pulled back. It made me feel good that someone, even if it was a man, was actually attracted to me.

They seemed like such a friendly lot, laughing and having a good time. There was no one in the toilets and when I flopped out my cock to piss, you should have seen the look on Frank's face. His eyes nearly popped and I must admit my chest swelled as his eyes devoured my member.

"Nice cock," he said.

"Never had any complaints," I laughed.

Next thing I knew he was on the floor sucking me off. I didn't know what to do. It all happened so fast. My cock grew and grew as he gobbled me down. Boy, did he give good head. I could feel my balls tighten as he looked up at me. I remembered how I felt when I was watching Brad and I thought, well, here's my chance, so when he beckoned me into a cubicle, I thought why not.

Before I had time to shut the door he had his trousers down to his ankles and was bending over, his arse cheeks wiggling at me as he whispered for me to hurry. I pulled his cheeks apart and his puckered hole winked back at me. I thought it's now or never and began to inch my knob in. Man, he was so tight. Once I got my knob in the rest was easy.

I was surprised at how easy it was and I loved my balls slapping against his arse as he pushed back. I gripped his hips, marvelling at his broad back, the tightness of his muscles. My hand moved further around and I managed to grab his shaft. It nearly drove me wild and I found myself slapping at his thighs, his arse and in no time I was shooting my load, just as a couple of other guys entered the toilets.

Zipping up my trousers I couldn't believe what had just happened, what I'd stooped to. Fucking a guy in a toilet in a gay bar. It was the most out-of-character thing I've ever done. I practically ran out of there, jumped into my car and drove home. The thing was I couldn't stop thinking about how my shaft disappeared into his arse, how his muscles gripped my cock, how fucking great it felt.

When I pulled up the driveway I wondered what to do about my wife. I'd completely forgotten about her and Brad, I was so caught up with myself. When I thought about it I realized she'd been complaining a lot, saying our sex life was boring, so maybe it was my fault that she had turned to our neighbour.

An idea began simmering in my brain. Brad had once told me about a swingers club he went to. Said anything you'd ever thought of you could have there. I wondered if she'd be in it. I wondered if I could fuck a guy while he was fucking her. The thought of it had my cock throbbing like crazy.

Yeah, that would be awesome. Or maybe another woman going down on her while I fucked her hot little pussy. I could see myself, my cock thick and hard, probing some other wo-man's fat pussy lips, sliding in, ramming into her while my wife looked on. Man, pre-come oozed from my slit. I hurried inside, found my wife relaxing in the spa and jumped in with her.

She was shocked when I suggested she bend over and I lather up her hole, give her a bit of a thrill. With suds clinging to her body, I soaped up my cock and with hardly any effort I slid right in. She loved it. Couldn't get enough. Before I knew it she'd turned into a tigress, slamming back into my groin, grinding her arse into my pelvis.

It was fucking amazing. We fucked our brains out all night, in every position imaginable. She asked what had happened, why I was doing stuff that she'd only ever fantasized about.

I never told her it was because I caught her and Brad. I thought me fucking Frank made up for it and I wasn't sure how she'd react knowing I'd just fucked a guy, so I said nothing, but I did hint that from now on she'd never know what surprises I'd come up with.

She giggled and threw her arms around me. Told me she loved the new me and to be honest so did I. There was so much I had to learn and I'm telling you it's going to be fun finding out what I've been missing out on.

I'd always been pretty conservative, maybe even a bit of a prude, so I suppose you could say that my wife having sex with our neighbour opened up a whole new chapter in my life.

I'm definitely not gay, but if the opportunity comes up for a threesome, or foursome, and nature takes its course, well, I'll be happy to participate and see what else I can learn but until then arse-fucking has become my favourite position.

IN HIS HANDS

Mary, Plymouth

Tom has been my boyfriend since college. He's a very sweet, attentive guy, and he loves to buy me little gifts. The best one by far was the remote-controlled vibrator he bought me for my birthday. I was totally confused when I opened the parcel; I just sat looking at this weird belt thing with what looked like a pager nestled next to it amongst the tissue paper. I asked him what the hell I was supposed to do with it, but Tom just smiled and told me I was going to have the best birthday ever. He'd booked us a table at a really nice restaurant for that evening, and he wanted me to wear the vibe. He said it would slip inside my knickers discreetly, and nobody would know it was there except me, and him. Then, he said, we'd go out for dinner and he'd keep the remote. He would be completely in charge of my pleasure for the evening and, when I was least expecting it, he'd give me the orgasm of my life.

I had to admit that the idea sounded appealing. I've always enjoyed the feeling I get from a toy, and the thought of giving Tom the power to buzz me into oblivion at any moment was quite arousing, but I definitely wasn't prepared to go out in public with a vibrator stuffed down my pants. I wanted to know what he thought we'd do if someone heard it, or if people started noticing what we were doing. It would be too embarrassing for words. Tom popped the batteries into the vibe and switched it on to show me how quiet it was, and he reminded me that restaurants aren't exactly the most silent of places. It took some wheedling, and even a little begging, but finally I agreed to wear it, on the condition that we wouldn't switch the vibe on until I felt ready.

Well, by the time we got to the restaurant that evening, I was feeling nervous. I had on my little black dress, with my black lace bra, knickers and stockings underneath, and the vibe belt on underneath that. It slipped firmly, not too tight, around my hips, with the unit itself resting just between my pussy lips. If I squeezed my thighs together, I could feel the pressure of it rubbing on my clit, and I was wishing we could have tested it out at home.

As I sat down, I was sure every other person in the restaurant knew what I had down my knickers. The people at the tables next to us were so close that I could have touched their elbows if I pulled my chair out. I'd never felt as naughty.

We ordered our food and a bottle of wine, and Tom asked me how I was feeling. I said I was all right, and he asked if I wanted to turn the vibe on. I wanted to wait a bit more, but after a couple of glasses of wine, I was less worried about it, so I excused myself to the ladies' and went to turn the unit on. When I got back, I saw Tom grinning at me across the restaurant, because he knew exactly what I'd been doing. I saw he had the remote in his hand, playing with it like it was a set of car keys or something, and I expected him to buzz me right there, but he didn't.

I sat down at the table again and it was like a normal meal, except I couldn't keep my eyes off that remote. I asked Tom when he was going to do it, and he just smiled at me. I called him a git and started eating my salad, and then I felt the vibrator start up. He didn't run it for long, and it was very low, just a little tickle on my clit, but I nearly spat lettuce all over the table.

Tom asked me if it felt good and I said yes. It was incredibly sexy to get that feeling sitting there in my posh frock, with all those other people around us, stuffing their faces and not having a clue what we were doing. The thought turned me on more than the vibe, and I was going to ask Tom to turn up the speed, but he shut it off again. It was then that I realized what his game was. He told me, in a very low voice, so the other diners couldn't hear us, that it wasn't the vibrator that was going to make me come, it was him.

All the way through the main course, Tom kept giving me little thrills with the vibe, just a few seconds at a time, and I had my work cut out not to gasp every time I felt it buzzing against my clit. I could feel myself getting wetter, and the anticipation was incredible. I could see Tom was getting really worked up. To anyone else's ears, we were carrying on a perfectly normal conversation about work, talking about Tom's chances for a promotion that was coming up, but he kept making little comments to me in a low voice, only for me. He kept telling me what a dirty girl I was, getting so horny in the middle of a posh restaurant. He kept pointing out people that he said were looking, and he told me he could tell how turned on I was just from the look on my face.

I could feel myself blushing, but I didn't feel embarrassed any more. All I could think about, all the way through dessert, was how much I wanted to push all the plates and glasses off the table and just bend over it and have him fuck me right there, in front of everybody. Tom asked me what I was thinking and I told him, leaning forwards so I could whisper to him. My breasts brushed the tablecloth and my nipples were so hard and sensitive by this time that I thought I was going to explode. Tom said he wished we could fuck like that too, but we both knew there was no chance. He said he was going to the loo and to pay the bill so we could go home, and I said I'd wait while he did.

I didn't realize that the vibe's remote had such a range, but he must have buzzed me from the gents', because Tom wasn't anywhere in sight when I got the most amazing sensation in my pussy. The vibe buzzed so hard I was sure it must be the loudest thing in the restaurant, but I didn't care. It felt so good. I was dripping wet, but it just kept pounding against my clit. I caught my breath, grabbed hold of the edge of the table and hung on. I knew if it kept up I wouldn't be able to keep from coming, and I could feel myself breathing faster. I started to grind my hips against the chair, and I was really aware of all the other people, but I could feel the climax coming up on me like a big wall of water, totally inevitable.

Tom was standing by the door, watching me, with his hand in his pocket. I turned my head slightly and I could just see him smiling at me as I came in a great big rush. I know I was panting, and I could feel my come soaking my knickers, making my thighs wet. I wriggled in my seat as my body trembled with little aftershocks, and the vibe stopped just as it was becoming painful on my oversensitive clit. I was amazed that no one looked at me.

Tom crossed the restaurant and stood behind me. "I think you're about ready, aren't you?" he said, touching my shoulder.

If I'd been able to stand up, I would have hit him. He slipped my coat on as I got to my feet and whispered, "Dirty girl," into my ear. By the time we got into the taxi I was getting horny again, and he played with the remote the whole journey home until I thought I was going to pass out.

That night, we fucked like we hadn't done for ages. I don't know if it was the excitement or the naughtiness of using the vibe in public, or putting myself completely in Tom's hands, but it did something pretty incredible for us. That evening in the restaurant was the first orgasm I'd ever had in public, but it hasn't been the last. These days, we use the remote vibe at work, in the pub, out shopping . . . anywhere, any time. I never imagined being completely in his hands could be so much fun!

MY MOTHER'S FIANCÉ

Selena, USA

When I was nineteen I went through a phase that I can only attribute to some kind of raging hormone imbalance. I was plagued with a physical disorder that had my sexual appetites skyrocketing out of control. My mind was dominated night and day with thoughts of sex and of ways to try to relieve myself of this tormenting sexual hunger.

I masturbated several times a day but the relief I got from it was short-lived and I constantly felt the gnawing need for something more.

I was so afraid an overpowering temptation would cause me to prostitute myself to some irresponsible, horny dork that would get me pregnant or give me some gruesome disease. So far I had not succumbed to that. I knew all about sex, or at least all one could know without having done it. I'd just never trusted anyone enough to let him fuck me. What I am about to tell you happened during the time I was having the aforementioned sexual problem. At that time my mother, who is assistant to the mayor of Green's Bluff where we live, was engaged to Alex Bromwell, a moderately wealthy man a few years her senior. He was and is an attractive, distinguished-looking man as well as a somewhat reserved, dignified gentleman. I was and am very fond of him. Until now I have never revealed this to a single soul, mainly because I promised Alex I would keep it our secret.

That particular day was a weekday, my mother was at work and I was in my bedroom frenetically trying to relieve myself of an intense onset of sexual arousal. I was masturbating and moaning in agonizing frustration over the gnawing hunger between my legs.

I heard my bedroom door open and looked up to see Alex standing there frozen in shock with a look of horror on his face. I screamed in humiliation, trying to cover myself but knowing that it was too late to bother. The man had seen me feverishly manipulating my clitoris, on the very threshold of an orgasm.

"Oh my God, Selena, I'm so sorry," he whispered. "I came in the front door and heard a noise. I thought you were hurt." His face was a deep wine colour. "I'm going to go now," he said.

"No, wait," I yelled at him, my voice hoarse with sexual agitation.

"I'm not going to say anything about this," he said, looking down at the carpet.

"No, it's not that, Alex. I desperately need your help," I pleaded, suffering from my approaching orgasm having been thwarted. "I'm begging you, stay."

"I don't understand, Selena, what is it?"

"Will you come sit here on the bed for a minute?"

Looking extremely uneasy he walked over to the bed and carefully sat down.

"I need to tell you about a serious problem I have," I told him, still panting. "It's a problem that's becoming more serious every day. I'm so embarrassed to tell you this, Alex, but I need help. I have to talk to someone and you're the only person I know I can trust."

I told him everything in detail – how tormenting it was, how often I had to masturbate, and the torture of the relentless gnawing emptiness in my vagina – and even telling him about it was arousing me.

He looked embarrassed but was not critical of me. He must have known it was a physical anomaly I couldn't be blamed for.

I also pointed out to him the dangerous temptations I was dealing with, the possible consequences of relieving myself through intercourse with some irresponsible guy that could get me pregnant or give me a disease.

"Have you had a man yet?" he asked me.

"No, I've managed to avoid that so far."

"Good, then your hymen is intact?"

"No," I told him. "I grew up a tomboy and when I was nine years old I fell out of a tree, landed on a woodpile and my hymen was ruptured on impact."

"I don't know what I can do for you."

"Well, it's obvious," I said, impatiently. "I want you to have intercourse with me, and don't say no, Alex. I'm begging you."

"Selena, no!" he said. "That's completely out of the question."

By now I was begging him, almost in tears. "What do you want me to do?" I said. "Go out and get pregnant or get some horrible disease? That would be great for my mother. Please, Alex, you're the only man in the world I can trust."

"Your mother would never forgive me if I did something like that."

"You don't think I would tell her, do you? I would never tell her, not ever!" Grabbing his hand I shoved it down between my legs, pushing my little mound up against his palm.

"Stop that," he said, jerking his hand away.

Immediately I grabbed his cock through his slacks and was shocked to discover that it was rigid. "You want me," I said.

"No, that's just a natural physical reaction to stimulus."

"Exactly," I said. "It's your cock saying it's ready and willing." I pulled one of my breasts out over the top of my low-cut knit shirt. The pink nipple was hard from my excitement.

His eyes were big, staring at it.

"Touch it," I murmured. "Suck it." I could see in his face that he was aroused though he was trying hard not to be. His hand cupped my breast, his fingers gently twisting my nipples and then he suddenly pulled away.

"Alex, I'm in agony here." I was whimpering again, begging. "Please help me," I whispered.

"Take your shorts all the way off," he said finally, not looking at me. "I won't fuck you, Selena, but there's something in here that might help you. I'll be right back."

He went to my mother's bedroom (I learned later), came back and plugged something into the outlet near the bed.

"What is that?" I asked him, and when he turned around he had something in his hand that looked like a big penis.

"That's what's called a dildo, little girl. Lie down. Open your legs," he whispered. "And Selena, don't you ever breathe a word of this."

"I won't," I said, my passion already spiralling up. I could see that his hands were trembling a little and that stimulated me more. I was breathing hard. "Hurry," I whispered.

"We can't hurry, Selena. You've never had anything inside that little pussy," he said. "This is going to take some time and patience."

It was shocking to hear a man like him say "pussy". I knew he had to be as aroused as I was to say something like that, but he didn't want me to know.

"When does your mother get home today?" he asked, stepping into the bathroom. He greased the thing down with petroleum jelly and came back. Sitting on the side of the bed he lifted my leg nearest to him and put it across his lap so my slit was wide open to him.

"She won't be home for hours yet," I said. "We have plenty of time."

"You better hope that's true, little girl, or we're both in a world of shit."

He must have believed me because with obvious pleasure he had begun gently tweaking my clitoris, squeezing and rolling it between his fingers and it felt wonderful. I was having a hard time equating this quiet, dignified gentleman with what he was so skilfully doing to me but I loved it.

"No guy my age would know how to make me feel like this," I whispered, squirming. It felt so good I couldn't be still.

Alex smiled and said nothing. The next thing he did had me begging for the penis thing in seconds. He put his hands under my butt and, holding onto each cheek, he slid down and lifted my pussy to his lips like he was going to drink wine from it. He put his mouth into my open slit, his tongue exploring me. Sliding his tongue up, he found my clitoris and lightly sucked it into his mouth, flicking it playfully with his tongue. This was driving me mad. I was groaning, squirming and suddenly I had to have my hand on him. Slipping my hand under my leg that was across his body I grasped his cock and was shocked at how stiff it was.

"Don't, Selena," he said crossly. "This is not easy for me, little girl. I'm trying to help you."

"I'm sorry," I said. "Please, keep going."

I felt the head of the penis thing as he gently inserted it in me about an inch. I was so aroused I thought I would come very quickly but I didn't want to. I wanted to find out how it felt to have that thing all the way in me. "Don't let me come yet," I whispered.

"Baby, I haven't even turned it on yet," he said, amused. He continued to work it in gently until it was almost all the way in and I was whimpering, making little animal sounds.

Without warning he flipped the switch and I squealed with delight. The thing was vibrating inside me as he pushed it deep into me. Then he began sliding it smoothly in, then out a little, then in deep, again and again, all the time using his other hand to roll my clitoris between his fingers. I was screaming in ecstasy as my orgasm swelled and peaked and exploded sending shock waves and shudders throughout my body.

And even as my orgasm began to fade I was already becoming aroused again, which wasn't surprising. One orgasm was never enough for me.

"Don't stop," I whispered. "I haven't had enough yet." I looked up at him and saw with gratification that he was in the throes of passion. I could see that watching my orgasm had pushed him over the edge.

Excited, I sat up and quickly unzipped his slacks pulling his cock out through his fly. It was hot and pulsating in my hand. "That's bigger than the penis thing. I want that," I said.

"Please, no, Selena." But his protest had become weaker.

"Yes," I said. "I want it! I want it, Alex – now!" I was pulling him on top of me, pushing my hips up to it. "Put it in. I don't know how to do it." I wanted it so desperately I was fighting him, trying to get it in. "Please, Alex. I need it so badly!"

I saw the expression on his face change and I knew he was

relenting. With a sigh he opened me with his fingers and slid it into my hot slit.

"Oh shit, Selena, what are you doing to me?" he muttered. He was panting with excitement as he pushed it in smoothly all the way down. "Don't move," he murmured, "or I won't be able to hold it."

"That sure is some good cock, Mr Bromwell," I whispered, teasing.

"Oh shit, Selena, stop it," he groaned, gripping me tight, not moving.

After calming down a little he began to move slow and deep in me.

"Alex, that's the most wonderful feeling I ever had," I whispered.

"What the hell am I doing, Selena?" he said, pushing deep into me, grunting. "This is wrong. I'm supposed to be marrying your mother." Even as he spoke he was pumping in and out of me with smooth, deep strokes, his breath panting with excitement.

"How could anything that feels this good be wrong?" I whispered, pushing my hips up to him in rhythm with his thrusts.

"You do have a point," he said. "This has to be our secret, Selena."

"Only if you let me have this every time I need it," I said, moaning with pleasure.

"Are you blackmailing me?"

"Yes."

"Well, you little shit." We were both climaxing.

Alex got me through a difficult time, taking care of me when I had to have relief. I couldn't get pregnant because he'd had a vasectomy years ago, and of course no one else ever knew about our guilty pleasures. He and my mother are happily married now. Alex comes to my apartment to see me sometimes.

JUST DESSERT

Siobhan, Norfolk

It was going out for a walk in the country that started it all . . .
but don't try this at home unless you have a large kitchen, that
can't be overlooked, with a quarry-tiled floor – and make sure
you put a sheet of polythene down first.

Mark and I have always enjoyed rambling. There are some
wonderful walks around the small Cotswold village where we
live and during the summer we think nothing of packing a light
picnic and taking off for the whole day.

And this particular one was glorious: we were way out in the
country, miles from anywhere. We were both only wearing
shorts and T-shirts, good boots of course, and had already been
going three or four hours and stopped for lunch.

Following a footpath alongside a small stream we came to a
point where the course bent quite sharply, we were on the
"inside" and had to bend down to get under an overhanging
tree.

To this day I don't know what happened but I somehow lost
my footing, slithered down the steep bank and ended up sitting
waist deep in the stream. The water was hardly cold, but I was a
lot hotter so it still made me gasp, and it was extremely muddy.

To start with Mark was quite shocked as I almost disappeared
before his eyes and then concerned to make sure I was all right
but after that we both started to giggle as you couldn't help but
see the funny side.

I tried to wash the mud off but it had gone everywhere, the
water in the stream wasn't much better and only seemed to be
making it worse.

Mark helped me out but without any clean clothes there was nothing to do but carry on. I started to dry out as we walked but was only too aware that mud had gone up inside my shorts and soaked my cotton panties. Although the smell wasn't all that good, the feel was something else – cool and smooth and slippery around my buttocks and my fanny. I can't say it was making me feel sexy but it was definitely making me think about sex.

Eventually, after another mile or two, the footpath actually took us through a small farmyard. There were three men in the yard, possibly the farmer and his sons or perhaps just a couple of younger workers. Mark went over to them, explained what had happened and asked if there was anything I could use to clean up.

The farmer pointed to a hose pipe coiled up over a hook on a wall and one of the other men disappeared into the barn and reappeared with what looked like a horse's grooming brush that he tossed to me.

Mark uncoiled an armful of the hose and turned on the tap. Walking back over to me he began to play the jet up and down my body.

It was bloody freezing, so cold it made me gasp for breath, and in seconds I was soaked again. My T-shirt clung to my chest and the cold had my nipples sticking out like chapel hat pegs even through my bra.

Despite the cold I blushed furiously and to cover my embarrassment began to scrub with the horse brush at my legs and shorts. It didn't take long to get clean and as I finished I kind of realized that things seemed to have gone very quiet. I glanced up at Mark and saw he was sporting a large erection through the front of his shorts. The three other men were also staring at me with an obvious mixture of lust and fascination.

"Well, thanks a lot," I said as breezily as I could through teeth that were beginning to chatter. "We'd better be getting along. Don't want to keep you any longer. Come along, darling."

It took us another two or three hours to get back home. I had a long hot shower, making sure I got myself really clean. Mark cooked us a pair of thumping great steaks that we washed down with splendid bottle of Aussie red. A good long walk always gives you a tremendous appetite.

Shortly after that we ended up in bed and had sex. Scrub that, we had great sex, fantastic sex. I certainly didn't think about it at the time but something had got me incredibly horny. I was all over Mark like a rash. I wanted him to be rough and tough with me and when I came it was hotter and harder and quicker than I'd done in ages.

Without making a big deal about it I kind of played our lovemaking over and over in my mind – the way you do after you've had a really good experience – and tried to figure out the how and the why of getting so turned on.

Finally I realized it had to be falling in the stream. It was getting soaked and covered in mud. It was dirty, it was filthy . . . and it felt so good. It was having it plastered all over me, sticking to me, up inside my knickers, matting my pubic hair.

Just thinking about it was enough to start me getting aroused and I knew I wanted to do it again, had to do it again, although without necessarily having to go to all the trouble of actually falling into a stream miles from anywhere this time.

I suppose that was when I started planning and it only took about a couple of weeks to get things organized. I picked a Friday night obviously because it was the start of the weekend and Mark is usually in a good mood when he gets home. But also because we pretty much had a Friday evening ritual: good meal in, watch TV if there's anything decent on or get a video – maybe something a little raunchy – and then early to bed and early to "rise"!

So this particular Friday evening everything was prepared. Around 7 p.m. I heard the key in the door and Mark's customary: "Hi, honey, I'm home."

"Hi, darling. Good day? I'm in the kitchen."

Then his equally predictable: "I'm starving, what's for dinner?"

"Me," I sang back. This was definitely not the usual response and although it was far too late to back out I couldn't help feeling that I might have just made a terrible mistake.

I heard Mark walk through the dining room until he reached the kitchen door . . . and stopped. He stood there with his jacket over his shoulder, tie loosened off and top button undone, clearly gobsmacked. "What the fuck's this?" he managed at last.

It must have come as something of a shock to him. There was his wife sat on a small stool in the middle of his kitchen on a large plastic sheet.

I had taken a lot of trouble with my dress and appearance. I was wearing a short denim skirt and a tight little long-sleeved cardigan in lavender: one of those furry things that feels like it's made out of mohair but is actually 100 per cent synthetic.

With the way I was sitting facing him with my legs apart, Mark could probably see I was also wearing white fishnet stockings – large mesh – stilettos and a cheap and tarty white lace push-up bra, suspender belt and briefs set. I had deliberately overdone the make-up and piled my auburn hair up on top of my head, plus put on the largest pair of gold hoop earrings I could find.

"Like it, darling?" I cooed. "I do hope so, 'cos I was serious. I'm dinner and I want you to eat me all up . . . but first I want you to 'prepare' me."

I could see from his open-mouthed blank look that Mark still hadn't caught on.

"If you look behind me on the work surface I think you'll find everything you need. There's chocolate blancmange, custard, aerosol cream, some soft ice cream, maple, toffee and banana syrups, honey, some fresh raspberries and even a selection of fresh cream cakes. So go to it, lover, and don't you dare disappoint me."

I could see the light come on in Mark's eyes but he still had to check: "You're not . . . You can't be serious?"

"Oh, but I am."

Mark threw his jacket over a chair, ripped his tie off, unbuttoned his cuffs and rolled his sleeves up. Some chance.

He walked across to me and then slowly all the way around me. He dipped his finger into the blancmange and then almost gingerly dabbed a spot onto the end of my nose.

"Come on, you're going to have to do much better than that," I said almost tauntingly. I stood up and grabbed a handful of raspberries from the bowl. Clutching them to my cleavage I squeezed hard, then wiped the sticky pulp across the top of my breasts before raising my open palm to my mouth and wiping it across my face, leaving it smeared with crimson.

It was like I'd just flicked Mark's switch: "So you want to play dirty, eh?"

Pulling open the front of my cardigan he scooped two great dollops of the blancmange down inside, then massaged it against my tits through the woolly material. Next he poured custard inside my knickers, front and back, before sitting me back down with a squelch.

The feeling was fantastic, possibly even better than I'd hoped. As I sat down I could feel the custard oozing out of the sides of my knickers and starting to slide down my legs. I could feel it squashing against my arse and fanny and being forced through the mesh of the briefs. It was cool and velvety and very definitely a turn-on.

"Oh Christ, that's wonderful! Do it some more," I implored.

Mark stood in front of me with the tube of banana syrup . . . and a tremendous hard-on. I reached for his fly but he quickly took a step back: "Don't you dare touch me, you dirty bitch."

And with that he started to squeeze the sticky syrup over my face, down onto my tits and then the cardigan and my skirt.

Of course it looked exactly like . . . Well, I'm sure I don't have to tell you. And so I stuck out my tongue for some "extras" and lapped up the sticky sweetness he dribbled into my mouth.

Mark picked a large chocolate éclair from the selection of cakes on the plate. Holding it to my lips he squeezed hard and watched as the cream squirted over my face and into my mouth. He then wiped the gooey mess off his hand with my hair.

Suddenly I couldn't wait any more. Teasingly slowly I unbuttoned my cardigan and slipped it off my shoulders, then standing up I unzipped the denim skirt and let that fall to the floor. Still in my outrageously tarty underwear I lay down on the plastic sheet and stretched out my arms and legs like a starfish.

"Finish me off," I gasped, "Tip it all over me. Cover me!"

But Mark had other ideas. First of all he sprayed the aerosol cream up and down my body: cold and almost fizzy against my bare skin as it began to melt almost at once. Then he stripped and his wonderful cock reared free as he removed his pants.

Picking up the bowl of ice cream he came and sat on the stool beside me and began flicking spoonfuls at me. Taking a scoop in each hand he shoved them down inside my bra cups and began rubbing it around my tits. The shock of the cold made me gasp and instantly had my nipples standing up on end. Another handful followed down the front of my knickers and I could feel it almost burning against my clit and pussy lips.

Standing over me he emptied the contents of the custard bowl over my body and the blancmange directly onto my head. I literally had a faceful: it was in my hair, my eyes, my mouth and even my nose. I had to wipe the gooey, brown stuff away just to be able to see.

I smeared it over me and started to roll around until my whole body was a marbled riot of reds and browns and yellows. Mark stared at me, almost hypnotized by the sight, and then hauled me to my feet and sat me back down on the stool. Fetching our sharpest kitchen knife Mark carefully hooked it under the front of my bra and with a single quick flick cut it away from me and then did the same with either side of my knickers until they also fell away, leaving me in just the stockings and suspenders. The cold steel against my skin caused my cunt to contract in a way I had never felt before: part fear and part pure passion.

"Sit still," Mark ordered and began to pour clear, thin honey over my breasts. It pooled between them before running down over my stomach and on into the "V" between my thighs.

Taking a soft pastry brush from the jar by the cooker Mark dipped it into the honey and then began flicking it across my nipples, coaxing them erect.

Kneeling between my spread thighs he started gently twirling it around the entrance to my hole until it responded to his insistent teasing, opening, almost unfurling, like the petals of a flower. Then I could feel the bristles of the brush inside me: little circular motions tickling the walls of my cunt where the skin is most sensitive, coating them with a lubrication of honey . . . and receiving a coating of my love juices in return.

Feeling my cunt close around the brush – sucking on it, trying to pull it deeper inside – was incredible and I shuddered and gasped in response. Mark immediately withdrew the brush and I moaned again – this time in sheer frustration.

Dipping it into the jar again he began to paint my pussy with honey using long strokes starting at my perineum and working up to the top of my slit. Dip, brush, left. Dip, brush, right. Dip, brush, dead centre.

It only took about a score of these before my first orgasm "b-rushed" up on me. I clung to Mark for support, pulling his face into my chest and feeling his tongue lapping at my blancmange-covered boobs and his teeth nipping at my nipples causing tiny aftershocks to course through my body.

Eventually the storm passed, I calmed down and Mark stood up – he was looking nearly as messy as I was by this time. Going over to the work surface he returned with a huge, peeled banana and the bowl of soft ice cream.

"Banana split," he said with a wicked grin. He dipped one end of the banana into the ice cream until it was thickly covered and then quickly pushed the whole thing inside me, leaving just an inch or so protruding like a little miniature penis.

The shock of the cold and the feel of the phallic fruit were too much for me and I climaxed again. I could actually feel my cunt squeezing against the banana as if it was a cock.

To make matters worse Mark was on his knees in front of me, literally eating me out. (Well, I had asked for it!) He ate noisily, chewing great lumps of the banana and then smearing it over my outer lips and into my pubic hair with his tongue. I grabbed his head and pushed his face hard into my groin, forcing him to feed in time with my own frenzy.

I felt the last mouthful of banana slip from inside me and then we were both down on the floor, rolling around in the gunk, covered from head to toe and fucking like rabbits. The floor was cold, hard and unforgiving but that just made me feel like more of a wanton slut than ever . . . exactly what I wanted.

We did it forwards, backwards, sideways, doggie-style, rodeo-style, sixty-nine different ways and all the time I was riding the crest of a honey-flavoured wave.

Finally Mark could stand no more, I could tell his own climax was coming fast.

"Not inside me," I pleaded, "I want to watch you come. I want you to come over my face, all over me."

That seemed to do the trick and within seconds I had jets of hot, creamy spunk in my mouth, dribbling down my chin and all over my tits – which I was contentedly trying to lick off like a cat that's got the cream.

"So that was dinner?" Mark eventually managed with an exhausted whisper.

"No," I replied sweetly, "just dessert."

THE CHEEK OF THOSE GIRLS

Derek, Calgary

A short time ago, my girlfriend's sister came to visit us for a week. Given that my girlfriend, Ashley, is an absolute knock-out, so, too, was her twin sister, Abigail. I couldn't tell the pair of them apart; they both had long, black hair and crystal-clear, blue eyes, high, firm tits and jutting nipples, slim waists and long, supple legs, and, best and most of all, plush derrières.

As an unrepentant butt man from way back – a guy who religiously tunes into women's volleyball, beach and otherwise, whenever it's on TV; eyeballs just about any magazine or tabloid that so much as mentions, and pictures, Jennifer Lopez; and, when he was single, spent many a Friday night scanning butt mags and bum vids at his neighbourhood porno store – the sight of those two big, tight asses prancing all over the place made for one of the most memorable weeks of my life.

On the last day of her stay, we took Abby snowboarding at a resort two hours outside of town. And after an invigorating morning and afternoon surfing the slopes, we made tracks for the lodge, for drinks and dinner and a dunk in one of the outdoor hot tubs. My cock had been a frozen cable all day long thanks to the heavenly vista of the girls' board-squatting, ski-pant-clad posteriors, and it didn't melt an inch in the bubbling chop of the soak tub, what with the two of them cavorting around in matching pink bikini tops and floss bottoms. Their heavy, heart-shaped asses, cheeks splayed into two glistening, golden-brown globes by the bum-cleaving thongs, were openly displayed for my erotic enjoyment.

And with my blood-alcohol level and waterlogged dong rising to near record heights, I boldly joked about going to bed with the wrong girl that night, at which point Ashley pulled her sister up out of the steaming froth and tugged down her thong, showed me a butterfly tattoo on Abby's lower abdomen. Ashley sports a tattoo in the exact same spot, only hers is a heart.

After more kidding and more drinks, we finally piled back into the car and drove home. I was totally beat, so I mumbled a slurred goodnight to the girls and poured myself what I hoped to be a long, fitful sleep. And I was sawing logs like a beaver operating a feller-forwarder when Ashley woke me up by pinching my nose. "Huh? What's up?" I grunted.

"I noticed that you had a bit of a 'hard' time today – keeping your eyes off my sister and me," she commented glibly, her eyes twinkling mischievously in the dim light of the bedside lamp. "Think you can give me a hard time – right now?"

I ran a wooden tongue over cracked lips, the fog in my brain quickly burning away thanks to Ashley's unexpected heat. "A man's gotta do . . . something," I mumbled, then rolled on top of her, my ever-ready dick pressing long and hard against her warm, flat stomach.

I slid my hands under her top and cupped and squeezed her pert titties, while swiping tongue and swapping spit with the raven-haired beauty. I jack-knifed up so that she could grab hold of my cock and stroke it with her hot little hand. We Frenched and fondled for a good long time, before I finally broke away from her wicked mouth and latched my lips onto her jugs. I sucked an obscenely swollen, mocha nipple into my mouth and tugged on it, then swallowed her whole blessed tit.

"God, that feels good," she breathed.

I sucked and sucked on her boobs, swirled my tongue all over and around her pointed, rubbery buds. Then I slipped a hand into her panties in prelude to pulling them off and steering my raging cock into her dripping pussy. But Ashley shocked the hell out of me by grabbing my wrist and saying, "I want it in the ass."

I stared at her, wide-eyed, for I well knew that she was an anal virgin, despite my repeated efforts in the past to pop her bung cherry. I thanked my Maker and scrambled off of her, flipped her over, and then fumbled a tube of lube out of the bed stand that I'd been saving for just such a special occasion. I anxiously rubbed the lube onto my straining prong as I gazed longingly at my girl's cushiony, brown pillows.

I wanted to sink my teeth into those fleshy bumpers, bury my tongue to the tonsils in between her hot buns, but first and foremost, I wanted to shove my fat cock into that girl's unviolated butt hole before she changed her mind about the whole thing. I pulled her cute little purple panties down and off and applied hand to ass – gripped her firm, round butt cheeks and squeezed them, kneaded them, playfully slapped them around a bit till they turned pink with embarrassment.

Ashley reached back and spread her cheeks in open invitation, and I swallowed hard and gripped my dick and pushed my big, bloated cock head up against her tiny bunghole. I had no idea how I'd fit all of my swollen pork into her ultra-small chute, but I was bound and determined to find a way.

"Fuck my ass with your big cock!" she bleated, cranking the sexual heat up another few notches.

As her silver-tipped fingernails dug into her lush butt flesh, and her body trembled with anticipation and nervousness, I recklessly ploughed my monster cock-top into her starfish, penetrating her petulant pucker, and then began easing my throbbing rod into her virgin anus. She moaned and buried her face in a pillow, before unexpectedly thrusting her ass backwards, helping me bury my greased bone almost to the balls in her gripping bum. My pole sank into her butt like a spike into the warm, wet earth.

I gripped the sheet on either side of her and churned my hips, slowly at first, barely moving my ass-embedded cock, then faster and faster and faster, torquing up the speed to the point where I was banging the babe's bum with an animal ferocity. I pounded my dick into her bouncing bottom, looming over the groaning girl and pummelling her ass. Great drops of sweat slid off my face and splashed down onto my sweetie, her tremulous ass rippling in time to my cock-spanking, my heavy balls loudly smacking her bronze booty.

"I'm coming!" I hollered, all too soon.

"Come in my ass!" she shrieked back, her head jerking to and fro.

I desperately slammed her ass a few more times, then threw back my head and bellowed and blasted white-hot semen up Ashley's jiggling bum. My body quivered like a sexual tuning fork as I rocketed load after load of sizzling jizz into her beautiful behind. I filled her sweat-dappled caboose to overflowing, my ruptured cock pouring what seemed like a gallon of come inside her.

When it was finally over, I collapsed on top of her, my cock and body drained. Then I tugged my wasted dick out of her vicelike petoot and rolled onto my back next to her, let blessed sleep hit me again like a ton of bricks.

"Derek!" someone hissed in my ear, seemingly only minutes later.

I groaned.

"It's Abby," the girl shaking my shoulder whispered. "I need to see you right away."

I groaned again, but allowed myself to be pulled out of bed, out of my bedroom, and into the neighbouring guest room. I rubbed sand out of my eyes and squinted at the spitting image of Ashley – right down to the skimpy, white T-shirt and purple panties. "What's up, Abby?"

She hooked a finger in between her pouty lips and stared down at her feet. "Well, um, I heard you and my sister having sex – I couldn't help it, you know, the walls are so thin – and, anyway, it got me really hot . . . and I was wondering if maybe you and I –"

"Hold it right there!" I blurted. Even half asleep and horny as hell, I still had enough sense to realize that I had too good a thing going with Ashley – especially with anal sex now added to the mix – to throw it away on a fling with her sister. "I can't cheat on Ashley. It wouldn't be right. We've –"

"I thought you'd say that, Derek," she interrupted, sliding her panties down to reveal a heart tattoo just to the left of her pussy – revealing that she was, in fact, my girlfriend, Ashley. "I was just checking. Now, how 'bout givin' me some of that butt-loving?"

I enthusiastically reamed her taut, oversized ass out for what I thought was the second time that magical night. To be honest, though, I'm not exactly sure who got bum-banged how many times, because both sisters were walking kind of funny the following day. And when Abby had left, Ashley coyly confided that, as twins, the two girls always shared everything, but since Abby was the more daring of the two, it was her job to try out new experiences first.

What I do know about that Ashley–Abby interlude, is that I fucked bodacious booty at least twice during one super-sexed night, and Ashley's lush bottom has been mine ever since.

AN AFTERNOON DRINK

Susannah, Bristol

This is a heck of a confession, and if my ex is reading this, then my secret will be out. Here goes, anyway.

I came out when I was twenty. I kind of knew I was gay all along, but it took a more confident girl showing an interest and showing me the ropes to make me make the change from wallflower into participant. This confession is about my first girlfriend – I'll call her Carla to spare her blushes.

We had been going out a few months and the French kissing and fully clothed fingering had progressed to oral sex. She was much better at it than me – I rarely made her come but she was a natural. I came the first time she kissed me down there and every time after that. All through the days in my first job I used to think of seeing her and having her go down on me.

Anyway, one summer afternoon I had been shopping in town and decided to surprise her. I took the bus and got off at her flat. She was in – just out of the bath and gorgeous in a towelling robe. We kissed and she pulled me straight into the bedroom with a wicked grin. We snogged on the bed for a while, feeling each other's tits and stroking hair and limbs. Then her hands went up my skirt and started playing in my knickers. The familiar warm glow went through my head and I settled down for a good licking. Soon the knickers were off and she had my thighs spread, lapping away at my pussy. It was at this stage I realized I needed the loo. I had felt like I needed to go on the bus but in the excitement of seeing Carla all pink from the bath it had slipped my mind. I wondered how long it would take me to come. I could have a wee after my orgasm, in the "interval" before getting Carla off with my fingers. I tried to focus on the pleasure, looking at Carla's naked form, her face buried in my pussy, her hand twiddling between her legs. The more I tried not to think about it, the more I needed to go. The two sensations became strangely mingled – a burning, prickling pleasure and a woozy, fuzzy pain. At one point I raised my torso and muttered "Carla," but she mumbled into my pussy and pushed me back down. I held on.

Suddenly she stopped and raised her glistening face (I was always a drippy girl and my juices were shining on her chin). "Sit on my face, sweetie," she said, and lying on her back, she wagged her long tongue in the air.

I tried to protest but she shushed me and slapped my bare bottom. She was very dominant and I was used to doing what I was told. I clambered up and straddled her face, lowering my wet cunt onto her waiting mouth, draping my skirt about her ears. I still had my shoes on. I faced away from her body and held onto the tubular steel of the headboard. The pressure in my bladder was extreme and it didn't help that as Carla ate me out, she held onto my hips, her thumbs tenderly massaging my stomach and loins. It was unbearable. Then a crisis came. The pain of holding on was getting unbearable and the pleasure was mounting. Carla was going to town – her long tongue intruding into my sex, lapping at the slick, swollen lips and flicking my hard clit side to side. I rested my bladder muscles for just a second, to ease the pain, and to my horror, a drop slipped out. I felt the warm, stinging sensation of the start of a wee. Carla's lapping stopped for a split second and then carried on as enthusiastically as before. Had she noticed? I panicked and tried to hold on but once I had broken the seal . . . Drop by drop, I began to leak piss, my wee dripping from me like champagne from a fizzing bottle. In my defence the relief was indescribable and coupled with the pleasure Carla's soft mouth was giving me I was dazed – not in my right mind. I have told you I was a very messy girl when it came to excitement and my cream was always plentiful. Carla slurped and gulped at my frothing crotch, guzzling down my offerings, not just pussy juice now but my pee as well.

I must have piddled away for minutes on end, moaning in ecstasy all the while as Carla twisted my nipples through my blouse and pinched my bottom with her sharp nails, licking my swollen clitoris. The piss was always tiny drops and each time I promised myself, through waves of pleasure, that this one was the last, that I had stopped now – that is until the next tiny drop. I pictured her lips smeared with my honeyed glaze, with tiny, secret drops of pee running across her tongue and down her throat. Finally – something we had been experimenting with – a slippery pinkie in my bottom made me come unexpectedly and joyously and I let the last teaspoonful of piss go in a hot, sweet spurt. I think she thought I'd ejaculated and probably promoted herself up the lesbian ladder for that little coup. Only I knew I had wilfully and with malice aforethought peed in my lover's mouth.

I climbed off, trembling (it had been a major orgasm) and kissed her passionately – the very least I could do. There was no untoward taste, to my relief, just her coppery breath and my own feminine musk. I finally went to the loo. Not a drop left. I never told her what had happened and she never spoke a word about it. To this day I wonder if she was oblivious, or if she knew, if she relished and welcomed the taste of my gift sparkling down her throat. I'll never know, but I know what I wish was true.

WITH A TWIST

Amber, Lancaster

It had been a long week for me. There were so many deadlines for me to meet that I had been in the office from 7 a.m. until well past midnight for four days solid, getting very little sleep and surviving on a cocktail of energy drinks and coffee.

Finally, I had everything finished, and managed to retire home in the early evening. Even though I was exhausted, a friend of mine had made me promise to go out clubbing with her that night. Topped up with plenty of caffeine, I got ready, slipping into my favourite dress, the slinky silver one that hugs my curves perfectly and really sets off my light blond hair. Stilettos buckled, I tottered out of the house to meet Jane.

When we hit the club it didn't take the adrenaline long to kick in – helped along by a couple of generous measures of boozy Red Bull. Jane and I were on fire, wiggling and grinding together on the dance floor, and laughing in the brief interludes when we paused to quench our thirst.

Towards midnight, we were approached by a pair of rather good-looking guys: one, Tyne, was just my type, tall, with blue eyes and a thick crop of lush black hair, and Jake, the other, well built with short sandy hair and twinkling green eyes. Fuelled by our drinks, we dragged the pair onto the dance floor with us, and shortly I found myself pressing up not only against Tyne's gorgeous body, but a throbbing hard boner, too. My eyes met his, and he must have sensed how turned on I was by being able to feel him so hard through his jeans, because he reached out to caress my breasts, giving the erect nipples of my double-Ds a squeeze with his strong fingertips. I let out a small moan of pleasure, my dancing momentarily forgotten, until it was broken by Jane.

"Come on, let's get out of here," she whispered into my ear, her breath hot and tainted with vodka as she tried to make herself heard over the music. "I've invited them back to my place, and I'm desperate to see what he's like under those clothes!"

Jane and Jake were wrapped in each other's arms from the moment we left the club, with him pressing her up against buildings as they went, thrusting his crotch at hers through their clothing while she moaned and giggled. Tyne and I were relatively more sedate, with him wrapping his arm around me, the hand reaching down every so often to tweak at my left nipple. It was such a simple gesture, but it turned me on so much that I had to suppress my moans.

Once we got in the taxi, I couldn't wait any longer. Jane and Jake were lip-locked, and I leaned over to whisper into Tyne's ear, "Let's give them a bit of competition, shall we?"

I was so horny I couldn't hold back, and without waiting for Tyne's reply, I slipped my hands up my skirt and quickly pulled down my thong. Tyne's eyes went wide with surprise, and my hand on his crotch could feel how hot and hard he was.

I didn't care that the taxi driver could see us – apparently he was up for a show as he didn't interrupt us at all during the ride home. By now, all I wanted was to feel Tyne's cock deep inside me, and so I straddled him, my breasts in his face, and gently rocked my hips back and forth, rubbing myself against his hard member through the rough fabric of his trousers. It felt so good that I began to unbutton them, releasing his dick so that it stood up proud, asking to be ridden. But rather than slip it inside me, I wrapped one arm around Tyne's neck, and with the other I started masturbating, making sure that he could feel my wet slit rubbing against him, making his trousers wet.

Tyne was enjoying it as much as I was, and I was almost at an orgasm when we reached the house. As I got out of the taxi, I knew that I was flashing my cheeks and, most likely, my sex to Jake and Tyne, but the thought of it (not to mention the look on the taxi driver's face!) just turned me on more.

As soon as we were through the door my frustration at not having come in the car got the better of me and, without caring about the other two, I snatched at Tyne's trousers, then quickly pulled them and his boxers down around his ankles. Though he was a little shy at first, he overcame it as soon as I got down on my knees and put his cock in my mouth.

I wouldn't let him come though, not yet, and when his little moans of ecstasy told me that he was close, I stood up and, pulling him by his shirt, led him into the living room, where Jane was already riding her man on the sofa. It's a situation I'm used to, so I didn't flinch. We're very close, and if ever there's a threesome opportunity she's the one who I'll invite, and vice versa.

Pushing Tyne down onto a chair, I decided to give him a show. Walking up behind Jane, I cupped her small breasts and squeezed her nipples hard, being rewarded with a heavy, sexy moan. I could see Jake shoot Tyne a look of complete surprise over my shoulder, which turned to a longing ogle as I began kissing my way up Jane's neck, flicking her shoulder-length brown hair out of the way until I reached her lips. I've always loved Jane's lips, they're so soft and full, they're just divine to kiss.

Being lip-locked with Jane I didn't notice Tyne get up, but I knew about it when he slipped his finger into my slit from behind me. Jake seized the opportunity too, and was groping at my breasts, his arms tangled with mine as I felt my friend's. Knowing where I wanted this to go, I wriggled backwards, drawing Jane with me, until the two of us were sitting on the floor. She reached out to pull my dress over my head, then unclipped my bra, tossing it to the side as I began to take off her top, loving that we were being watched by the two guys.

As I slid Jane's skirt down her thighs, I began kissing her stomach, slowly moving down to her sex. While we may be close we've never gone much further than fondling each other, but that night, something inside me wanted more. As I reached the line of her neatly shaped pubic hair she let out a gasp that told me it was OK, and so, for the first time, I went down on a girl. She was so wet, and I did what I knew I enjoyed, darting my tongue against her clitoris, gently teasing it with my teeth, feeling her love juices making my chin wet as she squirmed and squealed with pleasure. I was thrilled at how she reacted, and just the act of doing it brought me close to orgasm.

I could feel one of the guys come up and kneel down behind me, but I had no clue which one it was. He began to fondle my wet pussy, slipping in his fingers, one by one, making me moan and want nothing more than to feel whoever it was thrust his cock into me. It didn't take long for him to do it, and with that one, hard thrust, I very nearly came – it sent ripples of pleasure coursing through my body, and it was all I could do to hold myself, arse in the air. Jane wriggled out from beneath me, turning around so that Jake, who I could see over her shoulder, could fuck her, too, while she was face to face with me. It was such a turn-on, looking into her dark brown eyes as the two of us were fucked doggy-style, kissing whenever it was possible.

My orgasm was building up to be explosive, and I could tell that Tyne, Jake and Jane were enjoying it as much as I was. Finally, cliché as it may be, Tyne and I came together in one shuddering, mind-blowing orgasm that made my knees too weak to support me any longer. I could feel how wet I was all down the inside of my thighs, and so could Jane – she must have decided that she wanted to reciprocate the act I had done earlier, because she gently pushed my legs apart and edged forwards until she could reach at me with her tongue. Admittedly I've had much better head from men before, but the mere motion of her tongue against my clit brought my orgasm back up to full volume, causing me to claw at the carpet.

It all seemed to be over very quickly after that; Jake came, then brought Jane up to orgasm, until all four of us were lying naked in a contented stupor on the carpet, legs and arms entangled in a happy love mess, me pressed up against Jane.

I think I must have fallen asleep for a while, because there's a blank spot in my memory, but the next thing I remember was Jane nudging me gently.

"That was amazing," she whispered, giggling at me as we lay nearly nose to nose. "They're both asleep, but look at how they're lying."

I lifted myself up a little way and could see the two guys, practically next to each other, with their heads at opposite ends.

"If you're up for it, I've got an idea . . ." And Jane explained her idea to me; both of the guys had semi hard-ons, and she reckoned it wouldn't take much for them to be fully aroused. She wanted us to suck them off until they both woke up, then try something she said she'd seen on the internet – a spit-roast with a twist, she called it.

I was up for it, so the plan went into action, and I took Tyne's penis in my mouth, gently working it with my tongue and my hand until it was hard. When I looked up, Tyne was awake, and I gave him a saucy wink, before gently taking hold of Jane and lying her on the floor, me pressed on top of her, our breasts mashed together and my tongue exploring her mouth as my fingers worked on her clit. This must have woken up both guys, because they crawled across the floor towards us, kneeling with their cocks in hand, jacking off as they watched.

"Jake, fuck me from behind," I muttered between kisses, and he obediently did as he was told, coming up and sliding his hard dick into me slowly. He felt different to Tyne, shorter but much, much thicker, so much so that it almost hurt as he stretched my pussy with his, at first, gentle thrusts.

I just about managed to moan to Tyne that I wanted him in my mouth, but he got the idea pretty quickly, and soon I was being fucked from both ends; Jake's thick cock making me want to squeal with pleasure, Tyne's longer one suppressing it as he fucked my mouth deep and hard, almost causing me to gag with how far he was thrusting himself. I could feel my breasts bouncing against Jane's as I was rocked back and forth by the two men, her breath heavy on my chest as she slid her hand down to join mine in masturbating herself.

The whole situation was so hot that the men weren't long in coming – Jake pulled out and squirted his load all over my buttocks, while Tyne filled my mouth with his sticky, salty come. I reached my second orgasm of the night, and while it wasn't quite as mind-blowing as the first, it was still absolutely pleasurable, and I snuggled quite happily against Jane while we fell asleep.

That was the first time I'd ever had a foursome, and I can tell you now, it was the perfect ending to a totally crappy work week. When I woke up in the morning, Tyne and Jake were gone, but they had left their phone numbers – I guess we gave them as good a night as they gave us. I know for sure that I'll be doing it again!

NOT-SO-FOREIGN EXCHANGE

Melvin, Lincoln

I'm sixty years old, and seldom have sex with anyone over twenty. I know what you're thinking – dirty old man, right? Damn right! I've had more teenaged pussy than a high-school gym teacher. A strict religious upbringing and a frosty thirty-year marriage left me bursting with juice, and when my ex finally ran off with her butch aromatherapist, I vowed to make up for lost poon-time. And I've been making up and out ever since.

I live in an apartment complex that, by no coincidence, is situated right next to one of the city's universities, meaning that I have a plentiful supply of fresh meat to choose from. The place is literally crawling with sweet young things looking for some sexual mentoring from an experienced gent like myself. I give them a hard time, sure, but everyone's usually satisfied in the end.

One night, as I was dropping my dirty duds into one of the washers in the communal laundry room on the fifth floor, an Asian babe of not more than nineteen walked in with a basketful of clothes. I quickly stowed what was left of my load, twirled the dials on the machine, and hustled over to make my acquaintance with the Oriental pearl. "Hi," I said, in my deepest Barry White.

She smiled at me and nodded, her oval face as pretty and delicate as a geisha's.

"I'm Brendan," I lied. My real name is actually Melvin, but try picking up chicks with a handle like Melvin.

"Oh, yes, hi," she responded, nodding her head again and glancing uncertainly at my extended mitt. "My name is Lin."

I grabbed one of her warm, soft hands in both of my paws and squeezed, running my laser-sharpened eyes up and down the china doll's lithe, caramel-tinted body. She was wearing a pair of pink short shorts and a white crop top that said "Porn Star" across her girlish chest. Her legs were smooth and slender, flowing on forever out of her tiny shorts, while the nipples on her B-cup breasts pressed hard and yearning against the stretchy fabric of her top. Her eyes were dark and sparkling, her hair long and black and shiny.

My burgeoning boner told me to keep the conversation flowing. "Are you a foreign exchange . . ." My voice ground to a halt when I eyeballed the contents of Lin's laundry basket; it was loaded to the plastic brim with dirty clothing, all right, very, very dirty clothing. She had what looked like a year's worth of Victoria's Secret inventory in that naughty hamper of hers – sexy, silky thongs, panties, bras, stockings, negligees, nighties, teddies, corsets, baby-dolls, etc., etc. The seemingly innocent girl was either a lingerie model or the laundress for a whorehouse.

She followed my astonished eyes down to her basket of lewdly whispering seduction wear, then plucked a black, fishnet body stocking out of the pile and held it up for my inspection. "You like?" she asked.

"I likee!" I blurted. And then my stented ticker almost stopped cold when Lin walked over to the laundry room door, closed and locked it, then slipped out of her pint-sized duds and sandals and into the see-through body stocking. Her long, hard, chocolate-coloured nipples fought their way through the fishnet and filled my orbs. Her pussy was as bare as an unshucked oyster, save for a triangular patch of soft, black fur that crowned the top of her glistening slit.

"This is my favourite thing to get fucked in," she confided, her almond-shaped eyes staring at the bulge below my belt.

I restarted my heart and tugged down my sweats, let my swollen cock spring out into the open. Then I gathered the featherweight girl up in my arms and kissed her like it was an MIA homecoming. The exotic beauty was young, and her mother tongue probably wasn't even English, but she sure as hell knew how to use it. She twirled her tongue all around my tongue, speaking to me in the universal language of lust, and then she caught my taste buds between her glossy lips and sucked on my extended tongue like it was a juicy prick.

And after getting me all hot and bothered with her talented mouth, she dropped to her knees and without hesitation wrapped her lips around the end of my throbbing cock.

"Yeah, that's the way, honey," I groaned, as she earnestly sucked on my purple knob.

She popped my bloated hood in and out of her saucy mouth, her tongue scrubbing the sensitive underside of my prick, before swallowing my cap and hoovering my shaft. She rapidly inhaled a good two-thirds of my pulsating pole, and with her lips sealed tightly over the top of it, her mouth warm and moist and needy, she began sucking hard on my rod. Her head bobbed up and down on my dick like she was in the presence of Buddha himself.

Eventually, I had to pull the wet-vaccing babe to her feet, lest I blow foam down her throat. I wanted pussy, and I wanted it now. She instantly understood, bent forwards over the top of the washing machine and spread her sleek legs. I located a convenient cock-sized hole in her body stocking, right on target with her slickened snatch, and jammed my rod into the breach, filling her slit.

Her sex hole was dripping and gripping, and I savagely hammered the young hottie's puss, the washer rocking back and forth like it had a life of its own. Lin gripped the enamelled machinery and whimpered, her head bouncing to and fro, her silky hair flying all over the place, my heavy, hairy balls slapping her rippling, coffee-and-cream-coloured ass flesh as I bore into her.

"Sweet land of liberty!" I sang out, my cock exploding in her stretched-out love tunnel, rocketing sizzling jizz deep into her very being. As she herself was consumed by orgasm.

When we were straightening ourselves up afterwards, she more formally introduced herself. "My full name is actually Linda Jones," she said with a sassy smile, "and I'm originally from North Platte, Nebraska. I've felt a little like a foreigner these last few weeks, all alone in the big city. Until you made me feel welcome, that is."

BEST OF BOTH WORLDS

Ava, Ipswich

Steve and I have been married for almost ten years. I'm thirty-eight years old and he's thiry-four so if you like I'm the "older woman".

We went out for about eighteen months before we decided to get married and while Steve certainly wasn't a virgin it's also true to say that he wasn't terribly experienced sexually. Not like me!

We're very happy. With a little gentle help and guidance from me Steve has turned into a wonderful and attentive lover. He adores me . . . and that, if you like, is the problem.

Sexually I've always been the more adventurous of the two of us with a small but important masochistic streak. I like being a "naughty girl" and I like being punished. Not all the time, you understand, but maybe three or four times a year; it's like an urge than just keeps growing inside me, an itch I can't scratch.

To start with I tried talking to Steve about it. I bought a few mild S&M magazines and left them lying about. We even watched a blue bondage video. But it was no good; Steve just couldn't bring himself to "hurt" me. I tried explaining that I didn't really want to be hurt, just a decent "spanking" occasionally as part of a sex game. He tried, but it was a disaster and we both ended up in tears . . . of laughter, and no bad thing for that.

But it didn't solve my problem or cure my itch until one day I was reading a sex mag and came across the ad from The Master. It took several weeks and quite a lot of very subtle persuasion before Steve agreed to me making an appointment and even then he insisted on coming along that first time to make sure everything was properly above board.

Now when the itch starts coming on I start being deliberately naughty. I will stay out late without telling Steve, maybe come home drunk after a night on the tiles with the girls. I'll "forget" to cook his supper or serve up something I know he doesn't particularly like. I'm sure there are times when Steve deliberately pretends not to notice the signals and then – and only as a last resort when I'm getting crazy with frustration – I'll pretend to have a headache or be "too tired" when I know he's in the mood for love.

The session usually starts on a Thursday night, often just as we are going to bed. Steve will say something to me like: "You know you've been a bad girl so I've made an appointment for you tomorrow evening at 7 p.m."

That's all but it's still enough to have me spending the night – and most of the following day – tossing and turning in apprehension and, yes, anticipation.

When Steve gets home from work on Friday I'll have prepared a meal for him, definitely something that I know he likes. When he's finished he hands me a sealed letter for me to give my Master and it's time for me to leave.

My Master lives about a twenty-minute drive away. I will already have my uniform on: white, short-sleeved blouse, no bra, short, black miniskirt over white cotton panties and plain black shoes. I am allowed to wear stockings and suspenders – absolutely no tights – but I know my Master prefers me without so I am bare-legged. By the time I reach his house I will be feeling hot, body sheathed in a mist of perspiration and twitching with tiny shivers of fear. And yes I admit it, damp between my legs as well.

His large house is in an upmarket neighbourhood so I park the car in the drive and ring the bell. My Master opens the door; he is tall, distinguished with steel-grey hair, in his early forties and wearing casual slacks and an open-necked shirt.

"Ava, hello," he says as I silently hand him the letter. "It's been a long time, hasn't it? Do come in."

The house is beautifully and expensively furnished, although I have actually seen very little of it. He leads me into the large

drawing room. In the centre of the room is a small wooden stool
and he beckons me to sit on it. It is hard and uncomfortable and
so low that my knees are higher than my hips. My Master sits in
a white leather armchair directly in front of me and I am aware
that with my legs apart he will be able to see my white knickers
and the darker damp patch where the cotton is stretched tight
across my mound.

He opens the letter and reads it in silence, occasionally
glancing quizzically at me from over the top of the paper.
When he has finished he puts the letter back in the envelope
and says: "I'm very disappointed in you in, Ava. Stephen tells
me that he has had to get his own dinner three times in the last
two weeks. The bed is unmade and twice he has had to iron his
own shirt. He even says he asked for a blow job and you refused,
is this true?"

"Yes, Master," I reply.

"It seems you have learned nothing. What shall we do with
you, eh?"

"I need to be punished, Master."

"Yes, I think so. Stephen thinks you should choose your own
punishment. So tell me how many strokes you think will fit the
crime, please, Ava. But before you do, Stephen has also told me
how many he thinks you deserve. If your guess is higher than
that, of course, that is the number you will receive, but if
Stephen's is the higher – and you are trying to escape lightly
– then you will receive his figure plus the difference between the
two. So if you say ten and Stephen thinks you deserve fifteen
then I will give you twenty. Do you understand?"

I nod, but this is something new. The rules of the session are
strict and unbending. There is no sexual contact between my
Master and I, although occasionally he will caress me prior to
administering the punishment. Caresses which only serve to
make my skin more sensitive. Sometimes after the beating he
will order me to masturbate in front of him. I find this
particularly humiliating since I am invariably sopping wet
and climax within just a few seconds, with two or three fingers
rammed inside my throbbing pussy. An orgasm that I know
belongs to my husband and so feel each spasm as a betrayal.

More importantly my Master hasn't told me what implement he is going to use to punish me or where. Sometimes I will be tightly tied over a whipping bench or spreadeagled across his dining room table. On one occasion my wrists and ankles were trussed together and I was hauled into the air before he whipped my burning flesh with a cat-o'-nine-tails. On another he lashed my elbows tightly together behind my back and then used the flat of a springy plastic ruler on my breasts. I remember Steve melting ice cubes on them to ease the burning when I got home.

But possibly the worst and most humiliating is when he puts me over his knees and spanks my bare bottom. With certainty I know he has the power to reduce me to tears – the cheeks of my face redder than the cheeks of my arse, blubbing like a baby and begging him to stop – using just his hand.

What would it be tonight, I wondered: "T-t-ten," I whispered.

"Bravo. Good guess, but not quite good enough. Stephen, I'm afraid, thinks you deserved a dozen. And that means I get to give you fourteen. Stand up and remove your knickers."

As I do so my Master gets up and goes to a large fitted cupboard in one corner of the room. Inside are the instruments of my punishment – tawse, paddle, crop, cat – and he is truly master of them all. After a few moments' consideration he selects a thin bamboo cane and swishes it experimentally through the air. It makes a vicious hiss.

He crosses the room and sits in the middle of a large leather sofa, the arms of which end in carved wooden posts and around which I notice are tied lengths of braided golden rope. My Master summons me with his cane and I come and stand before him. He takes the knickers from my hand and raises them to his cheek: "My, Ava, you are a wicked girl. Now lie down here across my lap."

Obediently I do as I am told, head to his left. He pulls my arms out in front of me and ties my wrists together, before pulling the braid tight against the post. Once I am secured he moves his right leg away from under me and is then able to clasp my thighs tightly between his own, leaving me unable to move and completely helpless. Finally he pushes a cushion under my stomach so my buttocks are stretched taut and raised even more prominently before lifting my skirt clear of my hips.

My Master sits like this in silence for a minute or more before he starts to brush the skin of my thighs and buttocks with just his fingertips. Every touch makes me flinch, heat rising within me until I feel as if I am already on fire. With his left hand he reaches beneath me, undoes the buttons of my blouse. He cups my right breast and then squeezes the nipple between his thumb and forefinger, pulling down until I gasp with a mixture of pleasure and pain.

"Now we can start," he says. "Would you like me to gag you?"

I shake my head and instantly feel the first cut of the cane across my buttocks.

"I asked you a question." The swish and thwack of the cane making punctuation marks in the conversation.

"No. No, thank you, Master."

Swish, thwack. Three. Swish, thwack. Four. By now I am clenching my teeth against the pain. I know that sat in the sofa my Master isn't really able to swing the cane with enough force to really hurt me. But that doesn't stop the sudden blaze of each stroke and the heat building in my buttocks and raging outwards through my body like a bush fire. It doesn't stop it feeling like a line of bees marching in formation across my arse and then all stinging me at the same instant.

Swish, thwack. Five. Swish, thwack. Six. My Master is a real expert, laying the strokes carefully across my buttocks. I have been this far before but now I am entering unknown territory, possibly even an unknown world.

Swish, thwack. Seven and this one is laid precisely in the crease where my cheeks join my thighs and the skin is tenderest. Swish, thwack. Eight! The blow lands across the earlier strokes where the red welts are already beginning to rise.

"Aieee!" I howl and despite myself hot salt tears begin to course down my cheeks. "Please, no. Please, no more, that's enough. I'll be good, I promise. I swear. Ring Steve, please, tell him I'm sorry, tell him I'll be good. Tell him to come and get me," I babble.

My Master stops instantly. His hand begins to trace the welts across my buttocks, feeling the radiant heat and the way I wince from his touch, squirming downwards into his lap.

"Ava, you disappoint me," he says softly. "Have you learned nothing? This is what Stephen wants. It is what you want. It is what I want. It is what we do."

With that he reaches down over my forehead with his right hand, grasps my nose tightly and pulls my head upwards. As my mouth drops open helplessly he pushes my sodden panties into my mouth, effectively gagging me.

Swish, thwack. Nine. Swish, thwack. Ten. Suddenly the endorphins kick in. The pain is still there but now it is tinged with pleasure. I feel more alive than I have ever done in my life. Every cell in my body is on red alert. All my senses are heightened: even the scent and taste of my panties. A microsecond behind comes the familiar sexual rush: the dropping, dragging sensation in my womb and the gush of my love juices.

Swish, thwack. Eleven. Swish, thwack. Twelve. And my Master stops again, unties my hands and removes my gag.

"Kneel on the floor, Ava. Now sit back on your haunches," he commands, noticing the jolt of pain as my burning buttocks come in contact with the backs of my calves.

"Now listen carefully. I want you to open your blouse and cup each of your breasts. That's it, push them up nice and high. Now I want you to beg me to give you the last two strokes across your tits. Do you understand?"

"Yes, Master," I reply, although at that instant I don't know if I have the strength to do it or not and I feel my stomach flip with fear. "Please, Master, cane my tits. I beg you, please." My voice is wonderfully calm and firm.

The cane swishes down across my pillowed breasts and the fire follows an instant later.

"Now pinch your nipples, pull them up into the air as far as you can and lean backwards."

Silently I obey and the final stroke flicks upwards onto the delicate underside of my breasts. It is over and the agony is almost outweighed by the ecstasy of relief.

I straighten my clothing although my Master retains my soiled panties as "a reminder of you". I spend a few minutes recovering over a long cold glass of water and then set off to drive home, the rough material of the seat chafing against my still burning cheeks.

As I get out of the car I check my face in the mirror: eyes still a little red but apart from that I look shockingly normal. The pain has virtually gone although as I walk up the path I still feel stiff and sore, but nearly pleasantly so, like after a good workout at the gym. Experience tells me that the welts will probably be almost gone by the morning but that sitting down is still likely to be uncomfortable for most of the weekend

Steve lets me in and we go through to the lounge. He sits, I remain standing in front of him.

"Well?" he asks.

"I'm sorry I've been so awful to you lately. I really am. I've learned my lesson and I promise I won't do it again." As I say the words I mean them, I really do, but I also know that it will only last until the itch comes back.

"He caned me here and here," I say, pointing to my buttocks and my breasts.

"Take your clothes off."

That was easy. In two movements I pull the blouse over my head and drop the skirt down my legs, before stepping out of my shoes, noticing Steve's eyes widen as he realizes I'm not wearing my panties. Naked, I clasp my hands together at the back of my neck and pirouette in front of my husband.

"God," he breathes as he reaches out to trace the line of one of the welts across my backside. I flinch against the coolness of his fingertips.

He leads me upstairs and showers me. I stand passively as he plays the jet across my body – over my breasts, down my back and up between my legs – the barely warm water easing the stinging still further.

Steve dries me with a warm fluffy towel, just gently dabbing the tender spots. With infinite tenderness he rubs cooling body lotion into my breasts and buttocks before leading me to the bedroom.

We make love three times that night. It is the best sex I have ever had.

The last time he flips me over onto my stomach and then takes me doggy-style, his hands cupping breasts that seem fuller and heavier than ever before. My womb molten, I am filled with liquid fire. As Steve slides slowly backwards and forwards inside me, the caress of his pubic hair against the hypersensitive globes of my bottom seems as sharp and bright as the cut of the cane.

I come and cry. And cry and come, weeping tears of joy, not shame.

And when we have finished and are curled up close against each other Steve says in wonderment: "I just don't know why you do it, you know."

"Because I can," I reply. "Because it's what I want. Because it's what you want as well, even if you won't admit it. Because I love you so.

"And because this way I can have the best of both worlds . . . I can have my cane and beating too!"

BLOND BEAUTY

Karen, Blackburn

I entered the bedroom, dressed in a pair of tight-fitting jeans, work boots, and a second-hand "Official Bikini Inspector" T-shirt. My short, dark hair was slicked back and tucked in behind my ears, my strapped-on cock outrageously bulging the front of my jeans.

"What's taking so long?" I demanded, in a voice three octaves below normal. "Damn women always taking so long to make themselves pretty."

Chris was seated at my make-up table, his back to me, his long, blond hair fanned out across his shoulders. He turned his head and glanced at me, and his big, blue eyes looked just a little frightened under the black eyeliner and blue eye shadow. I gaped at him, at the well-applied blush and perfectly applied crimson lipstick, feeling even more frightened.

He slid off the stool and fully faced me – my husband, dressed in a short, black leather skirt and sleeveless, white satin blouse, black silk stockings on his legs and four-inch heels on his feet. "I'm ready," he stated, his voice gone high and squeaky, like a girl's. He twirled a strand of blond hair around his finger and gazed demurely down at the floor.

And as I stared at him/her, my fear of the kink slowly began to dissipate, my body surging with a heavy, tingling heat. He looked as sexy as hell, one damn fine-looking woman!

I ogled him guy-like, from the tip of his brushed blond head to the toes of his high-polish stilettos. I scrubbed under my nose with a pair of fingers, then hooked my thumbs into my belt. I would've spat on the floor, too, to heighten my masculine effect even more, but I just couldn't muster the saliva just then.

Chris clasped his scarlet-tipped fingers together over the front of his skirt and shyly looked up at me. "You like?" he asked, all peaches and cream.

I nodded, my pussy gluing to the leather platform of my harness with moisture, the flexible dong almost popping my zipper. We'd discussed it for months – cross-dressing – and now my only thought was: Why the hell had we wasted all that time talking instead of doing? Typical women.

"Looking good," I croaked, strolling over to the doll, my legs shaking.

He batted his lengthened eyelashes and licked his glossy lips, and my knees buckled. But I stood tall, like a man. I reached out and touched the dude-lady's bare shoulder with my trembling fingers. "Yup, looking real good."

The dialogue wasn't going to win any screenwriting awards, but the picture was the thing – Chris as I'd never seen him before, me as he and I had never seen me before – and the acting. I rubbed the smooth, bronze skin of his shoulder, and he giggled.

I trailed the quivering tips of my digits down Chris's arm, onto his hands, his skirt. Onto the raging erection that the skimpy wrap and a pair of panties could in no way, shape, or form fully contain. Chris yelped and spun away from me. He gripped the edge of the make-up table, his slender body shaking.

"H-hey now," I rasped, stroking the cutie's silky hair and staring at the taut, mounded buns that strained the seams of his short leather skirt. "Ain't no reason to be scared."

We hadn't really rehearsed any specific roles for the grand unveilings (though I seemed to be channelling redneck right then), deciding to play it by ear. But with the hot blood pounding in my ears, and pussy, I could barely hear the sound of my own voice, let alone Chris's.

I recklessly grabbed on to the babe, clasping his hot body tightly against my burning body. I pressed my rigged-up cock into the plush flesh of his bum, gripping his bra-padded breasts and squeezing. Man, I was as horny as a bullfrog.

I kissed his neck, nuzzled his hair, pasting my long, lean body to his and grinding my cock into his arse. "You want it bad as I do, don't you?" I breathed into his ear, before sticking my tongue in.

He arched his back against me in a feminine gesture, and I bit into the heated skin of his neck, inhaling his sweet perfume. "Yes!" he squealed, grabbing on to my head.

Chris and I had engaged in some mild kinkery in the course of our two-year marriage – some fairly well-hidden exhibitionism, a little tentative spanking (on both our ends), a few brief bursts of phone sex – but never anything this premeditatedly wild. The sheer crazy naughtiness of it all had my head spinning and pussy melting, as I excitedly licked at my man-turned-woman's bobbing Adam's apple.

Moaning, he pushed his butt harder into my hard-on, against my brimming pussy. I sang with sexual electricity. And when he spun around in my arms and I kissed the vixen full on his pouty, painted lips, it was all almost too much for my addled brain and blazing body to comprehend without premature ejaculation.

But I hung tough, roughly clutching Chris in my arms and savaging his pretty mouth. His cock pressed against my cock, breasts into my breasts. I drove my tongue into his mouth and just about down his throat, real-man style.

We swirled our slippery tongues together, hot, panting breath flooding our faces. I clawed Chris's skirt up and over his bum, grabbing me handfuls of thick arse flesh, lacy stocking top and frilly panty bottom, and squeezing. He moaned into my mouth, his fingers riffling through my hair.

Then the made-up babe was suddenly out of my arms and on his knees on the floor. He tore my oversized belt bucket open and my fly down, pulled my ever-hard cock out of my jeans. Gripping the pink, vein-ribbed shaft, he looked up at me and squeaked, "I'm going to suck you, mister."

I grunted something like, "Well, get to 'er then," and Chris took my mushroomed hood into his warm, wet mouth. I groaned, feeling it right down to my wildly tingling pussy, his thick lips tugging on my cock head, his hot little hand stroking up and down my shaft. I dug my fingers into his golden hair and rode his bobbing head, urging him to go deeper, suck harder.

He gazed up at me with sparkling eyes and inhaled as much of my cock as he could. His eyes went watery, face red. I pumped my hips, fucking the slut's mouth quick and hard and anxious, my pussy smouldering with the pressure.

He gripped my bare butt and hung on. Then slid a hand up and under my T-shirt and squeezed a buzzing breast, tweaked a numb-hard nipple. I almost came right in his mouth.

"I'm gonna fuck you, bitch!" I gasped, jerking my hips back, my cock out of his mouth.

We hadn't discussed just how far we were going to take things. But there was no room for discussion now. Not in the stifling sexual heat of that ultra-erotic moment.

I pulled him to his feet and dug under his skirt, yanked his pink panties down, my fingers brushing his throbbing erection. He staggered backwards and fell onto the bed. I ripped his panties away from his ankles and then gripped his spike heels, pushed his stockinged legs apart. His cock stood out huge and rigid above his hiked-up skirt.

I shouldered his silky limbs and then further greased up my mouth-wettened cock with the packet of lube I pulled from my pants pocket. Then I oiled up Chris's shaven crack.

He shrieked, "Yes, fuck my arse with your big, hard cock!"

"Here it comes, baby!" I hissed, gripping my dong and shoving the bloated cock head up against his virgin opening.

He whimpered, shuddered, as I ruthlessly popped his anal cherry and plunged inside of him. I dug my fingers into his corded thighs, my own thighs bumping up against his butt cheeks, my cock buried to the preformed balls in his bum.

He squealed and twisted his head around. I pumped my hips, sliding my engorged prick back and forth in the wanton slut's gripping anus. Surging with raw power and pleasure, I quickly stepped up the pace, urgently fucking the writhing girly-man, plundering his bum hole.

He grabbed onto his flapping hard-on and frantically pulled, as I clung to his jumping legs and pistoned his arse. The sharp crack of my flying thighs against his shuddering bottom ricocheted off the walls of the suffocating bedroom and filled our ears, our frenzied breathing and frayed passions crescendoing to the critical point, the wicked sexual pressure too much to contain.

Chris cried out with joy, jerking ropes of semen out of his ruptured cock, coating his blouse and skirt. Just as the wet-hot friction of the rocking dildo platform against my clit sent me sailing. I shook with one delicious, gushing orgasm after another, coming like a woman as I desperately fucked my man.

VILE SEDUCER

Simon, San Francisco

Take it from me: when you're pushing sixty, there's a certain
slightly queasy charm about having sex with a nineteen-year-old
kid who brings along his skateboard. A kid, that is, like Darrin.
When, thanks to the shop-at-home-for-sex services of Craigslist,
his baby face first showed up at my door, my dick and I were
suitably impressed. Darrin was enthusiastic, a little goofy, charmingly sweet. He'd told me via email that he was bi, that he'd
never had sex with a man before, that all he really wanted to do
was just talk . . . Which was fine with me, if potentially more than
a little frustrating. Actually, I'd somewhat duplicitously answered an ad of his that expressed an interest in "furries", those
folks who like to dress up as animals and sometimes, depending
upon their philosophical bent, have sex with other furries while in
beastie drag. So for the first ten minutes or so, I feigned an
overwhelming interest in boys in bunny suits.

For his part, Darrin sprawled back in my knock-off Barcelona
chair, legs spread wide, basket maybe showing despite his then-
fashionably baggy, low-slung pants. Did he realize how provocatively he was acting? How much I wanted him? Was he as
aware as I was that he was damn near young enough to be
my . . . grandson?

Yep, long ago, when I saw fellows my age (say, around
twenty-three back then) consorting with men old enough to
be their fathers – or granddads – I found myself somewhere
between puzzled and aghast. Little did I suspect that, in the
jizz-soaked autumn of my years, I would become a Predatory
Old Guy myself. Yes, a Vile Seducer. That's me.

Maybe some of it has to do with time's winged chariot rushing headlong towards the cliff of mortality; is my desire for youths simply a displaced longing for my *own* youth? Well, that sounds plausible, but simple fear of death doesn't really seem to explain my deep longing when confronted by fresh young flesh.

By Darrin's flesh, for instance. Had he been nervous, albeit charmingly so, when he first showed up at my door? Well, yeah. But then, so was I. Fear of rejection, fear of social awkwardness. Fear that I'd get what I wanted . . . Which, as it happened, I did. I suppose that, deep down, we both knew what was going to happen. Darrin didn't object when I slithered down to the floor, sitting between his feet, stroking my way up his well-formed legs, all the way up to his crotch. Hesitate. Unbutton. Unzip. He let me suck his astonishingly meaty, deliciously uncut young cock, a cock that was stiff from the moment I undid his pants.

And I soon discovered there were other pleasures to be had. Darrin's plump rump was not just lovely, but responsive as well, a hitherto unexplored land of heretofore untapped joys. Darrin had, he told me, played with it himself on occasion, but that had been all, no previous pricks had been in there. (But on the other hand, I later found out that when he'd told me he was bisexual, that he'd been with women, and that I was his first guy, none of those things – it somewhat disappointingly turned out – was quite the truth. Ah, the stuff we believe when it suits our egos. And when the guy telling the lies is cute.)

Be all that as it may, Darrin turned out to be a naturally voracious bottom boy, an epochal fuck. As a mostly top myself, I'm always gratified – if a bit stupidly surprised – to run across a fellow who thinks that getting screwed is the Very Best Thing in the World. Darrin's collegiate pucker was one of those Holes of a Lifetime. Whether the object in question was a probing fingertip, my tongue, or my eager cock, his ass was almost scarily insatiable. Had I created a fuck-boy Frankenstein?

It's not like I ever actually planned to become a lecher. But somewhere around the onset of middle age, depravity hit: I developed a yen for younger, much younger, dudes. I know, I know. Hardly original – letch-wise, I'm something of a walking cliché. With a hard-on. One that bobbles when I walk.

Sure, relationships are *always* fraught, but falling for a much younger dude is extra-likely to result in frustration, disappointment and unbecoming self-pity. He moves on, you move to a retirement home.

There were a number of boys back then, some of them beautiful, and most of my dealings with them ended on a decidedly ambiguous note. So by the time I met Darrin, one might have thought I'd learned my lesson, but no. He – I convinced myself – was different. Hell, he was a vegan anarchist! And he was into me, at least enough into me to let me bust his cherry. I, the first man ever to fuck him, fell pretty hard. At the risk of seeming an absolute jerk, I must confess there's something thoroughly bracing about plundering virgin ass. Sure, he was a little sloppy about answering emails, about keeping dates. But hell, he was young. And a stoner. And cute. And young. Allowances must be made. Even allowances that leave one feeling uncomfortably close to being a pathetic old fool.

And anyway, Darrin was – for want of a better word – fun. A whole lot of it. Sure, our relationship was pretty vanilla. Well, not all *that* vanilla, especially after Darrin had smoked a bowl. I did spank him a few times – more than a few – but who doesn't like to be spanked, at least a little? And yeah, I did drink his piss a few times as it jetted from his impressive foreskin. It was all rather nice, really. Even the time he showed up just having eaten a sandwich: I still recall the Proustian taste of tofu and onions when we kissed.

But somewhere around our first anniversary, things took a turn for the worse. After nearly a year of on-and-off fuck-buddydom, my calls and emails began to go utterly, unapologetically unanswered. Several dates were not just cancelled, but thoroughly blown off. I told myself that I was pretty sure that Darrin didn't actually want to hurt me – hell, he didn't even eat eggs. He was busy with classes, he told me. And with his family, who lived, scarily enough, just a short subway ride from my place. On those rare occasions we did get together, it was often a battle to get into his pants, though get into his now-just-past-teenaged pants I did. But finally the awful truth came out. Darrin had gone on the game. My sweet, innocent boy had started hustling. Yes, I'd fallen by the wayside when he began selling others what he'd given me for free. Men as old as I was – though, presumably, not working for a freelance writer's salary – were paying him 200 bucks for his big ol' tush. And hey, if there's anything worse than feeling unwanted, it's feeling underpaid.

Sure, in my brighter moods, I clearly recall the way that Darrin moaned when I expertly fucked him, how my well-honed butt-eating sent him into paroxysms of boyish joy . . . and what a tasty ass that was! I just trained his now-profitable collegiate *culo* too well, I guess. I have, though, published a bunch of pieces based on my experiences with him. (In fact, I showed him the first few, and he was delighted to be a star. And though the last one I published was a lot less laudatory, I doubt he's seen it. After all, it would be egotistical, even a shade pathetic, to believe that our time together has left him a fan of my writing.)

So, on at least some levels, the whole affair was mutually beneficial: he got training, I got material. Does that qualify as mutual exploitation? Well, fuck, what isn't? If sucking off young men is a form of psychic vampirism, it's a particularly ambiguous one. Because no matter how stiff I make a nubile fellow's dick, there's always the sneaky suspicion, given the general marketability of young flesh, that I'm a mercy fuck. And no matter how glorious the moment, being with a guy young enough to be my son is also a memento mori: *Odds are that this boy in my bed will outlive me by decades*. And hey, nobody likes a maudlin trick.

In a sense, all of this is like some twisted Buddhist lesson. In Nepal, I'm told, novice monks sleep with corpses, the better to realize the fleeting nature of life. And though I may wind up in bed with something a bit more animated, something named Shane or Zane or Jeremy, the end result is similar.

Because whatever else it's about, sex is a matter of the flesh. And flesh, desire, life are transitory. All things, like a dead Beatle said, must pass.

Even young ass. Even gorgeous young ass. Even Darrin's.

Hey, maybe a part of me chooses Unsuitable Objects of Desire *especially* because they are, in the final analysis, dead ends. Falling for a sweet but feckless boy like Darrin pretty much ensures that the roller coaster of lust won't threaten the mostly satisfying basics of my life.

What does threaten my life, most of all, is passing time. Not to get all melodramatic, but the ultimate bad date is Death. Yes, I know I should be more like a Buddhist. Or at least more like a sensible senior citizen. I should let go. Hell, I should stop thinking about Darrin, about his smile, about his hole, about his smiling hole. But desire is just so . . . sticky.

It's one of life's little ironies that with advancing years, you become more focused on the vicissitudes of your body, just when it starts deserting you. And with time's narrowing horizons, desire sharpens. At least mine sure as hell has.

So, dear reader, should you be in the bloom of youth, gather ye rosebuds while ye fucking may. Because from here on out, getting tricks will get trickier.

And for my fellow somewhat-senior citizens, a word of wisdom: Seize the moment, knowing full well it will pass. 'Cause that's all we've got. And sometimes – often – that's more than enough.

Sorry, Buddha.

Oh, and if you end up hiring Darrin's ass, please send me a finder's fee. I take PayPal.

BONFIRE NIGHT

Alisha, Edmonton

It was the final week of camp and my last chance to get into Ryan's tight white shorts. Ryan and I were counsellors at an exclusive summer retreat for rich kids. He was a blond, blue-eyed, beach-boy type. Bronzed and buff, with the biggest bulge I had ever seen. I had it for him bad, just had to have a taste. Unfortunately, he hadn't shown any interest in me all summer. I guess I was too slim, too dark. From what I could tell he preferred the blond bombshell type. Cindy was his current squeeze, huge tits, bobbed yellow hair, legs that just didn't quit. She was gorgeous. My own small, athletic frame and modest chest couldn't hope to compare, though he had said once that he liked my hair. It is one of my best features, these long, curling chestnut waves. My eyes are nice, too – large and dark brown – very expressive, I'm told.

Anyway, it was "sleep under the stars" night for the kiddies. That meant it was get drunk and wild around the bonfire night for the counsellors. At least, it was for those of us lucky enough to be left behind while the children slept on a nearby island. Cindy had drawn one of the short straws, and off she went, sulking prettily. I decided that if I was going to make my move it would have to be tonight. I enlisted the aid of Ryan's room-mate Tony. Tony was also a stud, tall and dark, a super guy with a great sense of humour. But alas, he was not the current object of my fascination. Tony agreed to help me and together we planned an evening of fun for the unsuspecting blond hunk.

As the party progressed I made sure that I was the centre of attention; gyrating to the boom box and teasing all of the boys with my impromptu striptease.

When I was down to my bra and thong Tony suggested I offer myself up for body shots, an idea I greeted with enthusiasm. It didn't take long before I was spreadeagled on the ground with a bunch of horny guys licking salt off of my torso. Some of the female counsellors joined in on the fun, too. I think it was Sara who removed my bra to create enough room for everyone.

Not bothering with the salt, Tony immediately popped one of my cherry nipples into his mouth, encouraging Ryan to follow suit. I was in heaven. Tony's tongue was rough, like a cat's, as he lapped and bit at my spiked flesh. Ryan was gentler, slow swirling strokes, soft suction. My sex was soaked from the combination. There had to be at least five other people licking and sucking at my skin; I lost track, but I knew I was going to come soon. I just needed a little help.

"For Christ's sake, somebody touch my pussy!' I begged, whipping my head from side to side.

My thong disappeared instantly and I felt someone lapping at my engorged clit. I looked down to see Sara crouched between my legs, her red hair shining in the firelight. I felt two long fingers slide into my hot slit and she began to finger-fuck me, fast and hard, just the way I like it, all the while thrumming my clit with her talented tongue. I came quicker than I ever have in my life, bucking and hollering. Ryan moved up a little to cover my lips with his. Having his tongue thrusting into my mouth quieted my screams, and gave me something else to concentrate on as Sara licked me clean.

Everyone except Sara, Ryan and Tony had moved off a little to enjoy the show I was putting on. Campfire night was turning into a private orgy, with me as the main event. I couldn't have been happier.

"This is so fucking hot," panted Tony, releasing my nipple with an audible pop.

Ryan and I both looked up as he stood and shimmied out of his white shorts and orange tank top. When he was naked I found myself looking up at about seven inches of dark, beautiful, uncircumcised meat.

"Bring that here, baby," I moaned.

Tony grinned. "Come and get it, sweetheart."

When I tried to rise to the delicious temptation Ryan placed his hand on my stomach, holding me firm against the ground.

"I think I can beat that," he whispered huskily against my ear.

Sara sat up between my knees and was treated to an eyeful as Ryan stood and skimmed his shorts down. He definitely could beat that. A flared purple head, the size of a ripe plum, drooled down at me as Ryan flaunted his wares. His cock was circumcised, and at least nine inches long, thick and ropy with veins. I had never seen a dick that huge before. Saliva flooded my mouth as I gaped up at him. My cunt rippled in anticipation.

"Oh my God!" breathed Sara, her eyes riveted on Ryan's massive erection.

Sara . . . I'd managed to forget about her. She looked so sexy sitting there between my legs, her pixie face coated with my sticky juices that, after giving her a sloppy tongued kiss, I generously offered her the first shot at Ryan.

As she tried to wrap her lips around that purple monster I knelt behind her and untied her bikini top. Then I pulled her shorts and underwear off of her slim, freckled legs, instructing her softly to lift first one knee, and then the other. Sara hardly noticed, so intent was she on trying to do the impossible – deep throat Ryan. When she was naked I motioned to Tony that he should join me. He'd been looking a little neglected, standing there idly stroking his own length and watching his room-mate get blown. He hurried to comply.

When he came down beside me I pulled him into a hard embrace, running my hands over his muscular back and ass. Our mouths were frantic as we kissed, a hot tangle of aggressive, wet tongue. Tony gasped when I took his cock in hand and he fucked my fist hungrily, pre-come slicking the way. I pulled back and threw him a smug grin before I lay down and inserted my head between Sara's thighs. My hand never let go of his dick.

"OK, baby, show me how it's done," I moaned, as I tugged him towards Sara's puffy slit.

He straddled my body and let me place him at her slick little hole. Sara was groaning, slurping and bobbing over Ryan's tool.

I don't think she even knew we were there until Tony plunged into her sopping cleft.

What a beautiful sight!

His dark Italian cock stretched her plump pink pussy to almost impossible dimensions. The contrast between her ginger hair and his black curls, her hot pink sex and his dark brown one, was so unbearably erotic that I only had to flick my finger once across my clit before I was coming again in huge, shuddering waves of pleasure. I screamed and arched my back, almost bucking the lovers apart as I slammed into Tony's ass with my torso. This was enough to throw Sara forwards and knock Ryan right out of her mouth. Oops.

Ryan had been watching the proceedings with a keen interest and, instead of inserting himself back between Sara's willing lips, he came around the grinding couple, tugged me out from underneath my own personal sex show, and knelt between my thighs. Tossing my legs up over his shoulders he teased me with his thick cock, sliding it along my swollen folds, circling my hypersensitive clit with its silky head. I was mindless with desire, thrashing against him, grabbing his ass and trying to impale myself on the beautiful, hot length of him.

"Please, please, please . . ." The litany fell from my lips as I writhed beneath him.

"Fuck yeah," he grunted, placing his huge mushroom head at the entrance of my pulsing quim. "Beg me, you horny bitch!"

"Please . . . now . . . fuck me now!" I cried, taking my hands off of his ass to pinch and twist my nipples.

Ryan chuckled and slammed his fat cock into my dripping pussy. I screamed. It felt like I'd been torn apart. The pain was outstanding and I instantly vibrated through another mind-blowing orgasm. Ryan didn't give me a chance to recover, just kept pistoning into my ravaged sex. My clit was getting tugged down against his cock as he drove into me and the sensations were so intense that I feared I was going to black out from the rough pleasure/pain of massive over-stimulation.

The sound of Sara's climax, signalled by high squealing moans, momentarily distracted me from the delicious torture of being fucked by a horse. I tilted my head back to watch her let go.

It was awesome.

She was bent over with her head resting in the dirt and Tony was simply fucking her into oblivion, ramming into her like there was no tomorrow. He must have felt my eyes on him, though, because he looked up to catch my gaze. His smile was pure perversion. I yelped as my womb pulsed from the wickedness of that leer alone.

When Sara was through squealing, Tony slipped out of her, still magnificently hard. Sara collapsed boneless to the ground and Tony flipped her over, scooping up as much of her juices as he could gather into the palm of his hand. His eyes never left mine. When he'd gathered all he could, he turned towards me and Ryan.

Ryan's movements had slowed as he'd watched the show Sara and Tony were putting on. Now they stopped altogether as his friend came over to us. I lay there panting, grateful for the reprieve, and enjoying the hard, full sensation deep within my body.

"Hey, man, is there room for one more?" Tony asked Ryan.

Ryan smirked and agreed that there was. He dropped my legs from his shoulders, hauled me up in his strong arms and sat back on his heels. His prick slipped even higher inside my swollen pussy. Then he lifted me almost off of him, and that was no good, I wanted him buried inside me again, but when I tried to thrust myself back down, he held me still. That's when I felt Tony spreading Sara's juices all around my virgin asshole. I stopped trying to move, both excited and scared at the thought of what was going to happen next. I was pretty afraid when Tony pressed his fat cock head against my tight pucker, but he and Ryan held themselves absolutely still, letting me lower myself as gently as I needed to over their twitching poles.

I think that was very sweet of them.

I let my weight rest against Tony's chest and tugged Ryan's head down for a wet, open-mouthed kiss as I slowly, so slowly, slid down their cocks. When they were both buried to the hilt inside my body, they began to move in a slick, synchronized rhythm. It occurred to me that they seemed to have done this before. They were too darn coordinated.

That was my last coherent thought.

The feel of those two big boys rubbing together, separated by only the thinnest of membranes, sent me into orgiastic overload. I wrenched my head away from Ryan to scream my pleasure through the woods.

Tony laughed and doubled his pace, pulling my head back against his shoulder. "You're going to bring the Ranger, babe," he said, before plunging his tongue into my mouth.

I didn't fucking care. Let him come.

One of Tony's hands moved down my body to tickle my clit. Ryan's hands were busy at my tits, manhandling the small orbs, twisting my nipples until I thought he was going to rip them off, and all the while they kept going faster and faster, fucking me like animals.

It was brutal.

It was fantastic.

When my next orgasm hit I clamped down so hard on their cocks that they were held immobile. Ryan was the first to lose it.

"Oh fuck," he groaned, as my pussy milked his length, "I can't hold it, man."

"Go for it," grunted Tony. His breath was heavy against my neck, in my ear. He surged into my spasming ass again and again.

The feel of Ryan shooting his load high up against my womb cranked my orgasm up another notch. My body lolled between the two studs, twitching and shuddering helplessly. The pulsing spurts must have set Tony off, too, because it wasn't even a second later when he clamped his teeth onto my shoulder and let loose, pounding viciously into my stretched and aching hole.

The surreal sensation of all that hot liquid flooding my ass sent me round the loop one more time, but by this point all I could do was whimper while my body flopped around, quite beyond my control. As Ryan slipped out of me Tony lost his balance and fell forwards. My breath whooshed out when Tony's weight landed on my back. Ryan grunted at the combined attack and fell backwards. We fell with him. It was vaguely uncomfortable, but the three of us were too nerveless to move right away.

At first, the only sounds I could hear were the crackle of the fire and our own laboured breaths. Then the clapping started, followed up with some wolf whistles. Tony chuckled and rolled off me, then climbed to his feet to bow to the mostly naked assembly. Almost everyone had separated into their own small fuck groups, but I guess our threesome had still been the centre stage, so to speak. I ignored the drunken crowd, content to just lie there comatose on Ryan's body.

Tony bent down and lifted me into his arms, nixing that plan. "The lusty lady will be performing again in twenty minutes, people." More hollering and whistles. "Only this time it will be a twosome," he whispered, before taking my mouth in the most unbelievably erotic kiss. His tongue was liquid sex as it traced my mouth, flicking against my upper lip suggestively, before thrusting inside in a wild rhythm I recognized all too well. "I've wanted you since the first day I saw you, babe," Tony broke away to say, "but you couldn't seem to tear your eyes away from the beach boy. So tonight, I thought I'd share in on a little of his action . . . hope you didn't mind."

I lay limp in his arms and gazed up at him in surprise. Did he really need to ask? As I was about to respond, Ryan gained his feet.

"That was great, babe," he said, giving my shoulder a friendly squeeze on his way over to Sara's current threesome.

I guess he hadn't had his fill of her yet. Rather than disappointment, I felt only satisfaction at the sight of his retreating back.

Don't get me wrong, he was great. And both of them together were lethal. I can honestly say I've never had better sex in my life. But I found myself hurrying Tony along as he carried me down to the lake for a quick clean up before our next show.

Turns out tall, dark and handsome flicks my switches, too. Who knew?

CHANGING BOUNDARIES

Rowan, Johannesburg

I see the statement once again in a magazine I'm reading and it takes me back to our courting days: "I'm not a virgin, I don't cook and if you think I'm going to take that thing in my mouth you can think again."

Jenni had actually said that to me, soon after we became an item. I think it must be a kind of policy summary for single girls.

We were getting along well, enjoying each other's company and the sex was great. I was beginning to think Jenni had long-term potential. She was attractive with a slender figure, small breasts, long, shapely legs and for me, sexiest of all, was her look of wholesome respectability. That the look was purely super-ficial was an added bonus.

My reaction must have shown. Her "If you don't like it you know what to do" showed a touch of overconfidence, I thought.

She'd got it from one of those women's magazines. I'd read it too. "Well, I didn't expect you to be a virgin and you can always learn to cook. It's the other one that worries me."

"Surely two out of three isn't bad?"

I had to laugh. "It's not good. You got a fail on the important one."

"Well, that's my boundary."

"Why put it out of bounds?"

"Because it's distasteful."

"Hmm. Well, if that's your boundary I suppose I have to respect it."

"Of course."

Smug complacency was creeping in. It was time to be cruel. "But 'not ever' is too long for me, Jen. I'm not going the rest of my life without that sublime experience now and again."

That got rid of the smug complacency but it took a moment for the words to sink in. "Are you dumping me?"

"No. Let's just say it's by mutual agreement."

"You bastard!"

"Don't be like that, Jen. We should just acknowledge that we're incompatible."

"No. It's blackmail."

"Please, Jen. Isn't it better to –"

"If I don't let you stick your prick in my mouth you won't go out with me." Her voice was becoming shrill.

She was happy enough for me to stick it in her cunt, I thought. I was starting to get irritated with her. I was getting another side of sweet little Jennikins.

"If that's not blackmail then what is?"

"Tell me, Jen. When you said 'not ever' did you mean it literally?"

"Yes, I did."

"Well then."

"Well then what? It's not meant for going in a girl's mouth. It's unnatural."

"Fair enough. I'll never put my prick in your mouth ever. Other girls think differently."

"Why are you so keen on it?"

"Have you ever thought how short a man's climax is compared to what a woman can experience?"

She obviously hadn't; not until then when she did think about it. I knew for a fact that Jenni was multi-orgasmic, provided I kept going long enough.

"Yes. I suppose so. So what?"

"Well, that's the way men are made and you can't change it. But with oral sex there's a special intense quality to the climax that makes up for its brevity."

"Oh." She was thinking about it.

"I don't know if it's the same for all guys but it certainly is for me. In some ways it's almost too much. A man only needs it now and again but it is special. Fond of you as I am, it's not a pleasure that I would deny myself. Not for ever."

That had given her something to think about. Of course it was mostly bullshit but a blow job is a particularly nice way to come and it had been all too rare an event in my life to date. Besides I think any woman worth her salt should give her man a blow job now and again.

"I didn't know that. You may have a point."

"No. I'm not going to force you to do anything you find distasteful. Not every girl does. Some even like doing it. They see it as a special gift from them to their man."

She looked like she didn't believe me.

"Look, a prick isn't dirty or unclean. Especially seeing as my mother had my foreskin cut off for you. Perhaps you tried it on someone who wasn't up to the mark with his personal hygiene?"

She looked shy. "I did try it once and gagged on it."

"Pity. You should make sure that the guy is lying on his back so you can control the penetration."

She was thinking frantically. Her hopes of a white wedding were fading fast. If we broke up she'd have to start from scratch all over again and she didn't want to do that. "Look, this is all something new and I need to think about it. Can you give us both some time before you . . . you do anything we might both regret?"

"All right, Jenni, but know that I mean what I say. If you really don't ever want to do it it's better to acknowledge it now. A messy divorce in a few years' time would be a lot worse." There was a hint of marriage implicit in that last remark. Perhaps that would help swing the balance.

I wouldn't have been so hard-assed about it except that she'd been so cocky saying she'd never do it. She'd brought it up in the first place as if she were challenging me. At heart I'm a nice guy and in the past I'd often let girls win those little challenges they come up with. They don't appreciate it. They think you're soft, not man enough to control them. They don't really want their man to lose the challenges they set. Now that I'd confronted her with it, Jenni was reconsidering her "immutable" boundary.

I put down the magazine and smiled. The compromise we came up with had been on special occasions: birthdays and anniversaries, Christmas and St Valentine's.

Jenni's happy about it too. As she brags to her friends, "My husband never forgets a birthday or our anniversary."

HUBBY'S BIRTHDAY TREAT

Susy, Buckinghamshire

It was my husband's birthday and as he has everything he could possibly want or need I was struggling with ideas for a present. One night we were lying in bed watching one of our favourite porn movies when he stated how horny it was watching me sucking his hard cock while watching two women licking and fingering each other's pussies. This gave me an idea.

Now other than the occasional fumble at school I have always been straight. Yet there is something about the shape of a woman's body that turns me on. I love it when my husband has been licking my wet cunt and then shoves his tongue into my mouth. I get so hot and wet sucking my juices from his face, or his cock. I found a local adult friend finder website and created an account. I thought I would have problems finding a woman who was prepared to join a couple in the bedroom who wouldn't want to be fucked by the husband. I was wrong. I placed the advert with the headline "Lesbian wanted must be willing to join couple and love the taste of come . . ." Within two days I had over twenty responses. I looked through the photos and found one woman who got me wet just looking at her. The thought of having my first real lesbian experience with my husband joining in got me so hot I had to thrust two fingers into my hot wet cunt and make myself come. I couldn't resist tasting my fingers after I'd come.

I emailed the woman, Jo, and after a couple of emails discussing what we would both like and dislike our emails became hotter and hotter until one night we met up online and were having such a filthy conversation I jumped on my husband, taking his cock deep into my mouth as soon as he walked in through the door. Before he had even taken his coat off I was bent over the stairs with his hot cock pounding my dripping cunt.

His birthday arrived and I had booked a hotel for the night halfway between our home and Jo's. The plan was that my hubby and I would go out for a meal and then we would go back to our room where I would instruct my hubby to go take a shower and make sure his cock was clean for a great sucking. I would say that I was going downstairs to get a bottle of champagne.

Before I went I decided that to be sure he was in for a real surprise I would gently tie his wrists to the bedpost with some silk scarves and blindfold him. I told him to lie there and wait for me to return. He did object slightly, but when I told him that if he did this for me I would suck his hard cock with champagne in my mouth he agreed. This is one of his favourite kinds of blow job. He loves the way I swill the bubbles around the head of his cock.

I left him alone tied to the bed and went to the bar to collect not only the champagne but Jo as well. We kissed deeply as soon as the lift doors had closed. This was our first meeting in person and neither of us was disappointed. It took all of our self-control not to strip each other in the lift. As we entered the room Jo was silent as she had promised. I told my hubby I had the champagne and that I hoped he was ready for the best birthday present ever. I dropped my clothes to the floor and Jo did the same. As we both stood there in nothing but our stockings and basques I could feel my cunt getting hot and wet. I took a mouthful of champagne and went down on my hubby. He started to moan as I swirled the bubbles around the head of his cock with my tongue. I gently stroked his balls and rubbed his asshole with a finger of my other hand. He began to fuck my face. At that moment I felt Jo kneel down on the edge of the bed and begin to rub my clit. I almost came in an instant. It was so hot having my face fucked and my clit rubbed by another woman. I let out a deep moan. This really excited him as I felt his huge cock grow even larger. He commented that although sucking him normally turned me on it never usually got me this hot.

I decided it was time to give him his true birthday present. I took my mouth away from his cock and kissed up his body, holding his hard member in my hand until I reached his face. I kissed him deep and hard. At that moment I felt Jo insert two fingers deep into my soaking wet cunt. I reached up and untied my hubby's wrists and slowly untied his blindfold. I then said, "Happy Birthday!" His face looked confused for a moment, then he saw Jo as she stood up beside the bed, grabbed my hips and turned me over. She shoved her face between my legs and began lapping at my cunt hungrily. I saw the look of confusion change to surprise then passion within a couple of seconds. I begged him to fuck my face hard but not to come as I had other plans for his gorgeous juices.

After a few minutes of him fucking my face while watching Jo licking me out, the combination of my moans and the visual effect of watching another woman eat his wife's pussy was almost too much for him. He was almost begging me to let him come. I told him I wanted him to fuck me hard while he watched Jo sit on my face. He didn't need to be asked twice. Before I knew it he had turned me over onto my knees and was shoving my face into Jo's cunt. At the same time he parted my ass cheeks and thrust his hard cock into my dripping wet pussy. He fucked me so hard I thought his balls would vanish up there as well. I licked Jo's cunt and fingered her until we all exploded in a fit of come within seconds of one another. It was the hardest I had come in a long time and I could tell by the way his juice was dripping out of my cunt even while his cock was still in there, that he had really enjoyed it too.

Once we had all recovered he turned to me and told me that was a great birthday present. I told him it wasn't over yet. I kissed him deeply and turned over to lie on my back. I could tell that kissing me while I tasted of another woman was turning him on again. Little did he know there was more in store for future birthdays!

PAPERBACK RIDER

Karl, Alabama

Back when I entertained delusions of becoming a successful
novelist, I often visited the local library for "research". I felt at
ease among the shelves of books I had no intention of reading.
Usually I sat at the table nearest the librarian's desk, a notebook
opened before me, and I'd stare at Rose sitting prim and proper
behind her desk.

While she read her romance novel I'd note the way she'd rub
her thighs together during what must have been the erotic
passages. I liked the way her long brown hair was severely
pulled back and wrapped up in a complicated concoction of pins
and barrettes. Her secretarial-style glasses teetered precariously
off the tip of her nose as though contemplating a suicide leap.

I'd be lying if I said she wasn't ordinarily my type. Guys like
me can't afford a type. I'm the sexual equivalent of flypaper. I
stick whatever sticks.

I began trying to impress her with the books I borrowed.
Dostoevsky, Hamsun, Gogol, Céline. Didn't even raise an
eyebrow. Hunter S. Thompson, Bukowski, Nersesian. I kept
waiting for Rose to compliment my choice in authors. Or, at the
very least, take note of the erection straining against denim.
Nothing.

Every day I sat across from Rose, pen poised above paper,
and fantasized about her approaching me (always as I affixed
the words "THE END" to a manuscript of blockbuster proportions) and saying, "So that's your new national book award
candidate of a novel, eh?" and I'd say, "Yep." She'd say, "I
heard six production studios are battling for the movie rights,"

and I'd modestly say, "You're goddamn right they are." Then she'd raise her burgundy skirt revealing an utter lack of undergarments or pubic hair. She'd climb the armrests of my chair and settle her gaping pussy on my face.

Fuck yeah! The fantasy struck me as inexplicably attainable. All I had to do was finish the goddamn novel and the rest would fall into place.

A month later, I'd managed to set down another 5,000 words, doubling my word count. Another 90,000 words and Rose would be mine. I wondered, Did she really shave her puss or go au naturel? And did it really matter to me at all?

Such were my thoughts that I scarcely registered the arrival of closing time. Having not had the chance to pick any books to impress her with, I simply grabbed a handful of paperbacks that had been left on the table next to mine by a woman much too heavy to stick to my flypaper. I didn't recognize the authors. I wouldn't be reading them anyway.

I set the books on the desk and handed Rose my library card. She raised her stamp and hesitated.

"Oh wow," Rose said. "You're a Stella Rider fan? I adore her Harlequins."

Harlequins? What the hell? I glanced at the book. The cover depicted a dashing pirate with the abdomen of a Bowflex endorser about to passionately embrace a scullery wench with hair like wildfire and a bosom of Californian proportions.

"Yeah. I'm a Harlequin fan from way back."

Her hard candy eyes melted into pools of luxuriant fudge. "Have you read the Forbidden Desires series? I swear I had to take a cold shower every ten minutes reading those books."

I thought about her pale thighs subtly massaging each other. What does she do in the privacy of her bedroom? As she talked I noticed the glint of metal from her tongue piercing. Outstanding. Women don't get their tongues pierced because they like to sit on the couch, Friday nights, reading the adventures of Cervais the lusty swashbuckler.

"No. Haven't had that pleasure."

"Omigod. You don't know what you're missing. Let me lock up real quick and I'll read you a few of my favourite passages."

She returned five minutes later with a handcart brimming with crack-spined literary treasures bearing such titles as *Forbidden Lust*, *Forbidden Fruits*, *Forbidden Toejam*. I'm gonna be here all night, I thought with a sort of manic glee, the epicentre of which was located between my forbidden legs.

We sat facing each other, our knees touching, at my table. The reading lamp cast an intimate circle of illumination around us. Her favourite passages included a lot of "throbbing manhoods" and the "licking of the flesh envelopes of love". Her soft voice could have made the telephone book sound sexy. As she read her thighs undulated like the tide. I could smell her musky scent, an undercurrent of her wetness beneath the waves of lavender wafting from her pale, smooth skin.

My hands brushed the outside of her knees. She opened her legs and slid down until only the top of her ass touched the seat of her chair.

As Rose continued reading the amorous exploits of Avery the well-hung aviator and Stash, the progressive airplane mechanic, I knelt between her legs, moving her skirt over her hips as I kissed my way up her inner thigh. She wore no panties, easy access to her joy button being imperative given the amount of eroticism she read during the course of her day.

Nearing her pussy was akin to crawling towards an open stove. Her heat baked my face, causing the tube of dough between my legs to rise. A barbell matching the piercing in her tongue lanced her clit hood. I sucked the jewellery into my mouth savouring the metallic taste. Her breath caught in her throat, a moment of silence like the inhalation before a scream, then she went back to reading.

"Stasha gasped with immense pleasure as Avery lugged out his perfectly proportioned ten-inch monkey wrench of bliss."

Ten inches? Fucking bullshit Harlequin setting me up for failure.

Her pussy, plump and engorged, two sizes too large for the rest of her body, seemed to pulsate against my mouth. She looked as though she'd been whacked between the legs with a fireman's axe and I buried my face in her wound, fanning the flames burning white hot within her.

My left hand curved around her leg, fingers splaying open her labes, exposing her erect clit. I break-danced my tongue against her bean as I fucked her with the index finger of my right hand, letting my pinkie finger dip into her asshole.

The words ejaculated from her lips in whispery gasps. "Oh . . . uh . . . throbbing . . . manhood . . . moist . . . flower . . . Hoboken."

Rose's hips contracted, raising her off the chair. I bore her weight with my chin and two fingers. She dropped the book and palmed the back of my head, pressing my face deeper against her cunt as though she wished to envelope my head with her pussy lips in a sort of reverse birth.

She came violently, and I could have sworn I heard a gurgling sound coming from her plumbing as she flooded my face with her juices. I rose up for air after being submerged for something like fifteen minutes. I eat so much pussy I've grown a pair of gills to adapt. Check behind my ears sometime if you don't believe me.

Rose reached down and pulled me up by my slippery chin. Our lips and tongue greeted each other before she went licking her come off my lower face.

"I love the way I taste," she said.

I'd long since destroyed my taste buds with a steady diet of corn liquor so I had to take her word for it.

"Read to me while I suck your cock," she ordered.

I didn't feel much like reading but feared I'd miss out on the blow job if I disobeyed. I chose *Forbidden Planet* from the stack. I opened it in the middle.

"The alien princess withdrew the spaceman's antenna from his aluminium pants and began polishing his helmet with her four tongues."

Rose licked the wet spot of pre-come on the denim jeans. Already I began to stutter. She unbuttoned my pants and yanked them down to my ankles. My dick bounced with the sudden motion, tapping against her spectacles. Her lips smiled against my tightening nut sack as she juggled my balls with her tongue.

She dribbled saliva up my shaft. Her tongue slathered up and down my cock, flicking across the circumcision scar. The stud in her tongue traced the engorged veins, feeling like the tip of a ballpoint pen scribbling happy faces all over my fuck stick.

"Purple . . . vagina . . . Uranus . . . so hot."

Enough. I threw the book on the handcart and knocked down the stacks blanketing the surface with paperbacks. I raised Rose up by her armpits, her mouth breaking suction with an audible pop. I sat her down on the bed of books. She unclasped her bra and leaned back allowing her breasts to loll.

Gripping her by the back of her knees and spreading her legs the wingspan of my arms, I eased myself into her incredibly tight pussy. Her vaginal walls constricted around me with each thrust. Her last boyfriend must have been hung like a cashew. Or perhaps she only dated Orientals.

Rose gritted her teeth as her cunt slowly expanded to accommodate my . . . uh . . . ten inches. Her tits bounced like pom-poms, cheering me on as I donkey-konged her puss. As we settled into a rhythm, I rocked the handcart with my foot letting it do the work for me. It allowed my hands the chance to roam like sex-crazed monks exploring the countryside of her body.

The sound of my balls slapping her ass was as loud as cannonade in the silence of the book sanctuary. Her groans and murmurs of pleasure like shouts in a monastery. We came simultaneously, silencing each other's cries of passion with deep tongue kisses. I pulled out, expelling come, mine and hers, down her ass crack, puddling onto *Forbidden Research* beneath her natal cleft. We used pages from *Forbidden Deformities* to wipe off with.

"So," Rose asked once we regained our breath, "what's this novel of yours about?"

"It's called *Vows Of Silence*. It's about a nun who quits the convent because she falls in love with a mime. So she enrols in mime school hoping to win his heart with pantomime."

"So do they live happily ever after or do they just fuck and run?"

"I don't know. I'm at the part now where the church sends out an albino assassin to kill them."

FLICKING THROUGH THE PAGES

Louise, Swansea

I have always been happy around books. As a little girl I loved the smell of a new book as you peeled it open and the sight of black words on a white page still does my heart good. This was an innocent pleasure until I reached young adulthood where my love of books developed into an interesting erotic quirk.

More and more as a young literature student I took to frequenting second-hand bookshops. I had texts to buy and a growing interest in writing and so I would spend many happy hours browsing the old volumes and newish paperbacks. I don't know what it was, but the places began to have an effect on me. Maybe it was the sheer mass of ideas contained in those shelves (I've always been a bit of a brain-fucker) or the aroma of ageing pages and cool, dry paper. Whichever, at some point, I began to get aroused purely by being in these shops. I would walk home in a slight daze, not knowing what to do with myself. I must add that this was nothing to do with the sexual content of the books. I love a bit of erotica as much as the next girl but the effect simply came from the books themselves. It was quite peculiar but very pervasive.

The first time things came to a head, I had come into this one shop out of the rain. My clothes were slightly damp and the books smelled green and grassy. I was lurking amongst the warren of ceiling-high, library-like shelves reading a collection of short stories when the usual erotic buzz of the place became overwhelming. I replaced the book and slipped into the small customer loo at the back of the shop. At first I just stood against the wall in silence and squeezed my breasts through the damp material. When this wasn't enough I pinched my cold nipples through the cotton of my bra until they stood out sore and hard. Before I knew it I had my right fingers in my knickers and my left hand inside my bra and I was quietly, firmly masturbating. As each fresh wave of pleasure developed between my legs I told myself that I would stop in a minute but soon felt the slipping sands of a climax beneath my feet. It was a soft, muted orgasm, dizzying because I was standing up. I walked home with a shocked smile on my face.

I visited that loo a few more times, on one occasion pulling up my sweater and cami top and baring my breasts under the strip light, watching myself come in the mirror, my hand gyrating beneath my underwear's straining nylon. However, after an accidentally noisy orgasm I decided that the obsession must stop. I didn't visit the shop for months and took a different bus to avoid it.

Then, one day, I was walking alone in the old neighbourhood when a coincidence struck me. I had, the night before, trimmed my pubic hair for the first time. I had previously kept a luxuriant bush of springy hair but in a fit of curiosity I had taken scissors and a razor to my curls and left behind a fine covering of hair which, while modest, showed a good deal of interesting detail. I had had some good fun the night before with a hand mirror, investigating my new look. It seemed to me that my newly styled pussy deserved to be introduced to the books, so I slipped inside. In the bookshop loo I raised my short skirt and took down my knickers to thigh level. My pussy looked lovely. I even teased apart the folds to see the pink pearl of my clit gleaming there amongst the short, newly shorn hairs. Then I had an outrageous idea. I arranged my clothes and with a beating heart explored the shop. I seemed to be the only browser in the labyrinth of discreet shelves and the owner was eating crisps, lost in a police procedural novel. I took myself off to the depths of the shop and found a spot I liked. There I bunched my skirt up around my hips and dropped my already moist knickers. I breathed in the raunchy scent of the books and, leaning against a shelf of hardbacks (I think I may have licked one of the spines), set to work.

It felt incredible, rubbing my cunt like that in public but at the same time in private, surrounded by these hot, dangerous volumes, the leather warm and sensuous on my bottom. I took my time, sometimes standing with my feet wide apart, once propping one booted leg up on a shelf to spread my legs further, masturbating in slow, hard circles, my cunt oozing creamy juice. A particularly good position was squatting, my bare bottom all but touching the dusty floorboards, my pussy pinched together around my rotating fingers. Sometimes I dipped in deep to my own warm honey; sometimes I tickled my rosebud with feathery strokes. In the end I came on my back, knees bent in the air, the heels of my boots pricking my bum cheeks. The orgasm was ferocious. I tasted it in my mouth before it arrived beneath my fingers and I remember flopping like a stranded fish as it tore through me, knocking the breath from my body. It travelled right down my legs into my boots and made my wrists tingle. Goodness only knows if I stayed quiet. I have no recollection. Dazed and seeing stars I arranged my clothing and left the shop on wobbly legs, saying goodbye to the (hopefully) oblivious bookseller, licking my sticky fingers as I went.

HARD WORKER

Kyle, Bellmead

A few weeks after I turned eighteen, my aunt – my stepfather's younger sister – came to visit and my parents put her in my room while I was stuck sleeping on the couch in the den.

In my haste one afternoon I pushed open my bedroom door without knocking. My aunt slowly turned to face me. Her towel drifted to the floor and her nude body glistened with water where she had failed to dry herself. She smiled, but said nothing.

I swallowed hard and backed out of the room, pulling the door closed as I went.

At dinner that night, I felt her feet on my shins, her bare toes grasping and pulling at the dark hair on my legs. I pulled my legs away, tucking them under my chair, and a moment later I felt her foot in my crotch.

Above the table, nothing seemed amiss. My aunt continued discussing her job prospects with my stepfather and my mother passed rolls to each of us.

My cock grew hard from my aunt's toe massage and I reached into my lap to stop her. I grabbed her toes and bent them backwards. She flinched in pain, but I doubt anyone else noticed.

When my hand returned from its trip into my lap, I held my napkin. I used it to wipe the corners of my mouth then I returned it to my lap. By then, my aunt's foot had returned to her side of the table.

The next day, I found myself alone in the house with my aunt. My parents were both at work and I was getting ready to go to my afternoon class at the junior college. My aunt returned earlier than expected from a job interview. I'd been sleeping on the couch ever since her arrival but my stuff was still my/her bedroom. I was standing in my room, wearing only a pair of boxer shorts while digging through my closet for a clean pair of jeans.

"My, aren't you a sight," she said, startling me.

I turned to find her standing at the bedroom door.

I held my jeans in front of me.

She stepped into my bedroom. "You've been avoiding me."

I shrugged.

My aunt took another step and stood so close I could feel the heat radiating from her body, could smell the delicate aroma of her perfume. She lowered her voice, almost whispering as she traced my jawline with the tip of her finger, "Do you think I bite?"

I shook my head.

"Of course not," she whispered huskily as she leaned in close. Her warm breath tickled my ear. "Something as tasty as you I'd want to lick."

She leaned even closer, pressing one breast against my arm, and then she licked the circumference of my ear with the tip of her tongue.

She used her fingertip to draw a line down my chest to my boxers. By then my cock was rock hard. She slipped her hand under the waistband and wrapped it around my cock. I was so surprised, I dropped my jeans.

My aunt released her grip on my cock, then hooked her fingers in the waistband of my boxers and pulled them down as she dropped to her knees. I felt her warm breath on my cock, then my eyes widened in surprise when she traced the entire length of my cock with the tip of her tongue from my balls to the mushroom cap. By then, a glistened drop of pre-come crowned my cock head and my aunt deftly licked it off.

She was still dressed for the interview, looking like a bright young businesswoman, but what she was doing to me was all pleasure. She took the head of my cock in her mouth and then wrapped her fist around my stiff shaft. She began pistoning her fist up and down while she caressed my cock head with her tongue.

I didn't know what to do. I wanted to grab the back of her head and pump my cock into her mouth. Instead, I braced myself on the closet door frame.

My heart began beating faster and my breath came in ragged gasps, and then I couldn't stop myself. I came in my aunt's mouth, squirting warm jism against the back of her throat. She swallowed every drop and then licked my cock clean.

She stood, looked me in the eye, and said, "Aren't you late for class?"

"Yeah – I – yeah," I stammered. I quickly pulled on my clothes and went to class, but my mind certainly wasn't on Introduction to Sociology, that's for sure.

That night, when my aunt's foot appeared in my crotch, kneading my rapidly swelling cock through the material of my jeans, I didn't push it away. I just smiled and continued discussing my grades.

That night, after my parents and my aunt had gone to bed, I lay on the couch tossing and turning, unable to get comfortable. I must have finally dozed off because at a quarter past two, I felt someone's hand on my shoulder, shaking me gently.

I opened my eyes to find my aunt bent over me. She pressed one finger to my lips to keep me from speaking, then took my hand and led me outside to my pickup. I parked in the back, between the fence and the garage where no one could see the truck from the house or the street. We climbed up into the bed area of the cabin where she had already spread a blanket from the linen closet.

She stripped off her thin robe, and lay naked in the back of my truck, her knees in the air and spread wide. I quickly tugged off my sweatpants, revealing my erect cock, and then I was on top of her, the head of my cock trapped against her abdomen.

We kissed, deep and hard. I sucked on her breasts, and I slipped a hand between her thighs to stroke the long slit of her swollen pussy lips.

"Fuck me now," she whispered hoarsely.

Then I was on top of her again and she guided my cock into her hot hole. She hooked her legs behind mine and grabbed my ass, pulling my cock deep inside her. I fucked her hard and fast, causing the truck to bounce up and down on its springs.

"Oh . . . God . . . yes," she whispered. Then she came, her entire body rigid, and she muffled her face against my chest so her scream didn't wake the neighbourhood.

I kept drilling into her until I came. With one last, powerful thrust, I buried my cock as deep inside her throbbing pussy as it would go, and then I filled her with hot jism.

I collapsed on top of her, barely able to breathe, and stayed there until my cock finally softened and slid free.

She kissed me on the forehead, pulled on her robe and returned to the house. It was twenty minutes before I could even move.

Well, my aunt found a job a couple of weeks later and moved into her own place before the semester ended. I sleep in my own room again, but my parents seem real proud that I visit my aunt a couple of times a week and help her do things around the house.

She tells my parents I'm a real hard worker.

GOLDEN GIRL

Tim, Burlington

I was taking a leak in the urinal, when a woman came out of a stall, got down on her knees next to me, and asked, "Do you mind?"

I was so shocked my stream cut off like someone had stepped on my hose. "What!?"

She had long, straight black hair, large brown eyes, bronze skin, and was wearing a gold bikini. She unfastened the top part, baring her pert, golden breasts. "Pee on me, please," she said.

I stared into her eyes, expecting to find nobody home. But they were sparkling with assurance, like she knew exactly what she was doing and, in her mind, why she was doing it. And that for her this was not an unusual request.

But it was unusual for me – way, way unusual. So far off the beaten path I was lost in the jungle. I twisted my head around, figuring maybe it was some kind of joke, or set-up.

But there was no one else I could see in that men's room. Just two other empty urinals and five empty stalls judging by the silence, a concrete floor with a drain in the middle, concrete walls, and a peaked wooden roof open at the sides. The place was entirely vacant, except for one stunned man standing there with his dick in his hand and one attractive, bare-chested woman kneeling next to him, waiting to be pissed on.

"You . . . You want me to ur-i-nate on you?" I asked, my throat gone dry as sand.

I'm a thirty-five-year-old accountant from a stable home with a stable job in a stable relationship with a fairly stable woman living in a medium-sized Midwestern city with a reputation for stability. Things like women asking me to pee on them just didn't happen – not even in the filthiest of my fantasies.

"Please," the woman replied, smiling. She cupped her breasts. "On my chest and face, if you don't mind."

She really meant it, wanted it. This was no joke, gag, or set-up. This was actually happening – to me. The gentle beach breeze drifting in through the open roof and the muted voices of normal people out on the beach, splashing around in the water, made the whole situation even more surreal.

Humdrum scenes of work and church and home flashed through my mind, of my parents and girlfriend waiting for me with a picnic lunch out on the public beach, as I stood there in my bare feet and pulled-down swim trunks gazing at the smiling, half-naked woman. Until the two bottles of ice water I'd downed on the hot summer's day – which I'd been anxiously draining from my overloaded system before the incredible interruption – claimed my attention again.

I shuffled around and faced the woman, pointed and pissed.

"Oh, God, yes!" she cried, taking my stream of warm pee on her chest, all over her breasts.

I don't why I did it. I don't know where I found the courage to do it. But I did it. She'd asked for it, and I'd obliged. And now I watched her shift rapturously back and forth on her knees, bathing in the golden shower from my cock.

I doused her tits, as she clutched and squeezed them, rolled her burnt-sugar nipples in the strong spray of my urine. "My face! Pee on my face!" she exclaimed. And I automatically raised my cock, catching her full in the pretty face.

Eyes and mouth closed, head wagging back and forth, lips spread wide in a grin of delight, she washed her face in my sheeting stream of pee. And then she opened her eyes, and mouth – wide – and I sprayed directly into her mouth.

She stuck out her tongue and my piss filled her mouth, gushed back out again, ran all over her chin and chest. My hand shook on my cock, shook my cock, splashing her nose and forehead with my water-coloured urine, before catching her in the mouth again. I'd never seen anything like it, never experienced anything so wild and dirty in all my thirty-five years of mundane living.

And when her throat started working, and she began drinking my piss, my cock grew hard in my hand.

My whole body shook, cock stiffening, straightening, balls tingling, as the woman eagerly gulped and gulped my urine. I had to adjust my aim, but the piss kept coming. Out of a cock gone fully erect and pulsing, the situation was sexual. She slid a hand into her bikini bottom and started rubbing her wettened pussy.

It had finally dawned on me just how wickedly erotic the whole thing was – a man spraying his hot bodily fluid all over a beautiful woman's face and chest, watching her revel in it, rub it into her gleaming skin, drink it in and make it a part of her. My sexual path had never strayed beyond missionary up until that point; but as I pissed all over the glistening, swallowing, stroking golden girl, I became turned on like never before, the sheer blazing wantonness and unexpectedness of it all shaking me to my sexual core.

I tentatively stroked my cock. Then not so tentatively, started fisting my throbbing organ.

The woman shuddered – with orgasm – her fingers flying in her soaked bikini, her mouth open and gulping and gasping. And that's when the urine stopped and the semen started. Bursting out of my cap and splashing onto her piss-drenched face and chest, into her open mouth.

I came ferociously, ecstasy coursing through my cock and body and being. And when it was over all too quickly, I staggered backwards, weak and wasted, the gleaming babe rising to her feet and stating simply, "Thank you."

She refastened her top, gave me one last warm, liquid smile, and then was gone, out the door of the men's washroom/change room.

Leaving me with one radically different perspective on sex, and life.

IN THE DEEP DARK

Sabina, Oakland

I wanted to tell you of the great changes in my life recently. I have become a submissive. I have been thinking a lot lately about my submissiveness and I want to tell you how it all got started. I was fortunate enough to encounter a man who took the time to get to know me, who observed me and saw what I really needed to release my deepest sexual nature and thus reach a level of erotic pleasure unknown to me up until that time. We had been meeting, and had already had a few increasingly intense erotic encounters when one day my whole world changed, like a door opening before me that I could not help but enter.

I was at work and I got a call. It was from him and, as soon as I heard his deep commanding voice, my pussy began to flow with wetness. He said, "Listen to me carefully. Make an excuse, leave work immediately but first step into the restroom and take off your panties, your pantyhose and your bra. Make sure you have a dress or skirt on. Then get into your car and drive to this address, park and go inside, look around, and you will find me. Be there at 2 p.m. sharp and don't keep me waiting." I started to say something, to ask a question but his voice stopped me. "Be quiet, do not ask anything, just be there," then I heard a click and he hung up.

I immediately complied with all his instructions. I went to the bathroom and I removed my panties, my bra and my pantyhose and stuffed them in my purse. I was already trembling with desire and anticipation. I got my car from the office garage and I drove to the address I had written down, which turned out to be a ratty old adult movie theatre in a run-down part of town. As I parked, I was nervous and hoping I hadn't fucked up and written down the wrong address. Also I was really apprehensive because I felt embarrassed to go into a place like that alone. I bought a ticket from the one bored and half-asleep ticket seller who perked up a bit when he noticed that I had no bra restraining my ample breasts. His hungry eyes on my body would ordinarily have been distasteful to me, but somehow they became part of the excitement building within me.

I proceeded inside, with heart pounding. The one I was to meet was not in the lobby, so I entered the theatre itself. It was very, very dark in there and the loud soundtrack of the XXX movie on the screen filled the room with loud moans and high squealing as some white woman was being fucked deep in her ass by a huge and very dark black man with an enormous dick. I stood just inside the door until my eyes adjusted to the darkness so I could search the room with my eyes and find where he was sitting. As I surveyed the room I noticed that there were only one or two men in the front centre section of the theatre and they seemed totally absorbed in the action on the screen. It was mid-afternoon on a weekday so not many patrons were there.

Finally my eyes spotted his familiar form in the far back corner of the theatre and I really started trembling then; my pussy was pouring juices down my inner thighs as I walked over towards him, my thighs sliding against each other making a wet slithery sound. I made my way down the aisle and then entered the long row and sidled my way to where he sat and I sat down next to him. I said nothing, nor did I look at him yet. I simply waited, with heart pounding. Then I heard his voice say, in a low whisper, "Well, I will say this for you, Sabina, you are on time. I like that." I smiled and was glad that he was pleased. His hand reached over and slid under my skirt and up my leg into my pussy, where, as he stroked me for a while, he could feel how moist and hot I was. "Yes, your eager white cunt is certainly ready for my dick," he said, and then took his hand out of my pussy and spread his own legs apart. He told me, "Now, I want you to kneel between my legs, bitch, unzip my pants, take out that black dick you want to suck so badly and get to it. I want you to lick and suck that cock until I tell you to stop, you nasty cunt."

I knelt on the floor. It was dirty and nasty and sticky down there and I could feel it on my knees but I didn't care. I would do anything he asked me to, I wanted his dick so badly. I unzipped his pants and pulled them back and away from his dick so they didn't get wet and took out that beautiful black cock. It was only semi-hard as of yet but I knew just what to do to have it as hard as a rock in no time. I knew that he loved to have my wet stiff tongue wrapping itself all around the head of his dick, flicking and tonguing right under the rim of it and then sucking the head of it up into my mouth. So far I was just sucking hard on the head of his cock while my saliva drooled down the sides so my hand, grasping the shaft, was slick and slid up and down easily to excite him. Then I stretched my wet lips and began to lower my face onto his dick so more and more of it entered my mouth and it went deeper into my throat. He grabbed my hair and pulled handfuls of it hard while I sucked and gagged on his dick. It was getting so fucking hard and his head was thrown back onto the back of the seat and he was moaning in pleasure. At first he was quiet as if not to arouse the attention of the other patrons in the front rows, but as I sucked and gagged on his cock and gave him the best blow job I knew how to, he stopped caring about the noises we were making.

Then he pulled my hair hard and whispered, "Stop," so I did and then he pulled his dick out of my mouth, pushed me back, partially stood and pulled his pants down his thighs a bit. He sat down and said, "OK, you come-loving cunt, I want you to stand up and turn around facing front. Sit down slowly and lower your pussy onto my cock until I am embedded all the way inside you. I want your pussy to fuck my black cock and my hands will guide you up and down. Follow my lead because you are gonna fuck me the way I want you to. You don't get to control anything, bitch."

I did what he asked and his dick felt so fucking good inside my vagina that I almost came right then. I contracted my vagina muscles and they gripped his cock. He chuckled. "That's it. Your white cunt loves this black cock, can't get enough of this dick – you're holding on to it for dear life!" He began to guide my movements up and down on his dick. When I came down on it, I came down on it hard and he loved that, me fucking his dick so deep and so hard with my dripping hot cunt, and I let out a pretty loud involuntary moan. I could see one of the men in the front row look back. He knew what we were up to; I am sure he could see me bobbing up and down and it excited me even more to know that he knew that this white slut was fucking that fine ass black man in the back corner. His dick was probably oozing come right now just thinking about it. I didn't think those men would do anything to interfere, as they wanted to hear what we were doing, and in fact were getting off hearing it. I moaned again and said in my normal voice, "Yes, I love your hard black dick in my cunt! Oh baby, fuck my hot, white snatch and come in me, baby. I want your hot come all in my pussy." By now, I didn't care who heard me, who knew that I was a nasty, white bitch with a sexy black man fucking the shit out of me in a public theatre and loving every second of it too. I couldn't contain myself and I started to come all over his cock, squirming on it and moaning, saying, "Yes, yes, oh, baby, fuck me, oh, fuck me. I'm coming, oh, I'm coming."

Once my head cleared a little, I saw that he had not come yet. He said to me, "Stand up a minute. Now I want you to bend, raise up your skirt, that's it – let me see that fine white Irish ass that I'm gonna fuck right now," and he bent me forwards, supported me with his arm around my waist and I held myself in place with my hands on the seat backs in front of me. I felt his slick, wet dick slide into my tight, puckered asshole and he grunted with pleasure as he forced it deeper and deeper into me and it felt so big and so tight in my ass and I loved the feeling, so full of his fine black dick. I realized that I lived for that moment in our relationship, that moment when his hard black cock rammed into my ass and he was fucking me until I saw stars. And he did fuck my tight ass, bent over me and pumping his hips as he thrust into me as deep as he could go. I could see that the guys down front were sneaking glances over their shoulders. I could see one man's shoulder moving, as his hand stroked his own inflamed dick. I knew he was listening and watching my man fucking me in the ass. I loved the fact that not only would he come in my ass but that jerk was gonna come all over his hand wishing it was his dick in my ass too.

I heard my man grunting and panting and fucking me hard. "Take all my come, you beautiful nasty white bitch – your ass is all mine, to fuck anytime I want and I *love* fucking your ass too. I am gonna come in your ass now, baby, now, take it all now," and he groaned loudly as his hot sperm shot into my bowels. He jerked over and over again and then slumped over me, spent for a few seconds. As this was happening behind me, I could see that man in the front moving faster and faster and throwing his head back and coming also; a slight groan came from the front. I smiled a wicked smile and loved the power of our session to so arouse the spectators too.

As he slid his cock out of me and wiped it off with some tissues he said, "OK, Sabina, I want to you to tighten up your ass and hold onto all that come as we walk out of the theatre. Don't you let a drop escape until I let you go to the bathroom." I lowered my skirt, smoothed it and adjusted my dress as he pulled up his pants and buckled the belt. And then we slowly exited the dark theatre with me holding my sphincter muscle so tight to keep all his hot come inside me. You see I will always do anything he asks of me.

Well, this was the beginning of the new me and perhaps in my next letter, I will tell you more about my strange, new life.

MY GUILTY, HOPELESS SECRET

Leanne, Stockport

I call it my hopeless secret because I just can't fight it. It's something I have to do, like eating and sleeping, but a lot more fun than either. Actually, fun isn't the best word, because without doubt I suffer for it, my partners see to that.

Put simply, I crave being tied up. There doesn't have to be anything else, because it's just the inability to move that gets me. You can leave me like that for hours and I get into a euphoric, trancelike state that's difficult to put into words if you don't have similar urges.

I tried tying myself up, particularly when I was a teenager, but it never really quite gets there. You always have to leave yourself a get-out, so it's never totally complete, though I did have a couple of mishaps. The first was when I was about eighteen and my parents had gone away for a weekend in the Lakes, leaving me alone in the house for most of Saturday and Sunday, including the whole of Saturday night. I'd actually been invited out to a mate's house for a party, but having the house to myself was far too good an opportunity to miss, so I feigned a stomach upset – that wasn't hard to do because the ideas I had made my insides churn up with anticipation.

I left a decent amount of time after they left, just to make sure they wouldn't come back for something they'd forgotten, but sitting there waiting wasn't easy. Finally I set my plan in motion, going out to the garage where I knew I'd hidden a new rope washing line I'd bought a few days before, then stripping naked in my bedroom in readiness. I cut the line into a few lengths and got a few other things I needed, then moved to the stairs, where I attached one length of the rope to the top banister rail and moved down a few steps. I sat and tied my ankles and knees tightly together, then put my knickers (the ones I'd taken off) over my head, cutting off my vision and covering my nose and mouth with the part that had got rather wet from my previous excitement. Maybe that idea would disgust people, but I guess I was trying to add to my self-humiliation by being forced to inhale my own secret scents and taste my own secret fluids. To add to the sensation I tied a rope around my face, making sure it pressed the knickers into my eyes, blindfolding me, and into my open mouth, acting as a very effective gag and keeping the fabric tight over my nose.

Of course it meant I couldn't see any more, and that, looking back, was stupid. But I wasn't thinking straight. I put my hands up above my head to find the end of the rope that was dangling from the top. I'd already made a loop in it using a slip knot, so it was relatively easy to slip my hands in the loop and pull tight, securing my hands high above my head. God knows what I looked like, but it felt great, even knowing that I could pull my hands wide at any time and get out of the loop.

Except it didn't quite work out that way. After an hour or so I seriously needed to masturbate, so I pulled. But the rope wouldn't budge at all. The curls of the plastic, added to my weight keeping it taut, wouldn't let the slip knot slide open. I tried climbing up a step, but I couldn't see and I couldn't get my feet far enough apart to make a step, and jumping would have been too risky. With mounting panic I realized I was stuck there. I kept tugging at the rope but it was hopeless, and I started to cry; not because I was afraid or anything, I was just having to face up to the fact my parents would arrive home – eventually – to find me naked, tied up and with a pair of my knickers tied tight across my face. Time slowed right down and it felt like an age. I could just about make out light and dark round the ropes and material across my eyes, so I knew when night came, and I even managed to sleep a bit, standing up and letting the rope support me, but after a while the rope would cut my circulation off and wake me up.

I won't bore you with the rest of the time, but I can still remember my dread when I heard their car draw up outside. I'd been desperately trying to think of some way to explain why I was like this, the most obvious being that someone had broken into the house and left me like it. But thinking that through made it totally implausible – there were no signs of any break-in, and there would be nothing missing. And besides, if some-one had broken in and done this to me, my parents would call the police and it would all result in a whole web of lies that I couldn't back out of.

I still didn't know what to say when I heard the door open. Luckily Mum had come in on her own, having dropped Dad off at the pub to meet his friend on the way. She obviously didn't see me at first – I heard her take her coat off and put the keys on the hook. Then I heard her: "Leanne? My God, what the hell's happened?" She was coming up the stairs to me. I just started to cry uncontrollably with the shame of it all.

She untied me without saying much else. I guess we all think of our parents as staid and ignorant of sexual things, but she realized straight away that what I'd done was sexual, and that made her back off saying too much once I'd answered her question that I was all right. After I was free she told me she didn't know what I'd been up to and wasn't going to pry, but if I did it again I should be much more careful in case I had an accident. I was so tired by then I just wanted to go to bed and sleep. As she closed the door, she finished by telling me she'd tell my dad I wasn't feeling well and then added something that floored me. She said to keep a pair of scissors handy next time. Somehow she knew what I'd done, and she understood it. Maybe, just maybe, it was hereditary.

It certainly took away some of the shame I felt, so I was able to drift off to sleep. But before I did I remembered back to the feeling of genuinely being unable to escape. My previous clumsy attempts at self-bondage had never gone that far, and I was totally hooked. OK, I admit it, I didn't go straight to sleep – I used my fingers first. Mum never mentioned it after that, and nor did Dad, so I guess she never told him.

TEAMING UP

Malcolm, Sioux Falls

When I hit fifty and flabby, I made a resolution to get back in shape before it was too late. I did not want to end up like a lot of my middle-aged insurance colleagues – nursing hernias and heart conditions and heavy loads over their belts that meant cock sightings only with mirrors and sex on the pay-away plan. I'd run the actuarial charts, so I knew where I was headed unless I took action.

And I took action. Along with a programme of early-morning weightlifting and walking, I test-drove a number of recreational sports: golf (too slow), basketball (too exhausting), racquetball (too claustrophobic), curling (don't know why I tried curling), before finally settling on softball; slo-pitch softball, to be exact. I'd played some hardball way back when, and I figured I could maybe work my way back up the horsehide ladder, and into better shape, via the slo route.

My secretary told me about a mixed league that was looking for players, and I signed up and met my teammates the following Tuesday on a gopher-holed field on the windy outskirts of the city. The Bronx Bombers they weren't, but neither were they the Bad News Bears. They were just a mixed bag of guys and gals used to fielding phone calls and inter-office memos rather than line-drives.

Except for the captain of the team, that is. Donovan was a long, lean, obviously athletic guy with short, rubbable black hair and brilliant, knee-sagging green eyes. He reminded me of Alex Rodriguez of the Yankees, and I could tell by the way he was throwing balls around during warm-up that he could really play the game.

We ended losing 21–19 to the Wheaties in a tight-scoring affair, but I had a good time and got a heck of a lot more exercise than I thought I would. Some of the old skills returned along with the arm soreness and the stitch in my side, and I found myself running the bases virtually every time I stepped up to the plate. And when our team captain saw I could field the ball without closing my eyes and offering a prayer, he put me in left field, which meant I was chasing down balls almost every inning, as well.

The best part of the game, though, was sporting young Donovan. He was decked out in a pair of tight, silky blue shorts and a blue-mesh muscle shirt. I reverentially watched him coil at the plate, knees bent and bum waggling, run the bases after a hit, powerful bronze thighs and arms pumping, loose cock flopping. And I had a good, unobstructed view of his big, rounded butt from my position in left field as he crouched in the hole between second and third. I fantasized about filling the stud's own hole with my bat and balls, field-dreaming that a fall-summer sexual encounter could be as natural as Roy Hobbs.

"Hey, you ever think of playing serious ball?" Donovan asked me after the game, when we were stowing the baseball gear in his equipment bag. "You're pretty good, you know."

"Thanks," I replied, beaming. "What do you mean – serious ball?"

"Well, I just play on this team for fun, and to recruit new talent. I'm on another team with a bunch of guys who play a lot harder. Thought you might be interested in stepping it up a notch."

"Uh, yeah, sure, I'm interested, absolutely," I blustered, lost in the guy's twinkling emerald eyes. I was willing to even play on the Tampa Bay Devil Rays if it meant spending more quality, sweaty time with the D-Man. "When do you guys play?"

Donovan cracked a blindingly white smile that lit up my small corner of the world. "Every Friday night. Why don't you come out this week?"

If I squeezed in a massage and a session with my chiropractor, I could just maybe make it to a Friday game in one piece.

"Great. I'd love to come . . . out," I enthused, watching Donovan's kitten-pink tongue part his thick lips and apply lubrication.

"Excellent. I'll give you my address. The guys always get together before the game to strategize and stuff."

They did take their diamond-ball seriously. Donovan gave me his address, and I memorized it like some guys memorize baseball stats.

That Friday night, I bumped the kerb a couple of doors down from Donovan's house at six o'clock sharp. He lived in the funky, elm-shaded neighbourhood we strait-laced, suburban Sioux Fallsians call the Yippie District. And Donovan's place turned out to be an old, refurbished, two-storey job painted a wild neon green with purple trim.

I wasn't absolutely sure of the young man's sexuality, but the house and the 'hood were sending out the right vibes. And so was the flamboyant tease with the pink hair and blue nose studs who answered the bell when I rang. "You must be Malcolm," he gushed, spilling some of his drink and his spit. He winked at me. "I hear you can really play."

Dressed in black leather pants and an unbuttoned Hawaiian shirt, drinking anything but Gatorade, the guy looked about as ready for a ball game as my dead uncle Clarence. "We're all in the backyard," he whispered, breathing booze in my face. Then he pirouetted and sashayed away down the hallway.

I followed his tight, twitching buns through the eclectically furnished house and out onto a creaking back porch that overlooked a small-size backyard. The yard was surrounded by an eight-foot-high cedar fence, and there were enough guys crammed into the green space to make up a ball team, all right; but they were playing a different kind of catch entirely.

A long-haired blond and a flat-top redhead were passionately making out in a shaded corner of the fence, Blondie gripping Red's head while Red gripped Blondie's ass, their tongues entwining like the ivy at Wrigley Field. Two more players were executing the ol' squeeze play on a third guy in another corner of the yard, their mouths attached to his sun-burnished nipples, sucking and licking and biting, their hands on his blue-jeaned equipment, rubbing and squeezing and stroking. The double-played dude had his back up against the fence and his shirt up around his neck, his hands on his buddies' heads, as he got licked and sucked and manhandled.

And smack in the middle of that miniature field of dreams, a guy suddenly sank to his knees in the grass and deftly unbelted and unzipped another guy. He tugged his pal's jeans down and said howdy-do to a slender, ebony-black cock rising up and sniffing the open air. The kneeling man fielded the standing man's cock like a pro, seizing it with his hand at the base, with his mouth at the head. The standing man grunted and tore off his T-shirt, exposing even more shining ebony skin. He started pinching and pulling his nipples, as his playmate got a good, hardcore sucking rhythm going, as I watched and drooled in amazement.

"What'd you think of the team?" someone asked, startling me like a voyeur caught with his pants down. Donovan casually threw an arm over my shoulder. "Think you can play with us?"

I looked at that muscular, brown arm, felt its soothing, sensuous warmth, looked out at that orgy unfolding in front of me, felt its raw, white-hot heat. Then I looked into Donovan's gleaming green eyes and gulped, "Game on."

He smiled, took my hand and led me down off the porch and onto the field of play. He pointed out the various players, told me their names, their favourite positions, then gestured at the guy with the pink hair and the skewed fashion sense to come on over. "Skeezer, Malcolm," he said by way of introduction. "Skeez here can really suck up the ground balls."

"Oh, yeah? How about that? We've, uh, already met," I mumbled.

"Not properly," Skeezer responded, grinning and touching my shoulder like I was "it". Then, without further ado or coaching, he dropped to his knees and stood his drink in the grass and popped open my Dockers. He had my pants and briefs down around my ankles before I could say, "Holy cow!"

I flinched when his warm, wet mouth engulfed my shocked cock, flinched again when Donovan slid his warm, wet tongue into my ear and swirled it around. My reflexes were still pretty quick for an old guy, though, my bat corked and balls juiced in a matter of seconds, thanks to Skeezer's loving lips and tongue and Donovan's whispered wet nothings.

"Jesus," I groaned, my wood filling the heated cauldron of Skeezer's mouth to the gag reflex and beyond.

But the ball boy didn't back down. He locked me tight and hot and wet in his mouth and throat, his nostrils flaring for air, his baby blues gazing up into my eyes. Donovan bit into my lobe and kissed my neck, his musky man-scent filling my dizzy head.

I'd only ever gone two men down once before in my life, in my wild youth, in a secluded barn with a pair of kissing cousins with no one to witness our wicked mischief other than a pair of disinterested cows and a one-eyed field mouse. This, on the other hand – Skeezer bobbing his pink head up and down on my pink cock now, Donovan tonguing and biting my neck – was wildly out in the open, ten other guys and who knew how many peeping Toms catching the action. I was overwhelmed by the thought, by the double-team sucking and kissing, and my knees buckled with the sheer erotic weight of it all. Thank God I'd been working out.

Donovan helped me unbutton my denim shirt, my hands shaking like a teenager showing his buddy his hidden stash of gay porn mags and wondering what would happen next. Donovan pushed my shirt off my shoulders, grabbed my pale pecs in his hot brown hands, and licked at my cherry-red nipples. I moaned as he twirled his thick tongue around first one nipple and then the other, as Skeezer hard-sucked my cock, almost pulling me off my feet with the intensity of his blow job.

Shivers of delight raced up and down my spine, like batters rounding the bases and heading for home, my balls tightening with imminent release. Donovan bit into a flaming nipple and pinched the other; Skeezer squeezing my tensed sack as he wet-vacced my cock.

"I can't take any more," I yelped.

"Swing for the fences, Mal," Donovan urged, mouth full of nipple. "We all do."

He stuck two of his fingers into my gaping mouth and I anxiously sucked on them, Skeezer taking me down to the matted hairline and back up again, over and over, sending me flying. I trembled out of control and my balls boiled over and my cock exploded. I blasted Skeezer's pretty mouth full of sizzling sperm and whimpered like a spoiled millionaire athlete, my body jolted by wicked orgasm again and again.

Skeezer took everything I had to give, like a true teammate, swallowing hard and sucking harder, milking my pulsing cock, draining my balls. And when I'd finally, blissfully, spurted my last dollop of sticky sunshine, I would've tumbled to my knees in gratitude and exhaustion had Donovan not held me up by the nipples and whispered in my ear, "Now you have to prove that *you're* a team player."

My eyes fluttered open and I stared at Blondie and Red staring back at me, cocks in their hands and grins on their kissers. I glanced down at Skeezer gently stroking my spent and slimy prick, noted the evil grin on his puffy lips. "I'll . . . I'll put out for the team," I gasped.

They were all over me like a guy getting mobbed at home plate after belting a game-winning dinger. They stripped me clean of clothing. Then the lube came out, Skeezer gleefully greasing my asshole and Donovan's cock. Sufficiently slickened, Donovan stretched out on a hastily unfolded lounger, long and hard and glistening in the hot sun. He gestured at me to stretch out on top of him.

I gingerly climbed onto the man's smooth, awesome physique, facing away from him, facing the crowd. His heavy cock squeezed up between my legs and pressed against my balls. Then he gripped my hips and pushed me upwards, easily holding me there with one hand while he grabbed his cock with the other and pushed its head into my butt cheeks, probing for my opening. I spread my trembling legs and positioned my feet, and Donovan's bloated hood quickly broached my asshole and punched up inside. He lowered me back down, burying his cock in my ass in one slow, sensual motion.

I closed my eyes and groaned, my body flooding with heat, a hard young cock up the ass feeling so very good, so very right.

But I wasn't expected to field just one cock. Blondie and Red stepped up to the plate, on either side of me, extending their erections towards my open mouth. Donovan had a secure grip on my waist, raising and lowering me on his cock like a pennant on a flagpole, so I reached out and grabbed on to Blondie's long cock and started stroking, pulled Red's thick little penis into my mouth and started sucking.

The fearsome foursome went on like that for an amazing few minutes, Donovan impaling me while I alternately tongued and tugged Red and Blondie's cocks. But then Skeezer got in on the action, grabbing my flopping cock and filling his mouth with it again. He got me hard as before, then greased the both of us up.

Donovan slowed his ass-pumping so the pink-haired guy with the rock star body could straddle the two of us, facing away from us. I knew what to do and I did it, plugging my numb cock into Skeezer's tight little hole, sinking deep into his quivering bum like a spike into the warm, wet sod.

I could hardly believe what was happening. Here I was, a respected, middle-aged business executive, getting reamed by one young stud, reaming another, while sucking and jerking off two others – in blazing backyard America. It pays to participate, I guess. And being a good sport certainly helps.

I licked and sucked and pulled on Red and Blondie's cocks as best I could, as Skeezer joyfully bounced up and down on my cock, as Donovan surged his cock back and forth in my tingling chute. It was a hard, intensely pleasurable workout, and I was soon wetly rewarded for all my efforts.

Red bellowed like he'd been hit by a pitch. He grabbed my head and poured molten semen into my mouth, just as Blondie started shaking on the end of my hand and I jacked his hot seed all over my face and his buddy's groin. And the sight and sound and smell of those spurting males quickly set off my two bum-buddies. Donovan dug his fingers into my slick flesh and grunted, unloaded in me, blasting my ass full of come. Then Skeezer shook like a stadium full of fans and fell back against me, sperm jetting out of his hand-cranked cock.

It was left to me to bat clean-up, my body arching and my brain melting as I rocketed spunk into Skeezer's dancing bum, as I hand and mouth and ass milked my teammates. A guy's never too old for this game.

TIRED OF BEING A VIRGIN

Joe, Wheat Ridge

Sex with a stranger. A woman who tells you her name five minutes before you fuck her. A woman that you have never met before and, the chances are good, you will never speak to or see again. That is how I lost my virginity when I was nineteen years old.

I've never been very comfortable around girls. I have many girls that are friends and I have no problem talking to them but to make that next step from friend to girlfriend or even just to fuck buddy, is the hardest thing in the world for me. I had wanted to have sex since I was fifteen. All of my friends were doing it, talking about it, enjoying it. I wanted to get in on the action. The only problem was, I didn't know how to ask any of the girls I knew if they wanted to sleep with me. Do it wrong and I could royally fuck up some pretty good friendships. I was such a wreck. Then when I turned nineteen, I finally decided that it was time. I was tired of being what felt like the only member of the V. Club.

The most logical way for me to go about losing my virginity, at least in my mind, was to put an ad on one of those online personal sites. I figured that being the only sexual partner I had ever had was my left hand I would be pretty bad at actual fucking and if I was able to lose it to someone I didn't know and would never have to look in the eye again it would be easier for me. So I summoned up all my courage and posted my ad:

Tired of Being A Virgin: I am a nineteen-year-old guy; five foot eight, one hundred thirty pounds. Average build.

Smooth chest, arms, legs, pits and ass. Trimmed down below. Nice sized cock. Big full balls. Shoulder-length brown hair. Blue eyes. Oh yeah, I'm also a virgin. I am looking for a girl to pop my guy cherry. I am unconcerned with age, race or looks, however you must be totally disease free. I just want to fuck. If you'd be interested in breaking in a virgin, give me a shout. I do have pics available if you want to see what I look like. Hope to hear from you soon. Joe

I reread my ad 100 times. I wanted to make sure that I said all I wanted to and that it was perfect. I took a breath and submitted the ad. My heart was pounding. My breath was rapid. I was sure that no one would respond. After all, how many girls want to be with a guy who probably won't be able to last long?

Later that night I checked my email and almost fainted when I saw that someone had responded to my ad. I started sweating and my heart felt like it was about to burst out of my chest as I opened the email. I smiled as I read the letter. It was full of sweetness. Innocence. A little bit of fear at responding to an ad online. I printed it out and still look at it from time to time when I'm feeling down and need something to put a smile on my face.

Dear Joe,

First let me say that I have never responded to an ad like yours before so I am a little nervous. Allow me to introduce myself. My name is Grace. I am going to tell you my age right now, just in case it turns you off. I am fifty-five years old. My husband died about six months ago and, even though I thought it would never happen, I have started having sexual urges. I have always had a fantasy of being with a younger guy and I thought maybe you and I could help each other out.

I am five foot four inches tall and weigh 115 pounds. My hair is long, stopping at my lower back, and grey. As per request, I am totally disease free. *[This part made me smile. It seemed like she had a good sense of humour.]*

I am enclosing a photo of myself. If you are interested in getting together, let me know. If you are interested, would you mind sending me a photo of you?

Take care and if I have offended you I am sorry.

Yours, Grace

I downloaded the photo and was pleasantly surprised at the woman I saw. She was really beautiful. She didn't look fifty-five. If I had just seen her on the street, I wouldn't have guessed that she was over forty.

I didn't even need to think. She was perfect. I immediately responded to her.

Dear Grace,

Thank you for responding. I really liked your photo. You are very beautiful. I am interested in meeting and am enclosing a photo of myself. Let me know when would be a good time.

Talk to you soon, Joe

I felt myself shaking slightly. This was it. I knew it. I wasn't going to be a virgin for long!

Grace and I made plans to meet the next day at a small coffee shop that was across from my house. That morning as I was picking out my clothes, I was a nervous wreck. I didn't know what a guy was supposed to wear to lose his virginity; something comfortable I guessed. No need to overdress. I settled on a pair of jeans, a black T-shirt and my Yankees hat. I walked over to the coffee shop, getting there fifteen minutes early so I would have time to calm down.

I sat down at a table by the window and tried my damnedest to concentrate on breathing evenly. I didn't want to appear scared. What if that turned her off? As I sat at that table, my mind began to wander into territory that I didn't want to think about. What if she didn't show? What if she smelled? What if I did? What if she didn't like me? What if I was bad in bed? What if I couldn't get an erection? Or hold one? What if I came too soon? What if she was a psycho? What if she had a disease? A knife? A gun? Stop! I commanded myself. If you get yourself all worked up then you're going to ruin this and you will be fucked. And not in the good way.

I saw her walk through the door and choked on my breath. Her picture didn't do her justice. She was really, really beautiful. Her hair was flowing freely. She was wearing a pair of white shorts that showed off her long legs; legs that could rival those belonging to the most desirable models. She was wearing a tank top that clung to her breasts, proudly displaying them. She saw me, smiled and walked over. I got up when she reached the table.

"Joe?" Even her voice sounded young.

"Grace?" I tried to match the calmness in her voice.

"Have you been waiting long?"

"No. I just got here. Did you have any problems finding the place?"

"No. I live five minutes from here."

"Really?" I asked surprised. "Wow. We're neighbours."

She laughed and we sat down.

"So . . ." she said. This made me feel a little better. At least she was nervous too.

"Yeah . . ." There was a pause between us for a few minutes. "I want to thank you for responding to my ad. I didn't think anyone would."

"To be honest, I was really scared about it. I've never done anything like this before. My husband, he was the only person I've ever slept with. When he died, I didn't think I would want to sleep with anyone else but . . ." Her voice trailed off.

"So, do you maybe want to go back to your place?"

I don't know what made me ask that so soon. I hadn't planned on it but it just seemed like the right time.

"I'd like that." She smiled at me.

It turned out that Grace only lived a few blocks from my house. I liked her house. It was a small, one-storey ranch with a neatly trimmed yard and small flower garden out front. We walked inside and I was immediately attacked by a small dog who resembled a hairball. Even the dog's face was completely covered in fur leaving barely enough room for two brown eyes to spy on the world.

"Cammy, be good," Grace told the dog. "Sorry about that."

"It's all right. I love dogs."

I sat down on the couch. Cammy jumped on my lap and vigorously licked my face. I smiled and petted the dog. "How old is she?" I asked.

"Four months. I got her because the house was too lonely. She's a good girl."

She sat down next to me and petted her small dog. We talked for a little bit, getting to know each other. She told me how she had met her husband. What he had done for a living. What she had done for a living. I told her about what I was studying in college. What I hoped to do with my life. Before we knew it we had run out of things to talk about.

"So," I said, throat suddenly dry, "where were you thinking of doing this?"

"Would it be OK if we went into the bedroom? Cammy won't bother us."

"I'd like that," I said. "Would it be OK if I get a glass of water?"

"Sure."

She went into the kitchen and got me a glass of water. I drank it with the intensity of a man dying of thirst.

We went into the bedroom. Grace closed the door. My hand was in hers. She led me over to the bed. We sat down.

"I really appreciate you doing this," I said stroking her hair.

"Same here." Her voice was soft.

I leaned in and kissed her. Her eyes were closed. Mine were open. Our mouths were joined. Her fingers were lightly, tentatively, caressing my back through my T-shirt. My hands were rubbing her shoulders. Our hearts were beating wildly. We were scared. Excited. Nervous.

"Get on top of me, Joe," she whispered softly while running her fingers through my hair.

Gently I eased her onto her back. We continued to kiss. My body was on top of hers. Our hands continued the exploration of each other's body.

My heart started pumping faster when she removed my T-shirt. Her hands caressed my back. My body was hot with desire; I wondered if she could feel it. It wasn't long before I had removed her shirt. My mouth travelled lower down her body. My lips made contact with her fleshy cleavage. Gently I kissed the tops of her breasts. Sucking the flesh. Licking it. I liked the taste of her. Her own skin was just as hot as mine. With shaking hands, I removed her bra. For a woman pushing sixty she had really nice breasts. They were perky. Didn't sag. Her nipples were erected. Gently I took her breast in my hand and placed it in my mouth. She moaned with pleasure and clutched my hair tightly as I sucked on her breasts, teasing her nipple with my tongue.

"That feels nice," she moaned, eyes closed.

I smiled and went to work on her other breast. Grace squealed and wrapped her legs around my waist. I gently rubbed my body against hers. My hard-on was throbbing, wanting to burst out of my pants. I was sure it would explode.

I planted a trail of kisses down her stomach. I unbuttoned her shorts and pulled them off her hips along with her panties. I started to sweat a little at seeing her nude. Her pubic hair was curly and neatly trimmed, just beginning to turn grey. I rubbed her legs, hoisted them over my shoulders and lowered my face to her vagina. I started out by kissing her flesh. Her legs wrapped themselves tighter around my neck. She moaned out my name. I gently sucked and bit the flesh. She shivered slightly when I stuck my tongue inside her. I thrusted in and out of her vagina. I flicked my tongue against her, stimulating her clit before burying it deeper inside her and swirling it around her.

"I thought you were a virgin," she moaned.

"I rented a porno last night so I would know what to do," I confessed.

She laughed. I continued my oral pleasure on her for about another fifteen minutes, then it was my turn. She rolled on top of me, unbuttoning my pants and discarding them and my boxers. Timidly she took a hold of my penis.

"You have a really nice body," she said gently stroking my penis and massaging my balls.

"Thanks. So do you," I said gently fingering her.

She lowered her head and sucked on my balls, licking them with her tongue before opening her mouth and swallowing me whole. She used a variety of techniques to get me off. She would bob her head up and down before kissing the tip of my penis and then licking the length up and down like an ice-cream cone.

"You're good at that." I smiled down at her, enjoying the sight of my penis in her mouth.

"Thanks." She smiled up at me. "I rented a porno last night too."

"Come here. Get on top of me. I want to do the sixty-nine."

She got on top of me, giving me a great view of her butt and, let me tell you, it was a butt that most twenty-year-olds wished they had. We licked, sucked and bit each other for about twenty minutes.

"I want you inside me, Joe," she said, out of breath.

"Do you want me to wear something?"

"No. Unless you want to."

I didn't. She mounted me and guided my penis into her vagina. We moaned in unison as we got used to the feel of each other. I enjoyed the feel of her wrapped around my penis. Slowly, she began to ride me. Up and down. Up and down. It was hypnotic watching her breasts jiggle and her vagina going up and down on my penis, wet with her juices. Her hands were on my chest, playing with my nipples. I had my hands around her butt, every once in a while slapping the flesh. We were moaning. My back was arching every few minutes.

I turned her over and thrusted in and out of her in perfect rhythm. Her fingers were gently tickling my back. Her eyes were closed. She was moaning. Head moving back and forth. My hands were getting lost in her hair. I was gently kissing her neck and chin, every once in a while biting her flesh. Her hands travelled lower and lower down my back until they clutched my butt. Her hands stayed on my butt for the rest of our love-making, pinching and squeezing the flesh. It drove me crazy.

I could feel myself reaching the point of no return. I picked up speed and thrust harder, deeper and faster inside Grace. Her moans became louder and more high-pitched. Her grasp became stronger. My hips were working like the pistons of a machine. Finally, I couldn't hold it in any longer and I had the most intense orgasm of my life. I let out a groan and collapsed on top of her. She ran her fingers through my hair and kissed my shoulder. I rolled off her and held her in my arms, naked flesh against naked flesh, for half an hour.

"That was great," I said.

"Yeah." She kissed my chest. "I had a lot of fun. Thank you."

"Same here."

A lot of people may not understand how a nineteen-year-old boy could have sex with a woman who was old enough to be his grandmother. I can't explain it myself. There was something about Grace. Something indescribable. I must say it wasn't a one-time thing we had. We would get together a few times a week and talk for a while before going into the bedroom where Cammy couldn't disturb us and have sex for a few hours. I am thankful that Grace came into my life. That she was brave enough to respond to an anonymous ad online and that I was brave enough to follow it through. I look back on the time I spent with her now and I smile.

SURPRISE ATTACK

Rebecca, Stockton-on-Tees

Galloping along the ridge I couldn't help but remember the last time I came along this way. That was about three weeks ago when Janet had cried off the afternoon ride. I'd soon got over it though because it is so gorgeous up here when the weather is this good and I really prefer to be on my own anyway – that way I can appreciate it all. Janet would just have kept chattering on about David, her latest boyfriend, and would have spoilt the peace. Days like this are too good to be spoiled by selfish girlfriends who only want to talk about themselves or other things, which of course involve them. I relax into Copper's rhythm and let my mind wander back to that momentous day.

Copper had been quite frisky and had been jumping all over the place so once we'd got up to the ridge I'd just given him his head to let him burn off some steam. Suddenly one of the "bushes" a couple of yards ahead moved and Copper jumped off to the side, unseating me, and I flew through the air and landed in a humiliating and very painful heap. As I was trying to catch my breath I realized the "bush" was now walking over to me.

"Are you OK? I didn't mean to spook your horse, but I suddenly heard this thudding behind me and thought I was about to be trampled."

I realized that the "bush" was actually a soldier obviously on some sort of exercise.

"I'm fine, I think," I gasped, still fighting for breath after being winded. "Where's Copper?"

"He's over there eating some grass," he said.

"What's going on?" I asked. "They always put a warning sign on the moor gate when there's an exercise on."

"They must have missed that gate. Are you sure you're OK, would you like to lie down for a bit? Here, rest your head on this," he said as he took off his combat jacket.

Even though I was still having trouble breathing I managed to notice that his body was quite well toned as he took the jacket off and bent over me to put it under my head.

He sat down beside me and took off his helmet, which was covered in leaves and other bits of greenery.

"At least you look human now," I said, as much to hide my embarrassment as anything else as he was quite attractive and I could feel myself blushing.

"I think you should take your hat off," he said. "You don't look very comfortable."

As I lifted my hands to take it off, he suddenly bent over me and loosened the strap. As his hand brushed against my cheek I felt a shiver run through me.

He carefully removed the hat from my head, but instead of sitting back he leaned over further and looked into my eyes. After a few seconds he moved further in and gently kissed me. I should have been shocked and shoved him off, but it felt so good as his tongue moved into my mouth that I just opened my mouth and kissed him back.

I ran my hands over his back and felt the hard smoothness of his muscles, which were well defined and powerful. His hand settled on my breast and I felt myself gasp as my nipple hardened. He played with the nipple between his fingers, pinching and pulling at it, which made my hips respond as the ripple of excitement spread through my body.

I lifted his T-shirt up and he opened my blouse. He took my bra off in a way that I knew he'd done that plenty of times before, but I was past caring. He kissed my tits and licked and nipped the nipples with his teeth. My hand had crept down his body until I could feel his cock through his trousers. I massaged and kneaded it until his breathing became quick and he suddenly stood up and took his trousers down. As I waited for him to take them off completely, I admired his well-toned body and the way his cock stood up proudly to attention. I felt my pussy clenching in anticipation of that gorgeous cock fucking it.

He unbuttoned my jodhpurs and kissed and licked down my midriff as he pulled them and my knickers down. When he got to my pussy he licked quickly into me and I groaned and my hips bucked at the sudden pleasure. Once he had taken off my jodhpurs completely he stood there looking down at me and I felt so wanton and dirty lying there in the grass totally naked with my legs spread open waiting for his cock. He knelt down and opened up the lips of my pussy wider with one hand and with the other he stroked me up and down gently. "Please fuck me," I begged, but instead he pushed two fingers into my pussy and played with me. As he was fingering me, he licked and sucked at my clitoris. I was writhing with pleasure. "Oh, please fuck me!" I begged again, more urgently this time.

"I am fucking you," he said.

"No, with your cock. Fuck me with your cock!" I demanded.

I knew he wanted to – I'd been wanking his cock with my hands so I knew how hard it had become.

"I want you to suck me first," he said, and moved round to the side of me so I could take his cock in my mouth.

I licked the end of his cock and it jumped in my hand. I slowly slid it into my mouth, playing with his balls with my hands. He gasped loudly and I started to move my mouth and tongue up and down his hard cock. I squeezed his balls and dug my nails in slightly and felt him tense but at the same time gasp with pleasure. I lightly nipped his cock with my teeth and he groaned out loud.

After a couple of minutes he suddenly pulled out of my mouth and said, "Now I'm going to fuck you," and drove his cock hard into my cunt. I screamed with pleasure at the sudden invasion and the wave of excitement that shook my body. As he drove his cock into me, I reached down and held onto his thighs. I could feel the muscles tense as he worked on fucking me. He had very powerful thighs and I felt even more excited when I realized the power that was behind his cock as it was driving in and out of my cunt.

Suddenly my whole body tingled and my cunt was clenching as I came. I think I screamed – I can't really remember as the orgasm was so good!

After a few minutes he slid out of me and said, "My name's Kev, by the way, just in case you were wondering."

"I can't say I'd really thought about it," I said. "But it's nice to meet you, I'm Rebecca."

"How about getting together later? A few of the lads and their partners are having a drink at the Fox Covert. I would quite like to fuck you again and maybe even get to know you too," he said with a grin.

"OK, I've nothing else to do later and I wouldn't mind another shag like that – once I've got over this one, that is!" I replied feeling my pussy clench again at the memory of that gorgeous cock thrusting in and out of it.

As I was slowly riding Copper back to his stable I was even more pleased that Janet couldn't be bothered to come that day. And now I have a great sex life, which I know I wouldn't have if she'd been there. All in all, even though I'd been really fed up with her for cancelling on me at first, she'd actually done me a huge favour!

ANONYMOUS

Siobhan, Manchester

I suppose I should tell someone about it. My little secret, that is. It makes me feel cheap each time I do it, but nobody will ever know it's me, I guess. And even though I feel cheap, I do enjoy it, and I know I'll keep on doing it, despite the risks. It's very simple. I like to have anonymous sex.

I can be a dirty bitch when I feel like it, and usually I can't control when I feel like it or when I don't. I just know I have to have it, and for a few days afterwards I'm OK. But sure enough, before too long has passed, I get the urge again, and I don't stop until I get it.

Don't get me wrong – I don't just want to get fucked. I like pretty much everything, the kinkier the better. I don't mean animals or kids or scat, but there's not much else I haven't tried or won't try, to the extent that a plain and simple marital fuck just bores me. I still do it with my hubby, but it's very routine and mechanical. But how could I tell him what I need without risking giving the game away or losing my nice, comfortable home?

The first time was at a party at our house. I'd been having lurid dreams for weeks. Well, more fantasies than dreams, and in every one I'd imagine this man, just his body, he never had or needed a face though often I'd imagine the back of his head bobbing as he stuck his mouth between my legs and speared me with his tongue. I'd get the itch and have to nip to the loo to satisfy the craving with my fingers while hubby watched *Match of the Day* on telly.

Then we had the party, for my birthday. We invited mainly friends but a few brought their friends that we'd never met before. One of them – God, I can't even remember his name now – kept eyeing me up then looking away when I saw him, and it gave me the hots. Not for him particularly, just the hots, so much so I was itching for relief as usual. But there was a steady stream of people using both bathrooms so I sneaked out into the garden, round the back of the shed. It was already getting a bit dark so it was easy to disappear for the few minutes I'd need. Except that the guy with the eyes must have seen me go, and a few minutes after I'd started he appeared silently around the corner, his eyes immediately darting to where my hand was busy pressing into my crotch through my party dress. I was shocked, to be sure, but there was something about the situation, assisted by the wine I'd had, that prevented me from stopping. I watched him watching me, and it was like I was full of molten liquid and that taking my hand away would somehow drain it from me.

He stood right in front of me and put his hands on my breasts, both of them, while I carried on below. When I didn't object he pulled the straps of my dress down and pulled my boobs free. I remember feeling like my nipples were going to explode in that night air. He bent and sucked them, one after the other, and his hand covered mine and pressed. I think I do myself better than anyone else with my fingers, but I let it pass and pushed back against his hand. More to show I was a girl of the world than anything else, I reached out my left hand and unzipped him, and I still can't remember why I did that, but he didn't complain. He was so hard. Then he was pulling up my skirt and pushing aside my panties and trying to push into me, and it all got very clumsy. I turned him round so he had his back to the wall and I held him, wanking his prick with my right hand and doing myself with my left. He tried to push my head down but I shook my head and he looked so pathetic. Instead I raised myself on tiptoe and he bent his knees and I slid him into me. It wasn't a great fuck in itself, but it was bloody exciting because it was so dangerous. I mean, we could hear the music and conversations inside the house.

He was humping me and I was humping him and I knew he was going to come, so I got off him and finished him with my hand. Dangerous or not, I was feeling really dirty and didn't try to avoid it when he spurted out all over my dress. Afterwards he just wanted to be away, so I said he should go back to the party and I quickly finished myself off after he'd gone, his semen still coating my fingers.

He'd gone when I got back inside. Then my friend Sue came across and said I'd got something on my dress. I looked and it was his come, but she said someone must have spilled something on me, and she took me to the kitchen and wiped it off, at the same time trying to imagine what it was in case it stained. I could have told her and she'd have been disgusted with me.

I did a lot of thinking after that. When I sobered up the next morning I felt mortified. But it didn't stop my roving fingers when I had a shower, and that set me thinking about what had got me so worked up. Certainly the fact we didn't know each other helped, and the cheapness of the whole thing, too. I knew then I ached for more.

Since then I've been felt up on the London tube trains, flashed at and rubbed a few trouser fronts in crowds. I'm totally brazen when I get in one of my moods. We had a guy in to fit some electrical sockets last year. He arrived and showed me his identity card but I deliberately didn't look at it because I had been in that mood all morning and I deliberately didn't want to know his name. That's always important to me. I knew he was coming during the morning – hubby kept reminding me to make sure I was going to be in (if only he knew) – and I'd been in the shower when he left for work. After he'd driven off, I dried myself and dressed in what I imagined the sparky would like, namely skimpy black underwear, stockings, suspenders and high heels, and I slipped a short dress on over it – not too short because I didn't want to appear too brazen just yet, but short enough so that if I was accidentally on purpose careless how I bent over or sat down he'd be in no doubt.

I was only just ready when he rang the doorbell. I invited him in and I thought I could sense him eyeing up my arse and legs as I led the way through to the kitchen where we wanted the extra sockets. I showed him then asked if he wanted a coffee. He did. And then he got down to work and was concentrating so much he didn't pay me much attention at all. Well, what could a girl do? Easy, though I doubt you'll believe what I did next. I pulled off my dress over my head, that's what I did, quietly so he didn't notice. Then I sat on the worktop and carried on chatting to him as he worked. I nearly laughed because he hadn't realized I was there to be had, only covered by a few scraps of black silk. But he did turn round eventually and his face was a picture. I just smiled at him as he stammered and asked what I was doing.

"Fucking the electricity man," I told him. That got his attention all right.

I stood up as he watched and went to him, ruffling his hair and pulling his head down to my boobs. I managed to get him turned round – I like doing that – until he was half sitting against the worktop, and I squatted down and unzipped him. He was nearly fully hard by the time I got it out and completed the job when I sucked him into my mouth, not using my hands at all. I made better use of them to unfasten my bra and drop it; then I slipped my panties aside and slid my fingers right up myself. Personally, I prefer to rub around my clitoris but men seemed to like it when girls push their fingers right in so I did that, making wet sloshing noises with them.

I kept at him, even when he tried to pull me up so he could fuck me. He even had the nerve to complain that I'd told him we were going to fuck and we weren't, but I was too busy being a cock-sucking whore. I kept at him till he gave up and held my head still, jerking his hips like he was fucking my mouth, just using me. He shouted out and spurted right into my mouth and I swallowed it all. Afterwards I just walked out and went upstairs, where I locked myself in my room with my fingers until he'd finished and left.

Sometimes you have to share things for them to have any real meaning, especially naughty things. It makes them feel extra naughty if you tell someone else.

SATURDAY, 5.30 A.M.

Giselle, Canada

I'm sleeping with a married man. There. I had to get that off my chest. You'll understand, I'm sure, if I don't tell you his name. After all, he could be someone you know. Or you may know his wife or his kids. I wouldn't want word to get back to them. And just because he's cheating doesn't mean he's a bad man. He isn't bad, he simply has needs. We all do.

So, what's it like? Well, last Saturday was a perfect example. At 5:30 in the morning, I heard his key in my door. That smooth metallic noise wakes me every time. It's better than an alarm clock. I had been looking forward to seeing him all week. I look forward to it every week.

He tells his wife he likes to jog early in the morning, before pollution envelops the city. He tells her he enjoys his run better when there are fewer people on the sidewalks, and when the sun hasn't yet risen. These are only half-truths, because he actually does jog all the way from his house to mine. I doubt if his wife even notices any more when he rolls out of bed before dawn. I doubt if she ever notices him at all. That's fine. I've taken it upon myself to notice him. In fact, I could notice him all day and all night, if I ever had the opportunity.

I emerged from the depths of slumber as he kicked off his shoes in my front hall. I scrambled out of bed and headed straight for the bathroom. When you only get to see your lover once a week, you always want to look and smell and taste perfect. And morning breath is a major turn-off. When I turned off the bathroom light, my eyes couldn't adjust fast enough to the darkness of my bedroom.

I asked, "Where are you?" as I walked straight into him. Ouch. "I couldn't stop thinking about you," I told him.

He concurred with his standard standby. "Likewise."

"All week I've been waking up and asking myself, 'Is it Saturday yet . . . ?'" That's all I managed to say before he kissed me. An entire week's worth of kisses in less than one minute.

When I opened my eyes I found that they had adjusted to the darkness and I could see my lover. Even after two and a half years, it's a thrill to see this man in my bedroom. He was still dressed, so I tore off his jogging shorts, followed by his red Reebok T-shirt, his running socks and his black underwear. I stepped back and, encircling him, took a good look at his tight butt and his athletic thighs. All that jogging . . . Then I ran my hands over his chest, smooth with only a touch of hair around his little pink nipples. He threw his arms around me and squeezed my body tightly against him. I've always loved that sensation of his chest and my breasts being separated only by my thin silk negligee.

I dropped to my knees to do what I know his wife won't. His cock was still lifeless when I took it between my lips. The sensation of a soft cock against the walls of my mouth was hilarious. What did it feel like? Like a snake, maybe. Malleable, like I could have tied it in a knot. I took it all in and, as I encircled his limp dick with my tongue, I started to feel it jerk and grow. As I sucked it, of course, it got bigger and bigger until his meat was so large I couldn't keep it all in my mouth any more.

Getting below him, I licked his balls, taking each in my mouth before working on the sensitive head of his penis. He made those noises I love to hear, sort of like a snort and a sigh, and he said my name while he stroked my hair. It's great to hear him say my name. I love that.

Anyway, I figured it was my turn, so I lay back on the bed to let him ravage me with his tongue. He licked my pussy lips hard with a warm, wet tongue. That really got the juices flowing. Then he sucked on my clit while squeezing my nipples through my silk negligee and, let me tell you, nothing else in the world feels that good. No, that's a lie, because what he did next was even better.

His cock was large with anticipation and just the sight of it made my pussy whimper. Oh, I just had to have it! I had to feel that big slab of meat inside of me and I don't mind saying so. The sight of my lover holding his cock by its base, guiding it towards me, made me quiver. My pussy opened up for him to ram it in me, hard and strong. I couldn't help but think how hot he looked while he was doing it. His lean stomach muscles, embraced by only the slightest layer of insulation, tightened with every thrust. I ran my fingers through the dark curls above his hard rod. He has the most incredible body!

Rolling onto my stomach, I half stood on the floor and half leaned against my bed. He came at me from behind, reaching around to rub my clit while I reached back to fondle his balls. I love the way they feel in my hand, squishy and soft. With both hands, he took firm hold of my hips and plunged into me so hard I could feel the pressure throughout my core. While his fingers grasped my hip bones and his thumbs dug into my butt, I hoped and prayed they would leave bruises. That way I would have something physical to remember him by throughout the week. I love to catch a glimpse of a lovely purple mark on my body and sheepishly recall the naughty act that created it.

As my man thrust faster, I explored the muscles of his thighs with my hands as he jutted forwards into me. They were eager and hard. His thighs are his favourite feature, but I've always been most fond of his cock. Rising to the balls of his feet, he held me aloft by my hips. God, those sexy arms! My feet weren't even touching the floor and I had to grab my duvet just to hold on to something. When I turned in near ecstasy to gaze at his face, it was practically scarlet, with one vein throbbing at the side of his forehead. The muscles in his athletic arms pulsed.

"Aren't I too heavy for this?" I asked, anticipating his response.

"Feathers," he said with strained laughter. "You're as heavy as feathers."

His cock had a mind of its own. It rammed so hard and fast into me, I knew my pussy would ache for days. So much the better. The dull pain would help me remember this morning throughout the week. I would do anything for that man. Thrusting his whole body into mine, he propelled me forwards so hard the mattress shifted sideways across the box spring. When he set my knees down on the dishevelled bed, I could feel his warm lips planting kisses across my back. He hugged me tightly around the waist, and I knew he was about to come.

Releasing a whimper like a child's cry, he collapsed on top of me on the displaced mattress, cuddling against my back. He may never say it, but that's how I know he loves me. We lay like that for a while, our blissed-out bodies in layers, flowing like a waterfall from heads on the mattress to knees on the box spring to feet on the floor. With his heavy body on top of me, I couldn't move if I wanted to.

Eventually, he got up and showered. I didn't move a muscle, just absorbed the scent of his body on my skin. After he dressed, he picked me up and reoriented me on the mattress, pushing it back into place. He tucked me into my sheets and duvet, then kissed my lips softly.

"I'll see you next week," he whispered, placing his gentle lips against my forehead. I listened to the metallic jingle of my lover's keys as he locked the door on his way out. It was not yet 6:30 a.m. and already I couldn't wait for the following Saturday.

Is it wrong to love a man with a wife and two kids? I don't know. Maybe it is. But I'm addicted to the very smell of him now, and to the feeling of ecstasy that lingers long after he's gone. Looking forward to his next visit gets me through the week. Anyway, I don't take up much of his time. Just an hour each Saturday at 5:30 a.m.

FOR GOD'S SAKE DON'T TELL MY WIFE

Robert, Wirral

OK, I confess. I did it. I screwed my wife's best friend. I'm only partly to blame. Only partly. Sophie should at least share the blame, even though she'd never admit it. But she knew. I never made any secret about what pushes my buttons and she pushed as many as she could reach.

She's one of those women who make you want to breathe in when you walk past them in the street and then hold your breath for as long as possible to keep their scent inside you. The first act in her capture.

My tastes have always been simple on the surface, but incredibly complex when you get under that surface. My public side, the one I always felt free to share with everyone, was a simple liking for most things that defined femininity to my albeit narrow mind. 'Black' falls into the list, as do 'lacy', 'frill', 'stocking', 'suspenders', 'underwear' and so on – I'm sure you get my drift.

And, like I said, Sophie knew it. She would wear clothes that not only inflamed my sight but also my senses of smell and hearing, the perfume of her and the way her clothes seemed to rustle as she moved. But, until that fateful day, the sense of her touch had eluded me. My eyes would dart each time she crossed her legs, hoping unsuccessfully to catch a glimpse of the stockings I was sure she wore, or perhaps the nirvana of bare skin above.

Oddly enough it was my writing that catalysed it all. I write erotic books. That's one of my less public secrets, because people have their prejudices and preconceptions, not least my wife, who thinks I'm twisted and sick. Not that her opinion affects me other than to make me smile at her mediocrity as a woman and as a person.

Since I've known Sophie and her husband for so many years, and, on this occasion, alcohol had been flowing rather too liberally at a Christmas party, I confessed to her, too. She'd seen some of my straight writing, but this time, goaded by the scents and the sounds and the sights, I told her about my bondage novels. I didn't get the reaction my fantasies had hoped for. I was relating the story of a woman who, to satisfy her dominant partner, had agreed to try to overcome claustrophobia be letting him lock her in a crate, suitably naked and thoroughly bound, for as long as he, not she, wished.

Sophie attacked. Why would a woman agree to such a thing? What could she, or her man, get out of the exercise, especially when, by their actions, they were physically separated by the boundaries of the wooden coffin that secured her?

But Sophie is not the only one who can push buttons. "If you have to ask, you'll never understand the dynamic," I countered.

That worked. I could feel her seething. Not that she'd ever admit I'd got to her. And then the subject changed, never to return.

Not that day anyway.

I'd almost forgotten the incident by the time she phoned my mobile. When I saw her name on the display the memory returned and I expected some barbed comment. Instead her tone was guarded and mysterious. The book I'd been talking about, could she by any chance read it? I waited a few moments for some reason, some excuse why she would want to read such a perverse book. None came. I promised I'd drop off a copy when I went to the supermarket later in the day. I waited a respectable amount of time before driving to her house. If she was in, she didn't answer the door, so I dropped it through her letterbox in a suitably ambiguous brown envelope.

Nothing happened until the following day, when a short text message on my mobile made things more serious. "Damn you," it said. "I can't get it out of my mind."

"Can we talk about it?" was my answer, a slight edge of concern that this would be some get-even plot hatched between Sophie and my wife.

"When?"

"Today. Two p.m."

"OK."

That got my heart rate going.

You could have cut the atmosphere with a knife when she let me in later the same day. She was polite and quiet, searching for the courage to open discussions. I guessed it fell to me.

"So," I started, "the book . . ."

She blushed and avoided my eye.

"What was it you couldn't get out of your mind?" I asked, adding, to help her, "the box?"

"No . . . all of it. Do people really behave like that?"

"Yes, lots of people do. Don't tell me Peter has never forced you to do something, or held you down?"

"He's very gentle," was her get-out. I had always thought them naive.

A pause from both of us. A long pause. Did we dare resume breathing?

"Tell you what," I offered, as light as I could be, "why don't we try something? No pressure. If you don't like it, just say and we'll stop. Immediately."

"Like a safe word?" she blurted. So she had read a lot.

"Yes. Choose one."

She answered too quickly. She'd already imagined this. "Mozart" betrayed her interest in classical music.

"Mozart it is." I smiled. "Just don't ask me to hum."

"What are you going to do?" she wanted to know, straight away.

"Let's go upstairs," I suggested.

A scared look. "I never agreed that we'd . . ." An unfinished doubt.

"One step at a time. You can't see in through the bedroom windows," I explained then gambled on, "and there's a bed to tie you to."

That hit home. She swallowed hard. "OK."

I followed her lovely rear view as we climbed the stairs and she led the way to their bedroom, then sat nervously on the bed and looked at the floor. A dressing gown hung behind the door, its belt an obvious invitation. I think she expected me to tie her hands with it, but instead I used it as a blindfold. To hide her from herself. She sat still as I fitted and knotted it.

"Something else. To tie you with," I told her, my voice husky with desire for her.

"Ties. Second door along."

Peter's ties. A betrayal of her marital status? Maybe. I didn't worry about that, taking a handful of ties and kneeling in front of her, wrapping the silk around her unprotesting wrists. Then another round her ankles. She stiffened as I raised her skirt.

"Your knees," I lied. Well, part lied. I did secure her just above the knees, but I also took time out to see her stockings and thighs.

"How do you feel?" I asked when she was no longer free.

"Peculiar," she replied. "Excited."

I reached forwards and cupped her breast, the reaction an involuntary intake of breath. But Mozart stayed dead. My hand grew bolder, feeling her flesh through her dress and bra, the nipple pushing back at me. I focused on it, pleased with her sighed response.

"Do you like being helpless?" I wanted to know.

"I'm not helpless," she whispered. "I can move my hands. I could stop you if I wanted."

She moved her bound hands upwards and nudged mine from her breast. But did she want? To paraphrase the Spice Girls, did she really, really want?

"I think you are starting to understand, Sophie," I ventured. "Let me change the question . . . *Would* you like being helpless?"

No answer. Just her rising and falling chest.

"Lie back on the bed," I suggested. No, it was more a demand than a suggestion. I had to teach her.

"What are you going to do?" But she settled back and swung her feet up on the bed without waiting for me to answer.

More ties. One more. I untied her hands long enough for me to wrap one tie around her left wrist and secure it to the bedhead. She made no move to resist, so it was easy for me to take the other arm and secure it to the opposite post, giving her an erotic Y shape.

She took her time settling, unfamiliar with the fact she now was helpless. She'd played with the words and played with the ideas and now she was there. But she didn't struggle, not yet.

After maybe five long minutes she spoke. "Are you going to keep me like this?"

"Any reason why I shouldn't? You have your safe word if you need it."

"I know," she added, a certain indication she wasn't going to use it, for the moment at least.

My hands returned to her breasts again, firmer this time, using both hands on both breasts. When no complaint came, I unfastened her dress. How thoughtful (and perhaps planned) of her to wear one that buttoned up the front. Beneath, as I always knew there would be, I found black lace. Not quite see-through but not far off. She tugged at her bonds, not so much to try to get free, I imagined, as to assure herself she couldn't.

A few minutes later my own impatience made me pull down the lacy cups of her bra and feast my eyes – closely followed by my hands and soon afterwards my mouth – on areas of her body I'd only ever fantasized about beforehand. I was getting uncomfortably excited and, judging from her jerky reactions, so was she.

"I can still move," she goaded, bringing her bound legs up off the bed to demonstrate. It was a clear challenge, one I was happy to accept. Untying her knees and her ankles, I used the two ties to secure her feet, turning her comfortable Y into a slightly stretched X, and causing her errant hemline to show me all of those sexy stockings and the suspenders that held them so erotically taut.

"Now you can't move," I reminded her.

"No," she said quietly.

I settled to caressing and kissing her breasts and neck again, rewarded by contented moans. My hands strayed too – downwards, over her rucked-up skirt and onto her surprisingly cool thighs, then down to feel the nylons and suspenders. Then, tentatively, upwards until they grazed the tiny strip of fabric that hid her remaining modesty. Her jerks continued as I pulled it aside and investigated her warm wetness.

"Fuck me," was all she could grunt out. Such language from such a naive lady. What could I do but oblige?

That started a relationship that goes on today. That's my confession. I screwed my wife's best friend. The fact I'm still doing it, experimenting in ways that are as far out as our combined imaginations can invent, including her very own isolation box. But all that is fact – I have no need to confess that to anyone.

SHE COMES IN COLOURS

Simon, Brisbane

Annie and I had been friends for years, and though we went out occasionally, we weren't really dating; she was cute, but skinny, and I preferred busty women – and so did she. But when she invited me to a sneak preview of the latest *Star Trek* movie organized by the local fan club, I decided it beat sitting home alone, and that's how I met Helena.

Annie and I had barely walked into the lobby when Helena emerged from the costumed crowd and rushed up to give Annie a hug. I looked down, and my eyes locked on to a magnificent display of creamy cleavage; it took a huge effort to look up again. She was rather plump, but breasts that large wouldn't have fitted on a skinny frame, any more than her grin would have fitted on a narrow face. "We haven't met, have we?" she purred.

Annie introduced us, and then introduced me to Paul, Helena's date. I resigned myself to watching the movie, but was pleasantly surprised when Helena sat next to me. Paul and Annie stared at the screen as though hypnotized, while Helena concentrated on entertaining me – shifting in her seat so that her tits swayed, dropping popcorn into her cleavage and fishing it out, even pressing her boobs against my arm and brushing her hand across my hard-on as she leaned over me to whisper to Annie. She kissed both of us goodbye after the movie and, as I drove Annie home, she commented, "You and Helena seemed to hit it off."

I shrugged. "How long have she and Paul been together?"

"They're not. She's just come over here for a few weeks to get over her divorce and make up for lost time, as she puts it." She said it warmly, without a hint of disapproval. "Look, it's the club's Christmas party on Saturday; do you want to come? You won't have to wear a costume."

I'm not sure why I said yes – maybe to make up for staring at another woman's breasts all night – but I'm glad I did. When I arrived, I saw Helena sitting on a chair in the kitchen clad only in an old towel and green body paint, which Annie was applying to her neck and back.

"I'm going as an Orion slave girl," Helena explained, "and Annie's doing the parts I can't see well enough to do myself. Do you want to help?"

I glanced at Annie, who grinned and handed me another pot of paint. "Uh . . . OK. Where should I start?"

In reply, Helena dropped the towel. The tops of her breasts were painted down to within an inch of her nipples, and her belly and thighs were also green, leaving only two narrow bands of pale pink. She grabbed both of her nipples – they were already swollen – and hoisted them up to her chin, saying, "I can't see below here."

I didn't need a second invitation. I scooped the paint onto my fingers, as Annie was doing, and began rubbing it onto the underside of Helena's sensational silken-soft breasts. She let go of her right nipple, and the full weight of that magnificent mountain fell into my hands. I saw Annie lean over Helena's shoulder and start nibbling her ear, and Helena grabbed the back of my neck and pushed my face into her cleavage, smearing my cheeks with green paint. More by good luck than good aim, one of her nipples found its way into my mouth, and I began sucking on it eagerly while she reached down and unfastened my jeans. I felt something brush against my ear, and looked over to see Annie sucking on Helena's other breast. A hand began stroking my cock, and when I reached between Helena's thighs, I found that Annie's hand had beaten me there and was already deep in her folds, her thumb expertly rubbing Helena's clit. The next thing I knew, I was sitting in the chair, with Helena kneeling between my thighs while straddling Annie's face. She wrapped her beautiful boobs around my cock, and grinned up at me before bending her neck and kissing and licking the head of my cock as it emerged from that heavenly valley. The warm smooth softness of her billowing breasts sliding along my shaft, her heartbeat close to my throbbing cock, the way she teased me with her tongue and lips, and her expression as she came, her mouth forming a perfect 'O', soon pushed me over the edge, sending my come fountaining into the air and splashing onto her face and tits. She giggled as she licked up as much of my jizz as her tongue could reach, and soon Annie emerged to lick up the rest. I watched, entranced, as they lay on the floor sucking on each other's breasts, then kissed their way down each other's bodies until they were sixty-nining in front of me.

After a few minutes, I suggested that we'd all be more comfortable on the bed, and they agreed. We staggered towards the bedroom with our arms around each other, then Annie collapsed onto the bed with her legs hanging over the edge. Helena dropped to her knees between Annie's thighs and began rubbing her boobs over her crotch, teasing her clit with her nipples, spreading her pussy lips with her milky flesh. Annie grabbed me and pulled me down towards her mouth, then quickly sucked me back to a full erection. Helena watched, a greedy gleam in her eyes. Annie rolled me onto my back, grabbed a condom out of the nightstand, and barely had time to put it on me before Helena pounced on me. She rode me frantically, coming time after time until I climaxed, while Annie sat on my face and kissed her, and we both fondled her awe-inspiring boobs. Finally, Helena collapsed onto the bed, and the three of us lay huddled together, touching each other gently, playfully, all smeared with come and pussy juice and green paint.

We never did make it to that party; in fact, we hardly left the apartment until we drove Helena back to the airport a week later! She's promised to come back soon – but whether she does or not, green is now definitely my favourite colour.

TENANCY AGREEMENT

Dave, Watford

My wife, Lesley, and I recently rented out a room in our house to a sexy young thing named Megan. We were careful in our selection, as we wanted just the right type of tenant – a quiet, well-behaved, good-looking girl who would take it any way we gave it to her. You see, she was to be our personal sex toy.

Megan fit the bill to a T. She was a shy, dark-haired nineteen-year-old with big, violet eyes, smooth, pale skin, a cute, round ass and a pair of jutting tits capped by hard, pink nipples. She was a bookworm and a depraved sex slave in one, her quiet demeanour belying the fiery need that burned deep within her.

The first day she was with us, we had a fairly conventional threesome; I banged her from behind while she ate out my wife. From there, however, things degenerated nicely. Bondage, spanking, water sports, you name it, we did it to Megan; and she took it and loved it. Then, one night, we interrupted the petite girl's studies by telling her that she was going to receive some DP.

"Bum and pussy at the same time?" she enquired, looking and sounding innocent, her eyes wide as she stared at the huge, black cock that dangled from Lesley's strap-on.

"Strip!" was how I responded to her impertinence.

She got up from behind her desk and did a slow, awkward striptease, first pulling off her sweater, and then unhooking her skirt and letting it fall at her feet. Lesley stroked my rigid cock as I pulled on her own flesh-feeling dong, as we watched our come girl remove her clothing. Megan unfastened and shrugged off her bra, and her ripe nipples swelled visibly in the humid air.

She kicked aside her shoes and tugged off her knee socks, then turned her back to us and slid her panties over and down her heart-shaped ass.

Once she was as naked as we were, she crawled onto her bed and lay on her back, tentatively slid a trembling hand down to her shaved pussy and rubbed her clit while she sucked her thumb and awaited further instructions. I nodded at Lesley, and we joined the wanton nympho on her bed. I ordered Megan to climb on top of me, and she quickly straddled my swollen cock with her plump ass cheeks. My wife lubed her cock and Megan's virgin asshole.

I told Megan what to do, and she gripped my long, hard rod and slowly lowered her tight, damp quim down onto my mushroomed dick head. She eased my straining prong into her glistening, baby-faced slit, until her bum touched my thighs and my cock was buried to the balls inside her cunt. I pulled the whimpering girl down to my chest, and then I grabbed her bottom and spread her butt cheeks, allowing Lesley to push her big, black cock top into Megan's tiny, petulant starfish.

The girl moaned into my mouth as I savagely Frenched her, as Lesley pushed forwards and ploughed her giant, ebony dong into Megan's gripping bunghole. Lesley's face was a mask of grim, sexual determination as she drove her thick faux-cock deep into Megan's quivering bum, then began churning her hips, fucking Megan's violated anus. I slid my own hard-on back and forth inside the groaning girl's drenched pussy, and Lesley and I were quickly pounding that reckless, obedient teenager from front and rear.

"God, she's tight!" Lesley hissed at me.

I grunted my agreement.

Lesley gripped the fuck doll's slim waist and plundered her ass with the hip-mounted dildo, spanking Megan's rippling butt cheeks each time she banged into her. I slammed the overwhelmed teen's pussy faster and faster and faster, keeping wicked time with my wife's full-bore ass assault. I squeezed and kneaded Megan's firm tits, pinched and pulled her rubbery nipples, as Lesley and I savaged the girl's stretched-out sex holes.

"Yes!" Megan squealed, her eyes shut tight, tears rolling down her lust-contorted face, her lush body dewy with sweat.

I pounded Megan's cunt with my enraged cock, while Lesley hammered the sex-crazed girl's rump. We relentlessly double-fucked our superheated sex toy for a long, long time, pummelling her glorious openings with our fire-hardened cocks.

Then I felt the come begin to boil in my balls, and I yelled at my wife to pull me out of Megan's hot, dripping pussy. She first ripped her own cock out of the moaning girl's gaping ass, and then tore me free and polished my coursing, juice-slick meat as I blasted thick, white-hot ropes of jism onto Megan's ass, onto my wife's night-shaded dong. My body jerked with ecstasy as Lesley hand-pumped my throbbing cock of its heavy load of sizzling semen.

When I'd spilled the last of my seed, Lesley brought her come-covered cock over to Megan's gasping mouth and ordered the girl to suck on it. Megan licked my sperm off my wife's ten-inch rod, before Lesley jammed it down her throat for a real blow job.

Megan was sore for a couple of days after that night, but we really didn't care. After all, she had to earn her keep like the rest of us.

MILKING MY LOVER

James, Oxford

My hottest sexual experience was with my married lover. She'd recently had a baby and her body was luscious with womanly curves and soft flesh. Peeling her clothes off revealed such a different figure than her pregnant form that I felt like I was with a new mistress; I wanted to run my tongue along every single stretch mark, to let my fingers explore all her new contours. But she was desperate for my cock; she barely allowed me the time to undress her before pulling and pushing me to the floor, unzipping my fly and plunging herself down on my hard prick. She rode me entirely for her own pleasure, she seemed totally oblivious to me, I could have been any man or even a lifeless sex toy. Her energy and attitude turned me on even more than her naked body; I was desperate to get her attention. I matched her strokes and thrust hard up into her; she didn't even look at me, her head thrown back, her mouth open, screaming out her ecstasy. I rubbed her clit with my thumb, grabbed her hand and sucked on her fingers, lightly brushed my fingers over her nipples, all the things that she normally loved, and even though they seemed to increase her enjoyment she still did not look at me. I was only a cock for her hungry cunt.

My attempts to get even the slightest acknowledgment from the woman who was pounding against my groin became increasingly difficult. I dug my fingers into her flesh, pulled on her long black hair, grabbed her arse and tried to pull her against me. She continued to ignore me, immersed entirely in her own waves of orgasms. She was a sexual goddess and I was desperate for her to see I was the one making her this happy. I began to pinch her nipples and slap her large swaying tits. At last she looked at me, her green eyes wide with the pleasure she was experiencing.

"Harder," she gasped at me.

I didn't want to hurt her but she became angry at my pause. She scratched her long nails down my chest.

"Harder," she commanded.

This time I immediately obeyed, pulling on her hard nipples, elongating them as far as I dared. Her gaze was fixed on me now, but I was mesmerized by the punishment I was giving her tits. I alternated pinching with slapping, leaving large red blushes on her huge white breasts. As she rode me hard I saw between her thrusts that my cock was covered with her come, the hair surrounding my prick soaked with her cream. Then I felt something warm and wet on my chest. Milk was freely squirting from her breasts; the sight was so beautiful I wanted to engrain it on my mind, but I couldn't resist for more than a moment. Her lactating tits were not meant for looking at, they were meant for sucking on. I latched my mouth onto one of her nipples and drank long and hard, thrusting my cock firmly up into her. We fucked like that until I couldn't hold back any longer and I spurted my juices into her, but even then I didn't give her nipples any rest from my hungry mouth. As we lay together afterwards I knew for certain that I wanted more of her sweet milk.

To date that was the best fuck I've ever had, but afterwards my mistress and I had a world of sexual adventures. We would push each other to do more daring things. I lifted her top in the cinema and drank from those huge tits through the whole film; I ripped her blouse open in a deserted part of town; put my mouth to her nipples at the back of a bus; completely undressed her and fucked and sucked her on a long train journey.

People might have seen us, and I hope they did, but the only time someone openly approached us it was in a park late at night. Her back was pressed against a tree; I'd pulled her tits out of the top of her dress and was drinking freely while my hand played under her skirts. It was probably her loud moaning that drew the attention of the man to this normally empty part of the park at such a dark hour of the day. I don't know how long he had been standing watching us, but at some point I noticed a change in my lover. It is hard to explain as she made no attempt to stop me or to hide her breasts, she did not suppress her loud gasps of pleasure, but I sensed that the focus of her attention had slightly changed.

I turned to see him; I couldn't make out any of his features, he was just a slight different shade in the shadows of the night. My initial reaction was fear: he was a stranger of unknown strength and fitness, my woman was exposed and I didn't know if I would be able to protect her. The man walked slowly towards us, the muscles in my body tensed, but when I glanced at my lover I saw she was smiling. She welcomed him with a kiss as if she'd known him all her life and then pushed his head down into her cleavage. My fear didn't entirely disappear but jealousy became my paramount emotion; even though she was married it was a new sensation to watch someone enjoying the pleasure of my mistress's body. The mixture of fear and jealousy added to the sexual tension I always felt in my lover's presence and when she beckoned me I put my head next to the stranger's and sucked on her other breast. The stranger did not stay for more than five minutes, he removed his mouth from my lover's breast and disappeared back into the shadows. I gave her the hardest fuck I'd ever given any woman that night.

When my mistress's milk stopped flowing I found I could not return back to our previous sex life. As beautiful as she was, sex with her now bored me. Our liaison ended but she'll always be special to me as she introduced me to the most erotic experience and she was the first one of my many breast-feeding lovers.

IT'S ALL IN THE TIMING

Steve, Clifton

"You have three minutes," Roxanne said twisting her kitchen timer, then placing it on my night table. "You don't come in that time you're not coming the entire night . . . and you get this."

Spreading her thick legs wide, her miniskirt hammocked between her dark thighs. Her back ramrod straight, she sat there on the ottoman, the dangerous rattan cane resting across her upturned palms, her thick purple lips pursed and shining, her deep brown eyes wide and set on my popping erection.

The ticking, her stare, the sight of the cane resting across her hands, her creamy chocolate thighs teetering up high there in her three-inch spikes: the full effect was the most unnerving sight I'd ever witnessed . . . and with Roxanne this past year I had witnessed plenty.

I simply grabbed hold and began stroking hard, the timer a torturous ticking cacophony in my ears as I attempted to concentrate. Though woefully turned on since Roxanne had knocked, come in, thrown off her coat, revealed her outfit – and that fucking cane and timer! – standing before her now I wasn't so sure I'd be able to come in the time allotted to do so.

"Two forty-five," Roxanne announced as I willed myself not to look at the timer.

"You are not going to like the cane, Steve," my girlfriend added. "It really hurts. Like a pinpoint rising heat."

Did I dare even imagine how she knew this?

"Fuck," I cried, pulling and huffing.

Roxanne smiled as I gulped, thrusting her crotch out to me even further. The bottom of her non-existent skirt shifted up her thick thighs; really all I had to do was dip my head to get the full view. Dangerously attracted to this voluptuous black girl as I was – obsessed actually – I could never really take my eyes off of any naked part of Roxanne when she presented it to me. It was mostly for this reason, my ache for Roxanne's body, sexuality, her mind, with her mind where it concerned her sexuality and body, that I had entertained the amount of kinkiness we got into. In all my thirty-one years I had never been so adventurous.

If I really considered it, this was why I had let the more submissive part of my sexual needs flourish here with this girl. This past year had been a whirlwind (at least for me), finding a girl like Roxanne who would play the dominant . . . and like doing so. God knows I had dabbled a few times with girlfriends who indulged me, but never to this degree, and with a partner who could think up shit like this timer game! In fact there had been more than a few instances when I feared I might not be able to take her latest torture, that I would disappoint her in my obvious naivety, that sooner or later I'd break under her and she'd find a better, more subservient man with a bigger cock and more experience.

And of course this imagined tenuous sexual entrance I was allowed made me want to please her all the more.

"I thought this would have been easy for you," Roxanne said. "I mean, don't you jerk off like ten times a day as it is? I can't believe you can't do this." Then, looking to her right at the timer, she added: "Two minutes. I don't know if you're gonna make it."

"Fuck!" I growled, managing my thumb and middle finger on either side, just below the head of my cock. This is the one position I know always provokes a release.

"Better hurry," my girlfriend cooed then leant well forwards, elbows on her spread knees, and the cane rolled to the edge of her fingers. She held that dangerous cane out like an offering between us.

"Looks like about a minute fifteen."

"Shzza, shnizz," the cane said as Roxanne sliced a wrist-flick of a space directly in front of her.

"Mmm, this is gonna leave welts."

Fuck.

I huffed. I jerked faster. I rolled up on my tiptoes.

"Tick tick tick," my girlfriend sang, then sat back once again and with her free hand pulled her skirt up so it bared her completely.

Staring at and into those glistening bald spread lips, I finally felt that unmistakable lurch right under my belly button. I spread the palm of my left hand right under that area and clutched my ass cheeks.

"Forty seconds, Steve." With this Roxanne stood. "You're gonna remember that sound a long time, I bet," she said looking back at the timer. She took six clicking-heeled steps to me, stood towering over me and looked down at my suffering purple cock.

"Time's running out."

"Roxanne!" I cried, writhing there, pulling, shucking. God, could I come?

Tick, tick.

"Not gonna make it."

I could smell her. I could feel her heavy tits poking me. Feel her warmth next to me . . .

Still . . . tick tick.

"Steve . . ."

Pre-come! Blessed, beautiful, clear and sticky pre-come.

Tick.

"Steve."

"Oh God."

Tick.

"You're not gonna make it," Roxanne teased.

Fuck!

"Bthling," the timer brayed. Roxanne laughed and a fount jettisoned out of my taut engorged head.

"Fuck, fuck, fuck," I managed while milking myself down onto my wooden floor. Roxanne held tight to me and she too began to shake, clutched tightly against the upper part of the side of my leg.

I could feel her pussy throbbing as she clutched round me tighter.

"St . . . Steve," she said, riding a shallow stuttering orgasm. Fuck.

I kept pumping the thick juice out of my cock as my girlfriend spread her legs on my thigh and rolled her pussy into me and came too.

"Wow," Roxanne said, coming down off her little crest finally. "We . . . we could not have timed that better," she continued, looking down with me at the puddle on the floor. "Wow, look at all that."

For that next minute we clutched each other and rode out the lasting effects of the entire escape (three minutes in the making as it had been!).

"You really were gonna use that, huh?" I asked, finally turning to kiss Roxanne.

"I still might," she said after releasing from the lip lock. "Now that you came the next time it's gonna be even harder."

"You are evil," I said.

"And you love it," my sweet Roxanne answered.

STOREROOM ANTICS

Lisa, Huddersfield

My mum used to tell me it was always the quiet ones that I should watch out for. I had never really paid much attention to that until one quiet Tuesday morning when I was sat behind the till.

I was stood reading the latest selection of women's magazines that had come in until the tinkling of the bell above the door let me know that someone had entered. Looking up, I could see him making his way over to the magazines. As guys go he was pretty good-looking; his chocolate-coloured hair flopped down slightly over his face in a cute, almost boyish way. He was dressed smartly in a suit of high-quality material, the type only someone with money can buy.

I continued to watch him, peering over my magazine; you can't be too careful these days, you have to watch everyone who comes in. He didn't notice me looking at him as he glanced up and down the aisle nervously. Once he had assured himself that no one else was around he reached up and pulled down one of the top-shelf magazines. Even from where I stood I could see he had gone bright red with embarrassment. Forcing back a smile I looked back down, trying to seem engrossed in my magazine. I sensed his presence at the counter before I looked up again, his scent winding over me: a musty earthy smell that made my stomach knot and knees go weak.

"Um . . . just this, please." His voice was soft as he spoke, the hushed tones of someone afraid their conversation would be overheard. I looked up and found myself gazing into his soft brown eyes, wishing he would speak more. His eyes sparkled with intelligence and I felt myself blushing just as much as he was. Biting my lip, something I do when I'm nervous, I rang the magazine through the till and placed it in a bag. As I handed it over our hands met, his warmth flooding through me. The moment passed and he smiled at me before leaving. After he left my mind filled with lots of naughty thoughts involving the two of us.

For the next month I found myself jumping every time the bell rang, looking to see if it was him, but he remained elusive although he filled my every waking hour and presented himself to me in my dreams. Although our meeting had been brief he seemed to have affected me like no man had done before.

At last the month came to an end, bringing with it the monthly magazines, all of which needed to be put out. A task I enjoy because it allows me to preview them and see what whets my appetite.

While I was putting the magazines out the bell tinkled.

"I'll be with you in a moment," I called, continuing to place the myriad of magazines on the shelves in their respective positions. I could hear soft shoes moving around the aisles. Finally I got to the last few magazines of the pile. As I started to put them out I felt the close presence of the person as they moved down to the magazine section. From the corner of my eye I saw to my delight it was the man I'd been hoping would come in.

Turning to look at him, my heart sang when he smiled at me and reached over. Unsure as to what was about to happen I stood still. Once more his soft voice surrounded me, and his delightfully sexy blush blossomed.

"Young lady, would you mind if I saved you the trouble of putting that on the shelves by buying it?"

Smiling at the "young lady" comment, which I took to be a compliment, I realized he was being a lot more forward this time around. Nodding, I let him take the magazine from my hands, relishing his touch. Side by side we walked back to the counter. I stopped as I got to the part of the counter that would allow me to pass and gain access to the till. I turned briefly to look at him as I did so. However, I had stopped so suddenly that he walked into me. Face to face, my body pressed against his. For a moment neither of us moved. I could feel the heat from his body. My heart pounded in my chest and all words failed me. Speechless I stood staring into his eyes, my legs wobbling. Reaching out, I held onto the countertop for stability. He looked at me and leaned down. Thinking he was going to kiss me and wanting it so badly, I tilted my head upwards ready to feel his lips upon mine. I was disappointed when he moved and lifted up the counter for me. From the way his eyes twinkled and the large grin he gained, I knew that he knew exactly what he was doing.

"Just this, thank you," he said disarmingly and placed it down on the desk. I turned, my face reddening, and tried to control my emotions. Walking behind the counter I heard him put the top down behind me. When I turned back I was able to smile and ring it through the till.

As I watched him leave I knew it would be another month before I saw him again, and I berated myself for not being more forward. As before, he was on my mind constantly and, although I kept second-guessing myself and his intentions, I looked forward to the day the new magazines arrived. On that day I turned up for work dressed as seductively as I could, determined to at least make an impression.

Time couldn't have gone slower that day. Nerves followed me around the shop as I worked and clock-watched. As time went on and it got later I became disheartened. Sat behind the till I kept staring at the shelves of magazines, including the one he always bought.

When the clock finally crawled its way to closing time I sighed and made my way through the aisles keys in hand. Just as I was turning the sign a figure moved across the door and attempted to open it. Pushing up against it with my foot I called out, "Sorry, we're closed." Prepared for an argument I held the keys tightly in my hands.

"Oh, I just want to get one magazine, but I'll understand if I can't." His sultry tones calmed me; when I realized who it was I opened up the door for him. Once he was in I continued to turn the sign and lock the door, telling myself that it was to prevent any other people thinking the shop was still open. As I locked it, a part of me knew that it was in hope of something happening between us.

He had already picked up the magazine and was waiting at the till by the time I had finished locking up. Straightening out my clothes I made my way over to him.

I had spent the whole day rehearsing what I wanted to say, but, as I walked towards him with a mix of nerves and annoyance at him being so late, I was filled with bravado.

I picked up the magazine and looked at the glossy cover. Images of women looked back at me, their bodies barely covered. It was obvious to me that the woman pictured in the centre had fake breasts. They looked too round and seemed almost to be two hemispheres stuck on her chest.

"I could show you some real ones if you like."

There was that bravado.

He looked up, and I found myself biting my lip nervously, but I needn't have worried. As I looked at him I could see the lust in his eyes.

Before he had a chance to say anything I lifted up the counter and took hold of his hand, leading him into the storeroom.

Leading him into the centre of the room and turning on the light I felt like a femme fatale. Nerves shot through me, and part of my mind kept screaming at me to stop, but I had got this far and I knew that if I did stop I would never be able to get the nerve to do it again. Besides, it wasn't as if he was protesting. By the time we got into the storeroom he had already loosened his tie.

"We don't have to do this, you know," he said as I closed the door behind me.

My body tingled at his voice, dripping as it was with desire and want. I looked at him as seductively as I could and began to unbutton my work blouse.

"But I want to, don't you?" I stopped, my hands poised at the last button. I looked at him, and when he nodded I undid the button and let the blouse open, revealing my rather ample breasts held presently in my best and most expensive bra. His eyes widened but since he didn't do anything I took his hands in mine and placed them upon my breasts.

Immediately his strong warm hands tentatively began squeezing them. I moaned at his touch, an act that caused him to move closer to me. One of his hands snaked around my back, fingers touching the bra clasp, expertly unhooking it while his other hand slipped up inside my bra. His fingers danced over my skin, and I felt my nipples being pinched and teased. I wanted him; the closeness of our bodies now allowed me to reach forwards and undo his belt. Quickly I undid his trousers, then slipped a hand in to feel his hardness hidden inside. I wasn't disappointed, and was rewarded by a groan from him. That spurred me on to free his cock, allowing me to get my first look at it. As I did so my pussy twitched with anticipation, and I imagined myself being taken by it.

I kissed him passionately, and found myself being pushed backwards against some of the boxes that lined the storeroom. Holding me close he planted quick kisses all the way down my neck. The world span when I first felt his lips around one of my nipples. His mouth was wet and warm, and he made full use of his tongue. My nipples puckered and hardened further than they had done before. I arched my back, moaning in pleasure, my head thrown back, resting on a box. Without thinking about it my hands entwined themselves in his hair, pushing him down onto more of my breast. I could feel his cock now pushed up hard against me; my muscles tightened and my breathing became haggard. When he pulled away from my breasts I cried out in frustration until I heard him speak: "Can I fuck you?"

I nodded frantically and felt myself being spun around.

Facing the boxes I could only guess at what was occurring behind me. I heard him rummage through pockets before the sound of something ripping could be heard.

I felt a sudden rush of cold air as my trousers and knickers were pulled down. His hands were on me again, squeezing my ass before cupping my pussy. I moaned as he slipped a finger into me, my moaning being echoed by him as he did so.

Each time his finger moved out of my pussy I tried to clamp down on him, not wanting him to leave. It had been a long time since I had been with a man and I didn't want him to stop. Waves of emotion crashed over me as his finger continued to investigate me. I rocked my hips and wriggled, pushing his finger deeper into me. With a sudden jerk I felt him pull out of me and an empty feeling washed over me. That emptiness was quickly filled however as, taking hold of my hips, he guided his cock gently into me.

I'm not the most patient person in the world, and when I felt him slowly entering me I tried to move back to force himself to be plunged into me, but his hands held too much of a grip on my hips and I was unable to move. It wasn't until my pussy had opened up and accepted half of him did he release his hold on me, at which point I slammed back onto him, screaming in delight at his full length pushing its way into me.

He grunted and became more animalistic; my body reacted accordingly. Grabbing hold of my hips he pounded into my pussy. The pleasure was intense, and so much more than I had thought it ever would be. Pushing against the wall with my hands, now only slightly aware of the boxes I was pressed against, I kept forcing my body backwards to coincide with each thrust he made. My body felt more alive than I could ever remember it being before as we had sex. It was passionate, wild and completely self-indulgent.

We remained in that position, our bodies relishing in the touch of the other. A burning ball of energy began building up inside of me; as my breathing became more ragged I knew I was close to coming. Pushing back harder I used one hand to hold myself up and the other to pinch and tease my nipples. My clit was being rubbed by the friction caused by the position we were in. As it began to pulse I started to see stars and the exquisite ecstasy of orgasm flooded through me. My muscles tightened and I screamed out in pleasure. As I did so I felt him thrusting deep into me one more time before his cock seemed to throb and he grunted loudly.

We remained still for a while in the room, now suddenly silent, his arms wrapped tightly around me. When we finally moved I turned to face him, smiling. He took me in his arms and kissed me.

"I should come in for magazines more often," he had said when he left.

Since then, we have seen each other outside the shop, but it's always much more fun in the stock room when I work late.

JUST DESERTS

Mrs Jones, Colchester

It was almost 6 p.m. and I had been sitting outside the Boss's office for over half an hour – deliberately, I was sure – when the buzzer rang and the green light came on outside his door, summoning me in.

I carefully smoothed my short black skirt down over my thighs before entering.

The Boss was sitting behind his spotless teak desk, a large full-length mirror behind him and beyond that a penthouse view out across the City of London to the Thames.

"Ah, Jones, come in," he said. And although there were plenty of spare chairs I noticed I wasn't being asked to sit down.

"It has come to my attention that you have been stealing money from the petty cash. No, there's no point trying to deny it," he continued as I feebly tried to interrupt, "the evidence is absolutely clear and incontrovertible.

"Now as you know we are a very old and well-established firm. I should call the police and have you arrested. But we don't like scandal here and we do things in a rather old-fashioned way. So I'm going to give you a choice. You will agree to accept your punishment here and now from me or . . ." He let the sentence die away but I knew what he meant.

"But, but I don't have any idea what it is," I protested.

"Nothing you can't endure and probably a damn sight less than you deserve. Let's say a good spanking. How about five strokes, on each cheek, over my knee."

"I don't really think I have much of a choice. I accept," I replied meekly.

"Right then, Jones, strip off, please."

"No one said anything about being naked."

"Make that six strokes on each cheek. You agreed to the punishment as I recall."

Reluctantly I removed my clothes: white blouse, black skirt, brassiere, shoes, knickers and tights until I stood naked before him.

"That's much better. Now come round here next to me."

The Boss turned his swivel chair so that it was facing the full-length mirror then had me stand facing it, with my back to him. He loosened his tie and then, still knotted, pulled it over his head. Roughly pulling my hands behind my back, he slipped the "noose" over both my wrists and then pulled it tight.

"Turn your toes out and then bend your knees like a ballet dancer, slut!" he commanded.

As I did so he pushed his right hand between my legs and roughly pinched my clit between thumb and forefinger. I gasped as he pulled my most sensitive morsel of flesh from between my outer lips. My position was all the more humiliating because I was being forced to stare at my own reflection and could see his hand protruding between my legs but I was glad that at least I had trimmed my pubic hair into a neat heart shape only a couple of days before.

Satisfied that I was suitably contrite and compliant, he released me, opened a drawer and produced a white linen napkin that he rolled into a sausage shape and laid across his left thigh.

"Come and stand between my legs, facing left, and then bend over. Please make sure your lips are parted and the napkin is between them."

As I did so the Boss crooked his right leg around my own, trapping them, and, taking hold of his tie with his left hand, pulled my arms up into the air, forcing my head down. I was completely helpless.

He gently caressed my upraised cheeks for a few seconds, and then allowed a finger to trail down between my buttocks and then up my gaping slit. I couldn't suppress an involuntary shiver: despite myself I could feel my love juices starting to flow.

Suddenly and without warning he raised his right arm and brought it down with a stinging slap that caused an instant blaze of heat and pain on my right cheek. As I gasped for breath his hand swept up and down again, this time on the other cheek.

Then he simply stopped as if waiting for something. Craning my neck to look over my shoulder I could see my arse reflected in the mirror . . . and the livid imprint of his palm on each cheek.

"I think we're forgetting our manners," he interrupted my reverie. "You forgot to count each stroke and thank me for it. I'm afraid we'll have to start all over again and add another couple just for good measure. So that's now seven on each cheek."

With that he began to spank me in earnest. Hard staccato blows, with a pause between each pair: "One, two. Thank you, Master. Three, four. Thank you, Master. Five, six. Thank you, Master."

By the time he had reached nine and ten my body was covered in a thin sheen of perspiration and by the time thirteen and fourteen landed, my cheeks were ablaze and I was crying like a baby, begging him to stop. But at the same time the friction of the napkin, wedged between my lips and erotically chafing my bud, had got me undeniably aroused.

"Bend over the desk, slut," he commanded.

"Oh no. Please, sir, please, not here . . ." I protested, but it was no use.

He bent me over the huge desk and used the tie to pull my arms up into the air until my face and breasts were pressed hard against the surface. I could smell and almost taste the leather and I could feel the hard edge of the desk pressing against my pubic bone before he once again pushed the rolled napkin up between my thighs.

Unzipping the trousers of his pinstripe suit the Boss pulled out his rampant cock and pushed it into me from behind. Almost at once he set a fast and furious pace, ramming himself into me at the end of each stroke and slapping against my still hot and tender behind.

I could feel that my pussy was tight and hot and wet. Despite myself I found I was arching my back and pushing backwards to meet each of his strokes. Almost before I knew it my climax was arriving and I found myself yelling and moaning incoherently, oblivious as to whether anyone could hear or if we were likely to be discovered.

As my climax subsided so the Boss's arrived, his spunk pumping into me as I lay passively beneath him.

Once he had finished, his cock limp and shrinking inside of me, he simply withdrew and zipped himself back up. He slipped his tie from around my wrists and began to knot it back around his neck, suddenly all businesslike again.

"Right, Jones. Let's have no more of this business with the petty cash, but in any event let that be a lesson to you and a taste of what's in store if you so much as step out of line again. Get your clothes and off you go."

And as I stepped out of his office, still naked with all my clothes across my arm, I could only reflect that just occasionally there were one or two advantages in being married to the Boss.

ROCK HARD FOR ED

Nels, Cleath

I met Ed in the seventh grade in 1987. He and I got along great from the start. We were a lot alike. We were both not popular and we were both picked on in junior school. I didn't discover that I was bisexual until I was twenty-four. I came out to all of my closest friends. But never in my wildest dreams did I ever think Ed was bisexual too.

A few times, Ed and I watched adult videos together but it never led to anything, not even masturbation. I mean, sure, we talked about it a few times but we never ever thought that what we do every so often now we would do then. And when it first happened, I was as nervous as a guy could get. Ed and I knew what was going to happen on that warm night in April 2004 but neither of us talked about it.

After several hours of boring chat, we were both anxious to watch the DVDs I brought with me. So, he loaded up the DVD program on his computer and I handed him the disk. He popped it into his drive and it started playing. I told him to forward a few chapters into the disk to get to the good part. We watched for a little bit. Then I made my first move. I unzipped my pants. Ed looked over at me a little embarrassed. I pushed my pants down a little, not really exposing anything. I put my hand inside my underwear.

"Ed, don't be embarrassed. It's OK to look," I said.

He looked over at me and then started unzipping his own pants. I was kind of nervous because I had never seen him in anything less than a pair of shorts. More than that, I was excited. Anyone who knows me well knows that I love to play with my cock. I do it at least once a day, unless it's impossible to do so. And I had not played with myself in front of anyone in a while so this was exciting to me. Most of the time I ended up in my room giving myself an arousing hand job.

I had, by this point, pulled my pants down to my knees along with my underwear. He had just unzipped his pants and had a hand inside. I could tell he was a lot more nervous than I was. I am a lot more uninhibited than he is. I was giving myself a fantastic hand job while we both watched the DVD on the screen in front of us. In no time at all, I was coming all over my hands. I quickly zipped up my pants and left the room so Ed could finish. I was kind of embarrassed because that was the first time we had ever done anything sexual together.

I went into the bathroom to wash my hands while Ed finished up. Then we went upstairs so he could drive me home. In the car I told him it was a lot of fun and I would like to do it again sometime soon. He agreed that it was fun and that we should do it again. I shook his hand and went into my house.

That night a lot of things were swirling in my head. I knew I wasn't romantically interested in Ed, I mean he is one of my oldest and dearest friends. But, suddenly in less than twenty-four hours, I was sexually interested in him. The next day I called him and told him that I had had a really good time playing with myself in front of him. He said the same thing. I told him my mom would be out of the house that coming Sunday evening and that I wanted him to come over for some more fun.

Then I asked him *the* question: "How do you feel about me sucking your dick?"

"I'm not sure. I'll think about it."

"I promise you that I'll be good."

"All right, I'll consider it."

That Sunday came and I was a little nervous. Ed came over and I put a long six-hour adult video into the VCR. We sat and talked for a while, glancing at the screen. We both knew what the other was thinking but neither of us spoke about it. Finally after about three-quarters of an hour talking about other stuff, I made my move. I pulled down and took off my pants and underwear so that I was sitting on the sofa next to him with nothing on but a shirt. I sat next to him for a moment or two, slowly getting harder and harder.

"I guess I should take off my clothes too," Ed said as he stood up and took off all of his clothes.

This was the very first time I had ever seen Ed completely naked and when I got my first glimpse of his ass I got as hard as a fucking rock. He turned around and saw my hard cock and smiled at me. We both sat back down on the sofa and began slowly stroking our own cocks, not touching each other yet. We continued to watch the video and slowly stroked our own cocks but we never touched each other. I was a little nervous but also excited.

After about ten minutes of us doing this, I made my move. I slid over next to him and put my hand on his cock. He looked at me and smiled a little bit. I slowly stroked his cock. I could tell that he liked what I was doing. Then I made my big move.

Keep in mind that because of some bad relationships he had had in the past, he was a virgin. Not even a hand job from another person. I felt so bad for the guy that I just wanted to make him feel good. And I knew just how to go about making him feel very, very good.

I leaned down and took his hard cock into my mouth. The sensation took Ed off guard. He didn't quite know what to think. I mean, I had sucked cock before but this guy was one of my best friends. This was a whole new thing for me. Plus, he had the biggest cock I have ever sucked. But, it went down smooth. It was wonderful.

The moan Ed let out was music to my ears. I could tell he was in heaven when I was sucking his cock. I sucked on it like an old pro, which I guess I sort of am. I was loving his cock in my mouth. It was wonderful.

I took his cock out of my mouth and started jacking him off fast and furious. I wanted Ed to come and come badly. And that he did. He shot out a load the likes of which I had never ever seen before. He came all over my hand and then some. Ed was in ecstasy. I could easily tell.

After he came and calmed down from his eruption, it was time to get me off. He stroked my cock like a man possessed. I never had a hand job like that before. It was great. I came in no time. I was so turned on that I came in less than two minutes.

We cleaned ourselves up and got dressed. A little while later, Ed went home. That was not the end of our fun. Oh hell, no. That was only the beginning.

About a month later, Ed called me and wanted to get together again. I was more than eager to oblige him. A few weeks before, I had purchased a blow-up doll from an online catalogue and I had had some fun with it but I wanted to share her with Ed. So, Ed came over that Friday night.

After about an hour I pulled out the blow-up doll. Ed was eager to get at her. So, I inflated her. Ed took off his clothes. My cock was as hard as a rock. He put some lube on his cock, lay down on the sofa in my bedroom and slammed his cock into the doll.

Then I made my big move. I lubed up my cock and while Ed fucked my doll, I slid my cock into his ass. His ass felt so good that I came in no time at all. I pumped his asshole like a man possessed. I slid my cock out of his ass and came all over his gorgeous cheeks. I was mesmerized. I watched in amazement while Ed fucked my doll. I got hard a few minutes later. I played with myself and came on Ed's ass one more time before he came.

We continued to suck each other and stroke each other off over the next few months. About a month ago, my girlfriend was out of town so I invited Ed over. He came over around nine o'clock. We bullshitted for a while. Then we took our clothes off. We then climbed into bed. I kissed him all over his neck, then I worked over his nipples. I made my way down to his cock. I sucked his big delicious cock for all it was worth. While I was sucking him, I worked over his nipples with my fingers.

You just have to see Ed's cock to believe it. It's nine inches long and has a nice thickness to it. It just looks like it was made to be sucked. And I love sucking it. It's great.

I continued to suck Ed for several more minutes. When he came, I held on to his cock with my mouth. I took every bit of his come down my throat without one single drop leaving my mouth. That was the very first time I ever swallowed someone's load and I really liked it.

A few months later, I moved back into my mom's house for a while. While living there, I sucked Ed off in my mom's backyard late at night a few times. It was so nice to suck his cock with the cool breeze blowing on my naked ass. That was super hot.

Ed and I plan to get together for more sex in the future. It's so fun to suck him off and come on his ass. Wow!

THE SWEET SMELL OF SUCCESS

Chrissy, Newcastle

The sign in the shop says WE ALWAYS PROSECUTE SHOPLIFTERS but it isn't entirely true. The way I have it as manager is I only prosecute the women who deserve it – and not the ones whose panties I want to sniff.

It might seem pretty outrageous for the manager of a fashion store to let people off the hook when they've been caught stealing, but the truth is we have so many and, to be honest, the amount of time it sometimes takes to get the police in and start the whole process isn't worth it. Usually the policy, with first-time offenders anyway, is to bring them to the manager's office, take our things back and tell the culprit in no uncertain terms that if we ever even see them in the shop again we will call the police.

Of course there are some who you have to prosecute: the hardliners, the ones who operate as part of a gang, who aren't stealing for themselves but to order. You know who they are as they go for the more expensive stuff, and in bulk. Then we always call the cops in and release the closed circuit TV images to other stores in the area.

No, what I'm talking about are the small-timers. It sometimes isn't worth prosecuting them as they are scared. Just occasionally you even feel a little sorry for them. Plus, there are those whose panties I want to sniff and I wouldn't want to prosecute them at all.

I sometimes can't believe I am the way I am. I am a forty-three-year-old respectable married woman and have been in retailing for years. I think head office regard me as one of their better local managers and have tried to get me to apply for jobs like regional manager. It would be good money no doubt but a lot more pressure too. I would also have to uproot from Tyneside and, more than anything, I wouldn't have the chance to practise my peculiar fetish.

It's a straightforward fetish in that I sniff other women's knickers. I know there are men who do it but what's sauce for the goose is sauce for the gander, and I guess there are more women like me out there who can't get enough of a noseful of the heady aroma from another's woman's crotch. I haven't met any females who admit to doing this but I can't be alone in getting off on the smell of another pussy, but that doesn't worry me. I get what I need whenever I can get it and I'm not into sharing experiences.

Because fashion is everything in a lively working city like this we get a lot of young women in our shop. Most of them are attractive even if the tendency these days seems to be they carry a bit more weight than they should. Well, I'm not going to make love to them so it hardly matters how they look. It's what they secrete between their legs that I'm after.

Usually we get an alert if there are shoplifters nearby, calls from other shops and so on. It's a pretty good network, though my fear is if there's someone wandering round stealing from other places they will get nabbed before they get to my store. I want to be the one who dresses them down, literally, in my office.

Take the other day, for example. We got a call from a fashion store that there was a young woman – blond, age twenty or so, about five foot three with a red coat – who was suspected of trying to take something without paying from a rival shop. So we were ready. Sure enough the girl came into our shop and did what most amateur thieves do: she looked guilty and wandered aimlessly back and forth, just as much concerned with looking over her shoulder and checking where the staff were than looking at the clothes. Believe me you don't have to be an expert in body language to see what's on their minds.

This woman – I'll call her Carol as that was the name she gave me when I spoke to her later – hadn't got a bag, which is the way a lot of this is done. I won't give any trade secrets away but it's obvious that the best way would be to drop something into a bag and slide out of the shop. But Carol didn't work that way.

She was walking between the racks of dresses, half looking at them and glancing round. You have to be careful as sometimes people are looking for a friend, or are simply just "butterfly" lookers, who alight on one thing and then move to another quickly without any seeming reason. But Carol here was someone who ostensibly was a customer who tried something on and didn't want it, but she would have hidden something under her coat. She would take another dress to the changing room and, under the pretext of trying on the obvious choice, would put the stolen item on under her coat. When she emerged from the changing room she would hand back the dress she didn't want and leave the store.

I was watching her on the TV screens in my office. Carol picked up not one but three tops and bundled them under her coat. She looked, almost, as if she were pregnant. Then she went to the underwear section and did the same with a couple of bras. Finally she selected a plain dress, almost without looking at it, and went to check it into the changing room.

When she came out she had her red coat buttoned up, handed over the unwanted dress, which didn't even look her size, and headed for the door. Two of my staff followed her out and onto the street, inviting her to come back in to my office. "Just to clear things up," as they always say.

Poor Carol looked utterly distraught. The amateurs usually do look devastated as they think that once they are on the street they have got away with it. The professionals always look hard or disinterested but then they have usually spirited the items away to someone else, and as they know where the cameras are we rarely get to see to whom they hand off to. Anyway, Carol was sat in my office and she was crying, saying there must be some mistake, that she's a good girl.

I asked her to take her coat off and she objected, but even though it was just me and her she knew there wasn't much chance of not doing what I wanted. It helps, I know, that I am tall and look intimidating under my somewhat stern hairstyle.

Carol undid her coat and sure enough she was wearing all three tops on top of each other. I told her we needed our property back and if she cooperated I wouldn't call the police this time.

Carol was glad to have a way out. She took off the three tops and put them on my desk. She was also wearing the two bras over her own and I told her I needed those returned too. She shed them and looked embarrassed.

"Now," I said, "I want the other thing you stole."

Carol looked astonished. "What other stuff?" she asked blankly. "That's all I took, honest."

Funny how she used the word "honest" here, but I was not smiling. "We saw you on the closed circuit cameras." I indicated the screens behind me, even if I didn't try to show the girl our images of her. "You went to the underwear section, right, where you took the two bras from?"

"Yes," she admitted.

"So I need the panties you took too."

Carol objected, but I told her firmly if she wanted me to press charges I would do so happily, reminding her that it was possible there would be a custodial sentence for shoplifting. But all she had to do to avoid more trouble was cooperate, hand over the panties and leave without ever coming back.

It usually takes a couple of minutes for them to realize that the best thing to do is not argue. Carol got to her feet, hiked up her skirt and took off the only pair of panties she was wearing. "They're not yours," she scowled one last time and dropped them on my desk. White cotton knickers, with little hearts all over them. Cute, really, even if it wasn't the sort of thing we normally sold.

The young woman straightened herself, glared at me, and I showed her the door before asking one of my staff to escort her out of the building. By the time she had left the store I was sat back at my desk with the cute knickers stretched over my head, the crotch against my nose, with my legs wide apart up on the desk and my hand between my legs. I played with myself furiously. I'd already examined the panties as soon as I had closed the office door and seen the skid marks from her cunt and her arse, a few streaks that suggested the knickers had been on a while. Stains are like gold to me.

The aroma from Carol's pussy was perfect as I drank it in. I'd like to think she hadn't changed the knickers in a couple of days as it was particularly rich. Mature, I call it.

I slipped my fingers into my wet sex as I sat there, skirt dragged back clear of my crotch as I didn't want to stain myself. I alternated fingering myself with stroking my clit, wallowing in the deep aroma and the thrillingly intimate muskiness of another female against my nose. I started to feel myself heat up and played with myself more intensely, even flicking my tongue out and straining it upwards to lick at the marked crotch, hoping to taste what I could smell.

I was also excited at the thought of Carol heading home without any knickers on. But then as I don't wear knickers myself I know how open she would have felt. When I came, as I always did like this, my senses were filled with the smell and even the taste of Carol's pretty cunt, her lovely stained knickers smothering my face.

As I recovered I carefully removed the panties and put them in a plastic bag and sealed it, then put them in a special drawer in my desk. I have something like forty pairs of knickers in sealed bags packed in the drawer, and most of them smell every bit as inviting as the day I got them from a shoplifter. As I always tell myself, there may be a week when we don't catch a shoplifter and it would never do to be without something delicious to sniff when the mood takes me.

KIDNAPPED

Katherine, London

When I called Roberta and asked her to kidnap me, I was
kidding. When she said, "OK – be a good girl and stay there,"
and hung up, she wasn't. I only found that out later.

I met the curvy Roberta at a kinky sex party. I was very new
to sex parties, and spent most of my time hiding by the wall. She
was one of the liveliest women at the party, about thirty, with
freckles dancing across her cheeks and a mischievous sparkle in
her eyes. I remember her blond hair was pulled back, a tiny top
hat balanced, precariously, on her head as she laughed and
joked with other partygoers. We exchanged a few words at the
bar. I had meant to be witty, and probably instead sounded in
awe as I complimented her outfit; still, she had exchanged
numbers with me, and a promise to get together sometime. I
was excited as I tucked the number into my bra, as I was new to
the area and glad to have made a friend. I watched her rounded
ass as she walked away, imagined what it must feel like to lick
those creamy, thick thighs. I was infatuated.

The first time I met her husband was at a local dungeon. It
was my birthday; they had given me a beautiful vintage purse
and a spanking. I remember I noticed how sexy he was, also in
his early thirties, with a slightly pudgy stomach and a short
brown goatee. I had recently discovered my attraction to
rounded stomachs and hairy men, and David was an excel-
lently presented example. He was silly, too, I remember – I
think it was a costume party we were at. He had dressed like a
caveman to his wife's sabre-toothed tiger; I had enjoyed her
fangs.

Our paths had crossed once or twice afterwards and we meant to get together to hang out. It never quite worked out, there was always some event going on. We did spend time together, but always at parties, in a whirl of faces and music that made it difficult to get to know each other.

But now, thanks to a random phone call, we were going to have dinner and chat at last. I remember how giddy I felt as I rushed around, putting on make-up and nicer clothes. I had been staying at my grandmother's house up in the hills. It had felt empty and dull for weeks since she was away on vacation. Alone in a dark house, I sat on the edge of the bed, purse in my hands, feeling excited and silly like it was a high-school date. When the knock echoed through the house, I jumped up, then tried to walk to the door like I hadn't been sitting and waiting.

I opened the door only to find two ski-masked people there, both in black. One was curvy, and had some tendrils of blond escaping out from under her hood, so I felt sure it was Roberta, and the other had the vague proportions of her husband.

"Candygram," they chorused, and entered the house, the door shutting behind them.

"Do you really want to be kidnapped?" the woman asked, and I sighed with relief as I recognized Roberta's voice.

I thought for a moment, then nodded, shyly. I wouldn't have been able to deny that my pussy was wet under my jeans, and kidnappings were a favourite fantasy of mine.

The other figure nodded. "OK," he said. "We're going to undress you and take you with us. You have a safe word, of course – it's 'red'. Use it if you need to. Otherwise, just do as we say. Can you do that?"

"Yes," I whispered, unable to believe this was really happening to me.

"Give me the house key so we can lock up," Roberta said as she started to undress me, pulling off my shirt and jeans and stuffing them into a duffel bag. I handed it to her out of my purse, which she also shoved into the bag. David blindfolded me, and I felt cool hands unclasping my bra and sliding off my underwear. Someone tied my hands together in front of me with something soft. Then I felt something itchy around me . . . I recognized it was my wool cape, which they wrapped around my body, tugging the hood up over my head.

"Think that'll work?" Roberta asked David. I didn't know what they meant. Work for what?

"Yeah, if we're careful," he answered. "We should probably not have the ski masks on, in case we get stopped. I don't want to try explaining this to police."

I giggled, feeling giddy. They pushed me along, opened the door and walked me into the night air. It was chilly, but not overly so. One of my kidnappers held me as the other locked the door to the house. Gently, telling me when to step up, they got me up the stairs into the driveway. I heard a car door open, and hands encouraged me to crawl into the back seat, where I was buckled in. I heard some more car doors open and shut, and the engine rev. We were in motion. But where were we going? I knew of a sex club in the city, but they wouldn't let me in the way I was, naked and bound!

It seemed like we were in the car for only a few minutes before it stopped. I heard the faint beep of a code being entered, and the car drove into an underground area, a parking lot, I thought to myself. And then I panicked. Had they brought me to their apartment? Was I crazy for just letting these people I barely knew carry me off? Probably, but at this point I wanted to see what would happen. And I had never been so wet as I was then. I prayed I wasn't leaving a smear of come in their car.

I was helped out of the vehicle and into another elevator. I heard someone step out and call back, "Clear!" before we moved again. The jingle of keys, the clank of a bolt sliding back, and I felt a rush of warm air that felt decadent against my skin. We were inside somewhere. I felt safe, in spite of the circumstances . . . I guess I've always enjoyed danger, and this was just the right amount of danger to get my juices running. My cape was unclasped and removed, and I was led forwards again, acutely aware of my nudity and a dribble of wetness that had begun to drip along my thigh. I was guided into a seat, my hands untied and retied separately to something that felt like chains. My blindfold was removed, and I blinked, my eyes adjusting to the light. I was in a bedroom, but not on the bed –

no, I was attached to a sex swing that dangled next to the bed from a hook Roberta and David must struggle to hide from visitors. I saw a closet overflowing with high-heeled boots and corsets, bits and pieces from costumes I had seen them in from time to time. There was a dresser with nipple clamps and rope scattered amongst perfume bottles and pocket change. I knew I was in for an exciting night, and David attached some cuffs to my ankles as if to confirm it. He clipped the ankle cuffs to the swing, leaving me feeling deliciously helpless and very, very exposed. There would be no hiding my arousal now.

Roberta appeared, now dressed only in a lacy black push-up bra and matching knickers, holding a ball gag in her hand. Her golden skin glittered slightly, her rounded tummy making her look like a modern Venus. "May I?" she asked, kindly, and I nodded hard, feeling thankful for anything that would take the pressure to say something off. The ball slid between my lips, just big enough to keep me from speaking but not so large I strained. Then, the double team act truly began, as she nibbled my neck and arms and David began to run his tongue along my slit. Her hands stroked my inner thighs, making me twitch and sigh; David laced his fingers into hers, and together they traced spirals over my pussy. Roberta languidly put her hand, now damp with my secretions, up to her lips and licked it clean. Her nails, I noticed, were clipped short and neat. I shuddered, feeling myself pulse with the desire to be used by my kidnappers.

David moved to my head and began to run his fingers through my hair, using them to push it aside. My neck exposed, he began to bite, gently at first, then harder, leaving a trail of bruises and saliva in his wake. His beard tickled the tender skin, and he used it to rasp my neck as he nibbled and nipped. Roberta was putting her smooth fingertips to good use in my cunt. Her middle finger slid in easily and curled gently to caress my G-spot. I moaned around the gag as she spit on my pink nub and rubbed her thumb on it, softly at first, then harder as I began to push my hips back into her. The biting continued, little shocks of pain intensified and then soothed by the ministrations of Roberta. I felt myself close to orgasm, but not quite there – how could I tell them I needed just a little bit more?

Green eyes met my pleading ones, and she smiled. "Bite her nipples," she told David, and he used his tongue to find them. He bit, and I shuddered, my pussy convulsing around her hand as I came hard.

"Your turn," Roberta said to her husband with a smile, as she removed the ball gag. She let me lick her fingers clean of my juices.

"Let's put her on the bed," he said, and began to free my ankles.

She deftly untied my hands from the chain, leaving the worn hemp rope on them as she directed me, now somewhat shaky with the aftershocks, towards their bed.

"Should we tie her hands to the frame like a good old-fashioned bondage scene, or something else?" David asked.

"Oh, I think we can leave her hands untied for now – I'll hold them down," his wife replied with a wicked smile, grabbing my hair and using it to pull my face to hers. We kissed, tentatively at first and then wildly. My thigh unconsciously moved between hers and pressed against her clit; the lace panties offered no real barrier. She pulled me away and, with a handful of my hair, she picked up a glass of water and drank. "Would you like some water? Wouldn't want to wear you out too fast!"

I nodded, and she opened my mouth and poured some water from her lips into my dry mouth. It was like I had never had water before. I swallowed greedily and opened my mouth for another. This time she let me drink from the cup, before spanking my ass.

"Now, get on the bed like a good pet, all fours," she ordered, and I complied. I positioned myself in the middle, unsure what was going to happen next but sure I was going to like it.

David removed his clothes, exposing a hairy chest and a raging erection. I was surprised and excited by his lack of underwear. Roberta grabbed a tin from the nightstand and opened it to reveal a variety of condoms; selecting a blue one from the bunch, she put the tin back and opened the condom wrapper. He crawled onto the bed and she rolled the condom onto his cock with her lips and tongue, her eyes on his as she licked and sucked the condom into place. He groaned, watching his wife, her pussy and ass close to my face as she worked. I got a sudden urge to pull her panties aside and let my tongue attack her pussy, but resisted. I didn't want to be punished.

David moved between my legs, lifting them until my calves rested on his shoulders. He grabbed a bottle of lubricant from the dresser. A little dribble covered my slit, cold and arousing. I could feel his latex-clad cock as it slid over my clitoris, making me shiver with desire.

"Do you want me to fuck you?" he asked softly, and I wanted it so badly I almost wept.

Instead I nodded, unsure I could speak.

"Tell me. Beg me to fuck you."

"Please." It came out a broken whisper, my voice cracking slightly. "Please, David, fuck me. I need to feel your cock inside me, so badly . . . so, so badly . . ." I was getting wetter with every word. I've always loved talking dirty; how did he know that?

"That's good enough," he said, kindly, and then Roberta's pussy, no longer trapped behind the lace knickers, suddenly smothered my mouth. She smelled musky and warm; her secretions were like fresh cream, thick and delicious. I let my nose rub against her clitoris as my tongue flicked over her opening, teasingly. My teeth lightly slid across her clit, then the tip of my tongue. I alternated between the two sensations, listening to her whimpers and trying to guess which she liked better.

I groaned into her labia lips as David entered me.

He had a short, thick cock, slightly curved at the tip, perfectly made to hook the edge of my G-spot with each slow thrust. When he slid out of my pussy and plunged back in, I cried out, the vibrations of my whimpers making her wriggle with delight. As he fucked me faster and deeper, my tongue grew wilder, plunging in and out of Roberta with abandon. She cried out, a deep, musical sound, and in between my moans I watched as David grabbed Roberta's hair and pulled her head back as she ground herself against my lips.

Her sandy pubic hair rubbed my lips raw, but I barely noticed. My feet hooked around his neck as he pushed me forwards a little, resting his weight on my thighs as he ripped Roberta's bra off, releasing her breasts. They were heavy, just over a handful each, bouncing in rhythm as he thrusted and she pushed her pussy into my tongue. I reached up and she let me capture her nipple between my fingers. I rolled each one around, lightly tugging as I lapped at her wetness. I came first, the squeezing of my cunt setting off David who groaned loudly as he shot into the condom. I shook my head back and forth quickly, my nose and tongue flickering over her pussy and clitoris until Roberta orgasmed with a contented sigh, my lips and cheeks covered with her cream.

We all sagged for a moment, spent. Then it was time for showers and dinner; they asked me to stay the night, and I gladly complied. I curled up between them, still throbbing, heart still racing. I could hardly believe any of it had happened to me. I was happy it had.

It may have been the first time, but luckily for me, it wasn't the last.

A SLAVE'S CONFESSION

Alexander, Horsham

Mistress Catherine and I, both of us naked, were in her living room that balmy evening. The gentlest of winds was pushing the curtain in slightly, revealing the dark of a starless, moonless sky outside. Catherine was seated on a black leather easy chair, one hand languorously caressing her sex, the other holding the handle of the rattan cane with which she'd just beaten me. I was kneeling on the floor by her side, gazing up at her adoringly. My backside was covered in smarting welts, my cock stiffly erect.

"Confess to me something wicked you've done in the past," my Mistress demanded. "I will then punish you for it."

"What sort of punishment, Mistress?" I asked nervously.

"I don't know yet," she replied, giving a slight flick of the shiny dark fringe that hung over her forehead. "It depends what you confess. I'll make the punishment fit the crime."

"I see, Mistress," I said, my voice hesitant.

"Come on, slave," Catherine pressed, a little impatient now. "There must be something you did in your guilt-ridden Catholic past you felt was particularly wicked, something that's contributed to those occasional bouts of angst that I have to beat out of you. Get it off your chest."

Thinking for a brief moment before replying, I said, "It goes back to when I was a teenager, Mistress. At the time in question I had hardly any experience of the opposite sex. I was also years away from recognizing my submissive and masochistic nature.

"I was a real late developer sexually and had only recently discovered masturbation. But I found it a guilty pleasure because, as you say, I'd been raised as a Catholic, a religion that teaches that self-pleasuring is sinful. What I'm about to confess would certainly be regarded as wicked by the Catholic Church. In fact they would call it a mortal sin."

"Go on," said Catherine. "You're beginning to interest me." She put the cane to the side of the chair and started to pleasure herself in earnest, working her fingers rhythmically between the lips of her sex.

"It all started on a Sunday, Mistress," I continued. "I was looking forward to the week ahead as it was a half-term holiday. I was attending Mass as usual, but instead of worshipping God I was on my knees worshipping the pretty blond altar server who was assisting the priest with the service.

"His name was Jerry and he was a year older than me. He lived nearby with his widowed mother. She and my mother were friendly through their involvement with the Church but Jerry and I were only passing acquaintances. On this occasion, though, as our mothers talked to one another after the service, Jerry and I also got into conversation and were getting on really well.

" 'What are you doing this week?' I asked.

" 'I've nothing planned,' he replied. 'How about the two of us going swimming tomorrow afternoon?'

"I said I thought this was a good idea and we made arrangements to meet.

"That night I couldn't resist the temptation to masturbate as I imagined what Jerry might look like without clothes – I was about to find that out, and a hell of a lot more besides.

"We got together the next day and made our way to the nearby open-air swimming pool. As we walked along, chatting about this and that, I allowed my gaze to wander up and down his body. I couldn't help thinking how good he looked in his tight jeans. I admired the perfect shape of his rear moulded into the denim and the impressive bulge at the front.

"Although the weather was reasonably mild that day, there were a lot of dark-looking clouds in the sky, and when we arrived we found that the pool was only sparsely attended. There was a slight breeze that ruffled the water, which looked downright cold. We went into the changing rooms and, at

Jerry's suggestion, shared a cubicle. As he stripped off, I was surprised, and turned on, to notice that he hadn't been wearing any underwear beneath those tight jeans. I was aware that my cock was starting to swell when I slipped into my swimming trunks, and found it a decided relief – an embarrassment averted – to run on ahead and plunge into the chilly water of the swimming pool.

"Jerry and I stayed in the pool for about an hour, splashing about, and it gradually warmed up. Every once in a while the sun even deigned to reveal itself through a break in the clouds, allowing reflected light to dance on the rippling blue water. Jerry and I swam and played in the pool – and, OK, maybe we did make physical contact a bit more than was strictly necessary in our games there.

"When we got out of the water the changing room was empty apart from ourselves. We dried off in the same cubicle, still in our swimming costumes. However, our bulges were becoming increasingly pronounced and when I took off my swimming trunks my cock sprang out erect.

" 'Mmm, that looks very nice,' said Jerry, who pulled down his trunks to reveal his own lengthening erection. 'Come on,' he said, his member now as full and stiff as my own. 'Let's jerk off together.'

"Feeling light-headed and extremely excited, I encircled my erect cock with my fingers as I watched Jerry bring a hand to his own erection. We both rubbed our cocks up and down vigorously, climaxing at pretty much the same time. And equally lavishly too, spraying out streams of sticky wetness onto each other with great force. It was an amazing feeling, it truly was – my first time masturbating with anyone else, and the most intense sexual experience that I'd so far had in my young life.

"We showered, dried ourselves, dressed and headed for home, both of us more than a little subdued. We said very little as we strode along, lost in our own guilty thoughts. Just as we were about to part, however, Jerry brightened. 'Fancy coming round to my house tomorrow?' he said. He told me that his mother would be at work so we'd have the place to ourselves.

" 'That'd be great,' I replied.

" 'It's a date, then. See you around eleven.' Jerry's face suddenly broadened into a grin. 'Hey and no more jerking off until then.'

"That proved easier said than done. I tossed and turned uneasily in my bed that night. My mind was in a whirl going over and over what Jerry and I had done together and what might happen tomorrow. According to my Church, all these 'impure thoughts' were a sin but the feelings of guilt this caused just seemed to make my cock harder. I was excited as much as anything by the intoxicating shame of my own arousal. Even so, although it took a deal of will power, I didn't touch myself that night.

"The next day I killed time earlier in the morning trying to decide what to wear for my 'date'. A clean white T-shirt and one of my pairs of jeans, I thought. On a whim, I removed my underwear, taking a leaf out of Jerry's book, and squeezed into the tightest pair of jeans I possessed.

"I set off, slightly nervous but very excited, the knot in my stomach no competition for the throbbing of my shaft. My growing sense of anticipation and the rough feel of the tight denim against my cock meant that I was in a high state of sexual arousal by the time I arrived at Jerry's house.

"When he answered the door I was struck anew by how devastatingly attractive he was, with his blond hair falling over his forehead, that pretty face and lithe, athletic body. He was wearing nothing but the jeans he'd worn the day before, which clung to his form like a second skin.

" 'Hi there, you're looking good,' he said, reaching over and squeezing the bulge in my jeans. I did the same to him, feeling the warmth of his cock beneath the skin-tight denim.

" 'Would you like a coffee or anything else to drink?' he asked.

" 'No thanks, I'm fine,' I replied.

" 'You sure are,' he said with a laugh. 'Follow me, we'll go up to my room and fool around.'

"Once in his bedroom we hastily stripped and were soon on his bed mutually masturbating, our excitement growing and growing. We climaxed simultaneously in great bursting spurts, and then lay together in the afterglow, the come on our bellies intermingling.

"We washed ourselves and put on our jeans, then went and had a snack and just hung out for a while. But it wasn't long before our lust erupted again and our swelling members were straining once more against the tight denim that covered them. We were soon naked and erect again, masturbating each other feverishly. And for most of the rest of that afternoon we simply couldn't keep our hands off each other.

" 'How about tomorrow?' asked Jerry, as I was about to leave.

" 'You bet,' I replied eagerly.

"It seemed like an eternity to me until we met the next day. I reckon Jerry must have felt much the same way because as soon as he'd let me into the house he pulled me towards him and kissed me hard. I kissed him right back, savouring the slick, demanding feel of his lips and frantic tongue, and reciprocating for all I was worth. Jerry and I carried on kissing passionately while rubbing our bulging cocks together, getting more and more turned on. We then went up to his room, stripped naked again and began mutually masturbating once more. Then the mood changed . . .

" 'Kneel down,' he said all of a sudden, his tone chilly with command. I obeyed in an instant. 'Now suck me off,' he added, 'and make a good job of it.'

"I was determined to do just that. I engulfed his stiff cock with my lips (it tasted *so* good, I can't tell you) and swirled my tongue around its swollen head. My tongue laved his cock, licking the thickness, my lips kissing and rubbing against it so that it flexed and strained against my mouth. Next I began sucking on his shaft with slow regular movements, then faster, then slower, then faster still. I felt as if I was born to give blow jobs. It made me feel deliciously wicked, thoroughly debauched and perverted and *sinful*.

"After I'd been blowing him for a while he announced, 'I'm going to climax real soon now.' His voice was full of sexual tension but just as commanding as before. 'When I do,' he added, 'I want you to swallow my come, every last drop.'

"I wanted to do that too, craved it. I could taste the beads of liquid seeping constantly from the slit of his cock and knew that there would soon be a gushing torrent. Then it happened. He emitted a strangled moan and erupted to a shuddering orgasm, his cock gushing wad after wad of creamy come deep into my mouth. And I did exactly as I'd been told. My head still furiously pumping, I drew down every ounce of the semen that spurted onto the back of my tongue, taking it deep into my throat.

"There's not a lot to add, Mistress. We carried on meeting in the same way for the rest of that week, and the following Sunday saw me at Mass on my knees again, my cock pulsing constantly as I worshipped that beautiful blond altar server. As a devout Roman Catholic I knew what I was feeling and what I'd done was sinful and wicked in the extreme, utterly depraved, but I just couldn't help myself. That, Mistress, is my shameful confession."

Mistress Catherine had been pleasuring herself constantly throughout my account, her fingers making an increasingly liquid sound. She now removed those fingers, wet with love juice, from between her swollen pussy lips and stood up. "That certainly was *extremely* wicked, slave," she said, her eyes shining. "Now remain on your knees and prepare to receive your punishment."

Catherine picked up the rattan cane again and gave it a practice swipe. She then went on to cane my already punished backside, beating me severely, one fierce stroke after another in swift succession, until the pain lacing through me was excruciating. I felt as if my body was ablaze as I tried frantically to contain the furious pain. At last I could take no more. "Mercy, Mistress, I beg you," I cried out, hot tears raining down my cheeks.

She stopped caning me immediately at that point and moved to my front. She placed herself on all fours, her rear splayed open, the pink opening of her anus twitching invitingly in my face. "Lick my asshole while I go back to pleasuring myself," she instructed, looking at me briefly from over her shoulder.

Needless to say, I obeyed and licked her pulsating anal hole for all I was worth. I darted my tongue in and out, feeling her anal muscles contracting around it as she continued to masturbate ever more furiously.

"Now bring yourself off," she demanded, her voice throaty with desire. "I want you to come over my asshole and then lick it all up, swallow the lot."

Again I did exactly as my Mistress told me. And as she used her fingers to bring herself, trembling ecstatically, to a violent orgasm, I too shuddered to a powerful climax. Convulsions shook my body as my cock erupted, pumping out a stream of ejaculate over her beautiful anus. Then, obedient slave that I am, I licked up and swallowed all that come – every last drop.

THE OPERA

Jane, Queensland

I was bored shitless. These operas were a total waste of my time. My boyfriend Brad's boss had given him free tickets in a private box and, at the last minute, had insisted he stay back and finish off a proposal. I was pissed off, I can tell you. This guy's voice was grating on my nerves. I had no idea what he was singing and why everyone seemed to be enthralled by him. I glanced over at the other side of the theatre, noting very little that interested me until I spied a very good-looking guy on the level above.

He too was in a box and by the looks of things his girlfriend, or whoever was up there with him, was glued to the stage. He looked down at me and at first I wondered if he was really looking at me or just observing the area. It wasn't until I saw him pick up his little opera glasses and hone in on me that I thought I too would check him out. Fortunately, Brad had insisted I take a pair along, didn't want me to miss out on anything interesting.

It was weird, spying on each other. He pulled back first, smirking seductively at me, raising his eyebrow as he pursed his lips, his eyes looking downwards. It took me a second to realize that he was indicating my lower half. I squirmed in my seat, eager for some fun.

With my eyes still glued to him, I lifted my skirt, exposing a good piece of my thigh. His hand indicated to go further, so I did. He nodded his head in approval. Being an exhibitionist by nature I pushed back in my seat and opened my legs.

I watched him lick his lips.

I shifted my gaze to his companion and the woman was still riveted to the stage. With one hand I managed to pull the crotch of my panties over. I could see him nodding his head. I lifted one leg and braced it against the balcony. Now I inserted a finger and began to explore myself. He leaned forwards and I rubbed my clit, enjoying the little show I was putting on for him.

Suddenly bright lights lit up the area and I quickly pulled my dress back down over my knees and sat up properly. It was the interval. Most people left their seats to have a glass of wine. I stayed where I was, disappointed at having to cut my fun short.

My mystery man spoke into the woman's ear and then rose and left. I stayed where I was, hoping it wouldn't be long before the curtains were back up and the lights dimmed. As the bell rang to indicate that the opera was ready to begin, I eagerly waited for the man to return to his seat.

Unfortunately he didn't and after peering through the lenses for at least five more minutes I finally placed the binoculars in my handbag and turned my attention back to the stage. A curtain behind me opened and the very man that I had been looking for sat in the seat that should have been Brad's.

Nervous now, I kept my eyes glued to the stage, unsure of what to do. He too seemed to be watching but suddenly his fingers were inching up my dress. I gasped. Should I stop him? Showing him was one thing but allowing him to have his way with me was, well, another. I held my breath as his hand slid under the material and between my thighs.

His fingers probed at the lacy edge of my panties and I wiggled in the seat, opening my legs for him to give him easier access. I thought I heard him chuckle softly and then his finger was sliding up and down my slit. I moaned with pleasure, leaning back in the chair, shifting my arse so it was hanging off the chair.

He slipped right in, my pussy wet from my own little play around earlier. My chest rose and fell and my passion built and then he was on the floor between my thighs, his head under my skirt, his warm breath tantalizing my inner thigh before his tongue flickered around my pussy lips. It was thrilling, I can tell you.

Still pretending to show interest with the opera I had the uncontrollable urge to grab hold of my breasts and tweak my nipples. I was so turned on as his fingers dug deep inside me, it took all my will power not to scream out with desire. He fingered me like that for a few minutes, really juicing me up. But I wanted more, needed more.

Tapping his head and indicating that I wanted him to move, I slid onto the floor, hoping that the balcony would serve its purpose and not allow anyone to see what we were up to.

He'd already undone his zip and had his cock in his hand. I flew down to it and gobbled it up into my mouth, sucking furiously, loving the feel of his knob as it slid over my lips and then his shaft was sliding down my throat while I squeezed his hairy balls.

I needed to be fucked and wasn't sure how much longer this opera would go on for. I worked my way up to his mouth and kissed him, our tongues lashing at each other's.

"Fuck me from behind," I said, rolling over and wiggling out of my panties.

He grabbed my hips and I rolled back a fraction, lifting my leg to place over his thigh. He guided his cock into my pussy and began to fuck me like I've never been fucked before.

It was wild, I can tell you. I had no idea who he was or where he came from, all I knew was that I didn't want him to stop. He grabbed hold of one of my tits and crushed it cruelly while he slammed into me. I was peaking, desperate to come but not wanting this to stop. He felt my pussy contracting and pumped harder, his breath coming out in gasps as he too climaxed.

We lay there together when it was over and then I felt him move away from me. I wanted to talk to him, find out who he was but he rushed through the curtains and then they fell back and I was all alone. Straightening up my clothing I sat back on the chair. I looked everywhere but couldn't find my panties.

On the other side of the theatre the guy was back in his box, whispering into the woman's ear. She looked over towards me and laughed. I rummaged in my bag and pulled out the binoculars, annoyed that they were laughing at my expense. Focusing in on them I noticed the woman had something red in her hand. She brought the fabric to her nose and seemed to be sniffing.

A hot sensation prickled me as I realized she was sniffing my panties. She put them in her handbag and smiled at me, kissing the guy full on the mouth. She seemed to be licking his lips, chin and cheeks. With her tongue licking him clean I knew it was me she was tasting and I promised myself as soon as this opera was over, I was going over there to introduce myself to them.

Just before the end though, Brad arrived. He hugged me, begging forgiveness at having to have left me alone. He said he'd make it up to me but the only thing I wanted then and there was another good fucking.

Grabbing his hand we raced out and into the car park. Like I said, I loved being an exhibitionist so I allowed him to take me over the bonnet, hoping beyond hope that someone would see us, would demand we stop. Unfortunately, though, no one did.

"Man, are you wet," Brad said.

"It's the opera, darling," I said. "I didn't think anything could turn me on so much."

"We'll have to come more often then," he laughed as he sunk his shaft in me.

"Yes, we'll have to *come* again and again."

DAGGERS

Angie, Wilmington

I stood motionless for a moment, staring at the empty hole in the wall, knowing exactly what Nicole expected of me.

"Ready?" Nicole chimed, her eyes flashing between mine and the hole. My thoughts were a blur of fear, arousal and, most of all, uncertainty. Did I really want this, despite what I had said?

"Well?" Nicole said. "Don't you want to?"

I do, I told myself. I did. Of course I did. Ever since Nicole had explained this to me I had wanted to, had fantasized about it. But it was just that: a fantasy, something I said to make myself seem wilder in front of my friends; something said when I was drunk. Just something I had said, with the assumption that I would never have to really decide, never have to act upon it.

I had no way of knowing what would happen if I did this – I didn't even know Nicole, not really – but somehow that excited me even more. I looked at her and felt a strange, wonderful fear. I thought then about how rare it is to experience something so totally unknown, so new. And I remembered the boast I had made earlier at the bar. I'd rather regret something I did than regret something I didn't do. I looked once more at the hole, and made my decision.

Nicole could see it in my eyes and smiled. "Good," she said. "I'll go tell them you're ready." And she turned and left me, closing the door behind her. I locked it and then stepped to the wall where I instinctively dropped to my knees on the dirty concrete.

I listened intently for sounds from the other side of the wall, but could hear nothing but the endless thumping of the music.

For what felt like an eternity I knelt by the wall, waiting for what I knew was coming. My eyes were fixed on the hole, watching, waiting.

A soft cock appeared in the opening, hanging limp over the edge, waiting to be sucked. I stared at it. I wasn't actually going to do this, was I? How could I? How could I not? My heart was racing as I looked over my shoulder, making sure I was indeed alone. I looked back at the waiting cock. I leaned forward, closing my eyes, and I slipped the warm cock between my lips. Instantly I felt it growing in my mouth, lengthening and thickening as I sucked on it. I tried to picture myself, on my knees in a dirty storage closet, sucking a cock stuck through a jagged hole in a wall. I felt ashamed, horrified almost at the depth to which Nicole could make me sink, yet exhilarated at the utter perversity of what I was doing.

I pulled the cock from my mouth and looked at it, fully erect now, and lapped at the swollen head, nibbled at its spongy softness. Once again I took it in my mouth, its hardness slipping through my wet lips. I tried to imagine who its owner was, what he looked like, how old he was. If he had a girlfriend. Or a wife. Was he tall? Had I seen him in the club? Maybe he was the guy that bought Nicole that drink. I thought suddenly then about protection. I had no idea who this man was, where he'd been. I pushed the thought aside. I couldn't stop now. Besides, this was part of the adventure, part of the danger. Taking chances. Taking risks.

Unable to see his face, to hear the sounds he made, made it nearly impossible to tell if he liked what I was doing to him, much less anticipate when he might come. Still, gauging by the hardness of his cock, I was doing just fine. I held and kneaded the large pouch of balls that had been pushed through the hole as well, caressing them as I moved my head back and forth on the cock. I felt it twitch ever so slightly on my tongue just before releasing its hot fluid into my mouth. I could feel the force of it spurting over my tongue and flooding my throat, could feel it coating my mouth, clinging to my teeth. I was almost frightened at how willing I was to suck anonymous cock, how easy it was for me to receive and swallow a complete stranger's come.

Even as I nursed the softening cock it was pulled abruptly from my mouth. Almost immediately another took its place. It was so long that it bumped against my nose before I could move out of its way. It hovered there, impatiently waiting to be sucked, and I crawled under it. Hesitation gone, I wrapped my lips hungrily around this new offering, imagining the smile on its owner's face as I did. I sucked my second cock of the night, working it into my mouth until the head was in my throat. I almost thought I heard him moan on the other side as I freed him momentarily to catch my breath, staring at his length, now shining wet with my saliva. I fed it back in, groaning loudly at the feel of it between my tingling lips. Back and forth I went, until I felt the warm jets of his come on my tongue. Connected to this man only by his cock, I could still feel his body trembling as he came and could hear him calling out his pleasure, hidden from me just inches away. He filled my mouth until I was leaking, sucking the whole time. Finally he expired and pulled away, disappearing quietly into the dark hole.

The hole was vacated, then just as quickly occupied again. And it went on, cock after cock magically appearing in the hole and just as mysteriously slipping from view after I had made it come. I was amazed at the variety of manhood offered to me— black and white, long and short, thick and thin. Each had its own unique taste and smell, its own feel. After the fourth, I stopped swallowing. I was afraid I would get sick and end up in the emergency room needing my stomach pumped like in some twisted urban legend. Instead, I let them come in my mouth and then pull out before I spit onto the floor below me. I wondered, suddenly, what a group of cocks would be called. A group of crows is a murder. There's a pod of whales. A pride of lions. What would a group of cocks be? A stab of cocks? A siege, maybe? How about a brace? After the seventh cock, the closet began to reek of sex, the thick taste of come filling my mouth, my pants legs splattered with it, a cloudy pool of it collecting below me.

Another cock skewered the hole in the wall like a dagger. A dagger, I thought. A dagger of cocks.

AFTERNOON ANAL SURPRISE

Eric, Ithaca

Looking back on this little incident I can see that she definitely planned the whole thing out systematically in advance. I did have a clue that something a little suspicious was going on that time when we went to the drugstore to pick up a prescription for me, and while I was there talking to the pharmacist I noticed her way down at the end of the aisle picking up a tube of lubricant and a package of condoms and taking them to the register at the other side of the store. I had never seen her buy such things before, and I thought that we really didn't need them. I didn't say anything to her about it, deciding that I would just wait her out and see if she was going to say anything. But she didn't. She worked as a nurse, so I assumed she must have bought these things because one of her nursing patients needed them. After a couple of weeks I just forgot about it.

Then one lazy, hot weekend afternoon while we were splashing around in the swimming pool, with some occasional playful fondling of each other, she asked me if I'd go up to the bedroom with her and "do something". Well, of course I would! I had always thought of her as being rather sexually conservative though so I figured that she was just in the mood for some good old-fashioned, traditional, ordinary fucking, as was usual for us.

When we got up to the bedroom this time though, she surprised me by asking if I'd be willing to do some anal play with her. I certainly didn't see anything wrong with that but I was a little bit stunned that she would actually suggest this, as she had never expressed any interest in anything anal during the whole four years that we had been together. She got out the KY and a couple of condoms. She told me to slip a condom over my finger and put some KY on it, and she did the same. She then had me lie on my back on the bed with my legs spread and my knees upraised. She was used to giving orders to her nursing patients and I felt almost as if I were one of them, passively following her orders and about to be subjected to some kind of unknown and mysterious procedure.

She got on the bed on her hands and knees beside me, with her ass pointing in the same direction as my head, and her face near my upraised thighs. She asked me to put my lubed finger in her ass and massage her anus, and at the same time she reached under my thigh and slid her finger in my ass, and began moving it in and out. She put her face down closer, peering around under my thigh, so that she could get a better look at my anus while she moved her finger in and out of it. She had an oddly serious look on her face, as if she were intent on giving me a physical exam.

At first both of the sensations, that of me fingering her butt and that of her fingering mine, seemed very strange and I felt awkward and silly. After a few minutes of it I started to get used to it and to feel pleasantly peaceful and relaxed, almost entranced. I think I would have been content to just stay there with the two of us massaging each other's butts for the rest of the afternoon. My cock seemed to have a mind of its own though, and it had become very stiff during the course of our anal play.

"Do you want to put your penis in there?" she said. I was not expecting this from her at all, and the businesslike and serious way in which she voiced this surprisingly kinky proposition almost made me laugh.

"Uh, sure."

"I think you should use a condom."

"OK."

I was amused by her professional nurse's caution and fussiness concerning hygiene. If it were up to me I would have simply skipped the use of the condoms, done the deed and then just washed up well afterwards but that was not her way, and I thought it best to simply follow her lead in this.

I pulled the condom off of my hand and threw it away, and got a new one and put it on my cock. I got up onto my knees and awkwardly manoeuvred around behind her on the bed. She was on her knees with her face pressed into a pillow and her breasts against the bed. Her butt was sticking almost straight up. I was awed and amazed at the sight of her body in this strangely submissive posture. I had never seen her like this before.

"Go ahead, put it in," she said, her voice muffled by the pillow.

I put the head of my cock against her anus. I started to push and it slipped out of position and almost went into her vagina. I tried it a couple more times but her anal muscles were tight and it kept slipping out.

"I can't get it to open up," I said.

She reached behind her and put her hand on my cock and positioned the head of it against her anus again. "Try it again," she said.

On the next try I pushed it in very slowly, but firmly, holding my cock in place with my hand as I pushed it in. It was very tight, much tighter than her vagina. I heard her inhale a long deep breath as it slid into her. When it was all the way in I stopped and stayed motionless behind her for a minute. I took a breath and held it for a few seconds.

"What's wrong? How come you're not moving? Are you all right?" she said.

"It's OK, just let me go slowly, all right? Let me take my time." In fact the sensation of my cock being gripped tightly by her rectum and anus was quite intense. I was embedded so deeply and so tightly in her that it felt like her whole body had become an extension of my cock. I tried to relax so that I wouldn't come right away. Gradually I started to feel calmer and more confident, and I started moving my cock in and out of her ass, slowly and gently. When I could be sure that it wasn't hurting her and that I wasn't going to come too soon, I increased my movement so that I was fucking her ass vigorously. I pushed her all the way down so that she was prone on the bed and I was lying on top of her back, still fucking her.

After humping her like that for a while I thought that I should do something different, and that maybe I could make her come, or at least try to make her come, if I stimulated her clit. I gripped her shoulders and rolled us both over in the bed so that I was on my back and she was lying on top of me, with her back to me and my cock still in her behind. I reached one hand down between her legs and into her pubic hair, and found her clit. I started rubbing it gently back and forth. To my surprise she came very soon, and it seemed to be quite an intense orgasm. She tensed up all over, panting heavily, and I could feel a wave of convulsions pass through her body. When she finally relaxed and I was sure that she was done coming I rolled her onto her side, with my cock still up her rectum. I decided it was time for me to come. I started plunging it in and out of her with long, forceful strokes while I squeezed and fondled her tits from behind. I fucked her pretty hard until I finally came. After my panting had subsided and I stopped moving, she turned her head and said over her shoulder, "You came, right?"

"Oh my God, yes."

We lay there on the bed for a few moments listening to the silence. I felt my cock relaxing and softening after my orgasm, so I started to pull it out of her. She said, "Are you pulling it out? Can't you stay in a while longer?"

"Sorry, my cock is through for now. I can't keep it in you."

I pulled off the condom, went into the bathroom and washed off my cock, then came back into the bedroom and collapsed on the bed beside her. We dozed off while the sunshine in the room gradually dimmed and the sky outside the windows darkened into night.

A WALK IN THE PARK

Seth, Cornwall

I'd first seen her as I'd taken Tess for a walk in the nearby city park. The day was overcast as the Labrador and I wandered along the path between the sparsely scattered trees and neatly trimmed grass.

She walked along the path towards me and her collie rounded on Tess when they drew close. The two dogs faced off with hackles raised. She and I both tugged on our respective leads and tried to bring some calm to the canine confrontation.

"Sorry about this," she said in a smooth voice which reminded me of honey, her dark hair cut short. That's when I noticed her hazel eyes for the first time. There was a sexual confidence in them that sent a thrilling tingle along my spine, my penis stirring.

I realized I was staring and turned my gaze away as the dogs decided to sniff each other's backsides rather than fight.

"I always find it embarrassing when Buster does that," she commented with a wry grin.

I nodded and looked at her face, high cheekbones and smooth skin touched by the trace of a light tan. Her lips had a natural pout and her nose was slightly upturned.

With a gentle yank of Buster's lead, she then continued through the park. "Bye," she said over her shoulder, her gaze briefly settling on my crotch before she turned away.

I looked down to see my erection pressing against my jeans and my blushing increased dramatically.

I watched her walking away, stared at her shapely backside, which was highlighted by the skirt she was wearing. I'd taken a late lunch and made a deal with myself to do the same the following day in order to meet her again.

I was living with someone called Stacy at the time, but our relationship had gone sour. We were snappy all the time and the sex was non-existent. She'd started seeing a psychotherapist called Dr Silverman, something she blamed on me. The signs were all there that the relationship was at an end; it was just that neither of us had said so out loud.

A few days after our first meeting, I saw her in the park again. "Great weather," I commented as we drew in the sunshine, wishing I'd been able to think of something more original to say.

She smiled at me, her white blouse revealing the upper slopes of her breasts, her pale bra visible beneath its thin material. "Let's hope it lasts," she replied as our dogs said hello in their own, special way.

"What a way to greet each other," she commented. "Imagine if we did that every time we met someone."

I smiled. "I wouldn't want to bump into a sweaty sumo wrestler."

She chuckled. "It could be quite fun with some people," she responded with a look which made my penis begin to enlarge. "If we were on leads it would be even more interesting," she added, her dark eyes sparkling with mischief as her gaze darted briefly to my crotch.

My cheeks reddened as a jogger passed between us and I became increasingly self-conscious.

"My name's Claire," she said.

"I'm Seth," I replied.

"So, Seth, do you come here every day?"

I nodded. "Tess would go nuts if she didn't get her daily walkies. Plus it gets me out of the house for a while."

"Things not good at home?" she asked, noting the change in my tone.

I shrugged. "Everyone's got their problems."

"And sharing them can make things a lot better. Do you fancy coming back to mine for a coffee and a chat?" she asked, her forwardness surprising me.

"OK," I said eventually with a nod, wondering what might happen once we were behind closed doors.

As it turned out all that happened behind the closed door of her terraced house was the consumption of a coffee coupled with a long chat. Claire listened. I told her about the relationship problems and she let me unload without voicing any judgment.

I got home feeling much better about everything, thinking that mine and Stacy's problems could be solved. How wrong was I?

That evening Stacy announced she'd met someone else and was going to leave at the weekend. That evening our five-year relationship finally reached the point of no return. It was over.

The following week the two-up two-down we'd been renting felt empty. Stacy had taken Tess with her. I was unable to concentrate on the magazine advert I was supposed to be designing. My thoughts kept drifting as I sat before the computer, but they surprised me. They weren't drifting to Stacy and pining after what had been lost, they were drifting to Claire and all that could be gained.

I finally decided to go to the park and try to see Claire. Failing that I already knew I'd go to hers and hope she'd be in.

I ended up sitting on a bench beside the path beneath the bright sun, letting my head rest back slightly, closing my eyes and feeling the warmth on my eyelids.

"Hi, Seth. No dog with you today?"

I looked up at Claire with a startled expression, not having heard her approach. I was immediately captured by the gravity of her dark eyes, pulled into their sensual depths. "No. Stacy left me and took Tess with her."

"I'm sorry to hear that. Maybe we can share Buster for a while. Why don't you join me?"

I smiled and then stood.

We strolled along the tarmac path without saying much. I could feel the charge of her presence beside me and felt her arm brushing mine from time to time. It gave me a tingling thrill and the desire within me was fanned by the light contact.

Our arms brushed again and she suddenly stopped in her tracks and turned to me. "Do you feel that?" she asked.

I knew what she was talking about, could see it in her eyes. I nodded. "Yes, it's like an electricity."

Without another word, we made our way back to her house, the dog almost being dragged the final distance. We knew what we wanted and we wanted it with growing urgency. My pulse quickened and my erection grew. My palms became clammy and I felt an almost feral wildness waiting to find its expression.

As soon as we were inside the front door of her house Claire pushed me against the wall and pushed her lips to mine. Her hands ran through my short brown hair, gripped the sides of my head as her tongue pushed into my mouth. Our breathing heavy, we embraced in the hallway, my hands sliding down her back and grasping her buttocks firmly, kneading them as my desire threatened to burst from me in the heat of lust.

Claire pulled my blue T-shirt up and her lips moved to my chest. She caressed it with hot kisses and ran her tongue across my quivering skin as my heart thundered in my chest. Trails of cooling saliva were left across my nipples as she licked and sucked them, nipped them gently between her teeth to make me gasp, my eyes closing as I was filled with pleasure.

Her hands went to the buttons of my jeans and her thin fingers hastily undid them. She yanked open the front and then pulled them down with surprising strength. My dark boxers were then taken down and my erection sprang up before her pouting lips as I glanced down at her.

Her tongue flicked out and cooled the burning tip of my penis. She took it into her mouth, her lips clamping about its thickness as she began to suck me. My eyes closed again and I leaned my head back against the cream-coloured wall, my mouth opening slightly.

She took me deep, her teeth lightly grazing my penis, tongue snaking about it as I felt the sensations of heat and moisture. My hands moved to her short, dark hair as I drew close to orgasm and I pulled her mouth from me. I brought her face up to mine and we kissed again.

Taking hold of her shoulders, I quickly pushed her across the hall and up against the wall opposite. My hands went to her breasts and squeezed them. Claire undid her pale blouse and let it fall open, then reached back and undid her bra, which fell away from her breasts. I cupped them, stroked them, pinched the nipples until they were raised and firm. Her cheeks flushed and she ran her nails over my chest, down to my stomach, the muscles twitching in response to her attentions.

Leaning forward, I took her nipples between my teeth one at a time. She bit at my neck, kissed my shoulders, her hot breath upon my skin.

Claire reached between us and took hold of my erection, her fingers clasping it tightly. "Condom," she said breathlessly, looking at me with her dark eyes hooded.

I shook my head.

"Wait here," she instructed, pushing me away, and quickly walked along the short hall and up the stairs to her bedroom.

I listened intently and heard the sound of hasty movements from upstairs. My breathing was heavy and I took a few deep breaths, sweat cooling on my forehead.

When Claire descended the stairs she was completely naked. Her dark pubes were neatly trimmed and I could see the petal-like lips of her vagina protruding from them, beckoning me to part them, to penetrate within.

She approached as she pulled the foil wrapping from the condom she'd retrieved and then quickly rolled it down my penis as I ran my fingers through her hair.

"Screw me against the wall," she whispered huskily. "Screw me hard."

She held my erection in one hand as I lifted her onto it and with the other hand she opened her fleshy lips. I slid into her warmth, deep between her legs. Claire let out a sigh of satisfaction and she wrapped her arms about my neck and I used the wall to support her weight. With her breasts pushed against my chest and legs about my hips, I gyrated and she moaned in response to the movements within her.

Then I began to move in and out. I could feel my penis sliding back and forth, moistened by her desire as her nails dug into my shoulders and she kissed my shoulders.

My movements became faster, my thrusts more powerful. I pushed into her as she bit my shoulder while stifling a yell of pleasure. Her buttocks slapped against the wall. My penis moved back and forth, parting her, penetrating her, bringing us both closer to orgasm.

The smell of sex and sweat filled the air. She moaned with growing intensity as my hips moved rapidly. The rhythm grew to a peak, our bodies entwined in the heat of the moment and our lust.

She let out a yell and I felt all the tension evaporate from her body as the warm waves of orgasm rolled through her. A moment later I found my own release, grunting with eyes closed as I bucked within her, my hips stilled, my erection buried between her legs.

We sank to the floor and she manoeuvred herself onto me. She turned her back, my penis still erect within her. I sat up and kissed the back of her neck as she ran her fingernails over my testicles. My hands reached round to caress her breasts, holding them, taking the stiff nipples between thumbs and fingers to pinch and roll them.

She began to move in gentle circles on my erection as her knees rested on the floor to either side of me. I stroked her inner thighs as I sat behind her, my fingertips making their way up between her legs. The index finger of my right hand moved between her damp lips as she began to move up and down on my erection. I rubbed at her clitoris, its stimulated nerve endings making her jump and shudder as another orgasm grew.

Pushing herself up time and again, Claire let herself drop with force onto me. Each time she let out a slight moan as her speed increased and I continued to rub her clitoris, my left hand moving back to her breasts.

The motions grew in intensity as she slammed herself down onto my hips, my penis penetrating deep inside her, filling her with its swollen stiffness. Claire bounced up and down, sweat covering her body, muscles jumping as her clitoris sent pulses of pleasure through her. Then, with a loud shout, she came for the second time, almost falling from her perch upon me as her body sagged, muscles trembling with the effort and the ecstasy.

She slowly climbed off me. "My eyesight's blurred," she said with a smile. She blinked a few times and then lay beside me.

I looked into her dark eyes as her right hand moved to my continuing erection and she gripped it tightly. With building momentum, she began to masturbate me and nuzzled my neck.

Then, with a temporary stiffness of my body, back arching slightly, I came. The movements of her hand ceased but she continued to grip me and felt the gentle bucking of my release, her smile growing.

I looked at her flushed cheeks and she took her hand from my rapidly fading erection. I stroked the small of her back with my fingertips and followed the upper contours of her buttocks. "You know, I think I'd be quite happy if we had to greet each other like dogs do," I said jokingly as I squeezed her backside.

She chuckled.

The doorbell suddenly rang and we both jumped.

"Shit! What's the time?" asked Claire in a hushed voice, glancing at the nearby front door.

I reached for my discarded jeans and took my mobile out of the right-hand pocket. "It's just gone two," I replied.

"That'll be my two o'clock client," she said as she got up, having to lean against the wall momentarily, her legs weak.

"Your two o'clock appointment?" I asked in confusion.

"I'm a psychotherapist. My lounge doubles as my consultation room. You'd better get your things together and hide in my bedroom until I've taken them through for their session."

"A psychotherapist," I echoed, keeping my voice low as I got to my feet.

She nodded. "Yes, Dr Claire Silverman," she replied as I looked at her in surprise.

COLLEGE REUNION

Liza, Denver

Every year, our class from technical college got together for an informal reunion. There were twelve of us who had been close – tearing our hair out as we tried to beat coursework deadlines, studying and partying with equal fervour, groaning through exams and then getting together afterwards in B.J.'s Bar to compare notes, drink pitchers of beer and devour the chicken wings.

After we graduated, most of us inevitably found jobs in other cities and moved away, but a core group of us faithfully attended every reunion. I had found work locally and still lived in the same town, so my small house was often the focus of our gatherings. We always had a lot of fun on those nights, sprawled in my living room with beer and pizza, reminiscing over our college days.

Steve, Mandy and Juan were my closest friends from college days. Mandy had been out with both of them at one time or the other, and loved to talk about what they were like in bed. The boys didn't mind being teased, and were quite happy to let her talk. They showed no jealousy, and even seemed to enjoy the camaraderie that sharing the same woman brings.

I'd always wished I had asked Juan out. He had a great sense of humour, and a way of holding your hand while gazing earnestly into your eyes that made you feel like the only person in his world. The soft friction of his thumb, rubbing over the back of my hand used to make me wonder what his fingers would feel like on other, more intimate parts of my body. But I never asked him out as, unlike Mandy who only wanted a good time, I thought I might fall hard for him, and maybe that would have spoiled the special friendship the four of us shared. So I contented myself with fantasies, and listened vicariously, whenever Mandy told me about what he was like in bed.

"His mouth, Liza," Mandy would sigh. "His wonderfully, devilish, exquisitely hot mouth. His tongue goes so far inside you it feels like a cock, and he has a way of fluttering it over your clit so that you just come and come again . . ." Her words tailed off as her eyes became unfocused. "Hell, I'd marry him for his tongue alone."

"So why don't you?" I asked curiously.

Mandy grinned. "Because a tongue's only part of it. There's also Steve's cock, Tony's fingers and Matt's cute little hairy ass."

Our five-year reunion started off as normal. As usual, Steve, Juan and Mandy planned to stay at my place. Mandy and I in my bed; Steve and Juan in the lounge. We met the others in B.J.'s and enjoyed a raucous evening of laughter, along with the obligatory pitchers of beer.

The evening was drawing to a close when Mandy pulled me to one side. "I won't be staying at your place, Liza," she said with an impish grin. "I'm going home with Raoul."

"Raoul?" I boggled slightly. Of all the men in our class he seemed the most unlikely to find Mandy's favours. Skinny and dark, he was the antithesis of her preferred type.

"Yeah." She looked anxious for a moment. "I really like him. I don't want to rush things, but I really think he could be The One."

I squeezed her arm reassuringly. "You go, girl! And come and see me before you leave tomorrow to give me the details. All the details!"

"Sure thing." She winked, and was gone, out into the night on Raoul's arm.

That left Steve, Juan and me. We made our weaving way back to my place and plunked on the couch. But it was late, and I was tired, so I soon made my excuses and headed off to bed.

Steve's question stopped me in my tracks. "Hey, could we sleep there with you?" he said. "Your king-size bed will hold three of us, and it's gotta be better than the floor."

I shrugged. "Sure, why not." I didn't see a problem; I'd known both of them for years and trusted them implicitly. Besides, what harm could I come to with both of them there? Even if I was tempted to oh-so accidentally roll against Juan while I was sleeping, and press myself against him, I could hardly do anything with Steve in the bed too.

I woke some hours later. I was in the middle between the two guys, on my side, facing towards Juan. He faced me, sleeping soundly. The covers were pushed down around his waist and his golden chest rose and fell slightly with each breath.

It was Steve who had woken me. He was spooned behind me, and I could tell he was awake by his erratic breathing. His hand had crept over my waist, and was gently stroking the skin between my shirt and my panties. His touch was hypnotic, as it traced the line of my panties, over and over.

As he breathed out his hips pushed forwards, just enough that I could feel the large ridge of his erection brushing my ass. He obviously thought I was still asleep, and he seemed to be very careful not to take advantage of me. His body was angled away from mine, so that I wouldn't feel how aroused he was. But the occasional light press of his cock against me was a dead give-away.

His fingertips stroked lightly around the top of my panties, hesitated a moment, as if they were going to dip down inside, before continuing on their aimless path. But they were having an effect. Arousal, hot and urgent, coiled deep in my belly, and my pussy throbbed with the need to be touched.

Still feigning sleep, I stole a look at Juan through half-closed eyelids. He was sleeping soundly, snoring lightly. I shifted slightly, as if in sleep, and pushed my bottom back against Steve's erection.

He gasped quietly, obviously thinking I was asleep, and gently tried to move back away from me. His fingers had stilled on my belly.

Subtlety wasn't enough. I drew in a shuddering breath to let him know I was awake and shifted so that his fingers slid inside my panties. I could feel them resting just above my pubic hair.

At the same time, I pressed back again and rubbed my bottom lightly up and down his cock.

He didn't need more of a hint. Spooning harder against me, Steve's fingers delved down between my legs, and one insinuated itself between my slick folds. I could hear the gentle squelch as he moved it into my wet pussy. He added a second finger to the first, and his thumb rubbed gently over my clit.

I was close to coming when he stopped and withdrew his hand. But I forgot about my frustration when I felt him moving behind me and his hands tugged at my panties. I lifted my hips slightly and let him pull them down my legs, and my eyes closed in anticipation when I felt his naked cock press down, seeking between my thighs. I raised a leg to give him access and the tip of his cock probed the folds of my cunt.

It was difficult, with the angle, but he dropped his hips down, and thrust up. My eyes shot open as he filled me, and his thick cock was clasped within my pussy walls.

So much for being silent. I was looking straight into Juan's warm, brown eyes. For a second I was mortified, then Steve started thrusting behind me, and his fingers came down over my belly again to finger my pussy.

Juan propped himself up on his side and smiled. His fingers deftly undid the front buttons of my shirt and he pulled it open so that he could see my breasts. When his fingertips touched my nipple, I exploded into orgasm, clenching around Steve's cock, as his fingers worked themselves frantically over my clit.

Aftershocks rippled through me as Steve continued to pump. With Juan awake, Steve abandoned any attempt at silence and fucked me hard, banging my ass with every thrust. With a roar his thrusts disintegrated into frantic spurts and he came hard, flooding me with his seed. He collapsed back, his cheek against my shoulder, his dick still embedded.

I exhaled in a great, shuddering breath, and Juan smiled. His hand came up to stroke my cheek, and he leaned forwards and kissed me. It was a tender kiss, a first kiss, a lover's kiss. It was the sweet goodnight kiss from a boyfriend, not the lusty just-fucked kiss bestowed upon a woman with another man's cock buried up to the hilt in her cunt.

I kissed him back just as tenderly, and for long moments we explored each other's mouth. Then his lips slid from mine, down my neck, kissing gently over my skin, until finally his lips closed over my nipple. His warm tongue swirled over the peak, sending ripples down my belly, so that my pussy shivered around Steve's cock. For long minutes, Juan laved each nipple in turn, before sliding lower, his lips running over my belly until they rested just above my pubes.

Behind me, Steve rose up to see, and his cock twitched and thickened, rising to half-mast inside me.

Oh God, I thought deliriously. He's not going to . . . Mandy's words about Juan's talented tongue came rushing back to me.

Juan's mouth dropped lower. With careful fingers, he parted the lips of my pussy and, uncaring of my slippery just-fucked state and of Steve's twitching cock still wedged inside, he put his lips to my clit and sucked. His tongue flickered, running over my throbbing nub. Mandy was right – he was a master. He seemed to know instinctively exactly the right pressure and speed, exactly how I love to be touched. My orgasm built inexorably, until I came with a gasp, my inner muscles spasming so hard that my stomach muscles ached.

Juan raised his glistening mouth, and I pulled him up to me by the hair. We kissed, tenderly, then fiercely, slurping and devouring each other. My hands delved down to his groin. He was hard, his cock a silky, steel shaft. Behind me, Steve was erect again, and starting to tentatively thrust, but I ignored him – it was Juan that I wanted.

Steve's thrusting held me pinned, so I tugged on Juan's arm until he took the hint and moved higher in the bed. His groin was level with my face, soft brown hair and musky scent. His cock pulsed in front of me. Bending towards him, I licked around its proud helmet, savouring the smoothness, the single salty drop of fluid that seeped from its tip.

Juan groaned, and his fingers clenched painfully in my hair. His hips moved forwards, instinctively, silently urging me to take him deeper.

Behind me, Steve was in fine fucking rhythm, holding my hips as he pummelled me from behind. He felt good, hard and fierce, and the aftershocks of orgasm rippled through me. Too soon for me to climb to my peak again, but the sheer eroticism of the moment made up for that. Two men, two glorious handsome men, taking me, loving me, fucking me. It was everything I'd ever fantasized about and then some.

Juan's cock bobbed enticingly in front of me. My tongue darted out and licked carefully around the rim, then, taking pity on him, I took the whole thing in my mouth. He wasn't particularly long, but he was thick, mouth-wateringly solid, dusky gold along the shaft, darker at the root.

I pushed on Juan's chest, rolling him over onto his back, and then I lifted myself away from Steve's cock, ignoring his moan of disappointment. My attention was fixed on the mouth-watering expanse of Juan's golden skin. Straddling him, I eased myself over his cock. Steve's seed was sticky on my thighs, sliding out of my cunt, but I didn't care. I wanted Juan's great golden cock, wanted to feel it inside me hammering my pussy as hard as it could. I wanted to come again and again, until my teeth ached.

Juan's eyes were slits of pleasure as I sank down over him, taking him inside in one smooth movement. His hands rested on my thighs, and he let me do the work, rising and falling on his prick with rhythmic motion. I was vaguely aware of Steve pumping his cock into his fist, but Juan filled my vision. His hips undulated in time to my motion, and his hands clenched and unclenched on my thighs.

The pressure built once more and I came hard, just as Juan thrusted up, spurting his juice into me, and Steve climaxed with a roar, spilling himself over his hand.

The next morning, the three of us shared breakfast as if nothing had happened. If it wasn't for the pleasurable ache between my legs, I might have thought I'd dreamed it all. Steve kissed me goodbye that afternoon and returned to Baltimore. Juan stayed, and we spent the afternoon lazily curled up on the couch, watching TV and caressing each other's skin, making love when the mood took us.

Around six, the door burst open and Mandy rushed in. "Liza! Have I got a story for you. You won't believe what Raoul is –" She broke off, her eyes wide, as she took in Juan and I, naked on the couch. "On second thoughts, you just might have the better story!"

TIA MARIA

Paul, Madrid

I had tired of the cities, of the hustle and the bustle, had had my fill of culture; I had seen Gaudi's Barcelona and Dali's Figueras, had visited the Prado and the Alhambra and the Escorial. Now I wanted something more peaceful, more rustic.

A two-hour bus journey took me inland, to such a nowhere place that I wondered why it should merit a bus service at all. A church at one end of the square was perhaps the most unremarkable I had seen during my months in Spain, the small hotel at the opposite end seemed clean and welcoming but could have been anywhere. There was nothing to distinguish the buildings and the town struck me as more a place to pass through rather than arrive at.

Arrive I had, though, so with my rucksack slung over my shoulder I strolled around the square, glanced in the windows of a shop or two, smoked a cigarette as I sat by the fountain in the centre of the square. There were quite a few people about, but not so many that they needed to compete for space, as they seemed to do in other places I had been, and none who were obviously tourists. Most seemed unhurried and contented, some smiled a silent greeting at me as they passed, and it occurred to me that the town's charm might be in its very anonymity, that the most remarkable aspect of it was that it was so unremarkable.

On an impulse I picked up my rucksack and walked briskly across the square to the hotel.

They had a room for me, the price was reasonable, within minutes I had deposited my things and changed into fresh clothes, was back out on the square again.

There were a number of bars, restaurants, cafes dotted around the square and I chose one at random, sat at a table outside.

The young woman who came out to me wore a long flowing skirt which was a little too old-fashioned for a person her age, it might have been more suited to her mother, if her mother had been a flamenco dancer. The blouse, too, was a little unflattering, a few too many frills about it, as if the fashions of ten years ago had only just reached that backwater. The way she moved, though, made any complaints about her dress immaterial, for she walked as other women might dance, her hips swaying, a gentle fluid motion making her whole body seem to undulate as she moved towards me.

"*Buenas tardes,*" she said with a smile.

"*Buenas tardes,*" I replied. "*Un cerveza por favor, y un . . . un bocadillo?*"

She sensed my hesitancy as I searched for the right word, asked in English, which was better than my Spanish, "And what would you like on your sandwich?"

"Erm . . . ham? And cheese?"

"*Bueno. Jamon y queso.*"

The beer was cold, her smile was warm as she served it to me; she brought me a dish of olives while the sandwich was prepared. There must have been few people inside for she was attentive in her service, unhurried.

I had a second beer, a third, and each time she served me she lingered a little longer at my table.

"*Me llamo* Paul," I introduced myself, and she said her name was Yolanda. I congratulated her on her English and she teasingly said that my Spanish was . . . understandable.

I laughed and invited her to sit a while if she had the time. She narrowed her eyes to peer into the dark interior of the bar, decided that no one needed her so took the seat beside me.

I told her of my travels, of the places I had visited and the sights I had seen, thinking to impress her with the sophistication, but though she listened with an interested smile there was no hint of envy in her soft brown eyes, no obvious yearning to visit these places for herself.

Finally she said, "Pah! These *Madrilenos* and the like, they are all very well with their fine clothes and their boutiques, their galleries full of art and libraries full of books, but still they are a little bit backward."

"Backward?" I laughed, first looking at the clothes she wore, then around me at her tiny town, and seeing not an iota of sophistication anywhere. If there was any place that was backward in that country then I had surely stumbled upon it.

"You doubt me?" Yolanda demanded, getting quickly to her feet, fists on hips and glaring down at me.

"No, I'm sure your small town has much to recommend it, and its people –"

"Do not think to condescend!" she cut me off, backing from me like a dancer, with a twitch of the hips and a single step. She spat a curse at me: "*Bruto campesino!* Ignorant peasant!"

The fire in those eyes! The lushness of the lips as she spat her curse! Her whole body trembled with anger, with passion, and before she could back further from me I reached out to grasp her wrist.

"I'm sorry, Yolanda, truly sorry," I said. "I didn't mean to offend you. It's my English sense of humour, I suppose."

"Unsophisticated?"

"Unsophisticated," I agreed, smiling. "Tell me, what time do you finish work here?"

"Why?" she asked.

"We might meet for a drink?" I hoped.

"I finish at eight, the house is at the back of the bar." She pointed, snatching her hand free, then turned on her heels and flounced off.

Yolanda greeted me more amiably than we had parted, with a smile and a kiss to each cheek.

She had changed from the skirt and blouse of earlier, wore a tight dress of black silk, its neckline low, its skirt short. Her hair had been drawn up, was held at the back with a large silver comb, her eyes had been darkened and her lips glossed a dark red. She looked stunning but still . . . a little out of fashion.

She stepped aside to let me enter, closed the door after me and then led me into the house, her arm linking through mine. The blinds were partly closed in the room I was taken to, keeping the air cool, the light soft. I cast my eyes around the room, making out objects in the muted light: the sofa and chairs, furniture of rich wood which might have been antique, the small table in one corner at which sat the dark shape of a woman.

I looked enquiringly at Yolanda, saying nothing but my puzzlement obvious.

"My aunt, Tia Maria." Yolanda grinned, and at the mention of her name her aunt's head lifted from the book she was reading.

"*Hola*," she said, regarding me sternly.

She was perhaps ten, fifteen years older than her niece, somewhere in her thirties, and dressed like a woman in mourning. Her long black skirt came to her ankles, her blouse was buttoned to the neck and hair as dark as Yolanda's was tied back from her face, though more severely than her niece's.

"Er . . . hello," I said, for the moment forgetting the little Spanish I knew, thinking that in her monochromatic harmony she resembled a portrait by Whistler. The artist's mother, maybe.

"Some wine?" Yolanda invited, crossing to an ancient cabinet.

"Just the one," her aunt said.

"Great," I said, without enthusiasm, wondering if Tio Pepe might be lurking somewhere in the background.

Yolanda nodded to me to sit on the sofa, poured two glasses and joined me there while her aunt returned to her book, her back almost, but not quite, turned to us.

I took a stiff drink, then asked in a whisper, "What's your aunt doing here?"

Smiling slyly over the rim of her glass, Yolanda said, "She is here as my *carabina* . . . my . . . how would you say? My chaperone?"

"Remind your young man that *carabina* can also mean carbine, gun," Yolanda's aunt said, without looking up from her book.

"Look, maybe I'd best leave," I said uncomfortably, setting my glass down, wondering how she might now dare challenge the idea that this town of hers could be anything but backward.

"No, please don't," said Yolanda, resting her hand on my knee to lean towards me, and in the instant before she kissed me I was offered an enticing view of her breasts, a sight which made me gasp, as if I was about to drown in them.

What Yolanda offered this time was no simple kiss of greeting, no light peck to each cheek, but a kiss as passionate as the Spanish sun was hot. I had never known lips so soft, her tongue when it slipped between mine was caressing rather than abrasive, and it felt as if my whole body was melting, sinking into hers.

When Yolanda broke the kiss, our faces inches apart, I cast an anxious glance over her shoulder, in the direction of her aunt. She was still seated as before, her back mostly turned to us, head bent over her book.

"Don't go?" Yolanda asked softly, her hand caressing my thigh.

If there was any temptation to leave, any cowardly impulse to run, it vanished the instant the tip of a finger reached my groin. A tingle that was electric coursed through my body and I leaned forwards to resume the kiss, my eyes still fixed on Yolanda's aunt at first, but soon feeling the lids flutter shut as I surrendered myself to the power of her kiss.

There was more than just the tip of a finger at my groin now, Yolanda had the palm of her hand pressed hard against my cock, her fingers were digging and probing beneath, clutching at my balls through the fabric of my trousers.

"Yolanda!" I hissed, softly but urgently.

"Yes?" she asked, her face pulling back to give me the sweetest, the wickedest of smiles, and her fingers pulled my zip down, searched around for my cock.

I bit my lip, closed my eyes and fought to keep my breathing even as Yolanda pulled out my cock, thinking: Oh shit! Oh shit!

Her fingers curled around me, she had me large enough to fill her and then some, and she squeezed me tightly, studying my face to enjoy my reaction, grinning to see me grimace as she tugged at me.

"No! No! No!" her aunt suddenly cried out, slamming her book shut, and my eyes flashed open to see her striding across the room towards us.

"Oh Christ!" I groaned, trying to rise from the sofa.

Yolanda kept firm hold of me, but only until her aunt reached us and slapped her hand away.

"No! No! No!" she said again. "Not like that, niece! You grip it like a club when you should be holding it like a brush, like a pen, something to be creative with!"

And before I had a chance to cover myself she was kneeling before us, taking hold of the cock Yolanda had relinquished.

"Take it as a conductor might take up his baton," she told her niece, gripping me with the lightest of touches. And to me she simply said, "Be still!"

As if to help keep me still Yolanda wrapped an arm around my neck to hold me to her and casually stroked my cheek as she gazed with interest at my lap.

I was astonished, aghast, lost for words and . . . growing harder than ever under the soft caress of this older woman.

Her fingertips ran lightly along the underside of my cock, from base to tip, at which point her nails grazed it, her thumb stroked once over the head.

"You see, Yolanda, how responsive a man can be with the right treatment?" she said, as my cock danced and pricked erect for her.

"Yes, Maria." Yolanda nodded, her gaze rapt, like a student attentive to her tutor.

"Right, you try," Maria said, releasing my cock and then slipping her hand beneath my balls to lift my genitals for her niece.

Yolanda's touch was as feather light as her aunt's this time; the soft pads of her fingers barely seemed to touch me as they ran along my shaft. The briefest brush of her thumb across the tip of my cock was such an exquisite delight that it brought an audible sob from me.

"You see, Yolanda? You can make him sing, you can make him dance, you can make him do anything you like," said

Maria, moving her hand around in small circles so that my balls rolled about her palm.

My eyes shivered open to check that what was happening was no dream, saw Yolanda looking down with longing at my ever-growing cock, her aunt Maria gazing directly into my face, her expression still a little stern, a little cold.

But then, as if she had just been waiting to get my attention, her face softened, she smiled at me and raised her free hand to the neck of her blouse.

"Of course, it is also possible to excite a man by exciting ourselves," she said, speaking to her niece but her eyes never leaving mine, burning into me as she slowly, almost fastidiously, began to unbutton her blouse.

Maria's bra, inevitably, was of black lace, and in contrast to this and the parted blouse which hung like a jet curtain to either side, her pale flesh took on the stark translucence of marble. She ran her hand over one breast, then the other, until I was aware of the nipples pricking against the fabric. Then she rose up on her knees and slipped one hand inside her bra to bare a breast.

I was now so hard in her niece's tender hand that the young woman began to make a low purring noise as her fingers slid back and forth, as if pleased with herself, as if pleased with me.

"Tia Maria," she said, looking up from my cock at last, switching her gaze to her aunt.

"Yes, Yolanda?"

"*Io deseo*, Tia Maria."

"*Entonces tomalo, sobrina.*"

The meaning of the words – "I want him, Aunt Maria" . . . "Then take him, niece"– was lost on me, but not the intention, as the aunt slid up onto the couch beside me, her fingers scratching up my balls as she released them, and Yolanda rose to stand before me. As if seen in a dream, as if the air was thick between us, Yolanda slipped the silk dress from her shoulders, pulled it down her body, revealing her nakedness inch by tantalizing inch. Her fingers then crept down her belly, between her thighs, splayed to part them until I could see her moist cunt.

"Slowly now, niece, take your pleasure slowly," said Maria, as Yolanda rested first one knee, then the other, on the couch astride me.

Hands wet with her own juices then moved from her groin to mine, took my erection and held it upright, positioning it carefully.

"Slowly! *Despacio!*" Maria repeated, and Yolanda rubbed the tip of my cock against her, then held it there and smiled down at me.

"So, my arrogant Englishman, who has experienced the sophistication of all our cities . . . you still think we are backward here?" she asked.

"No!" I gasped, as her body dipped slightly, taking just the head of my cock inside her.

"And the idea of a chaperone, a *carabina*, is not so old-fashioned after all?" she said, turning a moment to grin at her aunt.

"Not at all!"

Yolanda's body dropped lower, her cunt embracing my cock as she asked, "You speak from the heart?"

"From the heart!" I promised.

"Not from the genitals, but the heart?"

"From the heart! The heart!" I assured her, needing to be deep inside her, and then let out a scream as she sank hard onto me. "Ai! Ai! Ai!" I cried.

"Oh see, aunt, his Spanish *is* quite good after all!" Yolanda laughed, beginning to rise and fall with a steady rhythm.

Aunt Maria directed her niece as a maestro might an orchestra, conducting her movements, her rhythms, alternating the speed and the tempo until finally I was pleading, begging, asking them to put an end to my delight.

The first time I entreated them Maria silenced me by pressing her bared breast to my mouth. The second time Yolanda brought a halt to my sobs by holding her body poised above me, making me ache for her, and the third time . . . the third time Yolanda's glance to her aunt was as pleading as was mine to her.

"Yes, take your pleasure of him," Maria said with a nod, and Yolanda brought her body down on mine.

Just the once was enough for us both now; her muscles clenched around me and my body tensed beneath her. I gushed inside her and it seemed that she flowed over me.

But even as her body was softening against me, preparing to take me in her embrace, her aunt was gently but insistently easing her away.

"A drink I think, Yolanda," she said.

"Aunt?"

"Tia Maria!"

"Ah yes, Tia Maria!" Yolanda understood, beginning to laugh, and I opened my eyes to see her aunt lifting her long black skirt and baring her cunt, then lowering it towards my face.

"Drink long and deep of the Spanish drink, Englishman," she said. "So smooth and sweet. Drink long and deep of Tia Maria!"

A TATTOO FOR JOHN

Melissa, Perth

I love my boyfriend John so much that I'm willing to do anything to please him. My friends think he's a control freak but I don't, I think everything he says to me is just because he loves me. Anyway, he has a tattoo of a cobra on his arm and wanted me to get a matching one. I told my best friend, Sarah, and she freaked, told me I was nuts, so I thought I'd compromise by having a tattoo where no one else but John can see it. Little did I know how much that was going to change my life.

I'd booked in with the tattooist who does all of John's. His name is Marcus. He's Latin and absolutely gorgeous. We discussed the tattoo and when I suggested I wanted it on my arse so only John could see it, he suggested it would be better in the groin area, said it would turn John on.

"Really?" I asked.

"You bet," he said. "All guys like their women to have them there and if I could just make a suggestion?"

"Sure," I said.

"I did one last week for my girl . . . er, my friend. I had the snake's head, with its tongue flickering out, pointing right at her slit."

I blushed furiously. I wasn't a prude but talking like this to him was making me uncomfortable.

"I don't know," I mumbled.

"I'm telling you, it looks amazing. She's coming over later, we could wait and she can show you."

I thought about it. It certainly did sound erotic and the sort of thing that John would probably like, but I didn't know about

Marcus. I mean, I know it's his job and I'm sure people are always stripping off in front of him, but I didn't know if I should.

He was flicking through a book of illustrations as though he was uninterested in pushing it so I thought, OK, why not.

"Let's do it," I said.

I thought I noticed a quick smile puckering the side of his mouth.

"You'll have to strip off, only from the waist down," he said. "Cover yourself with this sheet and I'll be back in a minute."

He was gone so quickly that I didn't have time to protest about how short the sheet was. It was only about six inches wide. I didn't want to get caught midway in changing so I quickly whipped off my skirt and panties and lay down just in time.

He burst back through the curtain barely looking at me. He carefully pulled the sheet down and I was sure he'd be able to see my slit completely. I stared up at the ceiling as he drew the sketch pretending I was anywhere else but here.

The bell on the door rang and he excused himself. The curtain was slightly open and I saw a sexy-looking woman talking to him. She lifted her top and he inspected her large breasts. She had a tattoo on one of them. I couldn't quite make out what it was, but she was laughing as he bent his head to inspect it. She grabbed at his arse and pulled him in close to her. I didn't want to watch but couldn't help myself.

His hands roamed up her skirt, tugging it up to expose that she was wearing only a tiny G-string. He yanked the fabric over and I was shocked to see her flaps, exposed for me to see. She lifted a leg and before she wrapped it around his back I got a full shot of her gaping pussy. I've never seen another woman's and my pussy throbbed with excitement.

I knew I should have looked away but found my eyes riveted to what they were doing. I could only see his arm moving about so I assumed he was fingering her. My own pussy began to swell with excitement and I had the irresistible urge to rub at my clit. I kept my thighs shut tightly, which made it worse, made me even more aware of how sensitive it was.

He lifted her and had her sitting up on the counter. I saw his hand burrow back under her skirt and suddenly he ripped her G-string from her and discarded it on the floor. Both legs wrapped themselves around his back and he fiddled with his trousers.

The phone rang, disturbing them.

"Yeah," he said, snatching up the receiver. "Yeah, hi. Sure, she's here." He handed the woman the phone.

"Hi, darling. No, it's fine. Not infected at all. Marcus said it's just the dye. Oh, OK, I'll be right home."

She jumped down from the counter and whispered something in his ear. I looked away, my face flushed, my body tingling all over. I was disappointed I didn't get to see them fucking. I certainly never thought I'd be privy to a sex show and was wishing the phone hadn't rung. The door closed and a few minutes later Marcus appeared.

"Sorry," he said. "I nearly forgot you were here."

"That's OK," I stuttered.

He sat down on the chair and began to tattoo the outside of the sketch. I stared at the ceiling, hoping that my pussy hadn't gotten all juicy and that nothing was glistening on my lips. The pain wasn't too bad, actually, better than I thought. Marcus suggested a small glass of Scotch before he began the colouring.

"Sure, thanks," I said, pulling the sheet up a fraction as it had fallen down.

He had a drink too and I must admit I downed mine too quickly. He took it that I was nervous and gave me another. I drank without saying anything more, the alcohol spreading through my veins, relaxing me.

"You OK?" he said.

"Sure," I said.

"John's a lucky guy. Not many girls would mark their bodies for their man."

"Well, John's very special to me," I said, noting my words were slurring a bit.

"I can see why. You're gorgeous," he said, his eyes not leaving my face.

I flushed. "Thanks."

"No, I really mean it. If you were my woman I wouldn't let you out of my sight."

He was flirting with me and I liked it. Marcus could have any woman he wanted, that's how good-looking he is. I licked my lips nervously as he continued with his work.

The alcohol relaxed me and had my inhibitions falling away. Now when Marcus pulled the sheet a bit too far down I didn't really care. I lay there wondering what it would feel like to have him kiss me, to lift me up on the counter and fuck me in full view of anyone who might walk past.

The buzzing of the needle spread over the illustration and the hour just flew. The closer Marcus got to my slit the more I enjoyed it. At some stage the sheet totally disappeared and the buzzing began to turn me on. I kept my eyes closed as I didn't want to give away how I was feeling but Marcus is not stupid.

Suddenly a light buzzing grazed my clit. I kept my eyes closed and held my breath. Was it deliberate? Did it really happen or had I just imagined it? The buzzing continued. What was he doing? Fingers pulled gently at the hood over my clit and suddenly the buzzing zoned right in the centre of my nub. I gasped but kept my eyes tightly closed as if somehow that made it all right.

It was magical. I've never felt anything like it. It was nothing like the vibrator that I sometimes used and I just lay there, not wanting him to stop but too embarrassed to look at him. My body spasmed. I held my breath as an orgasm oozed from me. It was killing me not to scream. I wanted to open my legs and have him fuck me with whatever it was he was using.

Now the buzzing was roaming over my flaps and I did sneak a quick look and saw that he had the other end of the tattooing instrument, the blunt end, gliding over me. He was concentrating on what he was doing and I could see how intently he was focused on not hurting me.

I heard a growling coming from him and I quickly closed my eyes, and then his hand was pushing my thighs apart and indeed the buzzing entered my pussy. I sighed and he chuckled, stabbing me with it. Suddenly the buzzing stopped and a tongue lapped at me. It was heavenly, his tongue licked lovingly at me, much more lovingly than John had ever done. Now he was peeling open my flaps, digging into the folds with his tongue before it entered my pussy.

With his hands free he pushed up my tank top, exposing my breasts. His fingers were magical, touching, nipping, caressing. Then he was climbing up my body, his tongue leaving wet tracks as he found his way to my mouth.

Grabbing his head, I crushed him to my mouth, kissing him boldly, thrusting my tongue into his mouth to wrestle with his own. He was all over me, his hands touching me while his kisses drove me wild. Somehow he managed to get his trousers off and then he was between my open thighs, his cock probing my gaping cunt.

"Open your eyes," he said, his voice thick with emotion.

I did.

"You want this?" he said.

I whimpered and he sunk his shaft deep inside me. I swooned as he fucked me rhythmically, my pussy opening even further to welcome his girth. I was lost in a world of ecstasy, never having experienced sex like this before. John was always eager for me to suck him until he was about to come, and then he'd fuck me, but for only a few minutes. I'd always thought he was too excited to hold out too long for me to come too but now to have Marcus fuck me like this, well, it was absolute heaven.

"Fuck!" Marcus said, jumping away from me as the bell to the door sounded.

Startled into reality, I pulled down my tank top and reached over for the little sheet that had slipped to the floor. He adjusted himself and closed the curtains behind him.

"Oh, you're back," he said.

"Aren't you lucky," the voice – the same woman that had been here earlier – said.

"I'm a bit busy," he said.

"You told me you're never too busy for me," she chuckled, and I heard his zip come down.

"Hmm," she said. Then: "What the fuck!"

"What?" I heard him say.

"What have you been doing?"

"Nothing," he said.

"Then whose cunt can I taste on your cock?"

Fuck! Who was she? I panicked, looking about the room for somewhere to hide. Before I had a chance to do anything she yanked open the curtain and boldly entered the room.

"So, this is what you've been doing," she said, eyeing me, her eyes flashing wildly.

"Get out of here," Marcus said. "This is none of your business, Sheila."

"Isn't it?" she said, her eyebrow arching questioningly.

"No," he said, protectively, trying to steer her from the room. Her hand shot out to pull away the sheet. "A cobra. I should have known."

I tried clumsily to cover myself as her eyes devoured me.

"I thought I had the only cobra. That design is mine. You promised never to put it on anyone else."

Her eyes would not leave my body and I found myself becoming excited by her scrutiny. Even Marcus seemed to notice the change in the air. It was as though a surge of electrical current spread through the room. We all looked from one to the other. She moved closer to the bed I was lying on and gently removed my hands. She sniffed delicately.

"Your cunt smells divine," she said, and dived straight into my thighs that dropped open of their own accord.

Marcus pulled off his clothes and yanked at her skirt until it fell to the floor. She still had no panties on and as she nuzzled into my pussy he peeled her shirt off and yanked up my tank top, pulling it over my head. Now the three of us were naked.

Sheila climbed up on the table, her breasts dragging their way up my body, her nipples touching my legs, my slit, my stomach, then squashed against my own breasts, mashed together as her mouth came down on my own.

The taste of me on her lips had my head spinning. Somehow she manoeuvred her body off me, and then Marcus climbed up on the table. His cock thrust in and out of me as she smothered herself into my mouth. I grabbed at her tits, desperate to feel them and she laughed as she pulled away, dropping a tit into my open mouth.

I sucked at her nipples, suckling her like a baby would, loving the feel of her soft flesh as Marcus fucked me ferociously. She pushed him away, climbed up on the table and straddled my head. I looked up to see her cobra, to see the snake licking out at her slit. I hoped mine was the same, that mine would look as good as hers.

As she lowered herself over my open mouth, my tongue snaked out to lick at the cobra's head before sinking into her cunt. With her mouth tantalizing my clit I exploded into her mouth. She laughed manically and devoured me like a dog starved of food.

We spent the afternoon together, fucking, sucking and licking. Marcus took the phone off the hook and locked the doors. I broke up with John and now Marcus, Sheila and I are an item. She's married but I don't mind sharing her and neither does Marcus. I've already decided that I need to expand my lovemaking experiences and am eager to rope in new customers into our little web of lust.

But first on the list will be the hunk that helps Marcus out. He's as rough as a brick shit-house. A biker with long greasy hair, a full-length beard and who's covered in tats. I'm dying to have his beard rubbing against my hairless pussy, rubbing up against my clit. Just thinking about it makes me wet. He rides a Harley Davidson and I've been told that riding pillion with no panties is better than having sex. I find that hard to believe but can't wait to find out.

NO ONE HAS TO KNOW

Anon.

OK, I'm going to confess this humiliating story, all right? But there's no way in hell I'm going to tell you my name. Just thinking about it makes me cringe. And as bewildered as I am by my body's reaction to what happened, it also makes me incredibly horny.

He was a repulsive, licentious old man with the biggest, stiffest cock I'd ever seen. To this day when I think about it, which for some damn reason is often, I am completely mystified as to why this nasty, pasty-skinned old man made my cunt muscles contract in ravishing hunger.

He was the druggist and proprietor of the corner drugstore in the town where I lived, and it was no secret that he was your typical dirty old man. Everybody knew that. Every time I went in there for something he made no secret of looking me up and down as if he was mentally fucking me like one of those human-headed goats in Greek mythology.

My only excuse for what happened is that I was vulnerable at the time. I had broken up with my boyfriend, and hadn't had an orgasm generated by a real cock in almost five months. It gives me chills to have to admit that what happened was my own fault. I had been too damn picky. I had put off getting some dick for too long. By the time this happened I was so horny, I mean I was suffering so bad for some good cock I was no longer even rational. Let me give whoever is reading this a little advice from my own gruesome experience. Don't ever deprive yourself for that long, until you're that desperate. There's good cock all over the place. Hell, fuck your doctor, seduce your priest, fuck the shit out of your friend's dad, hump the plumber, the cable guy, the meter reader or your boss; just don't do without. Something could happen that could horrify you beyond belief. What happened to me happened because my primitive, cavewoman, wild animal libido rose up completely by surprise and over-powered me at the worst time imaginable.

What a sick joke. I passed up fine-looking studs because I was too picky, and suddenly, with no warning, I'm in the back room of the drugstore helping this old fart find my mother's medication and, unbeknownst to me, this revolting old bastard somehow knows without a doubt that he's about to score, big time!

I think he must have had some preternatural power that to this day I have no explanation for, or maybe I was putting out some kind of "in heat" smell like a bitch dog, or possibly his secret to his success was his dirty talk. "Those are some fine-looking pussy lips bulging through those tight jeans," he said admiringly, as though he had just commented on what a lovely day it was outside. "I'll bet that little cunt is all hot and wet."

I was shocked, and yet I wasn't. He made it sound so casual, like it was nothing.

"I have a sixth sense about these things, and I'm picking up that your little pussy is starving for some of what I've got right here," he said grabbing his crotch. Before I could respond by vomiting he slipped his hand between my thighs and squeezed me hard.

Jerking away horrified, I screamed, "How dare you!"

"Oh, I dare because when I massage a little cunt with this hand I can tell if it's deprived or not," he responded without hesitation, "and, girly, yours is suffering bad. I can feel your little cunt muscles contracting with hunger." He was licking his shiny, wet lips. "I can take care of that problem for you, Denise. I can make that little thing feel so good you'll be squealing in ecstasy."

I was in the corner of that small room with shelves of prescription medications on both sides of me and he was advancing towards me with the most evil, lusty look on his pasty old man face.

Paralysed with fear, I looked on in horror as he unzipped his pants, never taking his rheumy eyes from mine, and lifted out the biggest, stiffest, blue-veined cock I had ever seen. I mean that sucker would have made a prize bull proud.

"I won't tell anyone," he whispered, his creaky old voice raspy with passion. "No one ever has to know, Denise. This will be our little secret. I'm going to bury this monster cock in your sweet little pussy and I'm going to make you come so hard you're going to think your little cunt is exploding, and no one ever has to know."

His breath was frenetic, raspy, as he continued to come towards me, stroking his cock lovingly as he came close enough for me to see a big drop of pre-come oozing out of the eye.

I was horrified that looking at that huge cock was causing my pussy to respond instinctively with a pulsating need. That nauseating old fucker had cornered me against the wall and was rubbing that unyielding cock against my pussy through my clothes. "Nobody ever has to know," he was wheezing.

I couldn't believe my aching cunt was winning out. I was trying not to look at that thing. I needed to get out of there and go home so I could masturbate.

"Take those pants off," the old man said decisively. It wasn't a request; it was a command. "Strip from your waist down and get on the floor."

It was like I was watching from a far corner of the room as this young, attractive girl obediently unzipped her jeans, slid them down and stepped out of them.

"Take off those panties," he said, jamming his cock against me.

I took them off as though he had a gun to my head.

"Now lie down there on the floor and spread your legs, Denise," he said, his creaky old voice hoarse with passion. "I'm going to bury this horse cock in you and I'm going to fuck the shit out of you, baby. I'm going to make you come until there's no more orgasms left in you, and nobody is ever going to know." He had backed me against the wall and his hand was rubbing my sex. He had found my clitoris and was massaging it, rolling it between his fingers. "Get down on that floor and open your legs," he said again.

Paralysed in horror as I slid down to the floor, I was incredulous that my pussy was aching with a ravenous need while my mind was horror-struck that I was willingly spreading my thighs to let this repulsive old pervert shove his rigid cock into my gaping pussy.

Grunting as he climbed down on top of me, his old knees creaking, he said, "Get ready for the fuck of your life, girly. This is going to be the fuck by which every other fuck you ever have will be measured and found wanting."

I heard myself saying, "Hurry up, you old fucker." I was pushing up to him.

Cackling, he had his old gnarled fingers down there finger-fucking my pussy, which in itself was setting me on fire. Then he was spreading my lips and the fat plum of his monster cock was going in. His old flabby ass was pumping that rock-hard monster into me with the enthusiasm of a twenty-year-old.

"Ow!" I screamed as he pushed deeper into me. "That hurts; it's too big!" I was squirming, trying to back out of it.

Ignoring my screams he grabbed my ass with both hands, lifted it up and jerked me in towards him, which caused me to open up more. "That's better," he said, driving it all the way in with several forceful strokes while I continued to scream with a pain that hurt and felt wonderful at the same time.

"Oh God," I whimpered.

"Too late for prayers now, girly, I'm in there," he groaned. He was grunting like a pig in the throes of rapture. "I knew you could take it, baby. See, it's getting easier," he muttered, and even as he said this that huge cock had begun to thrust into me in deep smooth, rhythmic strokes. He had driven it all the way in without splitting me open and I'm humiliated to say I never felt anything so damn good in my life.

That old bastard had that fucking baseball bat buried in me as far as it would go, but he still had a couple of inches left. I was trying to take it all but it just wouldn't go any deeper. Now he was pumping it like a piledriver, his old bloodshot eyes rolling around in his head like a mental retard in the throes of an orgasm only he hadn't come yet, thank God, because at this point I had to have it.

I couldn't believe his stamina. He was gradually speeding up, huffing and puffing like a steam engine and that cock was stroking along like the pistons in a racing car.

"Oh shit, oh shit!" I screamed. A spewing geyser of an orgasm was building in the depths of my vagina shooting shock waves out to the tips of my fingers and toes. "Oh shit, you old fucker," I screamed, and he was riding me like a madman, those old hips stoking that thing in and out of me with the rhythm of a fine-tuned engine.

"I've got you covered, cunt," he yelled, and I exploded in the most gut-wrenching orgasm I ever had.

Oh my God, what have I done! "Let me up," I howled, so disgusted with myself I thought I'd puke all over both of us. I couldn't believe I was letting this old coffin dodger fuck me.

"You're dreaming, little girly. No way in hell I'm letting you up," he grunted, not even slowing down. That cock was still as stiff as a board and going strong. "I've got me some good pussy here, and I'm going to fuck it till I get enough if it takes till this time tomorrow."

I struggled wildly, trying to get out from under him but with incredible strength he held me pinned to the floor and all the time that cock was pumping into me as inflexible as a billy club.

To my horror my cunt was already responding to that thing working inside it and my vaginal muscles were involuntarily contracting, biting down on it, striving as hard as that cock was for my next orgasm. Even as I was coming he had jerked me up off the floor and with the strength of a bull he was twisting me around on his cock without ever missing a stroke. "Now I'm going to dog-fuck you," he said, huffing with the exertion of turning me over. I was on my knees and he was driving it into me from behind. He had put his hand around me and down between my legs, found my clit and was rolling and twisting it in his fingers while he fucked me. "You're getting it all now, baby," he said, grunting.

"I know," I moaned. I had just come and now I was coming again. "Ahhh! Ahhh! Ahhhhh, oh shit, oh shit, ahhhh."

While I was coming he had pulled something down off the shelf and plugged it into an outlet without even missing a stroke. Before I realized what he was doing he was sliding something long and slick into my rectum. "Goddamn it, stop!" I screamed. "Don't!" I was fighting him like crazy, trying to get loose, but he had me in a chokehold and I couldn't move.

"Shut up and be still," he said. "It's almost all the way in." He was holding me so tight I couldn't pull away as he continued to work it into my rectum until it was as far as it would go. All the time his cock was still pumping into me without even slowing down. Suddenly he flipped the switch and the thing was vibrating deep inside me. "Aaah yes," he groaned. "That feels gooood!"

My whole insides were vibrating as he continued to work that huge cock in me, smooth, rhythmic, deep, and he was still squeezing and rolling my swollen hard clit between his fingers. Soon I was coming and coming as it climbed higher and higher and, when it finally crested, the orgasm was so violent, I truly thought that this time I was going to die. I was screaming and I couldn't stop.

To make a long story short, that old piece of shit dog-fucked me for hours with that vibrator up my ass while he held me pinned to the floor, all the time massaging my clit, making me come so many times I lost track. And when he finally cut loose and blew that stored-up load of come he was riding my back, squealing like a hog, and squirting into me with such force it was filling me up and boiling out of me all over both of us.

When he finally let me up I was so weak from coming so many times my legs were trembling and it was a while before I could stand.

I swear I've never been fucked like that in my life. To this day I can't understand it. He was the most disgusting, revolting old geezer you could possibly imagine, and that was the most fantastic, mind-blowing fuck I ever had. I could barely walk for days. To this day I fantasize that he's fucking me when I masturbate. Sometimes I go by that drugstore and it takes all my will power to keep from going in, to keep from following that old bugger into the backroom.

PEEP SHOW

D.D., Queensland

My girlfriend Mary and I were backpacking around Europe. Staying in Amsterdam we decided to stroll through the red-light district. We were kind of nervous, unsure of how to act and found ourselves standing outside a peep-show entrance. I was shocked when Mary insisted on going in.

"Don't be such a prude," she said. "We said we'd do something outrageous and I've decided this is it."

Never in my wildest dreams did I think Mary would and I was rapt but didn't want to let on, didn't want her to think I was into that sort of thing, but I was. Anyway, I let her talk me into it and we were given our own booth.

We pulled the curtain around, leaving us in total darkness. My fingers shook as I dropped the coins into the slot. Suddenly the curtain rose and there lying on a bed was one of the sexiest-looking women I've ever seen.

She was lying on her side, one leg crossed over the other, giving her thigh a great line as it tapered down to her foot. She was wearing a black and red lace teddy, cut low at the front with her luscious breasts practically spilling out. I could just see the darkened flesh of her nipple peeking out.

She looked directly at us, although she couldn't have seen who we were as a bright light was shining directly over her bed, giving us the privacy we desired. My cock began to throb at the sight of her. I was thrilled that Mary had made me go through with it and I was hoping it was having the same effect on her.

The woman rose, stretched her arms up high over her head as she turned around. The high cut leg on the teddy rose until it practically disappeared up the crack of her arse. She began to sway as though dancing to music, then turned back to face us. As her shoulders moved about she allowed first one strap to fall, then the other, until her gorgeous breasts were free of the fabric and swayed of their own accord.

I've never seen anyone so hot in my life. She was totally comfortable with herself. It was as though we weren't even there.

Anyway Mary gasped as the woman began to peel the teddy down over her sexy hips, inching it down slowly, teasing us with quick glimpses of her pussy and then pulling it back up a fraction. Mary's hand sought out my thigh and it travelled upwards to my groin as the woman dropped the teddy and kicked the flimsy material away.

"Fuck, she's so sexy looking," Mary whispered.

I said nothing. She was!

She was only wearing black lace stay-up stockings, red stilettos and her jewellery. She sashayed towards us and I thought my heart would stop. My cock throbbed painfully as Mary's fingers caressed it through the fabric. She came right up to the glass and pressed her body against it, her breasts squashed, her pelvis thrust up hard as she gyrated her hips, pushing her mound over the glass, only six inches or so from my very eyes before turning her back on us and slowly walking back to the bed.

The curtain dropped.

I've never been so disappointed in my life. For the twenty dollars that I'd put in the slot we certainly got our money's worth but I wanted more.

"Fuck," Mary said. "That was great. I can't believe we did this." Her face was flushed with excitement.

"I know," I breathed as Mary playfully grabbed at my cock.

"What do we do now?" she giggled.

"I don't know."

"Should we put some more money in?'

"Do you want to?"

"Fucking oath," she laughed, slipping more coins in the slot.

As the curtain rose, the woman smiled our way, lay back against her pillows and opened her legs wide for us. She lifted them and placed her feet flat on the bed, then dropped her knees open. Man, it was such a turn-on. Both Mary and I held our breath wondering what she'd do next.

We didn't have long to wait as she pulled her pussy lips apart to slide a few fingers inside. She began to finger-fuck herself, half sitting up, pouting her lips, her tongue slipping over them before falling back against the pillows. Then she was pulling the hood of her clit back and rubbing the nub hard, her legs opening and closing as her passion rose.

I couldn't get enough of looking at her. Mary never masturbated in front of me. It was such a turn-on, not only for me but for Mary too. The next thing I knew my zip was down and my cock was being swallowed up by Mary.

She sucked hard and as she sucked I continued to watch the woman. My cock was bursting for release but Mary had other ideas. She lifted her skirt, pulled her panties aside and jumped up on my lap facing the glass so she could watch too. Within two seconds she was sliding down my shaft, her hot wet pussy hugging my cock, squeezing it as she contracted.

I pulled her T-shirt up and grabbed on to her breasts. One eye was still on the woman who was now in the middle of coming herself. She was up on both elbows, her breasts jutting forwards, her long brown hair cascading down her back. Her mouth was open and I could just see some glistening on her pussy lips as an orgasm escaped her.

The curtains dropped so I concentrated on Mary, crushing her breasts cruelly as her pussy juices oozed from her. She had her feet up on the seat now so she could slam down on me. My fingers roamed down her back and I grabbed hold of both cheeks, squeezing them before playing around her hole.

She clenched her arse cheeks together but a quick slap had her relaxing again so I inserted a finger deep into her rectum. She began to moan. The faster I fingered her hole, the louder she got. I knew a powerful orgasm was coming not just from her but from me too. We exploded together; our juices mingled while we caught our breath.

Giggling voices coming from the outside of our cubicle had us separating and quickly adjusting our clothing. Sheepishly we made our way out towards the exit sign. One cubicle hadn't drawn their curtain properly and with a quick peek their way I could see the woman giving the same show.

There were two guys in there. I wondered how they'd cope after witnessing what we had. A door opened and a man rushed out, heading for the entrance. I decided to take a quick peek in there and saw to my astonishment that the two guys that I'd just seen were on a small television screen.

I looked back to where they were and, yes, it was definitely them. I pulled Mary in with me and we watched with amusement when we saw the two of them undo their zips and begin to wank off. Mary was glued to the television and eventually I had to prise her away forcibly.

"Do you realize that guy must have been watching us too?" I said.

"What? Oh, no . . . don't say that," she said, reeling back in horror.

"They must have some sort of camera fitted in the rooms and that guy gets his rocks off watching others watching her."

"Well, I hope he didn't videotape us. I'd hate to end up on some peep-show porno."

The thought titillated me. It would make a great porno, I told her. The rest of the trip was spent checking out as many of these peep shows we could see and the whole time I was thinking how going into this business could become really profitable.

The problem was that it consumed me and in the end Mary and I broke up. She was disgusted with my ideas and about a year later didn't find what we'd done amusing and was furious when I told some friends.

The thing is I did have a tape of us together in Amsterdam, back in one of the hotel rooms after we'd been to a session. And, well, I'd become a bit of an exhibitionist. I wanted everyone to see it. Mary looked awesome in it and we played it up so much so that it turned into quite a professional-looking porno.

Mary didn't know I'd made two copies and when she insisted I destroy the only one she thought I did so willingly. I'd sent the other in to a production company and they loved it, wanted to buy it and the money was amazing. It's an overseas company so

I didn't think Mary would ever find out. I mean she did look different then, younger, thinner and her hair was totally wild so I signed the contract.

Thought all was well until this morning when I received a phone call. Mary is such a hit the public are demanding more, the producers want to pay her an absolute fortune to do a follow up. They don't want me . . . just her. I said we'd lost contact and they want to do a worldwide publicity search for her. I know I'm in deep shit and I haven't a clue how I'm going to get out of this one.

THE ADRENALINE MOMENT

Jonathan, Centennial

Lovers come and go. But events, the transformative ones, do not leave. Moreover, some events are not so much experiences as they are symbols. Like constellations in the heavens. To this day, I have yet to achieve the rush of one particular night – a night where I was both a voyeur and an exhibitionist.

Still, I remember nearly everything. I remember that I had just come from the shower, damp in the nearly airless and thick summery night.

It was pushing 2 a.m. and my girlfriend was asleep in the bedroom. This was the time of day that was allotted for myself. I had tucked her in and, typically, I used this time to write.

In the silent darkness of night I have always thrived. I love the cabalistic quiet that envelops me like a cloak. Always feeling that my moves were clandestine, it was as though I had a pact with the world; and that accord was rejuvenated and stamped for arrival every night that I held true to my aim: producing more work; finishing my current novel.

And so I was sitting on the couch, readying to either get some clothes on, or sit at the computer naked – which I often did when I was bogged down by the heat of August in Colorado. As I was lazily contemplating my next move, I reached down and felt my newly clean-shaven ass and water-softened cock. On this night, I had shaved it all, from the top of my cock down to my ass. I was at a point where this ritual of shaving myself was anything but pragmatic, or pedestrian. No, for me, the shaving sequence – with the highly anticipated first touch after the shower as the intoxicating dessert – still aroused me with an incredible, whirlpool force. Every time I became hard. Every time I had an orgasm, one way or another, immediately after shaving . . .

Still feeling and playing with myself, I went over and opened the window so I could have a post-shower smoke treatment. As I approached the window, I noticed our blinds were open. I realized this primarily because of the fact that I could see out in this dark of night, across our courtyard and into one of our neighbours' apartment. Her lights were on.

But it wasn't merely the light that caught my glance.

No, it was the head that was bobbing up and down . . .

And no, it wasn't the head of my overweight neighbour. Or my gay neighbour. It was the head of my hot neighbour – the one I had seen walking around in her panties late at night. I had never seen her on the street and would never in the future – I only knew her through our tunnel of paned-glass windows.

And her head, with her blond hair, bouncing up and down, was like a Fresnel lens, broadcasting its beacon out across the seas.

At this point, three years in to living in this apartment, I had become accustomed to the sounds and frequent sights that I was privileged to. I had thought that I had covered the continuum. I had heard gay men having sex, seen blow jobs through windows, seen the vague silhouette of people fucking, a girl getting eaten out, two girls making out, another girl shoving her boyfriend's hand up her shorts and then upon pulling his sticky fingers out she thrust them into her mouth. In this I thought I had heard and seen it all . . .

But what was about to occur illustrated that this world is much larger than I, always. Once again the world granted me its grand explication that yes, this continuum is always, always more robust than you think. Never believe you know it all or I will show you ignorance . . .

After spotting my sexy neighbour's bobbing head, I immediately froze. My first thought was that I should turn off the lights because I wanted to see this one. Stunned and naked and swirling with heat, I slowly backed up to the couch – light-headed, all the blood in my body settling at my midsection.

Without even looking down, I was hard and, moreover, throbbing.

Nearly paralysed, I fell into the cushions. My pulsating cock like a sailing mast, waving in the placid winds before the tempest.

Leaning into the couch and completely naked I began to stroke my cock in unison with the bobbing head across the way. Here I was not thinking about a civilized lot. Here I was unable to formulate anything cognitive, with any clarity. Instead, I felt a tingling in that primal core, deep inside me somewhere between my pelvis . . .

Then, her bouncing head disappeared.

Still I continued stroking myself. That, alone, was hot enough for me – simply to know that my hot neighbour was riding a cock. If nothing else, I was just wanting to see them both stand up, completely naked, if they were done. I wanted to see the post-coital ritual: the walks to the bathroom; the ice water from the fridge, the cigarettes, the windows opened. I wanted to see two naked bodies, trembling and still dripping with sex, rise up.

And that is exactly what they did. But by no means were they done. As soon as they stood, I was certain they spotted me – for they rose and both walked right up to the tall windows before them. Completely naked and erect he thrust her into the glass. They could have angled themselves any which way in the frame but, to my adrenaline delight, they were angled right towards me. As if they knew. As if they saw me before – waiting for them. Stroking my cock . . . Paralysed . . .

She tilted her head up as he seemed to whisper in her ear. At the same time he pushed her a little further into the glass, pinning her. Forcing her if she wasn't already willing. Then the guy settled into her, abruptly pulling her ass back into him.

With one hand assisting in the mounting of her, he pushed himself closer. With his other hand, he turned her head. Towards me.

With my light on, mine was probably the only well-lit apartment, considering the time of night. They were, *for certain* – at this point – watching me.

And I, for certain, was watching them. Stroking my cock – sitting upright; making sure that they had enough light to see me and my clean-shaved cock and balls.

And the way that they both looked at me, I will never forget. For it was two dichotomous emotions wrapped into one – a sight I have never seen before, for they looked both sheepishly and hungrily at the same time. They looked as though they wanted to tear into this entire situation with every sexual tooth they had, but at once they were stricken and confused with a conglomerate of urgency, fear and adrenaline.

This for me was the most thrilling eroticism that ever coursed through my body. Like a strike of electricity, finely tuned it was. In fact, the rush was so sharp, both of my legs were shaking. Not trembling, but shaking on the blades of knives. I couldn't stand. It was as though I was handcuffed and bound. *The world was not going to let this adrenaline moment slip away from me . . .*

My cock was pulsing beneath the skin, somehow carefully saving its eruption for the right minute. If nothing else, I was certain, I wanted to share my gratitude to – the couple, the world, the gods, whomever would watch – in the form of the enormous volcano that was boiling inside me.

In the frenzy that ensued, I remember little apart from a couple of details. She put her hands up against the glass – where once they were holding onto the frame of the window – as if she were afraid of falling through. Then, when they gained a nice tempo and his balls were slapping against her clit and the ecstasy of the moment took over, she was ready, and placed both palms against the glass; ready and bowled over by the pleasure of it all to fall completely through this glassy-eyed moment.

Then, several minutes later, just when an idea was mushrooming into my head – that I wanted more; that I wanted to go higher; that I wanted to fly across the courtyard and somehow magically join them – they switched positions. He violently turned her away from the window and, pulling her hands behind her and lacing them into one grip, in one of his hands, he took a free hand and wailed on her ass. From my apartment I could hear the skin smacking, kissing, breaking and cracking like a whip.

And he drilled her with his cock. She wailed and whimpered sweetly into the slightly ajar window. As the minutes went by, her body slowly folded over. Her legs, after a near eternity of this pounding, finally were giving out.

Then his muscles flexed and he pumped one long, hard, last time into her – emptying himself completely into her hotness. In that strong pause, he must have been shaking – but I couldn't see it from where I was. I heard no sounds from him.

He posted his orgasm-heavy weight on her; and she leaned into the couch next to them.

Then he pulled out of her and the two of them turned around and stood facing the windows. As if they were fixing themselves back up after the tremendous fucking. But no, they were only gathering themselves, to look back out at me.

This, I knew, *was really happening. This*, I knew, was *my moment*.

I began pumping violently at my cock. But it didn't take much. And with my abdominal muscles and every curve of my legs and ass tensed up; my feet off the floor in some rigor mortis severity, my cock pulsed and then catapulted a fiery jet of come all over my stomach – hitting me even in the neck.

It was as though I had been punched in the stomach. My lungs were paralysed for a long second. From the hips I began quivering, alternately bucking my hips into the couch and squiggling to the side.

Slowly, I came to. The lights became less blinding. And then when my cock ceased pulsing in my now-drenched hand, I looked up to the windows. The couple was gone.

Walking away from this moment, I was forced to redefine my sexuality. For ever were the answers going to be different to my questions of: What is erotic? What turns me on? How high is really high? How high do I want to go? How high *is safe*?

That was the first time I had seen another couple have sex in front of me. It was the first time anybody had seen me like that, with my cock out, naked and exposed so plainly. Before that night, I had never had an orgasm in front of a stranger.

This was a definite fulcrum point in my evolution as a sexual being. From this point onwards, I was for ever changed . . . Fire for ever burned a different hue . . .

To this day I strive to recreate the adrenaline and serotonin surge that I felt on that night.

Still, to this day, I have yet to achieve that rush.

LOUNGE SWEET

Chris, South Australia

I loved working as the front man for the family upholstery business. I spent two-thirds of every day driving around, visiting new locations and meeting new people. Getting your lounge suite re-covered isn't particularly cheap so most of my clients were over fifty and already financially secure. They were getting the house remodelled or the internal furnishings redone, probably for the last time. But sometimes life has a way of serving up a surprise that makes my job exceptional.

Graham Wishburn had come into the shop two days ago for discussions on having an old Chesterfield three-seater refurbished and re-covered. He'd picked out a few sample books of expensive fabrics for me to bring to his home the following day and requested I be there early. He'd indicated that I was to pick up the massive piece of furniture while I was there. Nothing better than a guaranteed sale. Graham looked to be in his thirties so I figured he'd be able to help me load it.

So bright and early yesterday morning, the sun found me in my trusty pickup truck, smiling happily at starting the day with an excellent bonus. I whistled mindlessly along with the radio until I pulled into the drive of the client's home. There were three geese blocking my way, honking and shitting everywhere. The grass looked like it hadn't been cut in a month and the paint was peeling from the house exterior.

His neighbours' homes were well-kept, medium-priced types but Graham Wishburn's house could best be described as ramshackle. Visions of my nice bonus flew out of the window.

Carefully stepping around the goose shit and doing my best to fend off the animals with my pattern books and briefcase, I made my way to the front door. I balanced my case under my arm and knocked loudly on the dilapidated front door.

I knocked three more times, still no response. A fucking wild goose chase, literally. One of the geese honked in agreement with my thought. I struggled to balance my pattern books as I shifted my briefcase back under my arm to try one final time. As I leaned forwards to knock, intending to do so with some force, the door suddenly opened.

I stumbled forwards, tripping on the raised doorstep. I managed to twist sideways as I went down, taking the brunt of the impact on my shoulder. Pattern books and briefcase scattered in all directions. I rolled to my back to look up into a startled set of wide grey eyes, peeking through a long fringe of unkempt blond hair.

She would have been in her early twenties, lean, with very modest breasts. From my angle and the fact that she wore only a white T-shirt, I could also tell the drapes matched the rug. She seemed unconcerned that I took a good long look at her uncovered pussy.

A voice from down the corridor announced the presence of another woman. "Kelly, what the fuck happened?"

The blonde above me glanced over her shoulder. "I guess this is the guy Graham said would be here to pick up the sofa."

Still on my back I raised my hand in greeting. "Hi, I'm Chris from Premier."

The smallest hint of a smile played across her light-pink lips as she clasped my hand. "Kelly, are you all right?"

I clambered back to my feet and gathered my books and case. Once I had everything back under control, I stood expectantly before her. She looked at me quizzically.

I suggested we should probably go have a look at the sofa. She nodded in agreement and led the way down the corridor. As we passed the doorway where her friend had appeared, I instinctively glanced in the opening.

Stretching before a full-length mirror was a naked brunette. Forgetting where I was, I stopped in my tracks to admire her.

From my vantage point I saw her reflection, the firm pert titties, the flat stomach and shaved bush. She was topped off by a brunette bob cut that framed a pleasant face. Her firm round buttocks and the play of muscles along her unblemished back added to the intensely erotic picture before me.

She opened her eyes and caught my gaze in the mirror, a similar half-smile playing across her lips that had been in evidence on Kelly's face only moments before. She made no move to cover herself. "Hi, I'm Kate."

I stammered out my name and tore my eyes away. Kelly had continued into the room at the end of the hall where the sofa lived. On changing my look from Kate to Kelly, I caught sight of the blonde bending over to retrieve a glass of water from the floor, next to the sofa. Her blond quim peeked out at me and caused me to again stop in mid-stride. My erection was now in full control of my faculties, leading me down the hallway. Soft padding feet from behind caused me to glance back. Still without a stitch, Kate followed in my wake. At this point in time, I couldn't give a fuck about a bonus, I was getting bonus enough.

The women stood side by side as I tried to appraise the couch, whispering in each other's ear. My cock was doing its best to break free of its confines and to let me know I should be doing other things rather than work. Finally I stopped and sat in the middle of the sofa. "Excuse me, ladies, but where is Graham?"

"He's only our landlord," said Kelly.

"He doesn't actually live with us," added Kate.

"So who was going to help me lift this onto the truck?"

Both women shrugged. Kelly said, "We were told to just choose a fabric and you'd sort out the rest, but you seem distracted." Both women had an eyebrow raised.

I'd had enough. I stood and undid my belt, button and zipper in record time, allowing my trousers and underwear to puddle around my ankles. Free at last, my cock bobbed in time to my rising pulse as pre-come threatened to drip from my tip.

Kelly peeled off her T-shirt as Kate knelt before me, tonguing up the drop of lubrication before swallowing me. She cupped my balls gently in her hand as she lavishly worked her tongue around my shaft. Kelly and I duelled with our tongues as I cupped her small breast and tweaked her pebble-hard nipple.

Kelly bent to join Kate at my feet. The immense pleasure of seeing two women at your feet, taking turns to engulf your knob while the other sucks on your balls is intense. When Kate started playing with Kelly's cunt, I erupted into Kelly's mouth, pumping my juices down her throat as she struggled to keep up.

Kate lay back on the huge Chesterfield and draped a leg over the backrest, exposing her shaved pussy to us both. Before I could react, Kelly positioned herself at Kate's hole and began to tongue her in earnest. With her butt raised in the air and her pussy again peeking at me, I couldn't help myself. I moved in behind the blonde and began tonguing her slit.

I sank to my knees on the bare floorboards for a better angle, allowing me to dip my tongue between her folds and coax her button out of hiding. I reached up and placed a thumb over her anus and began to massage there as I continued to tease her clit.

The moans coming from Kate suggested that Kelly was doing well in her own ministrations. I leaned in and latched on to Kelly's clit with my lips, sucking firmly to elicit a groan from her. A frustrated cry from Kate suggested that my pleasing Kelly was distracting her from finishing off the brunette.

I took it as a challenge. I inserted a finger into Kelly's cunt and coated it with her juices before allowing it to replace my thumb over her anus. Little by little I increased the pressure of my sucking and my finger. Suddenly Kelly's asshole relaxed and my finger slipped inside, gaining another response from both women.

My dick had now recovered and was straining to gain my attention; he wanted back in the game.

Keeping my finger in place I stood and ran my engorged head over Kelly's blond lips. She pushed her hips back at me, encouraging me to enter her. I pulled back.

Kelly forgot about Kate and glanced back at me. In response to her unanswered question I asked, "Rubbers?"

In annoyance she pointed at the coffee table where a large bowl held an assortment of prophylactics. Obviously this wasn't a completely new experience for these ladies. I randomly grabbed a foil packet and tore it open. Kelly had gone back to pleasuring Kate and without my distractions had managed to push her along. I slowly rolled on the ribbed strawberry-coloured sheath. I moved back into position behind Kelly but waited until Kate was truly into the throes of her orgasm before plunging into Kelly's pussy.

Her own lubrication mixed with that of the rubber, allowing me to slide all the way home in a single thrust. Her head reared back and a guttural groan escaped her lips. With measured, long strokes, I drilled her canal, slowly building up my pace.

From beneath us, Kate recovered enough to swing around so she could suck on Kelly's nipples and tease her clit with her fingers. With both of us working on her, Kelly's climax built quickly. Feeling her inner muscles beginning to contract, I shortened my strokes, my cock becoming a blur as I pounded into her, my finger still massaging her anus.

Her inner muscles clamped around my shaft. I endured a moment of intense pain as she squeezed and then she came. A torrent of juices washed against my pubic bone and ran down our thighs to soak into the upholstery. On feeling her obvious release I followed her lead and began to pump my load into the latex.

We found a number of different ways to fit all three of us into a daisy chain that morning but eventually I was too exhausted to get my dick to cooperate any more.

It struck me then that I still hadn't measured up the sofa, the women hadn't picked a fabric and there was still the problem of getting the thing onto the truck. My legs were shaky as it was. Lifting a huge antique sofa wasn't going to be easy.

Kate and Kelly gave me the solution. "Why don't you come back tomorrow with someone from work?" suggested Kelly.

"With two big strong men, it shouldn't be a problem getting it up . . . onto the truck," added Kate.

I didn't miss the innuendo or the sudden renewed interest these two were showing. I left the pattern books with them overnight so they could have a good look through them.

My biggest problem now is which of the lads from work should I take with me?

FRIDAY NIGHT SPICE

Jane, Powell River

When my partner and I bought a computer and discovered the Net, I decided it was time we expanded our horizons. We'd always had a pretty lively sex life but there was definitely something lacking somewhere. I couldn't quite put my finger on it. What was that elusive X factor? It dawned on me one evening when I was surfing the internet and came across a site about erotic corporal punishment.

I wanted to be spanked.

Suddenly, various pieces of a scattered puzzle fitted together with a satisfying click. My partner had always been fond of giving my cheeks an affectionate swat in the passing – could he rise to a full assault upon my rear? I decided to find out.

Peter and I are fond of watching a blue movie after our Friday night curry. The film inevitably leads to an extended session on the couch in our living room. For Spanking Night, I picked a new DVD from the adult video shop *Comeuppance – Tales of Wicked Schoolgirls*. The cover showed a nubile eighteen-year-old bending over, holding her ankles as a stern schoolmaster brandished a cane above her tight little behind. The "schoolgirl" wore a micro-mini kilt and a skimpy clingy top. I completed my shopping with a trip to Oxfam, where I found a school pinafore, perfect for flipping up to expose a naughty bottom.

When Peter arrived home that evening, he found me dressed in my new uniform. I had added sheer seamed stockings and shiny black stilettos with four-inch heels. The pinafore was very short and tight. I'm a big girl and my tits were crammed into the bodice, threatening to pop out any moment. Peter was speech-less. He put down his briefcase and stared at me. Then some-thing interesting happened.

"Bend over, Jane."

It was my turn to stare. I had set the evening up so carefully. Dinner first, then wine and *Comeuppance*. It looked as if Peter had his own ideas. We both breathed hard as I bent over the couch. My bottom felt vulnerable, clad in the flimsiest of black see-through panties. Suddenly, my pussy was extremely wet. I could sense Peter standing just behind me and a delicious blend of nerves and anticipation surged through me.

"You do have a lovely bum, Jane. And a very sexy one too."

I groaned and thrust my hips towards Peter like a horny slut. I wanted two things – a sound spanking and a hard fuck, preferably doggy-style. Cool fingers caressed the satiny flesh at the tops of my thighs. Moisture oozed from my swollen pussy and melted into the see-through panties. I imagined how my bottom would look to Peter. Wide and curvy, like a big luscious peach. I already wanted to come. Peter traced the soft lines of my hips with his fingertips and I shivered.

"I know what you need. A damn good spanking."

I swear, at that moment, I would've begged for it. Peter raised his hand and smacked my wriggling bum. A delicious warm tingle spread through my cheeks. My clit throbbed.

"Take your panties down, Jane."

Slowly, I did as I was instructed, savouring the wickedness. My pussy was hot and wet, my clit ready to explode with pleasure. Again and again his firm hand slapped against my tender exposed bum like a series of tiny bee stings and I ground my hips, crying out for Peter to fuck me. Quickly, he unzipped himself and I heard the familiar rustle of the condom wrapper. Groaning, he thrust his solid cock deep inside my velvety, melting cunt. My boobs popped out of the tiny pinafore as we fucked, doggy-style, and he squeezed their bouncing juici-ness as we pounded to a noisy climax.

I think the entire street must've heard us come that night. And, yes, we did get round to watching that DVD. Eventually . . .

SEDUCING MY DAUGHTER'S GIRLFRIEND

Isabelle, Chicago

When sweet little Tracy came to my front door asking if my daughter was home, I just about wet my panties right then and there. You see, the cute-as-a-button eighteen-year-old was scantily attired in a midriff-baring, pink halter top and a pair of tight, white shorty-shorts, her strawberry-blond hair braided into two impish ponytails.

"Uh, no, Tracy, I'm sorry," I said, running my eyes all over the burgeoning babe's body, "but Brianne won't be back until eight or so."

She turned to leave, and I impulsively shot out my hand and grabbed on to her bare arm. Her smooth, tanned skin felt so very good in my hand. In the split second that it took my pussy to dampen at the sight of the pretty teenager, I'd decided to try to put the moves on her.

Now normally, I steer clear of my daughter's boy and girlfriends, but months of involuntary celibacy had lowered my ethical standards, I guess, and inflamed my always seething passions to the flashpoint. Plus, I'd noticed the young hottie checking out my rather large chest on a number of previous occasions, and I was anxious to find out if where there was smoke there was fire.

"Why don't you come inside and wait for Brianne?" I suggested. "She'll be along soon, I'm sure."

The pert teen shrugged her buff shoulders and slipped past me, inside the house. Her girlish, fresh-scrubbed smell of innocence flooded my brain and stiffened my already hardened nipples to the aching point, as she brushed by. I ushered her into the living room, admiring her gleaming, sun-kissed legs and cheeky, twitching buttocks every prancing step of the way.

We sat down on the couch and stared at one another for a few awkward, silent moments. Then Tracy's shining brown eyes drifted away from my face and down to my chest. I'm a 38 DD, and my cups overflow.

I asked the girl what she was looking at, and her pretty face flushed red. She mumbled something about how much "bigger" I was than her – in a good way, she meant.

I smiled, my hot, stirred-up juices threatening to soak right through the front of my jeans. "You're a very attractive young woman yourself, Tracy," I said. "Even if your breasts aren't quite as large as mine."

We stared at each other some more. And just when I'd worked up the courage and urgency to take action, the impetuous teenager reached out and touched my left boob, jolting me right down to my sexual core.

"I've always wondered what they felt like," she whispered.

I swallowed hard, tingling all over. Then I breathed, "You'll never tell that way." And without further ado, I lifted my top off and flung it aside, pulled down my bra, letting the sweet young thing get a good look at my heavy, bronze jugs.

Her baby blues widened even further as I gripped her wrist and guided her hand back onto my tit. She tentatively caressed my bare breast, sending an electric charge coursing through my body. I heated up like a furnace, grabbing the girl's head and pulling her tight into my heaving chest.

"Suck my tits!" I moaned, my head swimming.

Tracy grasped my overblown boobs in her hot little hands and squeezed, the super-sensitive flesh overflowing her moist palms. I groaned. She stuck out her kitten-pink tongue and tickled one of my jutting nipples. I full-body shuddered. I clutched the girl's ponytails in sexual agony, urging her to fully explore my electrified breasts with her damp hands and mouth.

She didn't disappoint, tongue-lashing first one and then my other nipple to painful erection, earnestly lapping at the pair, swirling her tongue all around my pebbly areolae. Then she took one of my fully flowered buds into her wet-hot mouth and sucked on it, staring up at me with her big, bright eyes.

Tracy suckled my rubbery nipples hungrily and urgently, slurping away, slathering my tingling tits with her hot saliva. I bristled with the raw, wicked eroticism of it all, my pussy smouldering and my body on fire.

I finally pulled the ardent young lady off my glistening boobs and peeled away my jeans and panties, spread my legs open. I desperately needed to know if she was as good with twats as she was with tits. The pretty young thing showed the respect due her elders, promptly kneeling down on the carpet in front of me and gripping my fleshy thighs, burying her head in between my shaking legs.

"God, yes, Tracy!" I cried, almost coming in a blaze of pent-up lust as soon as she tongue-tapped my swollen clit.

I closed my eyes and clung to the girl's blond, bobbing head, as she excitedly lapped and lapped at my slit. She ran her velvet-sandpaper tongue all the way up from my butt hole to my clit, over and over again, driving me wild.

Then the darling girl suddenly stopped licking. She looked up at me and grinned, running her tongue over her slimy lips. I clutched her silky ponytails and yanked her face back down into my sopping pussy, and she clamped her pouty lips onto my button and sucked. I spasmed with joy, spasmed again when she boldly slid two of her purple-tipped fingers into my pussy and started plunging away.

The naughty young honey sucked on my buzzing clit and finger-fucked my slit. I went into meltdown, my overwrought body trembling out of control. The soft-lipped suction and squishy sawing away on my sex became too much for me to bear and I was jolted by orgasm. Again and again, coming multiple times, gushing tangy gratitude all over Tracy's pretty face and pumping fingers.

And only when the last of the white-hot lightning bolts of ecstasy had finally dissipated, leaving me wasted in body and soul, did I regain my senses enough to hear my daughter's car pull into the driveway.

"Brianne's home!" I squealed in warning, scrambling off the couch and into my clothes.

Tracy slowly got up off her knees, casually licking her fingers clean. I grabbed her by the shoulders and desperately kissed and tongued my come off her shiny nose and chin. Just as the front door creaked opened and Brianne strolled into the sex-funked living room.

I would have plenty of opportunity to thank my daughter's talented girlfriend more thoroughly in the hot days and nights and weeks that followed, before she skipped off to college in the fall.

THE ARCADE

Corinne, Seattle

I met Jerry at an orgy party in Portland when I was twenty-one. He was an older, more exciting man. Jerry was maybe five feet nine inches, but claimed he was six feet tall. A bit of a pot belly hung out over his jeans, blond hair, blue eyes and a baby face for being thirty-one. Someone who teased my senses. I wanted him to like me. Most of all I wanted to fuck him. From the moment I saw him, I wanted to shove his cock inside of me. Who cares about for ever, I would think to myself. The adventures Jerry and I had were beyond anything I've ever experienced again.

It was a hot summer day when Jerry and I drove down south for the day, stopping off at what seemed to be the only adult store in town because the reader board announced a huge arcade with windows between the booths.

"Booths with windows in their arcade. How weird is that?" I scrunched my nose a bit.

"The heat is killer," Jerry said slyly. "I think we should go inside and cool off."

Inside, the true seediness of this establishment was revealed. I love seediness. It lends to atmosphere. All the porno videos that were on display, covers with tits, pussies, cocks, assholes and a myriad of other visual stimuli, were right there in front of us. Even the guy at the counter was seedy, and unable to complete a coherent sentence. He had long greasy hair and was dressed in a wife-beater that gave him an aura of trailer trash.

A big neon red cursive sign to the back right of the counter advertised ARCADE. We walked back hand in hand. It smelled of old sex, love, hate and everything in between.

The inside of the booths were a little dark, but there was a window as promised. The window was covered with a set of blinds on the voyeur's side only. One wall had a TV screen and a slot to put your money in. Ads for Michael Nin films and the adult mega-star Jewel De'Nyle flashed on the screen in front of us. A bench with torn upholstery was the only furniture. The bench was covered in dingy green vinyl.

As I walked in I realized that our neighbour could hear us, and see us. I could feel dampness start to come from my honey hole. The walls didn't go all the way to the top. Jerry was smiling brightly at the realization that others could see and hear us.

The man beside us peeked through the window watching us. Pulling the slats from the blinds apart, he got a better view as I stripped completely out of my clothing. Our neighbour was balding and had glasses. I flashed him a smile. I heard the blinds come open fully. Now the middle-aged nameless man was staring at us openly. I started to think of him as Peeping Tom. He looked like an old elementary schoolteacher of mine.

"Bend over the bench, my little cunt." Jerry's voice had a sadistic edge to it. That edge is what always has and always will make my pussy wet. "Our neighbour wants to see your pussy," his voice teased me. I knew that both Jerry and Peeping Tom were staring. I wanted to give them the show of their lives.

Bending over, I spread my thighs. I felt our neighbour's eyes focusing on my cunt. Juicy is what Jerry called my pussy lips. He adored my plump round belly, the flab on my arms. All of it encased in golden olive skin. I have fine black ringlet curls on the top of my head, a full mouth and brown eyes that sparkle flecks of gold when I'm excited.

Still bending over the green vinyl bench staring at the concrete floor, I felt a sharp smack to my pussy.

"Ah!" I yelped. I jumped a little.

Jerry laughed. "You're so responsive." He leered at me. "Your pussy is weeping. God, you're a fuckin' whore." Cruelty was in his voice. His cruelty only made me wetter. I could feel juices dripping down the inside of my thighs.

"Ah." The moan came from a place deep inside my belly. Really it wasn't just my belly. It started at my clit, travelled up my womb, through my belly, then snaked its way out my mouth.

"Horny, bitch?" Rhetorical question. Of course I was fucking horny. I wanted to suck his big fat juicy cock right that instant, then shove it in my cunt. Jerry never let me have things when I wanted them though. I knew how the game worked. Jerry's fingers traced my lips. I could hear Mr Peeping Tom next door breathing heavily. He must have been choking his chicken. Hell, he had to have been. God, my cunt was dripping its silky smooth fluid. I could feel my lips swollen, engorging themselves with blood.

I felt a stinging sensation; Jerry was spanking me. The unmistakable crack of his palm on my ass cheek. The burning and stinging that followed. The muscles inside my hot wet hole were spasming and aching. All I wanted was something inside.

"He's looking at you, my wanton little slut." I couldn't see Jerry's face, but I knew what kind of grin was there. An evil one.

I felt Jerry's fingers probe into my slick hot hole. He pulled them out.

"Look at this. Little threads of girl come." Jerry shoved his fingers in front of my face. "My. You are a slut," he said. "I'm going to show our neighbour." He held his fingers coated in my silk up to the window. A grunt from the man at the window reached my ears.

"I think I like you best like this," Jerry told me cruelly.

"Uh-huh," came my reply. I don't know what I was replying to. Maybe just the reactions in my body. Maybe to Jerry. I never knew. I just knew that in those moments I was an object of desire. I only lived for his desire.

"What's that? A grunt of gratification, my little bitch?" He always knew exactly what to say to me. Jerry knew dirty talk just made me all the more wanton for him.

"Should I show our neighbour how much you like my cock in your pussy?"

I had been thinking that he would never ask. My hole was hungry for him.

"Please, Jerry." I was begging. I felt empty in my lower abdomen. It was always hard when he did this.

"I'm going to fuck your pussy," he said in a primal and growling voice. "Then I'm going to fuck your face. Of course I can't leave your asshole unattended." He stuck his finger in my asshole to emphasize the fact. I rose up on my tiptoes at the entrance of his finger. I loved and hated having my asshole violated. It was something I didn't want, but I needed.

"Oh God. You're so fucking wet." He was bent over me whispering in my ear. It was more of a hiss. I got off on it.

An unintelligible moan escaped my lips. I felt his cock probing my cunt opening. The probing was always torturous. It spread my hole just enough to let me know what was to come. I was wondering if the guy in the next booth over had died from a heart attack yet at this point. It wasn't every day that people got to see normal couples like Jerry and I fucking each other stupid in an adult arcade. I knew that most of the men who visited places like this weren't getting what they needed at home. It made me smile to think I might be filling that need in a vicarious way for someone.

Jerry's cock teased me mercilessly.

"Jerry, please fuck me." I almost screamed it. My need was so desperate.

"Not yet, whore." God, he was going to make me wait for ever. Damn him.

"Fuck you," I muttered under my breath.

"What was that?" He spanked me ten times. Those were very stingy. Retribution for what I knew he could not hear. It was one of our games. A small spanking that pretended to punish. I felt him shove his cock into my hungry pussy.

"Oh, Corinne. You're such a slut when I want you to be. What a dirty little bitch." He said it just loud enough for our neighbour to hear, as he pounded into me. I was grinding backwards taking in as much of him as I could. My pussy clenched on to him tightly. Oh God, how I wanted to come with him inside me. When he took his cock out I ached. I could feel the emptiness. I whimpered. He hated whimpering, because soon enough I'd have his dick back. Maybe not in the same hole.

"Kneel," he commanded me. Jerry was going to fuck my face. I knew it.

"Please, Jerry, fuck my cunt again," I begged him.

"I said kneel, cunt." It was an unforgiving command punctuated with a sharp smack to my thighs this time. I knelt as quickly as possible. Slaps to the butt made me more excited, but slaps to my thighs burned painfully. Of course, as soon as the sting had worn off I was at a new level of sensitivity. Everything in me became a raw nerve ending. Even my mouth.

"Suck my cock, bitch." Sharply he slapped my face. I heard Mr Peeping Tom taking deep laboured breaths. I moaned. My lips encircled his cock. I took all of him into my mouth, pumping my tongue along the length of his shaft.

It was Jerry's turn to moan. He pumped himself harder into my mouth.

His cock was hot and throbbing inside my mouth. He tasted and smelled musky. Musky and salty with sweat. I always relished that flavour. My own juices mingled with his. My own flavour was acidic and had its own musk. His cock had been in my pussy marinating in my juices. His cock soaked in my pussy was truly a gourmet experience.

I could feel Jerry getting closer to his climax. I always wished he'd do it in my mouth. Hot white come down my throat was always a huge treat; come was always slightly bitter, making my throat burn.

"You said something naughty to me." His voice was evil, patronizing, both these things at once. "You don't get to swallow today," he said to me. "I'm going to stretch your asshole out. Then I'm going to shoot my load into your ass. You're going to shit come ribbons. You little slut." His voice was gravelly.

"Fuck her ass for the love of God, please." It was Mr Peeping Tom from next door. He was obviously getting off on our show.

"Oh, I see someone else admires your slutty ass." Jerry smacked each cheek harshly. I was sure he was leaving handprints. My ass was always pink after us being together, this time was no exception.

"Bend back over the bench, whore." His voice was rough, commanding. I was so far into myself I barely heard him, but I understood that my mouth was no longer full. Jerry would want to finish in one of my holes, I knew that. He always had finished in my ass.

The head of his shaft traced my perineum. The sensation was like electricity, and even more electrical because I knew there was someone watching.

"Uh." Peeping Tom next to us was grunting. He should have been close. I liked to think that my display might have inspired him to a double orgasm.

"I'm gonna' fuck your ass, slut," Jerry told me roughly.

The rough burning sensation penetrated my asshole. I felt it stretch to accommodate his cock. The skin and hole stretched themselves to accommodate him. Sweet burning pain filled me. Jerry grunted behind me. His balls were slapping into my cheeks as he pumped in and out.

"Oh yes. Fuck that slut's ass." It was the neighbour. "Fuck her hard. Make her hurt." His breath and speaking were laboured. I could hear him stroking himself.

"Oh God," Peeping Tom yelled out. "Look, you nasty slut. I'm creaming all over myself because of your tight nasty little asshole." He was screaming.

I was able to feel Jerry still working in and out. The sensation filled me.

"Oh, Corinne, you fucking slut." His voice was raspy, on the edge of coming. "I am going to come in your asshole, bitch." As he said it he finished. The warm salty sting of his fluids filled my anus.

"Oh!" Peeping Tom managed to come too. I heard as he wiped himself down, and ran from the booth. Jerry was still in my ass. Slowly he worked himself out making a popping sound as the head came out.

I felt dirty, violated, and absolutely satisfied after being fucked. I especially loved that someone I didn't know was watching. I cleaned myself up and got dressed. I helped Jerry clean himself up. We left adult store hand in hand. The clerk smiled at us knowingly. I noticed there were cameras that could be focused into the booths to make sure everything was OK. So more people had been watching than I'd ever guessed. At least we had given them a good show.

Jerry and I parted ways soon after our video-store experience. He still contacts me from time to time telling me that I was the most fun he'd ever had with a woman. I smile to myself, never revealing he's the most fun I ever had with any man.

FORBIDDEN FANTASY

Lynne, Eindhoven

Getting off the coach, I peered around, though goodness knows what I was looking for. It may sound weird, but I'd never seen a photo of Paul. After sending him mine I had waited for him to return the favour, but nothing had arrived. I won't say it wasn't worrying. Perhaps he was ugly as sin, or an octogenarian with an extremely vivid imagination. Or, my God, perhaps he was actually a woman? He'd told me an awful lot about himself in his emails, but, as with most cyber stuff, there was no way I could prove any of it. I'd just trusted he was telling me the truth. I knew his address, but never even thought of checking out if it was genuine. Suddenly I was beginning to have major doubts about the whole idea. Some people might say it was a bit late to start questioning motives after a nine-hour journey to a foreign country, and some people would be right.

Again I stared around the bus station, searching out anyone who looked a likely candidate for a freelance bookseller, and came up blank. It was up to him to find me, and so I stood there, feeling, and probably looking, decidedly lost. After ten minutes no one was showing the slightest inclination of approaching me and I began to wonder if I was actually in the right place. I'd assumed he'd meet me off the bus, but perhaps he'd meant us to meet outside. Picking up my bag, I made my way to the exit, casting my gaze round the bustling terminus. The place was crowded, and getting more so with every passing moment. It would be so easy to miss each other, especially as I had no idea what Paul looked like. If he was here at all.

A quarter of an hour later I was in a panic. Pacing up and down, trying to look in all directions at once, I was beginning to attract strange glances. And then, when I'd given up all hope, a hand descended on my shoulder. Startled, I swung round. "Paul?" I squeaked. Could this be my fifty-year-old bookseller? It was hard to tell his age exactly because of the beard and long hair.

He raised his eyebrows. "I've been watching you for the last fifteen minutes. I've been sitting in my lorry, on my break, and didn't have much else to do. I take it you're supposed to be meeting someone?"

So, not Paul? "Well, yes, I am. But I've got a horrible feeling I've been stood up."

"A boyfriend, then?"

I blushed. "Sort of."

"Sort of?"

"It's a long story."

"I've got the time. Fancy a coffee? You can keep an eye on here from the restaurant."

"I – er, yeah, OK. I could do with a drink."

Over a hot chocolate I found myself telling the stranger the whole story. Well, almost the whole story. I doubted he was interested in the real reason behind my visit. A shared fantasy that was no one else's business but our own.

"You say you know where he lives?"

"Yes. That is, I know where he says he lives." I opened my bag and handed over a slip of paper with Paul's address.

"I know that area. It's just past the delivery depot. Look, how about I give you a lift there?"

"I don't know. I mean, I don't want to put you out."

"It's no trouble. In fact, I don't live too far from there myself."

"OK then. Thanks."

A small voice whispered that this might not be the most judicious decision I had ever made, but the whole trip seemed to have bypassed my sensible side. Anyway, I was tired, confused and lost for any other solution.

"It might take a while. I have to wait at the depot for a trailer swap."

"That's fine. It's not as if I have anything else planned."

Walking out of the bus station, I looked round one last time. No one rushed to greet me. I knew it was now up to me to find Paul.

My new friend helped me up into the cab of a huge lorry. Not the most elegant of manoeuvres and my long skirt didn't help, as it wrapped itself around my legs, depositing me with a thump in the passenger seat. An unladylike oath escaped my lips.

The trip was an interesting one. I had never seen the road from such an elevation and it was a diverting new experience. My companion was easy to talk to, and by the end of the journey I had pretty much told him my whole life story.

The wait at the depot was longer than expected and by the time we continued our journey it was already getting dark. The travelling was taking its toll and I felt my eyes closing and I drifted off. When I awoke I realized we were no longer moving. Opening my eyes I saw we were parked in a lay-by. My rescuer was staring at me with a very strange expression on his face. I smiled at him, but there was no response.

"I guess you're having a break?" My question was received in silence. "Um, do you think we'll be moving any time soon? I don't want to arrive at Paul's in the small hours."

Again, only silence. By now I was beginning to feel uncomfortable. In fact, more than uncomfortable. His stare was so intense it frightened me. "Hello . . . er . . ." I suddenly realized I didn't even know his name. "What do I call you?" I asked, trying to keep my voice from trembling.

"You can call me 'Sir'."

"Sorry? What did you just say?"

"I said you can call me 'Sir'. And from now on you'll only talk when I require it of you."

I stared at him in horror, my hand creeping to the door handle.

"It's locked."

Sure enough, however much I pushed the door wouldn't open. By now I was terrified. What sort of idiot had I been to get into a lorry with a complete stranger?

"Take off your knickers and unbutton that blouse."

I froze.

"Do as I say, Lynne. You will regret it if you don't."

Desperately I looked around for something to use as a weapon. There was nothing.

"Do it!"

Whimpering, I slowly began to unbutton my shirt. His hand reached out and pulled away the material to reveal my full breasts. His fingers closed around my nipple, tweaking it into erection. I gasped.

"And now the knickers."

"Please, please, don't make me do this . . ."

"You will do whatever I tell you to do. You are my property now. And didn't I tell you to call me 'Sir' when addressing me?"

"Yes."

"Yes, what?"

I knew I had no choice, terrified to think of what he would do to me if I disobeyed. "Yes, Sir."

"That's better. Now, take off those knickers."

With shaking hands I did as he asked. He pulled my skirt up to reveal my shaved pubes and grunted in satisfaction. His hand travelled up my stockinged leg and his finger brushed against my clit. Automatically I clenched my thighs together, and yelped in pain as the palm of his hand descended with a resounding slap. Immediately I opened my legs to his invading finger.

"Good, Lynne. You're learning. Now, keep that pose. I'm taking you home." And he started the engine.

Exposed and vulnerable, I had never felt so humiliated in my life. As the street lights flashed past us, I imagined that I was on show to the world, and a single tear trickled down my cheek. So, he was taking me home. I was not fool enough to think he meant my home, and it was then I realized just how helpless I really was. God, I'd even told him that my family and friends didn't know I'd left the country, so he knew they wouldn't be searching for me here. He could murder me and no one would ever know. My only option was to play along with his little game and try to find a way of escaping.

By now we were slowing down at the back of a row of terraced houses. I looked for a street name board, but couldn't see one. This could be any street, in any town, in England.

Turning off the engine he got out of the cab and opened my door. He yanked me out of the cab, his grip on my arm forestalling any attempt to run. I opened my mouth to scream and his hand closed over it. "Not a good idea, my sweet. And I shall remember that."

What did he mean? I had no idea, but knew it meant no good.

He pulled me into the house, slamming the door behind him, and dragged me up the stairs into a bedroom. At least, technically it was a bedroom, but its furnishings were more like those of an ancient torture chamber. Ropes, whips, handcuffs and some strange objects I didn't even recognize.

"Take off your skirt and blouse. Just leave on the stockings."

I hesitated.

"Take them off now! Or your punishment will be that much worse."

My punishment? Oh, my God. Hurriedly I obeyed him. Seconds later I was standing in front of him, naked except for a pair of black silk hold-up stockings.

"Now, kneel down on the bed with your hands behind your back."

This time I did as he said straight away. I watched, trembling, as he picked up a length of rope and proceeded to fasten it around my wrists, securing the other end around the bedpost. Secure in the knowledge that I couldn't escape, he picked up a long thonged flogger. I fought to suppress a scream. I had seen a ball gag amongst the paraphernalia on the bedside cabinet, and knew he would use it if I didn't keep quiet.

Although I knew what was coming I couldn't possibly prepare myself for it, as he raised the flogger and brought it down with a thwack on my naked shoulders. Despite my resolution to keep quiet I couldn't suppress the cry that rose to my lips.

"You will take your punishment in silence or I will use the gag."

I clenched my teeth as the flogger descended again, this time even harder. The leather bit into my back and the pain was unbearable. Again and again the lash flailed my body. Finally I could take no more and I collapsed onto the bed.

"So, now you know what happens when you don't obey me straight away. Have you learned your lesson?"

"Yes – yes, I have," I yelled, then remembered just in time, "Sir."

"Good. Now answer these questions. And, remember, you know the punishment if you don't answer them correctly. Who owns you?"

"You do, Sir."

"And what can I do to you?"

"Anything you wish, Sir."

"And why is that?"

"I . . . er . . ." The flogger whistled through the air, this time with all his strength behind it. A flame of pure agony flared through my back, and I buried my head in the mattress to muffle the scream I could no longer suppress.

"Because you are my slave. I own you body and soul. You only exist to obey my commands. You have no will of your own. You . . . are . . . my . . . property." The last words were emphasized by strokes of the whip. By now I would have said anything to make him stop.

"Yes, Sir. I am yours, and yours alone. I will do anything you say."

"I like that. Anything?"

"Yes, Sir. Anything."

"Very good. Get back on your knees, and open your mouth."

I felt a sinking feeling in the pit of my stomach. I had a very good idea of what he was going to ask me to do next. My worst thought was confirmed as I watched him undo his zip.

"Suck me, slave. Make me come." And he thrust himself into my mouth.

Knowing the consequence of refusal, I had no choice. Wrapping my lips around him, I took him deep into my mouth. My tongue flicked against him as my head moved up and down. I felt his whole body stiffen and he drove himself even deeper. Then, with a jerk, he came, his come filling my mouth.

"Thank you, Lynne. I'm very pleased with you. I think you deserve a rest. But first . . ." I watched as he picked up a camera and began to take photographs of me from every angle. "I shall enjoy viewing these when you are no longer here."

His words sent a jolt of terror flashing through me. What did he mean by no longer here? Was he planning to kill me when he'd had his fun with me? I had to get away. But the possibility of doing so became even more remote as he picked up more rope and bound my body to the bed. From some remote corner of my brain a small part of me actually admired his handiwork. He was quite an artist, the intricate rope work reminding me of a spider's web. Quite ironic really, considering my situation.

"I think I need some coffee. Feel free to wait for my return." I heard him chuckle as he left the room.

"Bastard!" I muttered, but not loud enough for him to hear.

He was gone for quite a time, leaving me alone with my tortured thoughts. Desperately I attempted to escape from the ropes, and had just succeeded in loosening one or two when he returned.

"Ah, I see you've been busy. Now, do I punish you or reward you for your efforts? Mmm, good question. I'm feeling generous, so I think the latter."

Approaching the bed, he clasped my breasts in his hands, his thumbs playing softly with my nipples. Then he took one in his mouth, rolling his tongue across the tip. His hand reached down between my thighs and he began to rub my clit. Despite myself I realized I was getting wet. Then his finger plunged into me. I gasped.

"Like that, did you? Well, you're going to like this even more then." And, after undoing the ropes that bound my legs, he stripped off his clothes. This was it then, what I'd really been dreading. He was going to rape me.

"So. And now it's your turn to ask me to do something for you. Come now, don't look so confused. You know what I want. You're going to beg me to fuck you, aren't you? I mean, I shall probably do it anyway, but I think you would appreciate it more if you do as I say, don't you think?"

He was right. Whatever I did or said now wouldn't stop him having my body, but I had a feeling it would be a lot less painful if I did as he said.

Gritting my teeth, I forced the words out of my mouth. "Please, Sir. Please fuck me. I want to feel you deep inside me. I want to be your true property. Please fuck me now."

"Very good. And because you have been so good I will give you my reward."

And then he was on top of me, his hands exploring every inch of my body. Then he took me, forcing my body into the mattress with every desperate stroke. As he came, I felt a shock reverberate through me as I reached my own climax. It was over.

"So, Lynne, my beautiful slave. Was that what you wanted?"

I smiled. "Yes, it was. It was everything I'd dreamed of, and so much more. Thank you, Sir. Or rather, thank you, Paul."

FITTING ROOM

Greg, Cleveland

I was standing around on a typically slow Monday afternoon when a customer walked into the store. I gave him the once-over and could tell from his houndstooth jacket, black turtleneck, gabardine slacks and polished leather shoes that he obviously had good fashion sense and wasn't afraid to spend a large sum on clothing.

"Looking for anything in particular?" I asked.

He regarded me with a pair of warm, brown eyes and smiled. "Yes. I need two or three new pairs of pants. Business-casual style pants."

"I think I know just what you're looking for," I told him confidently. "Right this way."

He followed me to the back of the store where the business-casual clothing was located, then bumped into me when I stopped short at a rack of dress pants. I felt his strong hands grip my slim waist as he steadied himself, and his considerable package pressed into my firm, round ass. "Sorry," he said unnecessarily.

I turned around and got a good look at him. He was about my height, six feet, with a lean, athletic build – broad in the shoulders, narrow at the waist. His hair was cut short and his facial features were fine, almost delicate. He appeared to be in his late twenties, maybe early thirties. "Here you go," I said, indicating the garments in question with a sweep of my arm.

He took some time carefully selecting four or five pairs of pants. Then I pointed him to the five closet-sized change compartments along the back wall, and he opened the door to one and walked in.

"Let me know if you need any help," I told him, as the door closed.

A few minutes later, I was idly rearranging some sports jackets that didn't need rearranging when a soft, muffled voice called out to me from behind, "Could you come in here a moment?"

I walked over to the cubicles, opened the door on an empty one, closed it, and then opened its neighbour and found my customer. He was standing on the narrow wooden bench against the wall. He was naked from the waist down, his huge, black cock pointing right at me!

"Hi," he said casually. "I'm having some trouble getting these pants on with this thing –" he stroked his monster erection and smiled "– like it is. Anything you can do to help?"

My knees went weak and blood drained out of my face and into my groin. I'd never seen a bigger, or blacker, cock in all my life – except in porno magazines, of course. It must have been ten inches long – at least; and it was straight and true and as blue-black as a long, thick piece of liquorice. "Uh, sure," I mumbled, my mouth drier than the Sahara Desert. I stumbled into the tiny change room and shut and latched the door before anyone else could grab an eyeful.

I moved closer to him, and he released his cock from his hand into mine. His body spasmed and he groaned as I firmly gripped his long, hard pole. He groaned again and closed his eyes when I quickly began jerking him off, pulling on his awesome length. His cock was beautiful, felt beautiful, and, amazingly, it grew even longer and thicker as my practised hand pumped it.

"Oh, yeah, that feels good," he said, abandoning his massive cock to my worshipping hand.

"You ain't felt nothin' yet," I told him, and bent down and teased the tip of his over-swollen manhood with my out-stretched tongue.

His body jerked and slammed back against the wall.

"Easy, big guy," I warned, vaguely recalling that there was a very public store beyond the thin partition of the change booth.

We'd have to keep things quiet. The sense of danger and urgency only hardened my cock further.

"Suck my dick," he whispered fiercely.

I grunted an affirmative, held his huge rod at its base, and proceeded to tongue-flog his cock head – teasing the sensitive underside, slapping my tongue across his slit, licking him up and down in long, hard, wet strokes. He thrust his hips forwards, begging me to get with some serious cock-sucking, and I did. I took the enormous head of his cock into my mouth and sucked on it – popped it in and out until its rich, full blackness gleamed with saliva under the muted lights.

He ran his fingers through my short, blond hair, urging me to suck deeper on his prick, spurring me on, pulling my head closer. The air grew thick with the smell of man inside the cramped cubicle. I opened my mouth wide and sucked up and down his shaft, taking more and more of his humungous cock into my mouth with each head bob. My mouth was a vacuum, and when I'd consumed almost half of his magnificent meat, his hood banged up against the back of my throat. I further relaxed my throat muscles and kept right on gulping down his cock.

"Jesus Christ!" he cried out.

I spun my eyes upwards and stared meaningfully at his incredulous face. Then I refocused on the pleasurable task at hand and continued on my way down his night-shaded cock. Inch by swollen inch I sucked his cock into my mouth and throat, taking my sweet time, enjoying the sensation of deep-throating this man's massive dick. His hands clutched desperately at my hair, and I felt sweat drip off his face and splash down onto mine – and what was left of his rapidly disappearing black battering ram.

"I'm gonna come in your mouth, baby!" he hissed.

It was time for the final push. I thrust my head forwards and gobbled down the remaining two inches of his ebony dong. It slid down easy. His entire cock was now packed into the warm, wet tightness of my mouth and throat. I pushed out my tongue and lapped at his pube-sprinkled balls.

It was all too much for him. He moaned and his body jerked and hot come gushed down my throat. His body spasmed over and over, and with each spasm came a stream of sizzling semen. He tore at my hair, grunted repeatedly, come pouring out of his ruptured cock and flooding my throat. The sensation was exhilarating for me, sheer ecstasy for him.

"Jesus Christ," he murmured, dazed and disoriented by the magnitude of his come-letting. He let go of my head and his hands dropped to his sides.

Then he watched in wasted wonderment, through half-closed eyes, as I slowly tugged his spent cock out of my throat, one sopping wet inch at a time. It tumbled out of my gaping maw like a python uncoiling, until, finally, I had only his cock head left in my mouth. I sucked hard on it, milking it, draining away and swallowing the last few drops of his salty-sweet goodness. "Now it's my turn," I said.

"Anything," he groaned. "Anything."

I kicked off my shoes and peeled off my pants and shorts. My cock rose stiff and sure in the super-heated air. It wasn't quite as long as his hardened rope, but it could still plug holes with the best of 'em. "I want to fuck you in the ass," I said frankly.

He smiled and dropped to the floor and onto his knees, propping his arms up on the bench and raising his big, black ass into the air, demanding some man-loving. I moved in behind him, took hold of his butt cheeks. They were round and taut and thick, and I kneaded them with my hands, caressed them, squeezed them, slapped the playful pair of them.

"Fuck my ass," he said, resting his chin on the bench, reaching back and pulling his butt cheeks apart.

I gazed into the blinding black nothingness of his asshole, and my pulse quickened another twenty beats per minute. I spat a couple of times into my trembling hand and then rubbed my cock with the warm saliva. I rubbed some of the spit into his bunghole and he moaned, and then I gently pushed my purple cock head against his pucker.

I pushed harder and my cock head slowly eased into his glorious ass. The sensation was pure heaven; he was tight – very, very tight. I shoved more of my rigid cock into his vice-like bum, more and more, until, unexpectedly, he thrust backwards and my cock sank all the way in. I was buried to the balls.

"Yeah," I groaned, the hot, tight feeling sending sexual shock waves crashing through my electrified body.

"Fuck my ass!" he pleaded.

I thrust in and out of him, slowly, slowly at first, then faster and faster. My steely seven inches cut him in two as I banged away at him, pounding my meat into his spectacular ass. My balls smacked against his rippling butt cheeks, the sharp sound rising above our muted moaning and groaning, and I slammed him over and over again.

There is no better sensation on this earth than the raw, unbridled, flaming sexual sensation of plundering a young man's heavy, gripping ass with a raging hard-on. I thumped my new lover's bottom for all I was worth, for as long and as hard as I could. And that wasn't long. "I'm gonna come!" I cried out hoarsely.

"Come in my ass!" he hissed.

My head started to swim and sweat poured off my face, and then searing semen raced the engorged length of my dick, roared out of the tip and erupted into his butt. "Fuck, yeah," I whimpered, my body jerking to and fro as I blasted that sweet man with load after load of jism. His butt cheeks bounced joyously as I kept pounding into him, filling his ass with come.

Somehow, we managed to pull ourselves back together, and I sold him the pants that he'd taken into the change room. Before he left, I gave him my business card – with my home phone number jotted in.

TEMPER TANTRUM

Charlotte, Stittsville

I'm a freak . . . Charlotte Davidson, a woman who doesn't orgasm. I've tried. I've had sex with numerous men. But I've never managed to come. I was resigned to spending my life as an orgasmic virgin. Then about a year ago, in a most unladylike display, I threw a temper tantrum.

I was a dinner guest of Alice and John, my best friends. Alice was constantly finding eligible men for me, hoping someone could solve my sexual difficulties. Tonight's "eligible man" was Nigel Roberts, a new faculty member at the college where we taught. Apparently Mr Roberts was very interested in me.

The dinner had gone well and Roberts was both interesting and charming. Then over cognac Alice asked, "Nigel, can you recommend a good sex manual for Charlie? She has a problem: she can't come during sex. She's fucked many men but nobody's managed to bring her to orgasm."

I blushed scarlet and squirmed in embarrassment at this public announcement of my sexual inadequacies.

Roberts looked puzzled. "You must have sex with the wrong men," he said. "Giving an orgasm is easy if you handle the woman properly."

His arrogance enraged me.

"So making a woman come is straightforward, is it?" I snapped. "Just follow the instructions in some manual and bingo . . . orgasm. Well, it's not like that with me. Every man has told me my cunt is too tight and I appear not to have a clitoris. So I'm a very difficult lay. I'll bet you can't make me come, Mr Roberts."

Roberts considered for several seconds. "I'll bet I can, Ms Davidson."

I was furious. "I think you're a conceited prick," I snarled. "How much do you want to bet? A hundred bucks."

"Done," he said.

When Alice and I were alone I hissed, "How could you do that, Alice?"

"Because Nigel's the right man for you, Charlie," she replied. "He's the nicest guy, he's good-looking and he's hot for you. So get over your temper tantrum. Just go to bed and fuck him."

But I thought Nigel Roberts a conceited male with an inflated ego and I intended to deflate it. As we left he said, "You're a challenging woman, Ms Davidson. I'll be in touch soon."

I expected we would meet in a bar some evening, and after a couple of drinks Roberts would take me back to his apartment for sex. Instead he arranged our encounter on a Saturday afternoon in the lobby of an upscale hotel. As we met, I did not offer to shake his hand but he raised mine to his lips to kiss. "You look beautiful, Ms Davidson," he murmured.

I am not beautiful and I know it. The bastard is mocking me, I thought. That'll make his humiliation especially pleasing.

"So, where do we fuck?" I asked.

"In one of the hotel rooms," he replied.

I was astonished. Roberts had booked a room in this expensive hotel for a sexual encounter that would last only a few minutes! The room was lavishly appointed with a luxurious king-size bed. Well, I thought, at least I'll be comfortable while he fumbles with me.

"Do you have any rules I must follow?" he asked.

I eyed him, trying to decide how far I could trust him. "No. You may do whatever you like, but I can stop you at any time." He nodded in agreement. "And you must undress first."

Roberts was taken aback, but reluctantly he complied. He was tall, slim and well toned, really quite handsome. But his cock . . . uh . . . feeble.

Roberts moved behind me and I stood motionless as he peeled off my top and unhooked my bra. He cupped my breasts, fondling them, playing with the nipples. "Your breasts are perfect, Ms Davidson," he whispered.

Lying bastard, I thought. I know my tits are too small.

He unfastened my skirt and slipped it over my hips. Suddenly, through my panties, I felt a hard ridge jammed against my ass. Holding my rear tight against his erection, Roberts slipped a hand down the front of my panties, stretching them as he cupped my mons, combing his fingers through my pubic hair. He moved lower, probing for my absent clitoris, then burrowed into my slit.

I realized with surprise that I liked his foreplay. Jesus, no! I thought. I'm here to humiliate this man.

Roberts knelt before me and pressed his face into my crotch. I felt his warm breath through my panties before he slowly pulled them down to my thighs. Suddenly I felt shy. I've undressed for innumerable men, so why should I feel embarrassed? But standing there in black stockings and high heels with my panties around my thighs I felt utterly naked.

"I think a woman is most sensuous when stripped as you are now, Ms Davidson. You are gorgeous." I blushed scarlet at the compliment.

Roberts pressed his face into the triangle of fur I left on my shaved pubis, then buried his nose in my crotch. "Your womanly aromas are intoxicating," he murmured.

Jesus, I thought, what's he going to do? I eyed his penis. No longer feeble, it was big and strong and eager. Suddenly he stood, picked me up, carried me to the bed and laid me on my back. I had to be careful my heels didn't tear the sheets.

Roberts leaned over me and kissed my eyes, licking the closed lids. His tongue traced a path along my throat then lapped in the hollow at the base. He took my breasts again, kneading them, squeezing them hard. They were swollen by his stimulation and he sucked hard on my engorged nipples.

I liked his smell and the feel of his tongue and mouth on me. No, I thought, this is not supposed to happen.

His tongue traced intricate patterns over my ribs, moved slowly down my belly and licked my pubis. Then Roberts put my legs up to his shoulders and very slowly pulled off my panties.

Without warning he lifted me so I was upside down, my head and shoulders resting on the bed with my ass in the air against his chest. Seizing my ankles, he splayed my legs wide to expose my genitals just inches from his face. He contemplated my pussy with rapt attention then put his face into my vulva and inhaled.

"The flower between your legs is exquisite," he breathed, "and its fragrance is divine. You are mouth-watering, Ms Davidson, the most erotic woman I have ever seen."

Me, erotic! He's delusional, I thought. But I didn't know what to do. I shouldn't have permitted him to inspect my private parts so brazenly, but it was exciting. Jesus, what was happening to me?

I was trying to decide whether to stop the experiment when Roberts began to lick my inner thighs. He worked slowly from one stocking top across my pussy to the other. I'd no idea my thighs could be so sensitive and he left me gasping for breath.

Releasing my ankles but keeping me inverted against his chest, Roberts opened me, spreading wide the inner lips to expose the pink flesh and red orifice.

Roberts studied these intimate structures for a long time then slowly began to lick my pussy. My rear squirmed against his chest as his tongue probed every fold and hollow and crevice. But when his tongue pushed into my opening, I went rigid, unable to breathe.

I knew that I should stop the experiment now, close my legs. But the sensations were so delicious I didn't want them to stop. I kept my legs splayed.

Roberts drew back my clitoral hood, inspected me, then hesitated, before slipping a finger up underneath it. I almost exploded. Whatever he had found up there was indescribably sensitive. I had never experienced such electrifying sensations. Licking his finger, he again went under the hood and rubbed what must be a clitoris, caressing it, swirling around it, squeezing it. When he pushed his tongue up and licked it, I convulsed.

I had to stop him; I needed time to think. With a supreme effort of will I closed my legs.

But he gave me no respite. Spreadeagling me on my back, he continued working my clitoris with his finger while sucking my tender nipples. I pulsed under the stimulation, moaning with pleasure.

Holding back the hood, Roberts again sucked the sensitive nodule. Then his finger eased into my orifice. I was wet but, as always, very tight and he had to work his finger slowly up my passage. It felt so good that I couldn't breathe as he held me pierced. Carefully he withdrew his finger and sucked it.

"Your juices taste like nectar, Ms Davidson," he said.

Again Roberts skewered me, pushing his finger carefully up my hole, then stirring, stretching, exploring while still sucking on my engorged teats. Suddenly, my body spasmed. Dear God, what was that? I thought. He rubbed the spot again, then again and my hips jerked uncontrollably every time he did so.

Could it really be a G-spot? I wondered in bewilderment.

He began pumping my vagina with his finger, alternating deep thrusts with pressure on the sensitive spot, all the while using his tongue on my wildly sensitive clitoris. My cries filled the room as I thrashed helplessly under the stimulation.

I realized I was losing control and should stop the experiment. But the sensations surging through me were heavenly. I thought I was losing my mind. If this was orgasm, I wanted it to go on forever. The waves of pleasure ravaged me as Roberts worked me into a frenzy. As the convulsions gripped my body I turned into a shrieking, feral woman.

Just when I thought I couldn't take any more I felt his cock nuzzle at my orifice. My juices soaked us as Roberts pushed the head of his stiff penis into my opening. His finger must have expanded my cunt, because as he kept pushing hard, I opened for him. Slow, very slowly, he forced his penis all the way in, penetrating me deeper than I ever believed possible.

His cock stretched my cunt to the limit, filling it completely. My vagina squeezed the throbbing penis as I savoured the feel of him inside me. But already he was moving. Slow at first, then as my tunnel enlarged for him, faster and faster, Roberts plunged into me. I thought he would split me in two. His assault rose to a crescendo driving me into shrieking hysteria. I was sure that

these were my last moments, that I would die from such indescribable rapture. As my brain shut down and my body disintegrated, my last coherent sensation was of an eruption deep
inside me. As I expired I could feel his come filling my cunt.

Slowly my scrambled brain regained awareness and my body
reassembled itself. Surprise, I was still alive! Roberts lay on his
back beside me. We were gasping, dripping with sweat. My
pubis and thighs were splattered with pussy juices, but I was in
a state of total bliss.

"That was miraculous," I breathed. "I've never been fully
penetrated before because it was just so painful. But you got
your penis in without hurting me at all, not even when you
thrust so hard I thought I would fall apart."

"I'd be appalled if I hurt you," Nigel said.

"You didn't, but you've given me the first real orgasm of my
life, a truly apocalyptic experience."

He rolled on top of me and I put my arms around his neck and
crossed my legs high on his back. I liked his body between my
thighs and his weight crushing me into the bed.

"I can't thank you enough. I thought I'd die from ecstasy. I
couldn't survive many of those."

"That's unfortunate," he declared, "because now I know
how to open you, you'll get them frequently. Every woman
needs regular orgasms to keep her healthy and happy. You're a
difficult lay, Charlotte, your clitoris and G-spot are hard to find
and your vagina is extremely tight. That means you have to get
laid by the right man. And that's me!"

I thought I would faint again; I was in turmoil. I had come
here to humiliate this man. Instead he had given me a mind-
blowing orgasm and now proposed to do it regularly.

Our lips brushed, our tongues entwined, then our mouths
coupled. The kiss liquefied my whole body. Nigel's tongue was
deep in my mouth when I felt his stiff penis nudging me.

"Jesus. You're hard again!" I exclaimed.

"That's what happens when I kiss you," he responded. "May
I have you again?"

I thought for a moment. "You don't have to do this," I said.
"You've already won the bet."

"Who cares about the bet," Nigel replied. "You're the sexiest woman on the planet, Charlotte. The sight of your naked body fills me with lust. I want to fuck you for ever."

Scarcely able to believe what was happening to me, I lay back and spread my legs for him.

My recollections of the next few hours are hazy. I know room service delivered supper and I know we rested and talked. But my dim memory is that Nigel explored many different ways of opening my cunt. I don't know how many times he made me come, but in the late evening I collapsed in complete exhaustion.

It was late morning when Nigel woke me and I lay drowsily as he peeled off my stockings. He looked gorgeous, and his penis was so sweet, unrecognizable as the rampant cock that had impaled me yesterday. He contemplated my naked body and murmured, "Ravishing," then carried me into the shower.

We crossed the crowded lobby holding hands. I tried to ignore the amused glances directed at me. But I knew my ungainly walk told every experienced woman I had a very tender pussy. And they would guess it was due to a night of wild sex with the man beside me. But I didn't care. For the first time in my life I was a fully orgasmed woman.

Alice was thrilled to hear the result of our encounter and I had to give her a detailed account of my initiation into orgasmic rapture. "Told you he was the man for you, Charlie," she said with a smirk. "He's right about frequent sex and good health. Make sure you get it four or five times a week, more if possible. You've waited a long time for this, Charlie. Go for it."

So that's how a temper tantrum led to the loss of my orgasmic virginity. I'll always be a difficult lay of course, but Nigel has discovered many different ways to ravish me and is always trying new ones. As promised, he keeps me fully sexed. I'm a blissfully happy (and exceedingly healthy) woman.

OPEN BORDERS

Alex, Bridgend

I know this might sound too fantastic but you can never tell what's going on in other people's minds, particularly if we're talking about other cultures and perspectives. I still shiver with excitement every time I relive what happened. I think knowing that my girlfriend will never know what happened to me that morning while she was on the way to work just makes it all the more delicious . . .

For weeks, I had seen them, standing there, outside that row of terraced houses. I started to try to imagine what or who they were waiting for. I knew there were a lot of workers from Eastern Europe there, and they just didn't look British some-how: one petite with that thick jet-black hair and those deep, almost black eyes that nearly, but never quite, caught mine as I passed her every day, and the other, blond, tall and Nordic looking. I walk to work, down into town and spend every boring day sat at my computer, accessing endless emails and answering the phone. I'd convinced myself that they were waiting for a lift to work, they couldn't be waiting for their boyfriends every day at 7.30, could they?

Almost subconsciously, I started to try to look better for them, my suits were cleaned more often, I wanted smarter shirts for them, and I never forgot to put my aftershave on, just for them really. One day, I actually did catch the dark one's eye and managed to splutter out a good morning. My reward was a smile to practically knock me into the road. Her lips almost pouted at me, and the way she ran her hand through that dark hair and the accent when she answered was enough to prove my instincts had been right: she wasn't a local girl. My heart was pounding and I just knew she had been thinking about me as well.

All my concentration disappeared that day at work; I couldn't stop thinking about the two of them. It was summer, so that morning, they had been wearing simple but beautiful dresses, one light blue and one cream and my mind was racing with how they would look without them. And that's when I made my mind up really.

It was no problem to get the day off, but Lorraine thought I was going to work as normal. I was shaking as I approached the row of houses, but there they were, today looking even better, the summer dresses were both white and I could see the outline of the blonde's nipples pressing against the fabric. The brunette was showing plenty of her tanned legs in that dress and I didn't care about anything else that day, I knew I wanted one of them. I can't believe where my courage came from but I just stopped, took her hand in mine, stared into those dark eyes and said, "I'm Alex. I've been thinking about you every day."

Dream girl one just squeezed my hand and, without a word, led me to her front door and let me in, her friend following behind. "Sara."

One word, with a shrug that maybe said, I don't know any more English, or maybe I don't want to talk, but the way she put her arms around me and kissed me told me everything I needed to know.

As she pressed her body against me, I felt myself getting hard and, as she broke away, she let her fingers trace a path against my crotch, my cock was straining against my trousers. That searing smile again but then she produced a strip of cloth from nowhere and I found myself blindfolded tightly. Almost immediately, my hands were pulled backwards, my shirt ripped off and I heard a click of handcuffs. So this was all some kind of trap. Was I going to be robbed? Murdered? Would I find the house full of muscle-bound men who had been in hiding all along? Somehow, I knew crying out wasn't going to help me, if I was going to be a victim I just wanted to focus on at least getting out alive.

But then, I felt the blindfold removed and I gasped at the sight of Sara, stripped and kneeling in front of me. She was smiling again, and she began to lick her fingers and then squeeze her nipples. Her tits were delicious, full and firm, but as she eased her body backwards, I was treated to the sight of her shaven pussy. Even from the angle I was at, I could see her lips were wet and full and I cried out in ecstasy as she inserted first one, then two fingers into her wet opening. Suddenly, I remembered the blindfold being taken off. Sara couldn't have done that and got in front of me that quickly so . . .

I felt long, probing fingers massage my chest, teasing my hair sharply. I began to turn my head to see blondie but suddenly Sara dived forwards and unzipped me, then yanked my trousers and my shorts down to my ankles. She took my cock in her right hand and my ever tightening balls in her left, and began vigorously rubbing me up. I almost fell forwards, but my attention was taken again by the sight of the taller woman coming from behind me. Naked as well, she had a thick bush of hair and her nipples were bullet hard, almost tilting up towards me and, as Sara carried on working on me, she lifted one leg onto the arm of the chair.

She began to play with herself, almost frantically pushing her fingers inside her soaking lips. I was aching to touch one of these women but I still had my hands cuffed, and that was obviously what they wanted. I felt I was close to coming and Sara felt it too because she abruptly broke away from me.

I was desperate to screw them, either of them, both of them, but they had planned this whole morning out, that was clear.

As I stood there, my cock pointing to the sky, I watched them fall onto each other hungrily. Sara yanked open her partner's legs and buried her face between them. I was close enough to see her tongue feverishly licking, lapping, almost biting at her wide open, completely saturated lips. I could see her tits bouncing up and down as she writhed in ecstasy, closer and closer to a climax. I was so excited I would have given anything just then to have been inside either of them but I saw the blonde's face, which told me that they were running this show and I just had to go with it.

Sara's tight, shapely bum was only a couple of feet from me and I burned to enter her from behind. My face must have made that obvious because I heard a few words whispered in a language I couldn't understand and, oh God, it happened for me. The blonde fetched a chair so she could perch on it, legs even wider open – I can't believe how swollen and bloated those lips were – and Sara backed onto my straining cock, her own lips closing around me. Then she began sliding backwards and forwards and resumed giving the blonde as much tongue as anyone could stand.

Keeping my balance was tough with my hands still cuffed but the feel of my shaft pumping inside her and the sight of Sara bringing her friend towards her own orgasm was the most erotic thing that had ever happened to me.

I'd never felt so big or hard but she had a way of moving, altering the angle of my thrusts so that I felt I was on the verge of coming but never quite doing so. The message was clear. You stay in me until I've had enough and I wasn't going to argue with her.

And then I couldn't carry on any more. I surged into her and I felt her tense and shiver as her orgasm shot through her.

We both collapsed onto the floor but the morning wasn't finished yet. Another few words I couldn't understand and it was clear that the other member of this trio still had an appetite for more. Still on the chair, her thighs suddenly closed around my neck and Sara guided my mouth onto her pussy although I could hardly miss a target like that.

I felt as if it were her lips playing with my tongue not the other way round and, as I found new ways of exploring her velvet soft lips, she closed her thighs and I felt the shiver of pleasure shooting through her body. I felt her juices pour onto my face and I wanted to make it fantastic for her. But finally she pushed me off, and sighed deeply.

I felt exhausted and looked around to see Sara, still naked, beaming at me.

As I dressed, I realized we had barely spoken. And then the blonde smiled and whispered, "Katya."

The next day, the road outside their house was empty and the next, and . . . So maybe that was it. Their last night in Wales, the last chance to let themselves go? I'll keep walking past in the morning; perhaps they haven't gone for good.

PARKING TICKET

Eva, Sydney

It was just after midnight and my car was the only one left at the railway station. As I hurried towards it I saw someone standing next to it. As luck would have it, it was a parking officer. Fuck! What the hell was he doing here at this time of night?

"This your car, ma'am?" he asked.

"Yes, is there a problem?" I said.

"No problem, just giving you a ticket." He smiled, as though he'd just offered me a bunch of flowers.

"What? It's only just run out by two minutes," I said checking my watch.

"Yeah, I know. I've been watching the time ever since I got here," he said.

Bastard! I knew how expensive the fine would be and money was a bit tight at the moment. I wondered if I could pay him another way.

"Please don't fill it out," I said, sidling up to him so that my breasts grazed his arm.

He looked down at me, his pen poised on the paper. "Why not?" he asked.

"Can't we settle this another way?" I asked, coyly.

"What did you have in mind?" he asked, his interest clearly piqued.

"What would you like?" I said, my fingers groping for his cock.

I was nervous as I'd never done this sort of thing before. I leaned in against him as I undid his fly. My hand stole down into his jocks where I felt his cock throb in the palm of my hand. Men were all the same. They'd do anything for a head job.

I lowered myself down to the ground where I pulled his cock quickly out of his trousers. It sprang towards me, the knob already glistening with pre-come as it oozed from the slit. Wow, you should have seen the size of it. I licked at it in the moonlight, marvelling at the way my tongue slid over the mushroomed knob.

I sucked on him for a while, surprised that it grew even further. My tongue rolled around the edges of the knob. He leaned back against the car and I heard him sigh. I give good head and know it, so I nibbled lightly on the edges, my tongue flickering over the slit, before I slathered saliva up and down his shaft.

Pumping with one hand my mouth did the rest until I could feel him just about ready to come. Good, I thought. It had been a long day and I was eager to be home in my own bed. He pulled back though, his cock dropping from my mouth, saliva dripping onto the car park concrete.

"Hey," I said. "What did you do that for?"

"Stand up," he commanded.

I did, annoyed he'd put a stop to the proceedings. My boyfriend would wonder where I was, getting home this late, and I was finding it easier than I'd thought.

"Lift up your skirt," he said.

"What?" I asked surprised.

"Your skirt, lift it up," he said again, this time with more authority in his voice.

I stared at him hard. He had a great body, broad shoulders and strong arms. He was good-looking too. Why not? I thought. I peered around, making sure no one was about.

I raised it demurely. I hadn't counted on this and so wasn't wearing my sexiest G-string. It didn't matter though because he wasn't looking, he was staring straight into my eyes, as though wanting me to defy him.

Suddenly, his hands groped beneath to latch onto my panties, his fingers tugging at the crutch. In one quick movement he ripped them right off my body. I gasped as the stinging pain from the elastic burned onto the top of my thighs.

"Hey," I complained. I'd thought he only wanted a quick peak to see what was underneath.

"Up on the bonnet," he said smugly, his cock jutting forwards, nearly poking me in the stomach.

His assertiveness sent a thrill through me. I wasn't used to men telling me what to do. My pussy began to throb as I looked from his cock back to his face.

"No," I said, half-heartedly.

"You want a ticket?" he asked.

"No." I pouted.

"Then get up there and fast," he ordered.

Cheeky bastard!

He lifted me up and dumped me on the bonnet. I gasped as the cold steel froze my arse cheeks.

"Lie down," he whispered.

I stared at him.

"I said, lie down."

I did.

"That's much better," he said, his hands roaming up over my thighs and then my mound. I struggled for breath as his hands electrified my body. Everywhere they touched seemed to ignite my passion further.

"Spread them," he said.

I did, gladly.

"Lift your feet up and place them on the bonnet. Yeah, like that. Now drop your knees apart."

I could see his eyes gleaming mischievously and I must say it was very erotic lying there practically naked on the bonnet of my own car with a complete stranger giving me orders. My eyes darted about, fearful that someone might stumble upon us.

I did as he asked, my legs splayed open for his approval, my chest heaving, my nipples straining against my bra, desperate to be freed. He held onto my knees with his hands and pushed them down further, my pussy gaping for him.

His finger touched my slit. "You're wet," he said. "Your pussy is very wet. You know that, don't you?"

I said nothing.

"You're hot for me, aren't you?" he said, as he opened my folds, the cool air tantalizing me further.

Still I said nothing, but my ragged breathing was giving me away.

"You want me, don't you?" he said, as his fingers slipped in and out of me.

I gasped but still said nothing. We both knew that I wanted him. I was desperate, desperate for a good fucking from a complete stranger. I couldn't hold out much longer. If he didn't fuck me soon I'd have to do him.

"I can smell your cunt from here. Tell me you want me," he whispered.

I flushed scarlet, whimpering, unable to speak.

"Tell me," he demanded loudly.

"I want you."

He lowered his head and his tongue snaked out. With my legs spread this wide he licked at my puckered hole causing me to clench my arse cheeks involuntarily. No one had ever done that to me before. My legs trembled and he chuckled while lapping at my pussy lips, nuzzling in, his nose rubbing over my clit.

"You're so fucking beautiful," he said.

I hadn't expected that.

He was grabbing at my hips, his fingers digging in cruelly as he gave me a tonguing like I've never had before. He was everywhere: in between the folds, inside my pussy, tantalizing the outer lips and driving my clit insane.

I undid the buttons on my blouse, eager to attack my own breasts, as I lifted them out of their cups. I kneaded the flesh roughly, wanting his hands over me, his fingers pulling at my nipples, his mouth and lips, licking and sucking as his tongue rolled over them. I nearly orgasmed just thinking about it.

I pushed up into his mouth, eager for more. A moan escaped me and I heard him chuckle again, knew that he knew I wanted him, needed him desperately.

Suddenly, he pulled me forwards and flipped me over, my skin burning against the bonnet. My legs hit the ground while his fingers roamed up the crack of my arse. Then his tongue was there, tantalizing the puckered skin around my hole before I felt his huge knob poking around.

I loved men being assertive and this guy certainly was, taking charge of everything, doing exactly what I wanted but thinking it was what *he* wanted.

I wiggled my arse up and into him, lying squashed against the cold steel of the bonnet, my hands reaching forwards, caressing the paintwork, scratching at the metal when in a flash his cock slipped straight into my saturated pussy.

"Oh God, yes," I moaned.

"Oh fuck," he whispered. "You're so hot my cock's on fire."

Encouraged, I pushed back into him while his fingers gripped my hips. He pulled me back towards him and fucked me hard, my tits rubbing hard against the cold bonnet, the nipples becoming even firmer against the friction. I wished now he'd made me strip completely; I would have loved to have felt the coldness of the night over my naked flesh. I had nothing to hang on to and I tried desperately to get a grip on something as he pounded into me.

"Oh fuck, yeah," I screamed out, as my body rippled with spasms.

"Your cunt is so hot," he said. "So fucking hot."

Pleased he was enjoying this as much as me, I pushed back into his groin until I was nearly standing. He leaned me forwards, reached for my breasts and crushed them cruelly while I reached under and grabbed hold of his balls giving them a gentle milking while his cock slammed in and out of me.

"Oh yeah," he said. "I knew you'd fucking love it."

He pulled out of me and turned me around in his arms, his head going down to latch onto a nipple while his cock probed at my stomach. I raised myself up on my toes, desperate to feel his cock again, yet not wanting his mouth to leave my breast.

I could feel the pressure mounting in me and knew I had to have his cock back inside me. I wiggled my arse back onto the car, lifted up my legs and wrapped them around his back, kicking into his arse as I shook with desire, trying to guide his cock back into my quivering cunt.

He laughed knowingly and pulled away, leaving me frustrated and on my back flat on the bonnet. He opened my legs and smothered his face into my pussy while his finger rubbed my clit until I was nearly insane, coming over and over again. He then climbed up my body, kissing my mouth so I could taste myself on him.

I felt the bonnet pop, the weight of us too much, wondering how I'd explain that to my boyfriend, but right now I didn't give a shit, all I could think about was what he was doing to me.

I didn't know what I wanted next, his cock inside my pussy or in my mouth. I was nearly insane as I licked his face clean of my juices. He looked down into my face before spearing me with his mighty cock, fucking me like a madman. The sound of my bonnet creaked and groaned beneath our weight, reverberating through the quiet night. Never in my life have I ever been so crazy with lust.

I pushed him from me, rolled him over and manoeuvred myself into the sixty-nine position. Balanced precariously I flattened my pussy over his mouth, grinding down as I flew onto his cock, gobbling and sucking until he came. I swallowed greedily, enjoying myself as come dribbled out of the side of my mouth. I disengaged myself and crawled around to kiss him. My nostrils flaring as our scents intoxicated me. Our juices mingling together, tasted beautiful.

Scrambling down we both adjusted our clothing and then without another word he was gone. As I sat behind the driver's seat and fired up the engine, I marvelled at the risk we'd both taken. Anyone could have come upon us and what would we have done then?

I can tell you it was the best fuck I've ever had and now I make sure I always let my ticket expire, hoping he'll be back to be of service to me again but so far no luck.

SERVICE CALL

Tony, South Australia

My job is boring. I work in information technology, meaning I walk around all day fixing computer problems for office staff that still look for the "any key". But in any large organization, a young, enthusiastic computer technician has plenty of equally young secretaries who call on him for help. Standing behind them while they show me what caused their latest problem, affords me a wonderful view down their conveniently agape jackets, camisoles and blouses.

Quite a few of the older secretaries also seem to forget the most rudimentary things concerning their computers at the oddest times. Only last week, Mrs Kennedy left an urgent message on my voicemail. In the overly superior tone she used with everyone younger than her she commanded me, "Tony, please come to my cubicle at your earliest convenience. My computer is completely broken. Even the TV thingy has gone black."

Something rather untoward must have occurred, as monitors simply don't implode. So I headed to the sixth floor with visions of spilled coffee flowing through the circuitry.

Mrs Kennedy has been at the firm for longer than anybody I know. She is in her early fifties and has been a widow for three years. All the girls on the lower floors gossip that she must be sleeping with at least one of the bosses to keep her position as Personal Assistant to the Board. If it is true, then good luck to whomever it is. She is a good twenty-five or so years older than me but still a very beautiful woman. Unfortunately she had never given me the time of day. A simple hello, in the elevator of a morning, was greeted with the barest of nods from her.

As the elevator door slid open, I pasted on my best smile and confidently strode towards her cubicle. I gently rapped my knuckles on the flimsy partition that separated her from the executive corridor. I was happy not to smell or see any telltale signs of coffee.

"Good morning, Mrs Kennedy," I said politely.

She glanced up with an annoyed look on her face, which was quickly replaced by a stunning smile when she realized it was me. "Oh thank God you came so quickly. I need to proofread an email for Mr Jenkins and get it sent out straight away, but everything's gone blank." She spread her hands forlornly towards her monitor.

I moved around behind her to look over the top of her head. Sure enough, everything looked dead. So I asked the first question all IT guys ask: "Can you tell me what you were doing when everything went black? It's probably an issue with the monitor. It'll need replacing but I need to show in the report that I looked into other options."

She glanced back at me with a very relieved look on her face. In one fell swoop I'd assured her of her innocence and blamed the dumb computer. I smiled back at her but the hint of lace I could see poking out at the top of her blouse drew my eye. She blushed and turned back towards the monitor.

After mentally berating myself for being an oversexed fool, I prompted her to retell her version of events. I nodded as she explained how she'd received the email, noted the importance attached to it, and swung in her chair to snatch up her glasses from her desk to read it. When she swung her chair back, everything was blank.

I asked her to move back from her position before the monitor, so I could get under the desk and check things like the cable connections – just in case.

A nervous look crossed her brow as I crawled into the space under her desk. I was beginning to think maybe all that swinging back and forth had caused her to kick a cable loose. Sure enough, lying in the corner of the chair recess was the unattached end of the monitor cable. I took my trusty pen torch out of my pocket. Holding the light in my teeth I carefully examined the pins. A couple had been bent but the connections to secure it to the back of the computer seemed fine. If they had been attached properly, it would have been very difficult for her to have kicked them out.

I crawled further into the space below her desk and pushed the monitor cable back into its housing on the back of the graphics card. An excited, "You've fixed it," came from Mrs Kennedy.

"You've fixed what, Sharon?" said a baritone voice from the other side of the partition.

Suddenly Sharon Kennedy's chair flew into the space that I was occupying. I leaned back and raised my hands to save my fingers from the wheels on the bottom of her chair. The light from my torch shone straight up her black skirt, clearly defining her crease behind sheer white panties.

Her knees tried to come together but trapped my raised hands between them. Mrs Kennedy never missed a beat. "Just a couple of minor mistakes in that email you sent me to look over. I was going to send it back to you for final approval after lunch."

The direction of Mr Jenkins' voice changed so it came from directly over my head. He must have moved to stand directly in front of Mrs Kennedy's desk. Slowly her knees relaxed their deathlike grip on my clenched hands. Before my stunned eyes, they moved further apart, affording me an uninterrupted view of her thinly veiled sex.

While the conversation went on overhead I thought it best for me to test the waters I was being offered. After removing the torch from my mouth, I leaned forwards and softly kissed the inside of an exposed knee. When she didn't jerk it away, I repeated the kiss on the other knee, which caused her to firmly plant her feet wide apart. I continued to trail kisses up her thighs until her chair stopped me from getting any closer to her core.

In the confined space below her desk, I could smell her musk as she warmed to my attentions. I rested my hands on her knees and softly stroked the inside of both, inching my way towards the hem of her skirt. Allowing my hand to continue massaging her left leg, I traced lazy circles down her inner right thigh with my other, continuing my advance under her skirt until the knuckles of my fingers brushed against the damp gusset of her panties.

Only the slightest catch in her voice betrayed her rising desire as Mr Jenkins continued to question her over the contents of his email.

I withdrew my hand from massaging her thigh and retrieved my pen torch. I placed half of it into my mouth, sucking on the metal casing and warming it with my saliva and tongue.

Just as I took it back out, judging it to be warm enough, Mr Jenkins finally bid farewell to Mrs Kennedy. I pulled both my hands back, sure that my brief minutes of fun were now over along with my further employment with this company. A sacking on grounds of sexual harassment would not look good on the CV. I slipped my torch back into my shirt pocket.

I waited for her to roll back the chair but instead her hands came down from her desk. She grasped the hem of her skirt and pulled it further up her thighs until she could hook her thumbs into the elastic of her underwear. As she wiggled her weight back and forth on the chair, she slipped her panties towards me. I didn't need a second invitation.

I reset the torch in my mouth before I placed my hands over hers. For a moment we lingered, fingers each caressing the other's. I reached past the point of our contact while she lightly rested her hands on my wrists. Curling my fingers under her waistband, I continued to lower her panties. Obediently she lifted one foot to allow me to slip them off and then the other. I stuffed them into my trouser pocket so I wouldn't have to look for them later.

The torch in my mouth never left the wonderful sight of her shaved slit before me. Who would have imagined that the office bitch was as smooth as a baby's bottom?

Free of her underwear and with her skirt hiked up past her thighs, she moved to the edge of her seat allowing me full access to her charms.

She only sat up twice during the time I spent under her desk that day, once to sign for a courier package and once to sign a card for one of the girls downstairs, who was going on maternity leave. The aroma of her was heavy in the air from my perspective; I kept waiting for someone to comment – none did.

Eventually her legs came together as she struggled through a silent orgasm, trapping my head between her thighs, my questing tongue still dancing within her folds. Without a word she passed a box of tissues to me, allowing me to clean up a little before casually rolling her chair back and straightening her skirt.

"Thank you, Tony," was all she said as I crawled out into the open space of her cubicle.

I stood, trying to surreptitiously adjust the evidence of my own excitement. A look of sympathy crossed her beautiful features before she reached forwards. I nervously glanced around to see if anyone was watching.

With a smile on her face, she carefully tucked the exposed portion of her panties deeper into my trouser pocket before she too looked around for any fellow workers. On seeing none she quickly patted my throbbing member. "I will have to thank you properly another time, I'm afraid. I really do need to finish that email."

I nodded and smiled at the offered promise of more to come. "If there is anything I can do for you in the future, don't hesitate to call me," I said. "I'm happy to help."

Like I said, that was last week and I've not heard from her since, at least not until I checked my messages before lunch. I'm booked to visit her workstation this afternoon, at the same time a board meeting is due to commence. Her message said I needed to fix a bug in her database program. I'm guessing I could be in her chair for quite some time.

STRAWBERRY YOGHURT

Laura, Worcestershire

My name is Laura and I have only been unfaithful to my husband once, but then I suppose once is enough. The thing is that it happened in the last place I expected, with someone I wasn't really attracted to and in a way I could never have imagined. It also stopped me buying strawberry yoghurt ever again, and this is why.

I am a thirty-eight-year-old woman, with a good husband and three children. We live on the edge of a small town not far from Birmingham and are quite comfortable. I have a part-time job as a receptionist in an accountant's office, my husband Bob earns a decent wage as a salesman and I don't want for anything much.

Odd then that one day I let another man do what he wanted with me in a way I had never imagined possible. A complete stranger, in a Tesco's car park, having me over the bonnet of my car.

I usually did all my weekly shopping at a supermarket in the town where we lived, but one October night I set off – for a reason I can never explain – to go to a neighbouring town and shop at the Tesco supermarket there. It was, I have to say, a bigger store than the one I was used to and maybe it was the vague thought that Christmas wasn't so far away that made me imagine I should go someplace else. For once too I had gone on my own. Usually at least the eldest of my three children, my daughter, accompanied me but tonight she was busy and the other two didn't want to come along so I happily left them at home with their father. Maybe I went further afield because I felt free, but I'll never know.

But while I can make all the excuses I want for my sudden choice, the fact remains I didn't have to do what I did. I arrived at this Tesco store, walked round the supermarket buying the usual things and piling my trolley up high, paid on credit card and made my way across the dark car park to where I had left my car. It was dark where I'd parked because one of the many lights around the car park had failed but even so I didn't feel in any danger as I started to unload my trolley into the boot of my car.

I was aware of a man standing close by, asking if he could help me. Now normally I wouldn't even entertain such an idea but he wasn't so much of a stranger. I had literally run into him three times going round the supermarket, the first time with our trolleys colliding so hard several things fell off both of them. He was smartly dressed, a pleasant enough personality though I have to say not exactly attractive to me, and he apologised profusely for his clumsiness (when in fact it was more me not looking than him). Having helped me pick everything up, he said goodbye. Then we had encountered each other again, though not so violently this time, exchanged smiles and a few words and when I bumped into him a third time we chatted a little more, especially as I asked him where the yoghurts were. You see, I am partial to strawberry yoghurts but no one else in our family likes them and I didn't know where they were in this new place. This man and I even went through the checkout together, and once outside he said I should be careful as I was heading towards the darkened part of the car park.

I had assured him I would be OK but perhaps he felt constrained to come over and see if I was OK in the dark corner. It was kind of him and, despite my protests I could manage, he still helped unload my trolley and put it in the boot of the car. It was then that he said the top had come off a pot of strawberry yoghurt and pointed out it would spill out in the bag. He extracted the half-open tub and asked if he should go and fetch me a new one. I said no, it didn't matter.

"It's a pity to waste it," he said as he held it up.

"Oh it won't be wasted," I said. "I can eat that now, before I set off home, as I like strawberry yoghurt and no one else at my house does."

The man said he had a better idea for it, and I was puzzled. "It makes a good lubricant for anal sex," he said calmly.

"Anal sex . . . You mean, up a person's bottom," I blurted out. "But why? Are you, uh, gay?" It was a stupid question but the man just laughed.

"Far from it, but that way the woman has pleasure and she doesn't get pregnant. You should try it."

At this point I should have fled, but I didn't. For a reason I cannot begin to fathom I just stared at him. I have never had anal sex and never planned to. Fortunately Bob has never asked and I would undoubtedly refuse. Yet here was a complete stranger holding up a leaking pot of yoghurt, suggesting I should try out having a prick up my rear hole.

I can remember saying: "You mean me try it?" And him responding, "Why not?" For some reason I couldn't think why not.

I don't know why I allowed it, but he took my arm and guided me to the front of my car. He set the pot down carefully, peeled open my coat and felt up my breasts. He pressed his lips to mine as he did so and I felt both revulsion and a wild wanton excitement. Among the panic that his hands were on me, I felt a strange burning in my sex. I hadn't felt this way since Bob and I used to have sex before we were married. Back then we had to do it at the back of a pub car park as neither of us would have been allowed to fuck in our respective family's homes. So here I was, reliving those days, though I always thought Bob was good-looking and this man wasn't. Just a stranger, that's all.

This man – I never did find out his name and never want to – had set something off in me. I felt I was a long way from home, safely hidden by the dark and with a fire in my belly like no other I had known for years. I allowed him to squeeze and fondle my boobs, feeling how hard my nipples had become, and then he broke the kiss and turned me to face the car.

"I'm scared," I said as he gently pushed me face down over the cold bonnet.

"Don't be, the yoghurt will stop it hurting."

I felt him lifting my skirt at the back and braced myself. It was insane what I was doing but I couldn't help myself. The yoghurt pot was right by my face and I stared at it as I felt him reach up and tug my panties down to my knees. I felt his hand easing my legs apart and I opened them as much as I could.

"It's my period," I said, in case he wanted to go in me the conventional, almost doggy-style way, but he said he didn't need to worry about my twat, as he called it.

I saw his hand reach for the open pot, scoop out a big dollop of the yoghurt and then I felt it smeared between my bum cheeks, his finger working up into the crevice and against my sphincter. I gasped as his finger worked the creamy substance up into my rear hole. I desperately tried to relax my back passage to allow him in. I was scared he would hurt me and equally scared the yoghurt would somehow, like horseradish sauce (I imagined) burn me.

But the yoghurt felt slick and cool and he expertly wormed his finger in, smoothing the yoghurt up into me. I suppose, though I didn't dare look or ask, he spread some along the shaft of his cock but in any event his prick was soon pressing against my anal opening. I wanted to scream as it pushed up into me – gently enough but insistent and I wished I had something to grip on to on the bonnet. I also wished I had something to bite on but he must have sensed this because he reached forwards with his dry hand and lifted the corner of my silk scarf so that I could take it between my teeth. It occurred to me this was a gentlemanly thing to do and I remember blushing at how ludicrous and bizarre a thought this was.

I also remember feeling his hard, long cock not only driving in but also it sawing in and out of me. I felt I was going to be split in two and wondered how anyone would even tolerate this for sexual union. But I more than tolerated it: I felt turned on being used like this and brought one of my hands round and stuffed more of my scarf in my mouth.

Behind me the man was grunting as he hammered up into me and I felt my cunt catch fire. What he was doing to me hurt but it was the most satisfying hurt I'd ever known and I could hear myself moaning into my simple gag. I could also feel, at every thrust, my body sliding on the car bonnet; my erect nipples rub against the cold, hard surface. I couldn't believe this humiliating near-rape was happening to me and equally I wanted his cock in deeper. I was mortified in case someone should come past and see me (thank goodness the scarf was acting as a reasonably effective gag as I bit on it so no one would hear my cries) and I was petrified in case somehow the lights on this side of the car park would suddenly flood me in a revealing glare.

In this state of terror and excitement I felt his balls slap against my cunt at every thrust and as his shaft slid into me there was an accompanying slurp from the strawberry yoghurt. He must have been doing this to me for a good five minutes but I didn't care about the time. He had one hand on my back, holding me down in case I tried to get up, but there was little danger of that. Above all I just wanted to come, but with a loud grunt he came first. He stopped his thrusting and at once his cock twitched as it began to pump his semen into my bowels.

After what seemed an eternity but was probably no longer than thirty seconds or so, his cock stopped pulsing and he began to withdraw, accompanied by a loud plop as it came free from my arsehole. His hand came away from my back. I lay, eyes closed on the bonnet of the car, both frustrated that he hadn't finished me off and glad it was all over and I hadn't been discovered like this.

I opened my eyes and turned to say to him I hoped he'd finished but the man was gone. I was all alone, legs apart, with knickers between my knees, my skirt up and a cold wind on my exposed rump. Hurriedly I stood and dragged my pants up and straightened my skirt, not caring if there was yoghurt on it.

I leaped into my car, my backside buzzing with the after-effects of the invasion and feeling wet and sore, and drove off as quickly as I could. The strawberry yoghurt pot on the bonnet slid off and no doubt splattered on the tarmac but I didn't care.

I got home in good time, rushed upstairs to get changed and despite feeling guilty spent a few minutes bringing myself off in the peace and quiet of the en suite. I felt both ashamed and relieved it was over. Thankful I had got away with it, I resolved never to go back to that store, nor do anything like that ever again. I have so far kept to my word.

But I can't look at another strawberry yoghurt without blushing, and I can never tell anyone why I just don't eat it any more.

BUSINESS SEALED

Liz, Edmonton

When my boss told me to fly to Vancouver to help a colleague with a sales call, I was more than a little pissed, for a couple of reasons. First, my associate in Vancouver was a total prick – and I don't mean that in the good, long, hard, stick-in-your-twat-and-gyrate sense of the word – and second, the guy we were calling on, Archibald Stevenson, was a notorious nutball. The entire Stevenson family was more eccentric than a Howard Hughes–Michael Jackson wedding.

But, as usual, I answered the bell. I packed a bag, a vibrator and an umbrella, and winged it for the Wet Coast. Stan, the inept B.C. rep for the large furniture manufacturer we both work for, met me at the airport, then drove directly to the offices of Stevenson Enterprises. S.E. Inc. was a family-run business octopus with a sticky tentacle in just about every type of financial endeavour, from fish farms to furniture stores.

"Be careful what you say, Liz," Stan told me as we flew up the executive elevator to the penthouse floor of the Stevenson Building. "This guy and his clan chew up and spit out sales-people like sunflower seeds."

I glanced at my overweight, middle-aged compatriot. His off-the-back-rack suit was two sizes too small, and his red-veined nose two sizes too large, but he could still dream big – he was ogling my voluptuous physique like it was an all-you-can-eat smorgasbord.

Fortunately, when we exited the nose-bleed express and walked up to the reception desk, the receptionist told my partner to take a seat – apparently Mr Stevenson wanted to deal exclusively with me. That was good; it meant that Stan couldn't screw things up, and I'd get whatever commission was coming.

The receptionist buzzed me through a thick, oak-panelled door, and I came face to face with another door – this one looking like it had been stripped off a bank vault. Eventually, this portal swung open, as well, revealing a stunning, statuesque brunette in a sapphire-blue dress, who claimed to be Mr Stevenson's private secretary. She used her long, silver-tipped fingers to punch a code into yet another hermetically sealed, bombproof door, and just when I thought we'd step onto the set of *Get Smart*, we finally entered a football field-sized office that housed reclusive tightwad Archibald Stevenson.

The supermodel secretary with the silky, black-stockinged legs and I traipsed 100 paces or so to the front of Stevenson's gigantic, mahogany desk, and the shrivelled tycoon pushed back his throne on wheels and stood up. His pants were down around his ankles, and he had his cock in his hand – stroking dick like the evil genius in an *Austin Powers* movie strokes fleshy cat!

My eyes bugged out and my jaw temporarily unhinged, both as a result of the unexpected greeting, and the incredible size of the tiny geezer's prick. He was hoisting an eight-inch tool in his right hand, and his practised stroke told me that he'd had a lot of experience in the meat-handling business.

"You and Claire are gonna fuck," the diminutive, well-endowed businessman growled, indicating his secretary with his prick. "Then maybe we'll sign some new contracts."

I glanced at the picturesque beauty standing next to me, and her exquisite face registered neither a hint of shock nor dismay. Business as usual on the funny farm, I concluded.

"Shall we, Ms Marsten?" Claire said, smoothly stripping off her dress before I could even say anything.

"Let's go, ladies," Stevenson grunted impatiently. "I've got a meeting with the Premier at noon."

Claire lifted her black, silver-tipped high heels out of her puddled dress, her lean, creamy-white body completely nude except for her shoes, her stockings and some expensive-looking silver jewellery. The sophisticated business slut was almost as blessed in the breast department as I was, her chew-toy nipples pink and jutting, and her brown, downy pussy fur was neatly shaved into a dollar sign, just above her slit. Her body was a hell of a lot sleeker than mine, but I bow down before no tart with my overripe femininity.

"Let's get it on, girls!" Stevenson urged, swirling his liver-spotted hand up and down his handsome prong.

Claire unclasped a couple of tortoise-shell barrettes, and her long, shimmering, chestnut hair tumbled down her buff shoulders, her arched back. She sashayed over to where I stood rooted and kissed me gently on the lips, began expertly un-fastening my skirt and unbuttoning my blouse. And before my Chanel No. 5-dizzy brain could even fully fathom the sexual depth of this naughty business deal, I was down to my shiny lavender panties and bra.

"Lots of kissin' and titty-suckin', then sixty-nine 'er," Stevenson croaked, pulling hard on his smooth, pink-shafted dong.

That finally woke me up. I popped my bulging bra, shed my damp panties and took control of the heated meeting, grabbing Claire's bountiful boobs in my hands and tonguing her swollen nipples. She gasped, her full, crimson lips breaking apart as she clasped my shoulders and sighed. I twirled my thick, wet tongue all over and around one of her engorged, bite-sized buds, then the other, excitedly painting the luxurious babe's inflamed nipples with my hot saliva.

"Hungry, eh, Liz?" Stevenson cracked, jacking his studly cock like he was pumping oil out of his Tar Sands property.

I greedily licked Claire's heaving tits and nipples, as it had, indeed, been a rather long spell between breast-feedings for me. I popped one of the trembling girl's blossomed nips into my mouth and pulled on it, tugging it almost off her tit before letting it snap back. Claire closed her ice-blue eyes and moaned, as I sucked and bit and licked her lush, round mounds.

"Kiss her on the mouth, Liz!" Stevenson roared, his with-ered hand travelling at light speed on his rock-hard cock.

I spat one of Claire's slobbered boobs out of my mouth and brought my flushed face up to her face, mashed my lips against her velvety lips and hard-kissed her. I kept on squeezing and kneading her slickened breasts, as I urgently sucked face with the posh secretary.

"Stick out your tongue," she murmured, when I pulled my mouth away to catch my breath.

I stuck it out, and she quickly vacuum-sealed her plush lips around my long tongue and started sucking up and down on it like it was a hardened cock. I groped her tits, she blew my tongue, and Stevenson fisted his dick, the three of us lost in the overwhelming eroticism of it all.

Claire eventually let go of my tongue, and me, and cleared away a spot for us on Stevenson's massive desk. We eagerly scaled the polished wood and climbed into the girly sixty-nine position. I was bottom and she top, and I gripped her round, taut butt cheeks and pulled her dripping pussy down to my mouth. Her rosy-red folds glistened with moisture, and I quickly spread her puffy lips apart with my fingers and pushed my tongue inside her, thrashed it around, lashing at her soft, wet love-tunnel walls.

She buried her face in between my fleshy thighs and groaned, and then expertly spread my own slick lips and speared my tingling clit with her warm tongue. I quivered like I was plugged into a wall socket, my body flushing with a heavy, languid heat as the sultry executive assistant tongue-tickled my button.

"Go for it, girls!" Stevenson exhorted, hovering close to us, his hand a blur on his joystick.

I jammed my tongue deep into Claire's tangy sex hole, ploughed in and out for a while, fucking her with my rigid, pink blade. Then I started lapping up and down on her slit, licking her from swollen clit to puckered bum hole in long, slow, sensual strokes. She panted like a rich bitch in heat, her hot, damp breath steaming against my pussy. Then she shoved two of her fingers into my cunt, started fucking me with her slender digits while she tongued my clit.

"I'm coming!" I squealed, after only an ultra-erotic minute or so of Claire's sensational finger and tongue-loving. I jerked up and down on the high-gloss desktop like a Mexican jumping bean, as multiple orgasms ripped me apart. I screamed into

Claire's luscious puss, and was rewarded with a juicy facial, as the undulating babe gushed all over me.

And just as us two sexed-up girls were being rocked by pussy-pulsing ecstasy, old man Stevenson let out a triumphant bellow and sprayed spurt after spurt of thick, sticky, white-hot semen into a strategically placed wastepaper basket. The three of us were racked by joyous orgasm for what seemed a blissful eternity, until we at last were still.

"You and Claire can sign the contracts, Liz," Stevenson stated brusquely, as I gently tongued his assistant's gooey snatch. "Her signature's as good as mine; she is my grand-daughter, after all."

I choked on Claire's juices. Eccentric really didn't do this business family justice.

CONVENIENCE

Amaris, Dunsborough

On the whole, a convenience-store clerk can't generally say they have the best night of their life during work hours but I did.

I do the eight-to-eight shift in a convenience store pretty much the same as every other store across the country. Being a woman means that people tend to raise an eyebrow when I say this but I figure we're all going to die sometime so if I'm due to go via a bullet from a masked assailant, well that's the way it is.

Anyway this night, the best one of my life, was a Wednesday night. This means it was slow, very slow. It was the kind of night where I had to read all the magazines in the stand to keep my eyes open. In fact, before about 1 a.m. it was so slow that I almost *wished* for an armed hold-up to distract me.

We have security guards and cops who come in for coffee and snacks. The company who owns the convenience store is too cheap to pay a company to do security so us clerks buddy up to the cops and guards that work the area by giving them free coffee and sometimes muffins. This means they come in at regular intervals and might feel honour bound to assist you, should you be in trouble.

I've always flirted with them, mainly because I was bored. It's the uniform though. I'm pretty sure even bus drivers get lucky because of the uniform. I have this thing about them, the police in particular. I am especially lucky with the eye candy because we were in the metro area and all new cops had to serve an amount of time there as probation when they first graduated from the academy. So each night I worked I saw a new pair of young, hot cops.

I felt I probably wasn't making quite the impression a girl would like to make, seeing as I was wearing my work uniform. The work uniform is something similar to those school dresses or nurses' dresses with the zip down the front. Pretty frumpy, I thought, and bright red to boot. We always wear them short and tight to try to combat the fact they haven't changed in a good twenty years. The only good thing about them is that if you wear a good bra, the neck is low cut enough to push your boobs into quite an attractive display.

Serving my young coppers each night I would watch them try to remain professional while their eyes wandered down and gazed hungrily at the rounded flesh peeking out of my neckline. This always gave me a thrill and I could go for hours thinking about what they might have been considering doing to me, should they have had the opportunity.

The best night of my life, I found out.

So there I was, bored out of my skull, beyond bored. I was honestly starting to go a little nuts working those night shifts. I was flicking through a magazine and in walks a young cop. I was a bit surprised because he was by himself and they almost always travel in pairs. He went and got two cups of coffee and two muffins. As he came up to the counter I can remember mentally growling with desire.

Hot was not the word. Seriously, if you were going to shoot a cover photo for a bad boy cop erotic book, this guy was your man. Average height, average build (as much as cops are ever average straight out of academy) but these gorgeous brown eyes that met my startled gaze without flinching. I had the uncanny sensation of being gazed into, as if he could read my mind, and I blushed hotly. This pretty much gave him the undeniable idea that I was perving and he cracked a stunner of a grin.

He put the coffee mugs on the counter with the muffins and crossed his arms, truly a cop stance. Obviously I'd lost my mind because instead of looking away and keeping my thoughts to myself I let my eyes slowly work over him from feet to head, meeting his eyes again. He watched me with an amused look and then started talking to me, telling me he and his partner were parked out front with the speed gun.

This explained why he was in there by himself and also planted an absurd thought in my mind. He wouldn't be missed if he took a little longer to return to the car. His partner was just sitting, listening to the radio, watching the speed numbers bleep up.

He then stopped talking and just watched me for a moment and I found I had opened my mouth. I felt like I was listening to someone else talking when it came out.

"You're hotter than they usually are."

He never even blinked. "Who?" he pressed. Even though he knew what I was talking about he made me say it anyway.

"Cops."

He licked his lips lightly and gave me a slow smile that made my panties moist.

"You like cops?" He raised one eyebrow and I noticed he had a dimple in one cheek. A cop with a dimple. I was speechless but managed a short nod.

He sighed and looked towards the door at the rear of the store. "Is that where your surveillance stuff is kept?" He was so casual considering I then knew I could have him if I wanted him. I felt like I was in one of my fantasies.

I managed another nod as he turned back, eyebrow still raised in question.

"Better check it out for you and make sure it's all in order; there've been a few stores hit in the area."

I wasn't sure if this was true but however flimsy the excuse, the important thing was he wanted me in the backroom with him. My legs jerked into action, feeling wobbly with excitement. I was aware he kept looking at them and my butt as I led him towards the door. His gaze was like a warm light moving over my skin, right through my clothes.

The backroom was in semi darkness, lights off, but the surveillance screens were throwing out a white light. As soon as we'd both cleared the threshold he shut the door quietly behind us. I didn't dare turn around but felt him come up behind me as I gazed at the flickering screens, which showed various angles of the store. He said nothing but when he pushed himself against my backside I could feel his hard cock.

I made a soft noise as he turned me around so I was leaning back against the desk and he pressed against the full length of my body. I suppose I should have been wishing we were both naked but I wanted to keep looking at him in that uniform.

He held my gaze for a moment, as if checking this was what I wanted, and then pulled the handcuffs off of his belt. He wrapped his arms around me and started handcuffing my hands behind my back. While he was doing this he leaned in and kissed me. His mouth was hot and hungry. I was so wet by that time that my thighs were sticky. I was being kissed by a hot cop who was handcuffing me, what more could a girl ask for?

When my hands were trapped he leaned back and slowly, very slowly, unzipped the front of my dress. Pushing it back a bit he surveyed my breasts and then bent down to nibble at them. Sliding one hand behind me, he undid my bra and they sprung out to meet him. His warm hands were suddenly working at them as he kissed my neck. My breathing was coming in short gasps and whimpers. The whole sight was almost too much for me.

He slid a hand up my thigh and I could feel him smile as he discovered how hot and wet my panties were. He then slipped his fingers under the elastic of my panties and into me.

I couldn't help it, I mewed. It's the only way to describe the noise that came out of me. I loved it. I wanted more though. I wanted to play out what I'd spent so many evenings imagining. I wanted to take out my frustration on him.

I surprised him when I dropped to my knees on the floor but he quickly understood as I gazed up at him from his crotch level, eyes wide with pleading.

He managed to unzip and expose his cock without taking a thing off. I was glad because it was the most delicious experience to suck him into my mouth like an errant citizen under arrest.

He was salty with pre-come and I relaxed my throat to take him deeply. His breathing deepened but he said nothing, didn't even thrust. He was getting me to do the work and his hands were on his hips.

I was only down there for a little bit before he hauled me to my feet, spun me around and bent me over the table. He used his knee like I'd seen them doing when patting someone down and he parted my legs. There was a sound of elastic on skin and I wasn't wearing panties any more. He slid himself straight into me, his balls pressing into my buttocks.

Again I surprised myself by crying out in need. He started to thrust, firmly and deeply, holding me by the handcuffs. Out of the corner of my eye I could see his face, expression unchanged, and I could feel the things on his belt smacking on my buttocks as he fucked me.

It was my dream come true. My hot young cop was now grinning at my whimpering. He had the power and we both loved it. He knew my weakness for his get-up and pulled out, spinning me round quickly. He lifted me up to sit me on the desk. I lay back to enjoy the view as he entered me again and resumed thrusting. The look on his face was one of complete authority.

As I felt my muscles start clenching for climax I allowed my eyes to drink up his hands gripping my hips, the gun on his belt swinging gently. Then I was gone, dropping over the edge of blissful oblivion and sighing softly. My climax must have been all he was waiting for because as soon as he saw it petering out he pulled himself up to kneel over my face on the desk. I remember sort of wishing my hands were free to grip his buttocks as he rode my face. I listened to his soft sighs as I swallowed down a mouthful of young law enforcement greedily. To me he tasted divine.

As soon as he'd finished he jumped off the desk. I sat myself up and watched him put himself away. He then leaned forwards and put his arms around me to undo the cuffs. I buried my face in his neck and took a deep breath of his musky scent, a mix of sweat and cologne.

He then stepped back to clip the cuffs back on his belt, winked, and left the room.

I recall that as the door swung slowly shut I watched his tight arse in his uniform pants as he strode over to the counter. I then quickly clipped my bra up, pulled my panties back on and zipped myself back into the red dress.

When I emerged he had gone and so had the coffees. I found his money on the counter and slowly rung the sale up in the till, gazing out the window into the night. My lips still tasted of him, my thighs still wet with my arousal.

As I said, best night of my life.

FUCK MY WIFE, PLEASE!

R.C., Danville

I wanted my wife just as much as he seemed to, judging by the huge rock in his jeans. My wife, Cindy, probably figured Rick was horny watching her dance in front of us in her bare feet. She tried to act oblivious to his reaction, but periodically I caught her checking out his bulge, which was by no coincidence much larger now than it had been when he had first arrived over four hours ago. Not to say he did not try to hide it with his hands rested on his lap, but this method proved futile when each swig of his beer exposed the beast.

Rick and I also pretended not to pay much attention to her, but this was hard to do.

"Who needs another beer?" Rick asked.

"Grab me one," I said.

"I'll take one," answered my wife, still shaking her taut, compact ass in her chequered, flannel pyjama bottoms, while hip-hop music bumped from the stereo speakers. It was a style of music I ordinarily would not want played, but as the scene was such a turn-on, I did not complain. Ken Russell's film *Salome's Last Dance* played out mutedly on the television screen.

We all seemed to be buzzing pretty good from the beer that we picked up after going to the restaurant, on top of the margaritas we had at dinner. We decided to continue our fun at home rather than hitting the bars, to save money. Rick was an old friend who lived over 200 miles away in a smaller city in central Illinois. We had worked construction there together until I completed my bachelor's degree in computer science and moved to Chicago. It had been the Windy City where I had met

Cindy, shortly after the move. She had at the time been working two jobs – at a retail store in the day and tending bar at night. We had married almost exactly one year ago. Rick had been one of the groomsmen, and that was the last time either of us had seen him. He had always been a good friend: easy to talk to and a fun drinking companion. He was physically much better built for construction work than I had been.

Rick returned from the kitchen with the beers. "Did I miss anything?" he asked.

"Cindy just flashed her tits," I joked.

"Damn, and I missed it?"

"Here, I'll do it again." She pulled up her pyjama top halfway and – likely inadvertently – flashed the bottom of her breasts. She was not wearing a bra.

"Wooo,woo!" hollered Rick. "That's some wife you got there, buddy."

"You're telling me." I could not believe she did it.

I had always had fantasies of Cindy taking on me and another man; and Cindy and I had played games in which she spoke of other men she would like to screw, while we fucked. Of course, those were only games. But when she had talked like that, in some mysterious way it made me both extremely jealous and extremely horny at the same time. It had brought on a tension so intense that not only would a heavy come release it, but it would also invariably result in a heavy come. I had always nailed her as hard as I could during those games. I had never thought in a million years that a penis other than mine would actually penetrate her.

Watching her now, dancing like a whore in front of us, and her likely knowing that she was turning Rick on – and with the effect the alcohol had on me – I decided I would try to have my darling wife do a threesome with Rick and me.

As we all tipped back a few more beers, my wife became a little tipsy. She finished the rest of the champagne Rick had brought over, and the empty bottle slipped from her hand and dropped to the floor. The opened end of the bottle pointed towards Rick. "Well, looks like you have to take your shirt off," my wife said to Rick and laughed.

Rick laughed too and looked at me a bit self-consciously. Apparently he did not know how I was taking this sexual bantering between the two of them and was trying to read my expression. When my wife went to the kitchen to grab another round of beers, I broke the ice with, "Looks like she likes you," and chuckled.

I was pretty sure, from knowing him, that Rick would be up for a threesome; and my wife was one sexy woman: adorable face; long, wavy brown hair; firm tits, and – as mentioned – a great ass. What I did not know was whether my wife would be up for it. I knew I had to think strategically for this to work.

"Hey, your shirt is still on," said my wife, returning to the living room with the three beers.

"Yeah, so is yours," I interjected.

"Well, I can fix that," my wife said, pretending she was going to remove her pyjama top and once again exposing only the bottoms of her breasts. She dropped two of the cans of beer. Leaning over to pick them up, with the pyjama top being loose and having the top two buttons undone, my wife's tits were in plain view for Rick and me, nipples and all. I actually saw Rick's boner moving in his pants.

Cindy struggled to pick up the two cans of beer and in the process dropped the third can – good thing none were opened. She dropped to her knees to retrieve the beers. Either Rick or I could have leaned off the couch to help her out, but we were busy enjoying the view of my wife's jiggling tanned boobs. She picked up one can and handed it to me; she picked up another and crawled over to Rick, laying it in his crotch. She grabbed the third can and climbed up onto the middle cushion of the sofa, between Rick and me. She sat straddling both Rick's leg and my leg closest to her – she was in a leg spread. Maybe this would not be as difficult as I had thought.

"How about a foot massage?" she asked, looking at us both and extending her pretty feet.

"You heard her, Rick."

Rick appeared hesitant, and then grabbed hold of her left foot, rubbing it as I massaged her right foot.

"Mmmm," my wife responded. I noticed her eyelids were drooping and knew I had better act before she passed out. I was hoping the foot massage to be foreplay, not a sleeping aid.

I held the side of her head, inched closer to her and began French kissing her, placing my other hand on her thigh. This seemed to rouse her. Rick continued on her foot. The implausible suddenly seemed plausible – I was in perfect position to get a three-way started.

My next statement could have been crossing the line – the point of no return – except I knew I could pretend I was joking, in light of the situation. "Why don't you suck her toes, Rick?"

My wife stopped kissing me.

She looked at me, studying me. I went too far, I thought. In a hushed tone – her former giddiness no longer seeming present – she asked, "Are you sure?" And I knew she was not merely asking about the toe-sucking – which Rick delayed acting upon; she was asking, *Are you sure you want to share me with your friend?*

"Yes," I whispered back.

"I love you."

"I love you."

My wife briskly repositioned herself and said, "You heard the man; suck my toe!" She crammed her toes into Rick's mouth to his obvious astonishment. Seeing my look of approval, he held her foot in both hands and sucked on her big toe. My wife breathed heavily as she unzipped my fly, pulled out my cock and began gobbling it up. Of all the blow jobs I'd had prior to our marriage, my wife gave the best. She sucked in corkscrew fashion, twisting her head from side to side as she moved her lips up and down my shaft.

"Rick, go ahead and play with my ass," Cindy said, and I nodded my approval to him. Rick began groping my beloved wife's ass through her soft pyjama bottoms while continuing to suck on her toes.

"You're doing a good job on those toes, Rick. Why don't you eat her pussy?" I suggested, floating in and out of consciousness from sheer pleasure.

"Yeah . . . eat my pussy, Rick!" exclaimed my wife, sassily, as she got on her knees – still on the couch – and pushed her ass out towards Rick.

Rick wasted no time in removing Cindy's pyjama bottoms and laying his tongue to her snatch from behind. He must have been inhaling the sent of her luscious ass because his nose was right up her butt crack.

"How's that ass smell, boy?" Cindy asked, an apparent rhetorical question.

My jealousy and arousal intensified times ten as compared to my wife's and my bedroom talk, watching this other man eat out my wife. Her moans were muffled as she sucked my cock. She had to stop periodically to release the pressure to moan freely, but would jack me off during these moments. I had never heard her moan like that when I licked her cunt. She was being a filthy whore – and I loved it!

"What are you waiting for? Fuck her, Rick."

Rick dropped his pants, positioned himself behind my darling wife, and drove his cock in. My wife grunted and groaned. He started slowly at first, gradually accelerating.

My wife removed her lips from around my cock, looked up at me and announced, "His dick feels so *fucking* good." Intense heat travelled throughout my body, and I shuddered all over.

I grabbed hold of the back of Cindy's hair and forced her back down around my dick. "Suck, bitch," I commanded. And she sucked hard and fast, deep-throating me as Rick ploughed her. Her moans caused pleasurable vibrations, and she cupped my balls in her hand.

My wife sporadically stopped sucking only to barrage me with comments such as, "Ooh, he is such a good fuck," and, "His dick is *so* big!" She would also blurt out commands to Rick. For example: "That's it, stud; fuck your friend's wife. Fuck that cunt good and hard!"

Rick laid into her with quick, jerky thrusts and was sopping with sweat.

"Stick a finger up my butt," my wife demanded of Rick. Rick slobbered on his large, middle finger and eased it into Cindy's butt hole. My wife moaned more loudly as he fingered her taut little ass.

"Come on, Rick, spank me with your other hand!" Cindy yelled. Rick did as told, slapping at both ass cheeks. He was leaving red handprints on her caboose.

I could not believe what I was experiencing, nor could I believe my wife was actually letting this happen and seeming to dig it.

"You fuck better than my husband!"

I was ablaze. I yanked my wife from around Rick's finger and cock, flipped her on her back, and fucked the living daylights out of her. She was yelling like crazy with pleasure until Rick shut her up with his dick down her throat. I ripped her pyjama top open and held her wrists so she could not move them. Rick groped at her breasts.

We all three came in unison, seemingly suspended in time; then we collapsed upon one another.

I slept the best sleep I'd had in years that night. Since then, adding to our various sexual implements – the dildos, the sex oils, the erotic films, and the anal beads – we had Rick, who seems to visit much more often nowadays.

SUMMER OF '69

Tony, Leicester

The other day I heard Bryan Adams singing "Summer of '69"
and it brought back all sorts of memories – not least of which
was Mrs Greening and her wonderful underwear. More spe-
cifically it reminded me of Mrs Greening's clothes line, and
what I saw there that summer. Just an ordinary clothes line
strung across our neighbour's garden but to me there was a
fascination about what she hung on it – mostly her underwear. I
was nineteen and old enough to know that women of a certain
age wore a certain kind of underwear, that they upholstered
themselves with things they called foundation garments. Nothing trivial or lightweight, not like the teenage girls I'd try to chat
up at the clubs around the city – exciting enough in their nylon
knickers and skimpy cotton bras, or even the ones who liked to
be daring and go round without any bra on at all, but nothing as
substantial as the things the woman next door wore.

Women like Mrs Greening weren't into anything trendy.
They wore real, functional underwear designed to enhance their
mature shape, to hold them in and push them up. Bras with
broad, white satin-like straps and pointed cups. Matching
girdles, shaped like a tulip with a zipper at the side and adorned
with metal clasp suspenders – those strange, almost ingenious
creations – and of course nylons. Nylons that gleamed with a
faint sheen that drew my eye. My friends, falling over themselves in their fantasies of possessing girls in miniskirts and
tights, seemed oblivious of the charms and styles of mature
women and what older women wore underneath their sensible,
knee-length dresses and skirts.

But then I told myself they hadn't seen Mrs Greening's clothes line, they hadn't seen her as I had pegging out her corsets and slips and all the rest of it. If they had seen what I'd seen, out on the line and drying in the sun, they would have understood too. It made me go hard just thinking about it, and the fact that Mrs Greening was wearing all that underwear every day.

I wondered if Mr Greening took any notice of it, but he always seemed to be out at the local pub, leaving his wife in on her own. They must have been happy enough with how they lived as I never heard them row, not like my mum and dad did at times. So I reasoned that Mr and Mrs Greening were content enough, even if he wasn't as turned on as me about the thought of the woman in her heavy-duty underwear.

I did agonize over this, fearing that my desire to masturbate over the thoughts of the woman and her lingerie was unique. I worried it made me some sort of pervert, wanting to think about a woman in her forties wearing all those tight girdles and long-line brassieres. But then it wasn't the underwear alone. It was the thought of Mrs Greening in them, and in my self-excited fantasies she was increasingly showing me herself in her underwear.

I even got off on the idea of her going out into the back garden in her underwear and pegging her normal clothes out on the line as if she had washed everything and had nothing else to wear. The thought of her wandering round the house in her underwear and stockings was the trigger I needed to send me into a fabulous climax.

In truth I didn't know Mrs Greening very well. I saw my mother talking to her across the fence in the garden, and several times slid close enough to try to listen in, hoping they would be discussing Mrs Greening's underwear. They weren't, I was disappointed to discover.

Mrs Greening was mature, though I had no real idea of how old she was. Not as old as my mum (who was forty-seven) but not far off. She was a brunette, not especially tall but well built with a narrow waist and good, round hips. Her bust jutted out invitingly and it took me no time at all to work out that her shape was no doubt mostly about what she wore under her outer clothes.

The thoughts that this was everyday stuff for Mrs Greening, that every morning she would clip and fasten and zip herself into her underwear, sent my fantasies into overdrive. It had briefly occurred to me that my mother might have underwear like Mrs Greening – my little sister Jane certainly didn't – but a surreptitious examination of laundry piles and drawers soon revealed my mother didn't feel the need to wear what Mrs Greening did. I resumed my interest in Mrs Greening's clothes line, relieved in a way my mother didn't wear what our neighbour did as it seemed entirely wrong to think these thoughts about my own family.

Then I found out what Mrs Greening was like.

For once I wasn't staring at the clothes line. For once I wasn't preoccupied with curves and containment. But a breeze, a sudden stiff gust, sprang up and one of Mrs Greening's white girdles – as the mercurial twist of fate would have it, not pegged properly to the line – finished up on our side of the fence. Under many circumstances, I might have felt it better to tell my mother, let her deal with it. But Mum was out and, feeling a little emboldened by the chance to touch Mrs Greening's underwear, I picked the girdle up, feeling its weight and texture, admiring the suspenders and the sheen on the panel at the front (at least I assumed it was the front).

It didn't surprise me that being so close to what had been so close to Mrs Greening made me erect, bulging the front of my trousers. I was however surprised that Mrs Greening emerged from her house at that moment and confronted me.

"So, young Tony," she intoned, one eyebrow raised, standing in front of me in a satin-like gown drawn and tied closed at the waist. "It's you that's been sneaking round taking my underwear off the clothes line, is it?"

I stared at the woman, my jaw sagging. I had last been in her garden three years before to retrieve a ball. But having been banned, after smashing a window at our own house, from playing football in the garden, I had no need to do anything but stay on my own side of the fence.

In truth it had never occurred to me to steal Mrs Greening's underwear. I couldn't even believe anyone would steal clothes from a line. My mum and dad hadn't said anything about thieves in the neighbourhood and Mrs Greening would have told them, I was sure.

"That's mine, I think you'll find. Looks like I've caught the culprit, red-handed." She seemed to have a smirk on her face as she said it.

Words failed me, but I managed to stutter something out along the lines of: "M-Mrs Greening . . . I hadn't . . . I mean, it isn't me . . . I don't steal . . . this . . . um, girdle blew over –"

"Hmm, you know what it is then," sighed the woman. "Please don't make it worse for yourself by lying."

I felt crushed. I wasn't lying and I thrust the offending girdle towards the woman, feeling ashamed and confused. But she didn't take it. Mrs Greening stood, hands on hips, and regarded me, her eyes going to my crotch. "I do understand, believe me. An attractive, mature woman's underwear on a clothes line always attracts young men. Excites them, too."

"Oh!" I gasped as I realized what the woman was looking at. Blushing red, I tried to cover my embarrassment by dropping my hands, still holding the girdle, over the front of my pants. Mrs Greening merely laughed.

"Tony, as you are so fascinated by my underwear, I suggest you come over here and gather all my clothes in off the line. Think of it as a test that you can touch my underwear without wanting to steal it. Bring them into my house, please, while I consider if I should tell your parents about what you have been up to." At that she turned and marched off into the house, leaving the kitchen door open.

I gulped, understanding at once that here was some get-out clause, that bringing all her underwear in would somehow help prove my innocence. I hopped over the fence and set about gathering the assortment of bras and girdles and stockings and even knickers – deep-waisted knickers, I noted – off the line. Under normal circumstances the chance to visit so much mature women's underwear would have made me swoon with delight, but this was more serious than that.

Mrs Greening was waiting in the kitchen and indicated I should drop the pile of clothes on the table. "It wasn't me," I said as I put them down. "You have to believe me, Mrs Greening. I wouldn't steal your clothes."

"Really? And yet you spend so much time staring at them, when I hang them out."

I felt my face burn. So she had noticed me, staring at the underwear on the line, and I earnestly wished the ground would open up and swallow me. "It . . . It isn't like that," I managed to say.

Mrs Greening was cool and very much in control. "Tell me what it is like, then."

"It's just that . . . um, your clothes. Seeing them –"

"My underwear," corrected the woman. "My skirts and blouses don't hold the same fascination for you, do they, Tony?"

I felt my face grow even redder. I started to say something vague about all women's clothes holding a fascination but it was not only gibberish that came from my mouth, but clearly a lie.

"I'm disappointed in you, Tony," said Mrs Greening gently, interrupting my implausible little speech. "I hoped you would understand better."

Understand? If I wasn't confused already I certainly was now. "Mrs Greening, please don't tell my –" But I didn't get any further. Mrs Greening had undone the tie at her waist and let her robe fall open.

The act revealed she was wearing a black bra and girdle complete with suspenders holding up her dark, almost black stockings. My jaw – for the second time that day – must have sagged open in disbelief as I saw her in her underwear. Underwear I had never seen on the clothes line. I remember hearing a strange gurgling noise coming from my throat, a mix of shock and delight I suppose.

"Do you like what you see?" Mrs Greening was almost purring, eyes on me. She put her hands on her hips, inside the robe, so it was held open even more, one nylon-adorned knee forward as a model might display what she was wearing. "Wouldn't you say my underwear is better on me than on the clothes line?"

Somehow, I nodded. I hardly dared blink in case this apparition disappeared. Then something happened that I would curse silently for another three years. There was a knock at the front door, my mother calling out: "Mrs Greening, are you in?" She sounded urgent.

Mrs Greening half shrugged, and drew her robe round her, fastening it again and hiding the vision of her in her black underwear. "I think you'd better go out of the back door, don't you? Before your mum sees you in here and starts to think strange thoughts."

I fled as suggested, and never did find out what those strange thoughts might be, but I soon found out why my mother's intervention was so urgent. There'd been a big accident at the factory where Mr Greening worked, with three people badly hurt – including Mr Greening. He wasn't expected to survive and didn't.

The funeral of Mr Greening ten days later was a sombre affair. I felt I should go, but there were so many going to the service, so many of the Greening family and friends were there, the chapel would be full to bursting. As a good friend my mother went, but no one else from our family did. I peeked out from behind the curtain as I saw the woman next door, dressed all in black, being helped into the lead car behind the hearse. Although it was a sad occasion I felt slightly guilty thinking about what the widow might be wearing under her black outfit.

I felt incredibly bad about such a thought at a time like this, but then I had come so close to something quite wonderful. I fantasized about fucking the woman (in her underwear, of course) but the opportunity had disappeared almost at once. I might have hoped that in time she would call me into her house again but within a week of the funeral Mrs Greening had moved to her sister's place, somewhere near Skegness.

Three years later it all seemed so far away. I had a girlfriend, had got engaged and was thinking about settling down when one day, out of the blue, a parcel arrived at the small flat where I was living. I didn't recognize the handwriting on it but it was clearly from a female. Not my mother's handwriting, or my fiancée's Denise or even my aunt Doreen who was convinced I couldn't possibly survive living on my own and usually sent some tins of ham over via my mother. But never a parcel.

I tore it open and was astonished to find a set of women's black underwear. As the items tumbled out I realized that they were one and the same that Mrs Greening had been wearing that afternoon when I had come so close to sex. At least, what I imagined was close to sex with the woman.

There was a bra – a heavy, long-line bra with wide shoulder straps and sort of pointed cups – and a black girdle with a satin front panel and metal suspenders. Plus there was a pair of stockings in black. There was also a note in with them.

"Dearest Tony," it began. "Please do not be alarmed at this: I obtained your address from your mother when I called her the other day and as I haven't forgotten our little time together in my kitchen, I thought you might like a little reminder of that day. Sorry to say that circumstances prevented what might have been a very special moment for you, but please accept these as a token. I hope you are well and can make good use of them. I believe you have a girlfriend now and are planning to marry: I am sure Denise (that is her name, I understand) will make you very happy. I am also quite sure this underwear will not fit her. But perhaps you can make use of it somehow. Every best wish for your future, Liz Greening."

I was shaking when I finished reading the note. Then I held the underwear up and examined it, knowing that it wouldn't fit Denise at all but understanding just what I was going to do with it.

I married Denise a year later and we moved into our first house together, but she never did discover where I'd hidden Mrs Greening's black bra and girdle, and for many years whenever my wife was away on business I got a chance to wear them. But then, I'd hardly been out of them when I was alone at my flat, remembering Mrs Greening and masturbating over what I planned to do to her when she'd worn them just for me that day in the summer of '69.

I CAN HAVE ANY WOMAN I WANT

Bob, Llandudno

Maybe this is more of a boast than a confession, but it's not quite as much of a boast as the title suggests. I can't have any woman I want, that would be impossible, but there was a time when it seemed as if I could come close.

I spent so many years married to a woman who, to use that ubiquitous cliché, simply didn't understand me. She was very strait-laced and anything sexual was confined to her beliefs that the word "sex" had to have the word "normal" appended to it. And she didn't think my desires were normal. That injured me at first, but I gradually realized that "normal" equates to "boring" or "dull" and became quite happy to be considered anything but normal.

So what were these tastes that were too outlandish for Anita? They fell into a few categories and her response was varied. My liking for sexy lingerie, black stockings (preferably with seams) and suspenders was tolerated rather than enjoyed. She'd wear such things and, aside from annoying comments like "bloody suspenders" and complaints about draughts, she'd indulge me on special occasions. High heels are an obvious accessory to the above, but were far too uncomfortable for her bunioned feet. Oral sex – well, I guess all men like that, or probably all men like receiving it, though not all that many seem to want to reciprocate, and those who do don't do it well. More of that later. Anita would do that for me, but I always got the impression that was the only reason she did it, there was no enjoyment whatsoever on her side. That takes the edge off, in some ways. More of that later, too.

And then there's bondage. I like it. No, I love it. I can't really explain why or where my liking originated, but it's been there ever since I was a small child. It has so many facets that explaining them to someone who can't, or won't, understand can be difficult. There's the visual appeal of a woman in ropes. There's the fact she cannot move, that she's put in positions not of her choice. That leads on to the whole power exchange thing, her helplessness increases along with my power over her. But she has to be willing, she has to submit. I'm no rapist, not without prior consent anyway. There are issues of trust – if she is helpless she has to be able to trust you not to go beyond agreed limits. Anita couldn't understand it. So she wasn't willing, she was scared. It just didn't work. We did try a few times and I got something out of it, but nothing to satisfy the craving.

As for pain and punishment, don't even go there. She didn't want to know and wouldn't even talk about it.

We were both members of an amateur theatre group. A few years ago we staged a play where a woman was kidnapped and held hostage in an old barn. I knew the woman – Jayne – well but had never fancied her, and – as far as I am aware – she'd never fancied me. But I was cast as the kidnapper and she was cast as the victim, with Anita cast as the female villain. The stage was a split set – by that I mean that half of it was an apartment and the other half was the barn. We had to bluff our way into the apartment, chloroform the wife that Jayne was playing, then, when she'd collapsed in my arms, carry her out and take her to the barn. Once there I had to dump her unconscious body on a straw bale, straddle her and tie her hands behind her back. During rehearsals we didn't actually tie her, of course, but as time went on she wanted to practise as she would be in the play, so I used my tie to tie her wrists. I can still remember having to bluff my way out of the fact I'd got quickly and powerfully erect while I was doing it, and Jayne magically appeared in my masturbation fantasies from then on.

It was only when we were doing the final rehearsals that I realized she actually liked it, and for sure it was the best performance she had ever given. We never took it any further, since we were both in committed marriages, but we would share glances now and again that betrayed we'd actually shared something neither of us fully understood.

That was what started me writing about it. I've written books before, under my own name, but now I started turning my attentions to erotic books, chiefly about bondage, punishments and so on. The very first was based on the play and Jayne, but beyond those first ideas was a work of pure fiction. I sent it to a niche publisher and they accepted it, which did my ego no harm at all.

Anita read the book and it did nothing to alleviate her reservations about my preferences. But by that time, for totally unrelated reasons, our marriage was starting to disintegrate anyway, and I found more pleasure with my own right hand and a fertile imagination than she'd provided for many years. Flushed with the success of my first BDSM book, I went on to write another, then another and so on, each triggered by something I'd witnessed in real life, rather than some ridiculous fantasy world of cruel prison guards mistreating gorgeous simpering women. My stance was that, in the reader's mind, all this could be happening just down the street, and that those taking part were just ordinary everyday people.

I never made any secret of the fact I'd written these books, and anyone who asked me was welcome to read them, be they man or woman. By the time I'd got to double figures I was being looked at by friends and acquaintances with varying views. Some were shocked; some found it distasteful. Others' reactions varied from interested to fascinated and, without doing anything to foster the view, some saw me as a kind of expert on the topic. My stories were all based on my opinion that if I could make them as realistic and everyday as possible, people would be able to identify with them and wonder if, just maybe, their neighbours could be getting up to all kinds of things belied by their outwardly respectable personae.

As people viewed me as a guru, my confidence and ego grew, so I unconsciously developed a kind of swagger that appeared to send messages to any woman who was tuned in. Sadly, that isn't all women, but it is a surprising number and quite enough to keep this pervert busy. Also sad is the fact I can't turn it on and off. It just happens, so maybe there's some sort of subliminal communication between people of complementary types that we don't understand and can't control.

But I do know when it happens because I feel different. The first time I noticed it was at a party given by a friend of mine who is obscenely wealthy. He is boss of a cosmetic surgery company and as such is always surrounded by lots of very good-looking women. Most of these women danced to the music as if they were one with it. I, meanwhile, was watching on the sidelines of the dance floor, since I am not good at dancing and prefer to watch. This time I was being watched back. A rather attractive thirty-something, whose name turned out to be Elaine, kept looking my way as she danced sinuously with a girlfriend. If I looked at her she'd lower her eyes and carry on dancing. Her movements were ever more sinuous and provocative from knowing I was watching. The guy next to me, Chris, was watching the dancers too, but that didn't matter – there was some communication going on between this girl and me without any need for anyone else.

Before many minutes had passed she danced her way over to me, took my hand and suggested I join her on the dance floor. I declined, but smiled as I did. She pouted, an image of a spoiled child. As she held my hand I twisted it from her grasp, round so I was holding hers, and when she moved her other hand in to play fight, I grasped that as well, holding both her wrists in front of her using my much larger hand. She could probably have twisted out of my grip if she had tried hard enough, but she didn't, accepting her position as submissive to my dominance. The feeling of power was very strong as I held her there, right in front of Chris who was all too happy to have this girl in our tiny gathering. She, meanwhile, just remained where she was, held fast as Chris and I continued to talk. It was as if she didn't really matter and remained there purely because I was keeping her there. We watched the dancers as the volume of music increased, and she backed into me, her body sliding seductively inside her silky dress, until I could growl into her ear, "I'm going to have you."

The words seemed to melt her. It was a farcical situation. She was several years younger than I, thousands of times more attractive, almost certainly wealthier and could probably have had any man in the room that she wanted. But she stayed with me and breathed hard as my words hit home.

"Where?" was her only response.

"Outside," I told her. "Be at the back of the pool in five minutes."

Maybe it was foolish to let her go, and maybe it was foolish to risk everything in such a public situation, but if her excitement at being told what to do was anywhere close to my own excitement for telling her, she'd be there. Chris had overheard and didn't quite believe it all, thinking this was some kind of set-up to wind him up. But I excused myself and left the room. I walked towards the toilets in case anyone was overly curious, but stepped out the back and made my way to the building that housed the swimming pool. Elaine was moments behind me, sliding her arms round my neck to be kissed. She smelled of the best perfume, yet fresh and perfect. With some women you want to breathe in the scent of them and never exhale, and Elaine was just such a woman.

"Tell me what to do," she asked.

"Take off your clothes," I responded, curious to know how daring she could be.

Answer: totally. She unzipped the dress and dropped it, showing all she had on beneath was a white thing, which soon followed her dress to the ground. I pushed her to a wooden bench and prised her legs apart, kissing up the insides of her thighs as she whimpered and moaned and she didn't know whether to pull my head in or push me away. She told me afterwards that I was very good at giving oral sex, which may have been flattery, but I enjoy it and do it when I can, and I've never had any complaints, so I guess I'm quite profi- cient. She tasted briefly sour, then sweet and liquid. And she didn't take very long, moaning out sufficiently loud that I had to put my hand across her mouth to quieten her. I unzipped and pushed inside her, meeting wet warmth and greedy suction. She was nearly there again before, at a whim, I pulled out and stood, holding her head while I erupted over her face.

I only ever had her once again after that night, oddly enough in that swimming pool. She called me and said our friend was away and she had use of the house, and asked if I'd like a replay. Of course I said yes, and she asked what I wanted. I told her I wanted her in the pool, dressed in underwear, black stockings and suspenders. When I turned up later she was nowhere to be seen, but eventually I found her in the pool, swimming slowly up and down in lilac suspenders, bra and thong, her stockings soaked. She was even wearing high heels to complete the picture. Our rapid fuck, with me standing in the pool and her balanced on the edge at just the right height, was fantastic, ending in me filling her with my emission. She ducked down under the water afterwards and sucked me clean and, after a suitable recovery time, sucked me all the way again until I filled her mouth.

But Elaine wasn't the only one. I just wish I could control it. There have been so many times I've tried, when some woman has taken my fancy and I've willed that I could exercise this strange power, yet nothing happens. At other times it's just there, and she and I both know it.

I started saying this wasn't a confession as much as a boast, but that's not strictly true. To some people out there, I confess: I've had your wife, your girlfriend, your sister, your mother . . . Ordinary women with whom there's a telepathic connection, so powerful there's nothing either of us can do about it. I've explored every inch of them. I've penetrated their every orifice. I've tied them up, whipped and spanked them, coated them inside and out – mouths, vaginas, back passages, bodies, faces, legs, hands, feet and hair – with my seed. And I intend to go on having them.

BRINGING EDDIE'S LUNCH

Jess, Mishawaka

My boyfriend, Eddie, is a remodelling contractor. Sometimes we fuck in other people's houses.

When Eddie is working, he's a walking sexual fantasy. He wears tight carpenter jeans, with a hammer hanging from the hammer loop. He wears white T-shirts that are always, no matter what time of year, soaked with his sweat. I love it when he's swamped with work, when he's too busy to get his hair cut. When he slicks his too-long hair back out of his eyes, he looks maddeningly sexy.

And, of course, when he's swamped with work, I have to bring him his lunch.

About a year ago, Eddie was refinishing the hardwood floors in a historic house by the river. The European couple who owned it, the Ellingtons, were both university professors. They were in Prague for the week while Eddie worked. Refinishing a hardwood floor is labour intensive, and Eddie didn't have time to break for lunch. That Monday, he asked me to take time off work to bring him a sandwich and a couple of beers. I was happy to. I bought myself a sandwich as well, and we ate together sitting on the back steps.

"Want to see what I've been doing?" Eddie asked me when we'd finished lunch.

I said I did, and he took me inside. It was a nice home, I guessed. I couldn't really tell, since the furniture was covered in tarps and piled into a carpeted room. In the middle of what I assumed was the dining room stood the floor sander. It looked like an oversized vacuum cleaner. As I walked over to inspect the floor, Eddie turned the sander on. It began to vibrate, humming loudly.

"I've been pushing this thing around all morning," Eddie told me. "Go ahead, give it a try."

I took hold of the handle. Instantly, the floor sander sent vibrations through my entire body. I'd been having my period, and Eddie and I hadn't had sex in five days. The vibrations reminded me of what I'd been missing, and my clit began to throb.

I looked over my shoulder at him, and I could tell Eddie was thinking the same thing.

"Pull down your pants," he said.

"Are you serious?" I said, looking around the room. "We've never done it in someone else's house before."

"Yeah, I'm serious," Eddie said. He reached around me to switch off the floor sander. Putting his arm around me, he guided me around it and backed me against the wall. "Pull your pants down and bend over the writing desk, Jess." He punctuated the sentence with a long kiss, probing my mouth with his tongue.

Eddie led me over to the writing desk, which was with the other furniture under the tarp. As I reached for my belt buckle, I said, "Are you sure the Ellingtons are in Prague?"

There was a devilish grin on Eddie's face. "No," he said. "I'm sure they're on their way home this minute. They could burst through the door at any time."

I frowned at his smart-ass remark as I lowered my skirt to the floor. The thought of the Ellingtons (or their kids, or the neighbours) bursting through the door at any time sent my heart racing.

Eddie helped me out of my panties, then stood back to admire the view. "Look at that cunt," he said, wrapping one muscular arm around my waist. "Bright pink and shiny wet. You should see it, Jess. It's beautiful."

"Oh yeah?" I said as he pressed his body against mine. "Are you just going to look at it, or are you going to fuck it?"

As if I had to ask. Eddie tried putting his cock in me, but I wasn't quite wet enough yet. After a series of soft kisses across the back of my neck, he licked his fingers. He spread the moisture all around my waiting cunt, then inside me. Slipping his fingers out, he licked them again, then slid his cock inside me.

Eddie started banging me slowly and gradually worked up speed. I reached back and put my hands on his hips, pulling him towards me again and again.

Eddie thrust into me hard, and I opened my eyes. I noticed a beautiful antique mirror across the room, in which I could see our reflection perfectly. I watched the hard muscle of Eddie's thighs pumping, watched my breasts bounce. We were beautiful together, a well-oiled fucking machine.

Right about then, Eddie opened his eyes and watched me watching the two of us.

"You like that?" he growled in my ear. By now he was slamming into me hard.

"Yeah," I said, my voice high and arching. I hadn't realized how hungry I'd been for his cock until he'd started pounding into me.

But Eddie was also eager, and he didn't need much more encouragement. "Can't wait," he said excitedly. "Gonna come."

It was now or never, and my pussy knew it. Seconds later, he was spurting hard inside me, and I was pulsating right along with him. He bit into his biceps to keep from screaming. I tried to hold back the shout that burst out of me, but it was no use. I hollered loudly. The sound echoed through the empty room behind us. It was like being in a cathedral. With my skirt down.

Eddie and I leaned over the writing desk, panting, as our juices began to run down our legs.

"We need to clean up," he said. I was far messier than him, so he added, "Stay here."

I waited, and watched the mixture of semen and pussy juice run down my leg, hoping Eddie would get back before it reached my shoes. He did. I mopped up my wet cunt as best I could with the paper towels he'd found, then pulled up my skirt.

Once we were cleaned up, as well as we were going to be under the circumstances, Eddie stuffed his cock back in his jeans and said, "Fun's over, Jess. I gotta get back to work."

He did, and so did I. All day long I smelled his sweat and sawdust, faintly, on my clothes and in my hair. I thought about him all day. When he finally came home that evening, I practically jumped him as soon as he walked through the door.

After that, Eddie asked me to bring him lunch more often. We got naked in more of his customers' houses. Once, we even had a quickie in the kitchen while the homeowner (eighty-five years old, and all but deaf) watched *Wheel of Fortune* in his basement. The thrill of being vulnerable, the chance of being caught at any moment was almost as big a turn-on as the way Eddie looked in those carpenter jeans.

And then there was Veronica's house.

Veronica was a schoolteacher. Eddie had been her regular handyman for years; she liked him because he cleaned up after himself. It would be an understatement to say that Veronica was a neat freak. There wasn't a speck of dust anywhere in her house – not even behind the dishwasher, and *everyone* has a horrible mess behind the dishwasher. Her cleaning products stood neatly organized on the pantry shelf, the outsides of the bottles wiped free of drips. Even the straws in her broom were clean. How could they be dirty? Dirt wasn't *allowed* in Veronica's house.

On the Saturday morning that I brought Eddie lunch at Veronica's, she'd hired him to take down and replace her kitchen cabinets. It was summer, and Veronica was away visiting her sister in Omaha. The thought of her kitchen disorganized – ripped apart, no less – was more than Veronica could bear.

"Let's get naked," Eddie said as I handed him his lunch. He set the lunch bag down on the counter and didn't give it a second thought; his eyes were focused on me.

"Not here," I said. "Anywhere but here. Veronica will know."

"So what if she does?" Eddie said. He slicked back his sweaty hair and smiled. He looked so hot, my resistance was rapidly melting. "If she has a video camera hidden somewhere, it'll give her the thrill of her dried-up old life. And if she doesn't, how's she going to know?"

"She'll smell it," I said, laughing. "I don't care how well you clean up after yourself. I'll bet she can detect one particle of the scent of my excited cunt per million parts of bleach and lemon cleaner."

Eddie massaged his cock through his jeans. "Say 'excited cunt' again," he said. "Get naked while you're saying it."

I was about to say something when Eddie pulled me in for a kiss, rubbing my nipples through my thin T-shirt. "Where should we go?" I asked him.

"Basement," he said. "There's a really nice leather couch down there, and besides, there aren't any really obvious windows." He led me downstairs, where we stripped totally naked. Eddie sank into the brown leather of the couch, and I climbed on top of him. This time, we didn't even need the spit lube.

"I hope she does have a camera," Eddie said breathlessly as I rode him hard. "I want to see this again, from the other angle."

I laughed, pushing my legs wider apart to drive his cock deeper into me. Eddie gasped. He might have been enjoying this performance, but though he was rubbing just the right spot inside me, I had a hard time letting myself come. I couldn't stop thinking about Veronica's disapproving face. I was fairly certain sex was no more welcome in her home than dirt.

"What's wrong?" Eddie asked me.

"We shouldn't be doing this to her furniture," I responded.

Eddie sighed. "Fine," he said. "Pick a spot on the carpet."

If it had been anyone but Eddie, I would have been offended by the suggestion. But I really wanted to finish what we'd started. Veronica's carpet was covered by the cleanest-smelling rug I've ever laid my bare ass on. Actually, Eddie laid my bare ass on it. This time, he got on top.

"There now," Eddie whispered in my ear. "I've got you nailed down, Jess. You couldn't get up if you wanted to. Even if Veronica walked in the door right now, she'd just have to stand there and watch you get fucked."

Eddie always did know the right things to say. Seconds later, we were coming together.

Veronica called the following week, letting us know that she loved her new kitchen cabinets. But, for some reason, she hasn't called Eddie back since then. He strongly suspects that she did have a hidden video camera.

Personally, I think it's the Ellingtons who had the hidden camera. Since Eddie and I fucked on their writing desk, they've had him put new windows in the pool house and a new roof on the carport. If that's not customer satisfaction, then I don't know what is.

CAROLINE'S BLACK AND BLUE BOTTOM

Michael, San Diego

I knew Caroline from the blogosphere. I knew she was twenty-nine, lived in LA, was into pain, worked as a submissive in a dungeon and constantly craved a Jamba Juice.

One time she wrote in her blog: "If anyone out there brings me a Jamba Juice to work, they'll get something special."

I wrote: "If I lived in LA, I'd bring you one every day."

Her user handle was SoozyQ, Caroline was her pro name and Elaine (apparently) her true name. She seemed obsessed with images of women in Nazi outfits and pictures of Edward Norton in *American History X*. For several months we exchanged blog posts about sex and drugs and loneliness. She kept late hours until sunrise like I did. One night she wrote she was upset because an ex-boyfriend had posted pictures of his dick entering her cunt on the internet, and she gave me the link. She told me how she loved crystal meth because it made her horny and kept her thin, but she had to stay away from the addictive drug; I certainly could relate to that. She told me how the one night someone gave her what she thought was XTC but was actually acid and she had to work in that state of mind. I told her about the massive amount of 'shrooms I'd been taking lately and she said she didn't like 'shrooms "because they make me see witches." When asked what was the nicest gift anyone could give her, she replied: "A family and a home."

That was a good answer.

Ever since joining the blog universe, I've struck up about a dozen online "relationships" with women all over the country, from ages eighteen to forty-eight, varying in degrees of flirtatious emails, cyber sex on Instant Messenger, late-night phone calls when their husbands, boyfriends or parents are asleep, to some of them flying, driving or taking the Amtrak into San Diego for a weekend to see if there is any chemistry "in the meat world", as they say in the vernacular. Usually, it's awkward and doesn't work out . . . so with this, I often suggest, before they make the trip, that we immediately jump into a quick, hard fuck. Why not? That's why they're coming to see me, and sex will be on our minds the whole time. You know: Who should make the first move? Will a move be made? Will there be sex? Will the sex be good? If the sex is taken care of right away, then there won't be all that tension and anticipation and we'll both know if the sex is good and if we should continue with the visit as friends or mere tricks.

So I was a little nervous about meeting Caroline in LA and she said she was too, but I wondered about that since our pre-arranged get-together was going to be brief and contrived; she was a professional, after all, and I was going to pay her for the time at the going rate plus a tip; and I knew there wasn't going to be any actual "sex" involved.

This was also going to be a new experience for me, dropping into an S/M dungeon; I felt better that I was going to be with a woman whom I'd at least communicated with and knew a little bit about, rather than a complete stranger.

I've never been into the BDSM or D/s scene much. The "lifestyle" fascinates me and I like the clothing and gear and attitude in an academic sort of way, but it simply doesn't turn me on, nor is it something I pursue with the kind of passion that many in "the scene" do with almost religious fervour and intent.

I set up a Sunday appointment with Caroline at 1.30 p.m. The dungeon was located across the street from LAX in a warehouse zone on South La Cienega Boulevard. If you didn't have the address and didn't know what it was, you'd never know such a place of business was among the rows of bland, cookie-cut rectangular buildings that look like they were erected in the 1950s. The windows were tinted and there was an American flag in front of the place in question. I was told there was a "discreet" back entrance for clients who didn't want to be seen going in or out but I didn't care; I pressed the intercom and said I had an appointment and was buzzed inside.

The lobby was appropriately dark; a fat, greasy man in a pastel shirt who looked like the clichéd smut peddler sat behind a wooden desk. He looked me up and down and seemed bored. On a leather couch to my left was a woman with short hair, wearing a teddy and chewing gum; at the desk to my right sat a short blond woman who was on a computer, doing something on the internet – I knew this was Caroline; she was often on-line at work and I recognized her from some photos I'd seen: long, thick curly hair, round face, slightly chubby body, big breasts and innocent-appearing blue eyes.

I had two Jamba Juices with me, orange and a berry flavour. She chose the orange and I had the berry.

She was shy and had a soft, high-pitched voice like a ten-year-old girl. She didn't look me in the eye when we shook hands, nor when she gave me a tour of the facility. But maybe this is what submissives are supposed to act like, what did I know?

This dungeon was a 7,000 square foot warehouse split up into various themed rooms. The Bastille Room – a jail cell with a rack; the Elizabethan Room – soft and pink and good for tickling; the "O" Room – minimal with plain white walls and some hardcore torturing devices; the Mae West Room for clients who liked to cross-dress and that door was closed; Windsor Hall was a classroom setting with half-a-dozen student chairs, a teacher's desk and a chalkboard; the Interrogation Room for some hardcore action had quite the fascist feel; Windsor Stables was the "pony training" area and the biggest – it was like a studio sound stage or small theatre.

"Movies could be made here," I said.

"Oh, there have been a few that have," Caroline said, looking at the floor.

"What kind?"

"What do you think?"

"S&M, I guess."

"And some porn."

I chose the Marquis de Sade Room, second biggest to Windsor Stables; everything in it was black or purple and there was a rack, cross, shackles, torture tower and a suspended cage connected to the ceiling and tracks, so it could be pushed from one side of the room to the other. I chose this room because it had a large, comfy couch with pillows. I would have wanted the classroom if Caroline had been wearing a schoolgirl outfit (she was in white lace) and I could be the perverted teacher and she the naughty nymph.

We went up front and told the fat man which room. "How long?" he asked me. I said half an hour and he said, "A hundred dollars." I already knew what the prices were going to be; an hour went for $160 and I almost took that but this was my first time, what if I got bored?

I gave the guy a $100 bill and Caroline took me to the equipment room, where I had the choice of dozens of whips, paddles, leather masks and so on. I had no idea what to do so I went for the obvious: handcuffs. Then I grabbed some clothespins because I remembered a blog post of Caroline's about how she liked them clamped on her nipples. Then I randomly grabbed a paddle. "Ohhh," said Caroline, "that one's the worst. It's so hard."

It was a pretty heavy paddle and looked like it was made of walnut.

In the room, I said, "OK, look, I told you I'm pretty chary of all this, so I have to say I don't know what to do."

"Well, it's all about fantasy," Caroline said.

"But what are the dos and don'ts?"

"There's no nudity, you can't touch me on my private parts underneath my bra and panties, and there's no exchange of bodily fluids."

"Let's keep it simple," I said. "What if I gave you a spanking?"

"OK. Where?"

"The couch."

I sat on the couch and she stood in front of me, looking quite demure.

"And I want you to call me Daddy the whole time," I told her.

"Daddy," she said, "lift up my skirt."

I did. She was wearing white thongs. She lay down across my lap. Her hair smelled like shampoo and I could also smell her pussy.

"Daddy, I've been so bad."

"Yes," I said, "you have," and I began to spank her, first on the left ass cheek and then on the right; back and forth like that, soft at first because I knew enough that you did this lightly and built your way up. Her ass was big and round and pink and her flesh jiggled.

I've had plenty of girlfriends who liked the occasional spanking – a smack on the rear while I fucked them in the ass or some playful stuff to get them excited, but I'd never done a "session" like this before.

As I spanked her harder, my hand began to hurt so I switched to the paddle. The hard wood against her butt made a reverberating sound in the de Sade Room. When I took my first hard swing, she tensed up and hissed and I saw that her ass cheek was bright red.

"I'm sorry," I said, "too hard?"

"Not at all, Daddy."

"Harder?"

"If you wish, Daddy. Hurt me good, Daddy."

So I did . . . and I got into it. It took me maybe fifteen minutes to get into what this was all about, and when I did, I loved it. Her butt was turning black and blue and she was crying out and squealing and sometimes her body went completely stiff and she'd shudder. But in my mind, she was no longer a woman I knew from the internet whom I was paying to do this to; she was Tara, my ex-girlfriend who had walked out of my life four months ago, who'd abandoned me and our cats and left me with the full rent and utilities to pay, who'd left me alone and never wanted to see or talk to me. Yes, she was Tara and I was punishing Caroline (Tara) for what Tara had done, for hurting me: I was hurting her back. "You bitch," I said (in my mind, not out loud) as I slammed the paddle down, "you cunt, you piece of worthless shit," and I guess I got too carried away because Caroline said, "OK, OK, that's too hard, not that hard, Daddy."

Her ass was completely red with several black and blue spots. Her body was shaking and covered in sweat. I was hot and sweating too. I felt bad that maybe I'd gone too far, so I rubbed her back and stroked her hair and ran my fingers up and down her legs; my hand moved between her legs, keeping above the thong panties, and she was wet – I could feel it, see it and smell it. She was enjoying this, I guess. She said, "Give me some more, Daddy."

So I did, but not too hard.

"You are bad," I said and began to use the paddle harder to keep my mind off the hard-on I had that was pressing against my stomach – one that she knew was there because she began to grind her torso into my crotch.

The buzzer went off, our half an hour was up. I could have gone for another thirty minutes but this was good enough. Caroline stood up; her make-up was smeared and there were tears down her bright pink face.

"OK?" I asked.

She smiled. "I would've been more verbal but I was just trying to survive that paddle. Oh man –" she lifted her skirt and looked at her backside in the mirror on the wall "– my ass is gonna be a mess tomorrow."

I got up and we both grabbed some cheap motel-style towels to wipe off sweat and tears. We stopped and looked at each other and then hugged.

I gave her a $50 bill as a tip, hoping it was a good tip.

I then gave her a kiss and she closed her eyes and smiled.

"Thanks for the new experience," I said.

"Come back again when you're in LA."

"I will."

"Maybe get a second girl, double your fun."

The other girl was asleep on the couch in the lobby. The fat man nodded at me. I walked out of the dungeon like I was being released from county jail and the sun was very bright. I didn't feel dirty like I thought I would. I felt – fuck if I know – cleansed in a way. I felt less angry. I may have even been a little happy.*

(* I was worried I'd crossed the line with her, that I damaged her flesh beyond $100 and a $50 tip. I emailed her about it and she replied: "Not at all. If you had gone too far I would have TOLD YOU. Oh, my ass is really black and blue, YOU. It's beyond my skin and muscle, it's a bruise right down to the bone. It hurts to sit. That's so COOL-IO!)

IN PLAIN SIGHT

M.G., Enfield

First, let me assure you, I am not some sort of creepy peeper. I do not make a habit of skulking around spying on young ladies, nothing like this ever happened to me before. It really was an accident that I discovered her sunbathing habits, and I only approached her because I was sure she had no idea how exposed she was out on her balcony. From there things just sort of spiralled downhill.

I had best start at the beginning. A friend of mine had offered me her condominium for the week. It was right on the beach with a great view of the sunrises. The "Salida Del Sol" complex was five high-rise buildings facing the ocean in a giant U shape, the four buildings on the wings were six storeys high and the one at the base stood one floor taller. My friend Cindy bought into the top floor of the tallest one, just her nature, I suppose.

It was late February, a little early for the college kids' spring break and still too cold for the oldsters. They tended to migrate further south this time of year. That meant the place wasn't crowded and those of us there didn't hit the beach until midday when it really started to warm up.

Now I tend to be up late and sleep in later so I never expected to catch one of the sunrises that gave this place its name. Best laid plans and all; Sunday night I went out drinking, found a friendly native and followed her home, I didn't stumble back to my place until just before six in the a.m.

I stepped out onto the balcony hoping some fresh air would revive me and realized the sun was just about to pop over the horizon. I wasn't that tired so I went and got my camera equipment and set up the Nikon on a tripod. The sun rose with all the splendour and majesty the place advertised and I snapped maybe a dozen photos. I was just about to take down my equipment when something out there caught my eye. A Northern Right whale and her calf were heading north just about 400 yards off the beach. That's not something you see every day so I quickly flipped on my 500mm telephoto zoom lens and started following the pair as they headed up the coast. Before I'd focused and snapped five frames, they were disappearing behind the northernmost building of the complex; that's when I spotted her.

She was cute, a thirtyish body that was not fat or thin but curvy. A short mop of coppery red hair, a sharp little nose and lips a tad too thick, she wasn't beautiful, not in the classic sense, but she was enough of an eyeful to give me pause. The fact that she was stark naked may have lengthened that pause a bit.

Well, she was almost naked; she was lying out on her flattened lounge chair with one of those sleeping masks covering her eyes while she soaked up the early morning sunshine. It was barely seventy degrees and that seemed somewhat cool to be outside in the altogether. With my big lens, I zoomed in and, sure enough, her nipples were tight little nubs. Yeah, I suspect I could have counted the hairs on her pubes with that lens; I didn't try though, she'd shaved. I could almost make out goosebumps on her arms. I only checked because it had to be rather cold out there. Still I guess someone coming down from Canada or New England might think seventy was warm.

I refrained from snapping the picture; after all, I'm a gentleman, am I not? In fact, after taking inventory for a few seconds I walked away. I was up now so I went in and made my breakfast. Taking my coffee out to the balcony I casually glanced over. Even without the help of my camera lens, I could see she'd rolled over onto her belly. I went to check her at full zoom and admired her firm little bottom. No visible tattoos is always a good sign. I tried reading out there on the balcony and checked on her a few more times before I dozed off. When I woke up around two, she was gone.

The next morning I set my alarm for six. Once again, she was outside before seven catching the early morning sun. I checked on her at regular intervals, not spying on her really, just concerned that she not be disturbed. She did seem to be sleeping but rolled over several times. Right around noon she got up, slipped on a pink bikini, and headed off to the beach.

I followed along shortly; she seemed to be alone. She flirted with some of the wanna-be surfers and laughed gently when they tried to pick her up. She retreated into one of the condo association's striped cabanas, seeking shelter from the midday sun. Stretching out on a beach chair, she seemed to be reading. Around two in the afternoon, she took a brief dip in the ocean and then went back up to her condominium. To be honest, I'd been working myself up to approach her, but I still wasn't sure what I wanted to do or say.

Wednesday morning I finally did decide to do something. I was concerned about sunburn, and was quite sure she had no idea how many people could be watching her morning ritual. After several false starts and running an opening speech through my head a couple of times, I set off for her building. I took the elevator up to the top floor and turned left down the corridor. Hers was the outermost flat, closest to the ocean.

I politely knocked on the door, feeling a bit awkward and imagining how badly she might react to my news.

There was no answer. I tried the bell but heard nothing; I supposed it was broken. I knocked louder but still no response. Just as I was turning to head back to my place, I checked the doorknob. It turned easily.

That gave me pause. If this was like every other morning, the lady was asleep out on her balcony, quite naked, with her flat wide open. Anyone could walk in on her. I pushed the door open and gave a tentative "Hello."

No answer.

Cautiously I let myself in, I didn't want to startle her, but clearly, she wasn't aware of just how vulnerable she was. I quietly threaded my way through the suite. The layout was identical to the one I was staying at and I made my way quickly through the kitchen area and living room. The sliding glass doors to the balcony stood open and I could hear soft snoring coming from outside.

I stepped onto the balcony and took in the sight of her. She lay face down on the lounge chair, her chin turned away from me, her perky little bottom uncomfortably close. From a distance she had been a cute eyeful, here in the flesh she was achingly real. I could smell her fresh shampoo, hear her rasping breath, and I reached a trembling hand towards her. I knew in some deep recess that if I touched her, if I woke her, she'd scream. Then all hell would break loose. Who knew, I could end this vacation at the police station trying to explain what I was doing here. The trouble was I wasn't quite sure myself.

In the end, my hand decided for me. I simply couldn't resist. First, my fingertips touched, and then my full palm stroked that delicate little rump. She tensed, her breath caught at mid-snore. Belatedly I thought I should have put a hand over her mouth, just to buy a moment before she started yelling. That wasn't what happened. Without a word, she pushed herself up onto her elbows. While I ogled her newly exposed breasts, she reached towards her sleeping mask.

"Don't do that," I snapped, my voice a little harsher than I intended.

She nodded, then sat up wordlessly, mask still in place.

"Do you realize your door was unlocked? Anyone could come in here and find you like this."

Again, she nodded then bowed her head as if in contrition. We paused in awkward silence. This wasn't going at all as I'd imagined, I was at a loss as to how to proceed. She had yet to say a word. After the silence had stretched too long she took matters into her own hands. She knelt down by the lounge chair and bent across its width, presenting her bottom to me.

I was shocked and grinning all at the same time. How could she know? Certainly the saner part of me was a little leery, but this wasn't something I was about to pass up. I debated a moment, palm or strap? Then with a tug, I pulled my belt free of its loops. The first firm slap of leather on flesh brought a gasp of surprise but she snuggled her belly down and pushed her bottom back towards me. That was all the encouragement I needed. I slapped and smacked away with enthusiasm feeling myself grow harder with each blow. I wasn't counting but it must have taken about forty smacks to brighten her arse to my tastes. I was careful to lay the leather on the meaty portion of her bottom, but if she planned to wear her bikini that day, some stripes were going to show.

She was moaning when I finished up but I couldn't say for sure if that was from pain. I waited a moment, admiring the warm glow of her bottom, but I was ready to walk away. She sensed that, I suspect. Her knees parted further as she rolled her hips towards me. I licked my lips.

"Please," she said.

That was the only word she ever said to me, but it spoke volumes. I was on my knees behind her in a flash. She was wet and eager. I sank into her with a leisurely arrogance that made her twitch with anticipation. She tried to press back towards me. My hands gripped her hips and pushed her down into the seat cushion. I steadily pressed forwards and, once I'd fully impaled her, I curled my belly against the curve of her welted bottom. Her contented sigh only served to annoy me.

We hung motionless for an endless moment, and then I gave free rein to my lust. I reared back and slammed into her; I held nothing back, pummelling her body as it shuddered under my assault. I didn't last long; I didn't care. Usually I try to please the lady I'm with, but this time that just wasn't important. When I was finished with her, I pulled away, releasing my grip and letting her collapse.

"I hope you've learned to lock your door," I muttered, not knowing what else to say.

She may have nodded; I didn't look back. I made my way across her suite and hurried back to my own. Once there, I couldn't help but go out to my balcony and check. She was inside. I spent most of the day fretting, half expecting the police to show up. In the afternoon, I went to the beach but she was nowhere to be found. By evening, I was breathing a bit easier, so I headed out for a night on the town.

I got in late and didn't set the alarm yet somehow I was wide awake when the sun peeked over the horizon. Shaking my head,

I walked out onto the balcony and looked down. There she was, waiting for me. Her mask was in place and she lay belly down. The telephoto lens confirmed her bottom still bore the marks from yesterday's encounter. I didn't rush right over; after all, I'd ordered her to lock her door. I figured she was just taunting me. She only rolled over with an effort and didn't stay on her back for long. By eight thirty, I had to know. I stood before her door for a full minute before I turned the knob. Sure enough, it opened for me.

This time the light in the kitchen was on. A key sat on the counter on top of a note. "Please drop this off Saturday morning," it said. I grinned, pocketed the key and headed out to the balcony. She never did give me her name.

THE MODEL

Peter, London

I used to work as a freelance portrait photographer, advertising my services in the newspaper. I took pictures of whoever wanted to have a portrait: men, women, children, couples, families, pets. I didn't exactly get rich from it, but I did make a decent enough living.

One day, a man called me and said he wanted some photographs of his wife. That suited me just fine. They lived in a stylish split-level home on a quiet street in the suburbs. The man answered the door and ushered me inside. His wife was standing in the hallway, looking at me expectantly.

"We'll do it in the bedroom," the woman said, and led the way down the hall, her husband bringing up the rear. To my considerable surprise, the woman started to get undressed as soon as we were in the bedroom.

"I wanted some nude photographs of my wife," the husband explained, rather unnecessarily, I thought. "I just didn't want to tell you over the phone."

I had done some nude photography before, so I knew pretty well what kind of poses worked. While I took my camera out of my carrying bag and readied myself for the task, I watched the woman stripping down to her panties and sit down on the bed. She didn't seem to mind at all that I was watching her. She was completely relaxed and at ease with herself and her body. I was glad; it would make my job a lot easier.

I stepped up to her, aimed my camera at her, and looked at her through my viewfinder to see what she looked like in the frame. It didn't take me long to figure out the best ways to photograph her. She was an easy model, as I had suspected. She followed my instructions with ease, moved where and when I wanted her to move, struck the poses I suggested to her, and even added a few of her own. When I felt I had enough different pictures to make a good selection, I went to put my camera away.

"Just a minute," her husband stopped me. "I want some pictures of her pussy, too."

The woman peeled off her panties, looking directly at me, and spread out on the bed, parting her legs and pulling up her knees to allow me the best view. I knelt down beside the bed, aimed my camera at her again, and began my work. It was amazing, the details I was able to see through my lens. I took several long shots, then moved in to shoot some close-ups. I was getting close to finishing when she reached down and parted her labia with her fingers to reveal her clit and the insides of her pussy, so I kept shooting until my roll of film was full.

I rose to my feet and looked at the husband. "Anything else?" I asked, not really expecting him to respond.

"There is something else," he said, tentatively. "We were wondering if you would be interested in having sex with my wife while I watch." He stopped, then added, almost like an afterthought although it obviously wasn't, "We'll pay you double your fee."

I hadn't expected that. I looked at him with consternation, but he seemed to be quite serious. I looked at his wife. She nodded encouragingly. How could I refuse? I didn't want to refuse, strange as the request seemed to me at the time. I was young, and quite turned on from the photo session. She was a nice enough looking woman with good breasts, and I could certainly use the money.

"All right," I said after a moment's hesitation. "I think we could do that."

"I'm glad," he said while the woman was rearranging herself on the bed.

I walked around to the other side of the bed and began to take off my clothes. I happened to look up and saw, to my further consternation, that the husband was taking off his clothes, too. I was going to say something, but then decided to let it go and wait and see what would develop. So I took off the rest of my clothes and climbed on the bed beside the woman.

She proved to be a proficient and skilful lover. She made me feel as good as I was hoping I was making her feel. Her frequent moans and cries certainly seemed to indicate that I was. The husband had faded into the background and I was hardly aware of him any more. He was sitting on a chair against the wall and just watching, as he had said he would. We completed our performance to our mutual satisfaction, and I rolled off on my back.

The husband rose from his chair and stepped up to the bed. He looked at me. "Now she has to be punished," he said sternly. "She's been a bad girl and I don't tolerate that."

What a strange development, I thought, but it was their house and their game, whatever it was, and I didn't say anything.

He turned to his wife. "Say it!" he barked at her.

"I've been a bad girl," the woman repeated her husband's words. "Punish me now, please!"

She rolled over on her stomach, took hold of two newels in the headboard with her hands, and buried her face in the pillow. Her husband took a long whip out of a cupboard and flicked it in the air a couple of times as he walked back to the bed.

"I'd like some pictures of this, too," he said.

I scampered off the bed and picked up my camera. He waited until I was ready, then lifted the whip over his head and let it come down on her buttocks, leaving a faint red line across her white skin. She winced, but didn't make a sound. The whip went into the air a second time and came down on her, causing her to yelp, the sound muffled by the pillow. The husband raised the whip a third time and let it come down on her. This time she screamed, but then she lifted her head and looked at her husband over her shoulder.

"More," she moaned. "Punish me more!"

At this point, I really wasn't sure at all just how hard the whip came down on the wife's buttocks, nor just how genuine her screams were. Whatever was the case, the two of them seemed to be enjoying themselves in their own ways, and I was capturing everything on film.

The husband whipped his wife for a fourth time, and again she screamed, louder and more plaintively than after the last stroke. The whip came down for a fifth time, and she screamed, this time into the pillow to muffle the sound. Her husband dropped the whip on the floor.

"That's enough for today," he announced. He climbed on the bed between her legs, put his hands on her hips, and lifted her up until she was on her knees. Her hands were still gripping the headboard newels, her knuckles white from the effort of holding on, her face still buried in the pillow. He mounted her from behind and began to ride her with forceful, determined strokes.

I kept shooting pictures of the two of them until my film ran out. A few moments later, the husband threw back his head and groaned with the ecstasy of his orgasm. He dismounted and flopped down on the bed. The wife turned on her back beside him, a look of deep satisfaction on her face.

I assumed that this signalled the end of my assignment. I put my clothes back on and packed my camera into my carrying case.

"Thank you," the husband said from the bed. "We're really very happy and grateful that you stayed."

"You were wonderful," the wife sighed.

When I went back to bring them the photographs a few days later, they were sitting in their living room, looking like a regular suburban couple spending a quiet evening at home. They loved the photographs. The husband handed me the balance of my fee, and I left them to their own devices. I half wished they would call me back, but I never did hear from them again.

COCKSUCKER

Drew, Winston-Salem

"Do you like it?" Sabrina used to ask.

"You know I do," I'd lie as I tried to ignore her incisors, her uselessly shallow insertion, and tried to convince myself she was every bit the fellatrix I told her she was. I'd close my eyes and imagine Sabrina acting as if she was starving for my cock and in my mind she was feeding on me, trying her best to consume my cock, wanting nothing more than to be rewarded with my come.

The feel of my cock in her mouth would fill her senses; the smoothness of the head as it slipped into her open throat, the hard shaft, sliding in and out of her wet lips. With concupiscent eyes and breathless moans she would show me just how much she loved it, how she was there only to please.

But she didn't love it. Not really. She didn't even like it. Giving me head was just another chore to her. Another inconvenience she had to endure to keep me from complaining. Like going to visit my mom. Or watching horror movies with me.

"Is this good?" Sabrina would ask when she'd pull my cock from her mouth to catch her breath, using her hands for twice as long as she did her mouth before finally going back down. But in my mind, she knew it was good, staring into my eyes as she begged me to call her my filthy whore, my dirty little cocksucker. She'd gaze at my cock, amazed at its size and its perfect shape, and she'd tell me so as she'd rub it all over her upturned face, inhaling its raw, wet scent as she ran its length under her nose, like it was some fine cigar. It would smell like the ocean to her, and she'd plunge her mouth down over it again and simply devour me. And I'd tell her, over and over again, how good she was, how beautiful she was.

And then she'd make me come. And I'd watch her face as she went through all the motions, swallowing it as if it were some kind of nectar, as if finishing a blow job any other way would be utterly wrong, a waste of a precious gift. And then she'd look up at me, her eyes narrowing as she smiled around my cock, and I'd try to tell her "Thank you" but I'd be unable to speak.

But Sabrina, quite simply, is not good at sucking cock. And Sabrina is not here right now. And I'm a firm believer that if you want something done right you have to do it yourself. So I lie back, raise my knees to chest, pull myself tight and coil up, shoulders pressing into the mattress with the full weight of my body, until the room is upside down before me. For a moment I have no weight, no equilibrium, I can see only my thighs, and between them, my inverted cock, pointing down at my face. With both hands, I cling to my buttocks, pulling myself in until I'm almost straddling my own face. I can smell the stains on the sheets from this morning, where Sabrina, not realizing at first I was coming, gagged and ejected my still-spurting cock from her mouth, spilling a mouthful of semen onto our bed.

My cock hovers above my face, just inches from my mouth. I strain my neck to reach it, but can't yet. The bed creaks and sinks as I condense my body further, my bare toes clutching and curling under the headboard, like fulcrum and lever, and the tip of my cock suddenly brushes my lips. I extend my tongue, use it to guide my cock towards the opening of my mouth. I seal my lips around the plump head and I feel my cock begin to stiffen, responding immediately to my attentions. I kiss it, lap at it, causing it to harden further, lengthening and straightening until it juts purposefully from my groin, straining towards my face.

My body sinks onto itself, my abdomen pressing onto my chest, my stomach crushing against my ribcage. My hands clutch at the backs of my thighs, my knees bending as my body folds. My cock seems to leap at me from between my legs, as if trying to reach my mouth of its own will. I take it in my hands and wrestle it into my empty mouth, its width stretching my lips to a familiar shape. I moan as I taste myself again at last. An eternity has seemingly passed since I last had my cock in my mouth. Immediately I begin to move my head back and forth on it, feeling it fatten and strengthen, growing harder yet between my lips. I clamp my toes under the headboard and use the big muscles in my thighs to tighten my body in on itself, pushing my cock deeper into my mouth so I can suck on it.

Starving, I swallow it whole, the trained muscles in my stomach contracting, helping me move the fat head in and out of my lips. My cock is the connection, the link that joins me to my own body. It's at its hardest now, perfectly erect, and I brace myself against the headboard and begin to buck up from the bed, fucking my own face, my head pressing into the mattress. I suck hungrily on my cock as it fills my mouth, draw it in until my throat contracts around it, squeeze my lips around it until I can feel the blood pulsing through it.

With a gasp I free my cock and let it rest against my face while I breathe again for just a moment. It smells like sweat and bleach and I close my mouth around it again, as deeply as I want now, my head pinned between my thighs. My weight forces my cock into my throat, the penetration deeper than before. I focus alternately on my mouth and my cock and try to decide which is giving and which is receiving. Does the mouth pleasure the cock or does the cock please the mouth? I think of Sabrina for a moment and I wonder what she thinks of when she is sucking my cock, and then realize I probably don't want to know.

I'm going to come. I'm ready; I can feel it – something that Sabrina, I'm sure, can never quite do. I listen to my breath bursting out of my nostrils as I go all the way down on myself, as far as I can, until my lips sink into my groin. I can feel the vibrations of my moans through my cock. My thighs tremble on either side of my head and, helplessly, I begin to come, the thick, swimming mass sliding down my throat. It's warm and briny and it pulses into my mouth in a series of clinching spasms and I think about the long journey it's made from deep inside my body, through my sucked cock and into my mouth, back within my body, where it had came from, never once leaving me.

I release myself, my body snapping open like a spring, and collapse on the bed. The knotted muscles in my back and thighs slowly soften and I take a few deep breaths when I finally think to. I lie there for a long time and watch my cock as it rests on my left thigh and slowly begins to deflate.

I don't want to think about Sabrina, but just for the first few minutes after I come, I do. I am so much better than Sabrina.

SLAVE'S BIRTHDAY TREAT

I.G., Oregon

I love Mistress very much, but I really miss having a man in my life. Yesterday, for my twenty-eighth birthday, she gave me a most wonderful present. I had asked to go to a local pizza place that has an indoor mini-golf course – a chance to forget my age and indulge in juvenile pursuits. Mistress, who is quite a bit older, took me, but made it clear she would not play golf. When she went to purchase a round of golf, she asked me with whom I would play.

I shrugged. "I know you're not interested; I guess I'll just play by myself."

She looked up at me. At home, when I'm usually on my knees in her presence, it's easy to forget how tiny she is and that I'm almost a foot taller. "You could play with him." She pointed to someone behind me.

I turned and found a friend who I hadn't seen in several weeks standing there with a huge grin on his face. "Liam!" I said with delight and gave him a big hug. Liam is one of Mistress's play partners so I'd seen him naked often enough at parties. I do admit I have the hots for him, but Mistress doesn't permit me to have sex with anyone but her. Still, I was delighted just to have someone my own age to play golf with.

Mistress ordered pizza, paid for two mini-golf games, and told them to bring the food out after we played. I enjoyed the game immensely. We got 3D glasses that made it hard to hit the ball accurately, but embellished all the black-lit pirate scenes. I beat Liam by a couple of strokes and Mistress took pictures of us with the "pirates".

After the luscious pizza, Mistress invited Liam to come to the house and visit for a bit before he drove back home – he lives an hour and a half away. When we arrived, Mistress sent me upstairs to strip and take care of some quick chores. I came back down and saw Liam had a great big bow tied around his neck.

"You may unwrap your present now, boy," Mistress said, twirling a strand of her long, auburn hair around her finger.

I just stared at her.

"Don't you like your present?" She had a wicked glint in her green eyes.

I tilted my head to one side. "Um, what do I get to do with it?"

"Anything he will let you." Mistress smiled, but I had a hard time believing she meant I could have sex with him.

"Anything? As in I can go down on him if I want?"

"Of course."

"If I wanted him to do me, that would be OK?"

"Yes."

I almost wept for joy. "Oh, thank you, Mistress." I got down on my knees and kissed her pretty feet. "Thank you so very, very much."

My hands shook when I unbuttoned Liam's khaki shirt and unbuckled his leather belt. He has broad shoulders and he works out so his pecs and abs are nice and firm. I ran my hand over his muscular chest, enjoying the feel of another man. When I pulled down his jeans and cotton boxers, his beautiful penis practically jumped into my mouth. I hadn't touched one in so long. It felt soft and smooth in my hands. The absolute exquisiteness on my tongue caused my own pecker to respond rather abruptly. I wrapped my lips around his rod and let it slide across my tongue until it hit the back of my throat. I moaned in between his thighs, and I could hear Liam sigh with pleasure. With one fist at the base of his penis and the other hand holding one of his plush cheeks, I slid him in and out of my mouth.

Pain seared across my butt. Out of the corner of my eye, I could see Mistress bringing her cane down for another strike. I winced, but I knew better than to do anything to try to avoid or deflect the blow. I concentrated on enjoying the plump succulence in my mouth, but I couldn't help a little muffled yelp when the second blow struck close on the first welt – Mistress has a rather good aim. Liam and Mistress laughed at the same time at my distress.

Mistress handed Liam a bag of colourful plastic clothespins. He leaned down to attach them to my thighs, my arms and my nipples while I kept my mouth firmly attached to his crotch. They pinched a bit, but I knew that depending on how long he left them on, they would really hurt when he removed them. When another stinging blow from Mistress's cane cut into my arse cheeks, I stopped long enough to cry out. With Liam's cock shoved deep in my throat it came out kind of gurgly. He seemed to like the sensation, though, because he grabbed my hair, and face-fucked me until he jabbed the top of his crotch onto my eyes and sent warm, slightly salty come down the back of my throat. I swallowed every drop and milked him dry until, to my surprise, he became hard and ready again.

I heard Mistress snap her fingers and I looked up to see her sitting on the sofa, her legs spread apart. I crawled over to her and kissed her feet, sucking her toes one at a time until she wiggled her rear and I could smell her arousal. Then I kissed my way up the soft skin of her plump legs, ducking under her black, ruffled skirt, until I could push aside her silk thong with my nose and dive into her luscious moistness. While I lapped up her sweet juices, Liam removed the clothespins slowly so I fully experienced the pain of each one. I didn't let that distract me from taking care of my Mistress though.

I felt first one and then two cold, lube-slick fingers work their way into my arse. I winced and Mistress grabbed my hair, pulling my face deeper into her warm folds. Liam slid his sheathed cock into my hole and grabbed my thighs as though they were handlebars. I squirmed in ecstasy while he banged me. I had my face smothered in the flesh between my Mistress's legs and a cock ramming the shit out of my arse. What a ride. I wished I could stroke my own hardness, but Mistress doesn't permit me to touch myself. While I enjoyed my appetizing position, I could only hope if I pleased Mistress she would eventually allow me some kind of relief.

Liam's engorged cock carved me up beyond what I'd ever experienced. Mistress's juices covered my face as she grabbed my hair and shuddered all over with one of the most intense orgasms I have ever felt from her. I guess she enjoyed watching Liam ram me while I sucked her. When I had licked up all her come, Mistress slid down in her seat and grabbed a fistful of my hair. She pulled me up slowly so I could slide my own cock into her without escaping Liam. He grabbed my hips and drove himself into me with a fierceness that made me shudder with delight. When he pulled back, I drew out of Mistress and let his thrust push me deep inside of her. She clamped down on my cock with her muscles and I had a hard time maintaining control, but I'm not allowed to have an orgasm without her permission.

Mistress and Liam came at the same time, his bellow drowning out her ecstatic cry and his grip on my hips leaving marks on my skin. When he pulled out, Mistress finally said: "You may come, boy."

"Thank you, Mistress!" Without Liam behind me, I could move in and out enough to finally come, so grateful for every moment of delight she had given me. I buried my face in the pillows of Mistress's chest and enjoyed the spasms in my cock. Once my breathing became regular and my heartbeat slowed to normal, Mistress yanked my face up. "Clean up your mess, boy." I eased out of her, and knelt down so I could suck my own come out of her. It didn't taste nearly as good as Liam's, but mixed with her juices, it wasn't bad and I got to give her another orgasm.

When she pulled my hair to let me know I could stop, I leaned my head against her thighs and wrapped my arms around her hips. "Thank you so much, Mistress, for such a wonderful birthday present. Today I had the absolutely best birthday I have ever had."

PAINFUL PLEASURES

Debra, Doncaster

I have to admit here and now to having a pain fetish. It is a strange quirk in my nature. It has always been there; well, it has since I discovered sex. That fine line between pain and pleasure does exist; it is not simply a cliché. But I must take you back in time to demonstrate this fine balance.

I met Gary, blond and bold, when I was in my early twenties. He was the first man to understand my need for pain. He could tie me to the bed and whip me for a good twenty minutes without ejaculating all over the place. Most men come in seconds if a woman allows them a dominant role. Not Gary. With him I moved on a stage. Whipping my arse didn't really create that much pain, so I turned over. I loved to spread my legs and catch my breath as the whip crashed down between them. My pussy would jerk at the harsh attention but grow wet with the thought of the next stroke of stinging leather. However, the problem with pain is you have to keep upping the ante. You soon become used to pain and when you do the pleasure stops. This was happening to me, so Gary looked on the internet and found an interesting place.

Walking into the club was like walking onto the set of an old-fashioned horror movie. It was dark, very dark. Low lighting and weird music almost gave a sense of threat. I could feel excitement and tension in the air. Gary went off to find the bar, while I soaked up the atmosphere.

Suddenly someone grabbed my hand and I was being dragged to the back of the room. The guy had a mask on, the type like a balaclava, but made of leather. I could see blond hair curling at his neck. I knew it was Gary.

I was pulled through a set of huge doors and dragged down a short flight of stairs. Then I was pushed through a black painted door. I landed on the floor, panting. I got up and went to fondle Gary but he shoved me away and gestured to me to undress. I got the message: pain first, pleasure second. I couldn't get my clothes off quick enough; I was so wet.

My hands were placed in metal handcuffs that were attached to the wall by chains. I was naked apart from my leather thong. Gary still didn't speak but he came over and stood in front of me. He grabbed a nipple in each hand and squeezed hard. He rubbed his thumb and finger together and ground away at my nipples. It was fantastically painful. I could feel how wet my pussy was, it was starting to drip out onto my thigh. I waited to see what he would do next.

He stood in front of me again. He had a large candle on his hand. He lifted one of my legs and I watched as he poured the hot candle wax onto my thigh. I whimpered with the pain. This was different. This really hurt. I could feel the heat sinking into my leg; it seemed to last for ages. Then it cooled to leave a steady tingle under my skin. I wanted it again. This time he lifted my leg higher and pushed my thong to one side. He dropped the hot wax in my groin and it trickled slowly towards my pussy, stopping just short. I had my head bent forwards to watch but the pain forced my head back and I screamed. For the first time I lost my breath and my knees buckled. The first of the heat diminished and the steady tingle toyed with my soaking pussy.

I was sweating with pain and excitement. Would he do anything else? He came forwards again. He took hold of one breast and squeezed it so that the nipple was almost facing the ceiling. Then he poured the hot candle wax over my nipple. I almost climaxed before the wax hit me, such was my fervour. The wax sent arrows of pain down my body and my hips started to jerk as my pussy demanded some kind of release. Then I felt my thong being ripped off and Gary pushing me back against the wall. He rammed into me and I bucked against him, delirious with sexual excitement. The combination of hot burning wax on my nipples and a huge cock surging in to me was beyond anything. I was so wet he was almost slipping out of me and I had to bring my legs up to anchor him to me. I climaxed again and again, but as I came back down to earth I was aware that I might never match this experience.

Afterwards, Gary released me and left me to clean myself up. I looked at the pink marks left on my skin from the wax. I could still feel the tingle. I got dressed and left the room.

Gary spotted me straight away. "Here's your drink. I've found out where we go and what the carry on is. So when you're ready."

I knew then that I had just had sex with a stranger. Perfect sex. Lots of pain and lots of pleasure. I am still with Gary and we still go to the club but what Gary doesn't know is that I go to the club on my own sometimes. Not often, just sometimes. I never know who the guy is, maybe it is always a different guy. But it is exciting because I never know how far they'll go or how much I can take. It will be my downfall one day but not yet. No, not yet.

THE WASP VICTORY

Carmel, Hove

It was already hot that summer, and it got hotter after Jen
arrived. The grass was crisp under our feet by June and the boys
pulled off their shirts as soon as we left college, exposing lean
torsos already burned matt brown by the sun until they were the
colour of chocolate ice cream. I thought about licking that dark
smoothness and the thought made me hotter than hot, until I
was certain I would melt to the pavement and gloop there – a
puddle of longing. Until Jen.

She was older than us and if she hadn't been ill she wouldn't
have hung around with a bunch of teenagers. But glandular
fever had made her value simple pleasures – she reached back a
few years to her own late teens as though they were a comfort
blanket and joined in our lives, sharing again the things that
seemed so complicated and important to us but were probably
infantile to her.

Like me. From the first time she gave me her "lazy" glance I
knew. I walked back with her to her aunt's house where she was
recuperating. Jen led me up to her room, talking calmly, sat me
on her bed, lit a cigarette and then braced one hand on the
bedside table and the other on the mattress beside me as she
pressed her mouth to mine and offered her mouthful of tobacco
to me like a grey prayer. I knew women did this stuff, I knew
what lesbians were. But they weren't sexy, orchid-lipped, hip-
swinging girls like Jen, or I didn't think they were.

Every boy in my class was crazy about her – the kind of crazy
that made them crumple their discarded shirts and hold them
over their crotches to hide the way she made them swell inside

their trousers. And she was giving me the slowest kiss in the history of the universe. I felt my spine melt, just the way I had feared it would when I thought about the chocolate boys, and I rolled slowly down to lie on her bed and she rolled down too, fitting her body against mine.

As soon as I felt the softness of her body, like mine, unlike mine, I realized I couldn't stop. All I could feel was the sensation of giving way to her, her thigh between my legs, her breast softer than clouds against mine, her mouth as gentle as moonshine, making its way from mine, still trailing its tobacco cloud, down my neck. I didn't look, that first time. I didn't want to spoil the magic.

But after that I looked. I saw how her hips curved around mine to lock her thighs around me. I saw how the rosy flesh between her legs swelled like a stormy pink sea under my fingers, and how it became like a handful of wet silk, slippery with pleasure and ripe with the insistence of near orgasm. I saw how the sweep of my long hair could shudder her small nipples into tightness, and how, when she was sated afterwards, they relaxed again to gentle halos crowning her sweet breasts. I saw how her face darkened with excitement, how she bit her lips to hold back from coming. And I saw how she came.

She could do me in ten seconds, I swear. Her hand, her tongue, even the blade of her thigh could bring me off so fast I wouldn't have time to protest. But when I watched her, I saw I couldn't do what she did. When she was ready to come, she would gather herself up, like a predator and then she would use me, use whatever I was doing to her, to make it happen. I couldn't do it to her – I was an instrument of pleasure, not a conductor. At some point in that hot summer, it started to matter.

I wanted to make her melt like I did. I wanted to possess her and hold her on the point of orgasm and watch eyes unfocus and turn inwards on the moment of absolute pleasure when her face would go slack and her toes would point away and her calves would bunch, bring the coral heart of her sex up to my hand as though magnetized, begging, demanding, pleading without words. I wanted to make her come without her orchestrating it – and I couldn't.

I began to plan. First I took her along the river, to a place I knew where an old punt lay half-hidden. I led her to the boat and showed her how we could strip off and rest on the wide wooden planks of the ancient craft, in the blood-warm water of the river, surrounded by the scent of bulrushes and the thrum of insects. For an hour we lazed, and then I moved my fingers to enter her, like the river entered her, warm and insinuating, secret and languid. And she came of course, but there was still that moment where she gathered herself around my hand, and I saw the calculation as she lifted her spine and pressed down with her shoulders and rocked her hips to get me just "there", where she needed me, and I knew I hadn't given her the orgasm. She'd taken it – again.

I tried a moonlit evening in the park. The two of us lay entwined on a bench, knowing that nearby a young man was watching us with the strained delight of someone who couldn't believe his luck.

I tried the top of a double-decker bus, with a hot wind blowing through the open windows and the seats scorching her thighs as I knelt and lapped at her clit – one eye trying to peer round her to see any passengers who might be climbing the stairs to surprise us. But each time I felt the way she organized herself around her needs and shaped what I was doing to deliver what she wanted. It began to drive me crazy.

Then I brought her to my parents' house one day when they were both out. I stole a bottle of champagne from them, telling myself that they'd promised me a magnum when I graduated and this was a kind of graduation. It was going to be the day I made Jen lose control. I took care that she drank most of it while we sat in the garden, feeling the sun pressing down on us like a physical being, an insistent lover. The heat burned along the partings in our hair, slipped inside our ears, curled itself into the whorls of our navels – exposed by our bikinis – and even found its way to the root of every pubic hair, striking so hard on our tight bikini pants that we could feel the sunshine trapped there.

When I led her upstairs she had a wonderful smell, like baked bread, and she was vaguely drunk. For a while we just lay tangled on my bed, listening to the sound of lawnmowers outside, and then I remembered I had a task, a grail to find. I began to please her, moving down her body, peeling the bikini away and anointing every inch of the flesh it had covered with kisses. She sighed. I used my fingers to bring her nipples to tight buds, pinching gently so that she shuddered with pleasure-pain. I straddled her and began to sweep my fingers from her neck to her thighs and, as I did, I heard a wasp, trapped against the window, trying to get out. As I hypnotized Jen with my hands, I watched the wasp, quietly murmuring its way up the glass and then falling back to the window sill in a bad-tempered crescendo of loud buzzes. Instinctively I timed my movements to the wasp's, travelling slowly and easily around the contours beneath me, then cupping my hand over her sex and pushing hard against her pubic bone in time with the insect's irritable descent.

Her breathing became laboured. Next time the wasp fell, I slid my index finger inside her, and pressed my thumb down hard on her pubis as if trying to join it to my finger. Her back arched. I pulled back and stroked her labia, as dark and ripe as plums, as the wasp industriously climbed the window again. Jen's eyes searched mine, looking for something that I'd never been able to give her before. I looked away, watching the wasp.

For a second it hung at the top of the window, and then began to tumble. I closed my eyes and listened to the bittersweet note of its descent as I thrust three fingers into Jen and felt her explode around my hand.

We stayed together all summer, but it was never the same again. I could never forget the moment I took her, and she could never forgive me for doing it.

THE SECRET TO A CLEAN HOME

Di, Barnsley

It's no secret that I'm a lazy bitch. I *hate* housework with a passion. Unfortunately, it is one of the evils of life and has to be faced.

A few months ago, I developed a strategy, which has made housework bearable. More than bearable in fact. My friends and family have commented on the previously unknown order that now reigns in the house. Cupboards are tidy, dust no longer coats the surfaces and rather than the lingering odour of last night's takeaway assailing the nostrils of visitors, the fresh aroma of furniture polish now greets them.

My secret? I am the proud owner of a cylinder vacuum cleaner. So what? I hear you cry. Well, the truth is I have discovered that my vacuum cleaner is useful for more than picking up dust. Now I actually enjoy cleaning.

I am not sure where the inspiration came from, but I am so pleased the idea occurred to me. Maybe it was the purchase of a new vibrator that triggered it. If I get pleasure from the vibration of a nine-inch piece of plastic with the power of two AA batteries, then what would the vibrations of a 2,000-watt motor do for me?

The first time I plugged the vacuum cleaner into the wall socket, I got turned on too. The vibrations began to spread from the hardwood floor, through the soles of my feet. They rapidly moved up my calves to my thighs where they hit their target with exquisite perfection.

The powerful motor caused my pussy to quiver. I pulled out the extendable pipe. The metal felt cool in my hot palm. I slowly prised the shiny chrome to its full length, sliding my sweaty hand along the shaft.

I closed my eyes momentarily, relishing the smell of the heat from the motor. I moved the cleaner across the floor, removing any offending particles of detritus, relishing the vibrations emanating from the machine, spreading up my arms, sending tingles to my breasts where the nipples had now formed tight, hard buds.

I cleaned the living room last. By the time I reached this room my thighs were slick with my juices and I was eager now to finish the cleaning. My aching pussy needed attention.

I left the vacuum cleaner running and sat on the leather sofa. The smell of the leather added to my arousal. The soft material was cool to my bare buttocks. (Did I mention I was naked?)

I pulled the body of the vacuum cleaner to within reach of my left hand, which hung languidly over the side of the sofa. With my right hand I began to pay attention to my tight nipples. I started gently, rubbing my palm over the hard, pointy bud. My fingers almost formed a claw as the sensation tickled my hand as well as my breasts.

Tweaking and pulling at the tight tip, my toes curled. I cupped my breast in my hand, forcefully kneading the soft mound of flesh. My breathing became increasingly shallow as my arousal level grew.

The vibrations from the throbbing motor shot from my left hand, through my arms, across my shoulders to the tips of my right hand. My juices were trickling continuously now, forming a puddle on the smooth black leather.

With practised skill I ran my red-painted fingernail down the length of my tanned torso. I stopped momentarily at my navel toying with the pool of sweat that had collected in the wrinkled hollow. Slowly I moved to the tight dark curls covering my mound. I stroked the smooth freshly shaved crevice of my groin. I teased myself; my swollen clit was screaming for attention and the folds of my sex ached for my touch.

Unable to resist any longer I pulled at my lips before sliding my finger up my sopping slit to my swollen clit. As I rubbed the sensitive nub yet more liquid oozed from my depths.

Unable to restrain myself any further, I inserted a finger into my wet opening. I moaned softly as I felt my muscles contract. I explored my centre further, inserting my digit to the first knuckle. A spasm of pleasure swept through me and I plunged a second finger deep inside myself.

Hot liquid was expelled forcefully from my body, adding to the pool spreading underneath me; my buttocks were sticky and wet. The smell of my fluids mingled erotically with that of the leather. The motor of the vacuum cleaner still hummed, covering the sound of my throaty moans.

As the heat in my core built, I thrust my fingers deeper inside myself. With increasing speed, I pushed them in and out, all the while my other hand continued to stroke my twitching clit.

My breath was now coming in short sharp gasps as my climax built. My hips had risen off the sofa without any conscious effort on my part, allowing deeper penetration.

As my juices were flowing liberally I decide to treat myself. I brought my heels up to my buttocks and allowed my knees to fall to the sides. I now had access to my most sacred hole.

My tight bum hole was already wet, but I lubricated it more with juice from my pussy. I licked my index finger before running it around the dark rim of my anus. More fluid squirted from my pussy as I began to insert my finger.

I gasped loudly as the muscles in my bum hole objected to the initial intrusion. Slowly and carefully I worked my finger deeper into the reluctant opening. The exquisite pain made me slightly dizzy, until suddenly the screaming muscles relaxed and I sank my finger into the smooth tunnel.

It never fails to amaze me how two holes so close to each other can feel so different and provide such pleasure.

As I added a second finger, I continued to roll my clit between the thumb and forefinger of my other hand. I fought to control my breathing. Lights flashed behind my tightly closed eyelids. My heart thumped against my ribs and I knew I was close to a massive orgasm.

The muscles in my thighs contracted almost painfully as my orgasm swept through my entire body. Hot sweet liquid spewed from my cunt as the muscles in both holes spasmed delightfully. My clit throbbed and I began to shake uncontrollably.

I lay there for a moment or two revelling in my post-orgasmic haze. As I came down slightly and my breathing became less ragged, I began to contemplate the joy of what was to follow.

I would need to clean the sofa. The smell of the leather polish would, I knew, turn me on once again. The act of wiping up my fluids with a soft damp cloth before spraying the supple leather with the aromatic polish was suddenly very appealing.

I groaned softly again as an orgasmic aftershock shuddered through my body. I turned off the vacuum cleaner; the sudden silence was almost deafening. I sighed contentedly.

It has taken me many years to find the motivation to keep a tidy house. Now I have the motivation, the house is spotless, cleaned every day. A friend has asked me to do her cleaning. I have considered it.

The added excitement of masturbating on someone else's sofa is tempting, and she does have a leather sofa. Unlike my soft black leather one, hers is an ox-blood red Chesterfield couch with firm seats and brass buttons adorning the back. I have wondered whether the difference in style will add to my pleasure. Maybe I will take her up on the suggestion. Of course the reason for my new-found enthusiasm would remain my secret!

MOTHER AND DAUGHTER

Alex, Wales

I suppose going out with a girl as posh as Amy was the turn-on to begin with, but she was gorgeous anyway. That long black hair, down to her shoulders, that golden skin and those big dark eyes, almost black really, would have got any bloke going. The first time I saw her stripped was even better than all my fantasies. She had small, beautifully shaped tits, her belly button was decorated with that expensive-looking bit of jewellery and that pussy! Just the vertical strip of sleek black hair, tantalizing me, making me want to run the fingers of one hand through it while the other hand was opening up, parting those luscious lips so I could slide inside her and explore her fully. And I did.

When she asked me to come to her parents' house (Vanessa and Richard) for the weekend, I knew it wouldn't be a little terrace house or on a council estate, but I still wasn't prepared for the mansion as the car swung onto the drive that was longer than my street.

Her dad was a very senior judge apparently, nice enough I guess, but I just knew he was measuring me, weighing up his offspring's latest. Her mother? Well, you could tell she would have been tasty once, the same colouring and features as Amy, but a good bit heavier all over the place, particularly what I could see of her boobs pushing against that blouse. So what? she was thinking. You're just my daughter's bit of rough, it won't last. She'll end up with the nice rich son of this friend or that one.

Let's face it, I thought, she could be right. Amy and I are in our mid-twenties, lots of time left to sleep with lots more people. Just enjoy it while you can.

I had the guided tour from Amy. The house had quite a history, but I was disappointed to learn there was no resident ghost. The evening meal was a bit of a trial though. The butler (yes, I know!) served us everything, the courses lasted for ever, and I struggled to cope with what knife, fork, God knows what to use, but I was kept going by the promise of the night to come. Amy had made it clear that, even though my room was discreetly way down the corridor from hers, she was going to pay me a very physical visit once it was late enough for her parents to be deep in sleep. I made sure I didn't overdo the drink, partly because I didn't want to let her down in front of Mummy and Daddy but, all right, I admit it, more because I wanted to be fully fit to perform. I'd seen that bed, huge for a single guest, and those silky sheets were going to see plenty of action if things went well.

Half past two, dead on time, the door opened and there she stood. The nightdress was more substantial that I would have liked but I guessed she had to have some insurance in case she was seen; "Just going to the loo, Mummy, go back to bed . . ." And it wasn't as if it stayed on long. I was hard in seconds and then she was on all fours on the bed with my fingers fondling, stroking, massaging those lips as she tilted that pert bum up towards me. Then, I drove into her, reaching forwards to cup those boobs in both hands, relishing her gasps as she adjusted her body position to allow me further inside her. We were both facing the door and so I guess we froze at exactly the same time as it swung open to reveal a very angry-looking Mummy. I was rock hard when the look on her face hit me but I'd never got so soft so quickly. Amy fell forwards out of me, sitting up and saying, stupidly, "Oh, Mummy, we were just . . ."

"I can see what you were just, Amy. I've told you before: when you're in our house, you obey our rules. If you want to roll around with these men you pick up, I can't stop you, but not here."

Conscious that Vanessa was staring at my naked body and now embarrassingly limp cock, I grabbed a sheet and just waited for her next comment. I didn't have to wait long.

"Right, young woman, back to your room. I really should call your father this minute . . ."

"No please, don't do that, it won't happen again."

"Just go. I want a stern word with this young man."

Amy seemed quite happy to let me face her mother's wrath on my own but I couldn't blame her. I thought I just needed to grovel a bit, talk about respect and how much I cared for Amy. I hoped I would just get thrown out in the morning as opposed to the judge bringing out his black cap and sentencing me to death.

Then, for the first time really, I saw that Vanessa was wearing a pretty revealing nightdress herself. Dark blue, classy and frilly, it was giving me a tantalizing glimpse of those impressive boobs and enough hint of bush to tell me she wasn't into shaving neat patterns like her daughter. I must have been too obvious with it though.

"Christ, not content with screwing my daughter under our own roof, you lie there gawping at me as well. That sheet isn't a lot of good just now, is it?" I looked down and saw, as she had done, the return of my erection, rising up from the silk sheet, standing to attention. Natural reaction or not, God was I in trouble now.

Well, maybe not actually because Vanessa was talking again.

"If you really can't take your eyes off me, you might as well get a proper look."

And with that, she ripped off the nightdress, so roughly that her boobs bounced for a few seconds, only confirming my earlier impressions of a woman very well blessed in that area. It wasn't just the breasts; the nipples were huge, very dark and, best of all, very hard. My eyes (of course) travelled down further and I gasped involuntarily at the sight of that thick, jet-black triangle of hair between her legs and, even from where I lay, I could see that the lips of her pussy were swollen and bloated. Vanessa gave me a smile that was like the smile on the face of a tiger before he eats his prey and sprang forwards, pulling off the sheet and exposing my by now very hard shaft. Grabbing it with her left hand, she began yanking it backwards and forwards.

"At least my stupid daughter has picked somebody well hung for a change."

The implication that Vanessa had tried out all of Amy's previous men in bed flashed into my head but I was too turned on to care.

"I'll make you a deal, Alex. You make sure I leave this room happy, and I won't feel the need to tell Richard how you repay his hospitality. But we do things my way, OK?"

She stood up suddenly and backed away from the bed.

"Get down on your knees, now, in front of me. I want your tongue here and don't you dare stop until I tell you to."

I ran my tongue across the surface of that ever-widening opening and, as I did so, Vanessa hooked her right leg behind me and clamped my face onto her lips. I licked and sucked her; she was soaking so quickly I thought my tongue would drown in her juices but she wanted more. The folds of that velvet-soft pussy just kept contracting and expanding, I felt the raised, hardened nub of her clitoris against my mouth. My tongue was almost numb; I felt I couldn't give her any more pleasure but then, with a cry that I was terrified would bring in her husband with a shotgun, she released me from her grip and I slid backwards.

I still had a huge erection and I was praying she would return the favour to me now. The thought of my cock being devoured by her mouth was wildly erotic, but she had other plans for me. Motioning me to lie on my back on the floor, Vanessa lingered over me, teasing me, letting first one, then the other of those fabulous nipples brush against my straining cock. Then, she moved her still wide open, saturated lips onto my shaft and sat back almost savagely. She arched her back even more, until I was completely horizontal inside her. But then, God, she began to almost bounce up and down on me, her incredible lips controlling, gripping, manoeuvring me. As she bounced, those playboy model type tits bounced wildly. If I had had the strength I would have tried to reach out and grab them but I knew I was close to coming now and I just knew so was she.

And then we came together and she fell off me, panting but not as much as I was.

Only seconds passed before she gave me that "I give the orders here" look again.

"I can see why my daughter enjoys you. Well, Alex, it's four o'clock. Only a couple of hours and I might let you get some sleep."

What? I thought. More? How can I . . . ?

She took my hand in hers and placed them on the still rock-like nipples and, as I began to squeeze them, I watched transfixed as her own hand strayed between her legs and she began playing with her still wide open lips, vigorously, almost fiercely. I was more turned on than I ever had been in my life and although I needed time to recover, Vanessa was using her other hand to squeeze my balls, and then it moved up my cock and nothing was going to stop me hardening again. Watching her play with that amazing pussy, feeling her nipples in my hands but most of all shivering at the expert touch making me as hard as she wanted, I just knew that tomorrow she would be saying a polite goodbye and that maybe I had to find someone else.

Being in bed with Amy was a hell of an anti-climax from then on.

CREAM AND PUNISHMENT

Clarabelle, Winnipeg

You might say I'm good to myself. I make lots of money. I like to eat well and wear nice clothes and drive a lovely old Jaguar type E. I'm tall, buxom, thirtyish and strong. Lots of lipstick. I dress well, if a little unconventionally, and wear bold clothes and fine boots with big heels that make a lot of noise.

Yes, I call myself a woman. But I have a cock. You can argue about what label to use for me, but at the moment I don't care. And I'm not in transition from one thing to the other.

At any rate, I can afford to be choosy, and I am. You might say I tend to attract and take command. I can seduce and dominate. I don't often want it, but when I do, I want it bad. And I get it. I wouldn't even have mentioned all this, but you might find it puts this story into perspective.

It all started with me going for a walk.

I got up that morning, one of those early winter days when fall feels like it's over, but there's no snow yet, and after my shower I painted my face, careful to use lots of shadow and mascara to bring out my white skin and green eyes.

My hair is as black as ebony, and I have it cut like Queen Cleopatra's.

I hooked myself into my sturdy black under-wire and my wide, waist-cinching black garter belt. Then I pulled on my stockings. Yeah, I'm one of those women who hates pantyhose. In fact, I don't even own any. I always wear the more traditional lingerie because it makes me feel special. And I have a bit of a tum-tum that has to be hauled in. What of it? I don't make a pig of myself, but I told you I like to eat.

I also pulled my nicest black Jane Belt out of the drawer. A Jane Belt, for those of you unfamiliar with such accoutrements, bundles you all together and pulls it all down, but doesn't have as severely binding a nature as a transvestite's gaff. It is a little like a jockstrap, but without the hard cup, and will hide your bulge if you are wearing a loose skirt. The quality ones, like mine, are not made of some cheap elastic, but a thick, soft material which comprises a pouch and three wide strands of belt or sash: two that go around your hips and a third that comes up between your cheeks. You tie all three together in a special little bow: as important a bit of ropery as the four-in-hand is to men and their ties.

So I tied on my soft black Jane Belt, wound myself into my heavy-pleated, wrap-around black leather mid-thigh skirt, and pulled on my long, thick, grey sweater with the cowl, which comes down to the hips.

Then I squeezed into and zipped shut my tall, black leather platform boots and I was ready to go.

Leaves danced and skittered on the city sidewalks as I walked through the Fisby Gate area feeling a sense of – oh, I don't know – that vague but exciting sense of personal power and potential one sometimes gets when one has chosen just the right clothes or falls into just the right frame of mind.

Sometimes I get that sense, you see, that something can happen. No, I'm not talking about sex, just that indefinable something. Call it inspiration if you like. It almost never does happen when you get down to it. I go home, I take off my fine clothes, get into my pyjamas and watch a stupid video. So it goes.

I walked into the little shop and smiled at the old lady at the counter and she nodded back. It was a marvellous little place I went to from time to time, festooned with old-time remedies, herbal cures, obscure Asian foods in beautiful little packages, unheard of beauty products from the four corners of the earth and deli products. I made my way to the magazines and flipped through a few.

Then I made my way to the smoked meats section.

I've got to admit it. I'm a bit of a shoplifter. Not a real kleptomaniac, but sometimes I just like the thrill of stealing something – the secretiveness of it. Why do I do it? I just love the kind of smug feeling it gives me. Like I'm getting away with something. And the desire to do it tends to spring forth with that feeling of possibility I just told you about. OK, so this old lady probably has worked hard all her life and it isn't fair to her, is it? But I don't do this very often at any one store. Besides, they overcharge here. She'll never miss her salami.

I looked to the right, and to the left.

But I didn't happen to look right behind me, assuming that no one was there to begin with.

Then I took the salami and slipped it into my purse. I waited a moment, braced for that terrible cry of "You there!" or whatever they say when they spy a shoplifter.

It didn't come. And I allowed myself a little, secretive smile.

Then I thought I felt my skirt rise at the back, but assumed that since that was impossible, it was just a child or someone gently bumping into me.

There was a tug on the bow of my Jane Belt, and with disbelief, I felt the whole thing unravel with a swish as my cock and balls bounced down to their natural position.

"Huh?" I spun around, dumbfounded.

The old lady was holding my Jane Belt up in one hand, her elbow in the other hand, looking up to give me the evil eye.

"Since you've seen fit to steal from me, young lady, I'll take something from you, if you don't mind."

I darted glances throughout the store to see if anyone was looking. Fortunately, not. "Give that back!"

She said nothing, but turned, holding the Jane Belt up and clutched in her fist as if it were testament to some shameful truth only she could expose, and marched off towards the backroom.

"Hey! That's mine! You have to give it back!" I darted after her, feeling self-conscious about my bouncing genitals despite the fact my skirt was easily long enough to cover them. Bursting through the swinging door after her, I shouted, "Hey! You can't just . . ." It was kind of dark back there. I bumped against a stack of pallets, turned, walked a few steps. "Hello?" How could the old broad have disappeared so fast? "I don't know what kind of game you think you're playing, old lady, but . . ." I gasped as something darted under my skirt and grabbed my dick: hard. "Help! Ouch! What the . . . ?"

The old lady was before me and she kept a firm grip as she looked me in the eye in a no-nonsense fashion. "You take my salami, young lady, I'll take yours."

To my horror I started to get hard. "What the hell are you doing? Let me go!"

"There's surveillance cameras in my store just in case you hadn't noticed, young lady, so you have two choices. I can call the police or . . ."

I was grasping ineffectually at her arm. "Help! Let me go!"

"Huh? Say, you're getting hard awful fast. Tsk. Young girls are so slutty these days. You know I'm old enough to be your mother, easy. Maybe your grandmother."

"How dare you! That's just a natural reaction, it's just . . . Please! I'm sorry I took your salami. It's in my purse. I'll give it back. Or pay for it."

She shook her head. "Hear me out, dearie. Just letting you go isn't in the cards. Now a few of the products I make in this store, some of the natural skin products and the longevity potions, require certain ingredients that are very expensive. I like to get them myself when I can." She squeezed a little harder and pulled me closer to her.

"Oh! This is so humiliating. Please . . . I promise I won't come back. I have lots of money in my purse I can give you. Just let me go, please."

"Shhh. You panic too easy, dear. One of the ingredients I use is the sort that comes right from this thingamajig of yours here. I can get something kind of like it from men, but it's not nearly as good. This," she said, waggling it, "is the real McCoy."

"You can't get away with this. What you're doing is illegal."

"Yeah, but nobody would believe it, a big strong girl like you. Besides, there are no surveillance cameras in the backroom here, dear. So you see, the cops would be on my side."

"Please don't call them. I'll be ruined."

"Ruined? Oh. Your reputation, I suppose. Don't worry, dear, it's not like we're in public now. There ain't going to be any headlines saying, YOUNG HUSSY WANKED BY OLD LADY. Now, let me show you something."

She pointed to a sturdy rubber hose threaded through a steel loop hanging from the ceiling. One end of the hose led to some kind of machine with a control panel and some kind of motor, it seemed. The other end dangled downwards, attached to a transparent, flexible plastic cylinder almost ten inches long.

With her left hand she undid my skirt snaps, one after the other, as I writhed helplessly in her grasp, then she carefully dropped the skirt on a table next to us. She reached up and grabbed the cylinder, then pulled it down, the long sturdy tube following.

"This has already been well lubed, dear, but it'll be tight. You're a big one. It should automatically adjust to your thickness in there and give you a nice comfy hug."

I still didn't understand. I knew only that she had her hand on my precious thing. Strong as I was, I could not break her grip on me because she had me by the . . . well, you know. She began to stuff me in. I'm afraid I squealed. Like a stuck pig. The tube was warm and mooshy, but very firm.

"What are you doing?" I groaned, even as my cock bucked in her grip.

"Whoa, girlie, settle down there, hon', ol' Betsy ain't gonna hurt you. It's all hygienically clean and lubed for you so don't worry."

"That looks like something they . . . they milk cows with, for crying out loud."

"Same principle, dear. A dick is much like a teat. At least, for my purposes it is. I'm not getting off on this in case you're wondering – unlike your Jane Junior here – this is strictly business for me."

"I am *not* getting . . ."

"Oh, don't be an idiot. You're as humiliated as hell and wondering how a fine, intelligent (even if thieving) young woman like yourself is ever going to get over having her pretty thing shanghaied by a grandmother – but you also like it, so just shut your pretty mouth . . . Dang! If this isn't a tight fit. Got to go nice and slow with this one . . ."

"What are you doing? I'll get stuck! Unh! Oh! You brute! You horrible old . . . You can't get away with . . ." Finally, my cock was all in.

"So much for the teat. Now let's see how the cow does. That's you, dear." She let go of the cone and took the hem of my long sweater in her hands. In a couple of swift motions, she had it up and over my head, and then off me. She laid it neatly by the skirt with some comment about it not being in the way any more, and began to make adjustments to the control panel.

Automatically, I reached for the cone and began to pull at it, desperate to get it off and escape before I, now a helpless cock-slut stripped to bra, garter belt and stockings, shamed myself in front of her in the most spectacularly possible way. I whined and whimpered, bit my lower lip, couldn't believe it was all happening . . . "Oh God! I'm stuck!"

Immediately she smacked me hard on my bare ass, and when I yelped and reached back automatically to touch it, she swiftly tied my wrists together with my own Jane Belt.

"None of that now. I've got to get this temperamental milking machine going and I can't have you fidgeting about." She flicked a switch and immediately there was a chugging sound. "Feel any suction?"

"God! Yes! What the hell are you doing to me? My cock! Oh my God, my cock!"

There was a kind of rubber scritchy sound as my cock swelled even more into the tube and forced it to expand. Involuntarily, I backed up, trying to pull myself out. The hose grew taut, but held firm. My dick was stuck.

"Get me out of here! Help!"

"You're not as bright as you look, are you, dear? Either that or you weren't listening. I'm milking your sausage for my health and beauty products and the odd potion or two. I hope I don't have to explain that again."

"Ohhh! Ohhhhh! You're gonna make me . . . You're gonna make me . . . You fucking witch!"

"I'll thank you to mind your language, young lady. But I don't want you to come too quick, dear." She turned the suction down, but only a little. "I find if you make 'em wait a while you get a larger, higher quality load."

"You're fucking mental!" I stamped the floor with my boots. The tube jiggled. "This is fucking rape! This is fucking cock rape!"

"The moment you want, dear, I'll turn the machine off and turn you loose. I'll turn the tapes over to the cops too. The choice is still yours."

I sniffled. My cock swelled. I danced obscenely at the end of the hose. I felt the urge to moo with shame and arousal.

"Phew!" she said, looking into the transparent and swelling tube. "You're gettin' *huge*. This should be a good haul. Just hang in, dear, and don't come too early. Would you like me to play some nice music on the radio? That should help you relax a little. You like country? Can't stand it myself. But lots of my girls find it more relaxin'."

I bucked and wiggled, trying to get out without increasing my arousal. I was desperate.

"You've got to come sooner or later. Now where's that salami you stole?" She rummaged in my purse and found it. Holding it up before me, she had an evil glint in her eye. "I know just where to put this to get young Bossy to perform. Would you look at that! The very item that got you in this trouble to begin with. Can you spell irony?"

I stamped my feet. "Let me go! Let me go!"

"Really, hon, your hypocrisy is getting very tiring."

The door back into the shop sprang open and a spry old man wheeling boxes on a dolly came in. I didn't see him that well because I think I was practically cross-eyed by then.

"Morning, Edna."

"Morning, Frank."

"Milking time?"

"Yep."

"Looks like a fine young heifer."

"Premium dairy, Frank. Champing at the bit though, thinks herself hard done by."

"Tch. Kids these days."

"And now she has her hands tied behind her and her dick up a spout. And why? Because little Miss Greedy Guts couldn't keep her fingers out of the cookie jar."

"Oh-oh. Shoplifter, eh?"

"Yep."

"Say, she looks familiar . . . Yeah, works at the investment centre in town, I think. Seen her drive a fancy old Jaguar around. Must be doing well, all right. And a shoplifter for all that? Shameful."

"Some people never get enough."

"Ain't it the truth."

"Well, I ain't getting any out of her yet. Say, Frank, maybe you can help me a little. I want to keep my eye on the suction here. Can you just lube this up and keyster our big friend here?"

I couldn't believe it. The old man scratched his chin and looked at my gartered thighs and burgeoning cock like you'd appraise horseflesh.

"Wait a minute," said the old lady. "You don't have a problem with men, do you, dear? Cause if you're some kind of radical lesbian or something I wouldn't want to force old Frank here on you. I'll just do it myself. He's gay, by the way, bless his soul, so he won't get any more out of it than I would."

I stared at her in disbelief.

"Fine then. Take that stool, Frank, and set yourself in behind her. Don't forget to work it in real slow."

She bent me gently over and supported my shoulders while Frank pulled up a stool.

"Investment centre, eh? What does she do there?" asked the old lady.

"Some kind of investment analyst, I guess."

"What is that, exactly?"

"Tells people how to make money with their money."

"I always thought it was just work that did that. No wonder the girl's a thief. No idea what's what for all her intelligence, so she diddles about with money and steals salami. 'Investment' my bottom!"

"Hold her still, Edna, I've got to invest something in this bottom here." Frank began to twist and push. I bellowed with ignominious delight.

"O Lordy, we've got a screamer. Any customers out front, Frank?"

"Yeah, but Isabel's takin' care of them."

"Don't want them to hear this. Might give them the wrong idea."

"This, my dear –" she held forth a ball gag "– is for bad little moo-moos who make too much noise." And she gagged me.

Frank continued. The old lady cranked up the suction. I was still bent over, and felt the salami oozing and twisting its way up me.

I felt the old lady unhook my bra at the back. "I'll just massage her titties for a bit. That should help too."

I felt I was going to go blind from joy and die of humiliation. I mooed. That's what I did, deliberately. I mooed. Through the gag as well as I could. I'm a cow, I wanted to cry out to the world, milk me milk me milk me. Let my semen fill every pore and wrinkle on every sad face in the world. Let my dick stir potions for love and happiness. Just make me come, come, come. I stomped my feet and shook, wiggled, squealed . . .

"Whoo-ee, will you look at that, Frank! She's a regular geyser. That's it, Bossy, squoosh, squoosh. Frank, look at her go!"

"I know, I know. Is that collection bottle going to be big enough?"

"Just barely. No one's ever come close to filling it before."

I stomped my boots on the floor, bellowed and mooed. Every last ounce of pride and power gushed out of me through my pinioned tap. I was crazy.

When it was all over she shut down the machine, unhooked me from it and removed the ball gag, then soaped and rinsed my tired cock with clean, damp sponges, as I stood there perfectly helpless and stunned. She gently cleaned the lube from the crack of my ass with warm soap and water, and even powdered me down when she was done. She got me all dressed, hooking my bra on expertly and snugly tying the Jane Belt for me, snapping me back into my skirt and pulling my sweater over my head. In the washroom, she even readjusted my make-up for me with the expert precision of one who had been in the business.

Leading me into a tiny parlour with an enormous puffy armchair in it, she said, "Sit down here, dear, and recover your strength. You've been badly humiliated and totally drained of every last ounce of spunk and energy."

She brought me a cup of hot tea and went out front to tend to customers, leaving me to think my thoughts.

I had been broken and milked by two old people whose bones I could have broken with my bare hands.

After a while I collected myself, shouldered my purse and went into the store. She was counting money at the till. I stood, for a moment, taking in the whole store. The store I was going to steal from not that long ago. I felt quiet and peaceful inside. I walked up to her. "Would you like me to come back?" I said timidly.

"Would I? I took a whiff of your spunk, honey, and I can tell it's top-notch for my purposes. You bet. Come back as long as you've got a spring in your skirt and I can use you. You have a boyfriend, dear?"

"No."

"A girlfriend maybe?"

"Not that either."

"Well, that shouldn't last long. You're a real looker."

"Thanks."

"But until you get yourself a sweetie, sweetie, don't go blowing your wad into a sock or something. I can always use more. Here's your share, hon." She put $150 on the counter before me. "This is after deducting the price of the salami, dear. I can't sell that, now, can I?"

"What? For me?"

"You don't think I was going to steal your spunk did you, honey? Now what's the moral of this story after all? Don't steal. Haven't you learned that now?"

"I'll say. And I'll never forget it, thanks to you. Stealing is wrong. But, ah, what about prostitution?"

"I paid you for semen, dear, not sex. I didn't turn you into a sperm cow for my own titillation. You see, dear, I just did it to acquire the raw fixin's for my product – and to teach you a lesson, of course."

"I want you to keep the money. I mean, I don't know how to say this but, degrading as it all was, I really enjoyed myself."

"So you have a good time and then give me $150 worth of merchandise? That would make me the whore, dear. Let's just look at it this way: what if a Guernsey enjoys getting milked? She doesn't owe the farmer anything. The farmer has her milk, doesn't she?"

I thought about that. "OK," I said. I took the money and put it in my purse. I had no idea what I was going to do with it. Buy myself something pretty? Give it to Oxfam?

"There's just one thing I want to ask."

"Yes, dear."

"Can you please not call me 'Bossy' again?"

"As you wish, hon. What is your name by the way?"

"Portia. But I want you to call me . . ."

"Yes?"

"Clarabelle."

"Clarabelle it is then."

"Moo." I winked at her and she smiled, closing the till.

YOU HAVE THE RIGHT TO REMAIN SILENT

Kathleen, Liverpool

When there had still been some romance in him, in our earliest years together, Alan had said that he could never make a drama of our love; any satisfactory story had to have an end, he told me, and what we shared would have no ending. Twenty years on, though, I had come to realize that no ending was just as unfulfilling as a bad ending.

What passion there was Alan had put into his work, into the stories and novels he wrote, the plays and television dramas; there was no passion in my life, only in his, which he lived as if it was a novel, he its hero, driven on by some anonymous but omnipotent author.

Now I was so desperate for love that I could share it with anyone but my husband.

"But a policeman, Alan? Did you have to?" I asked, as I set the places at the dining table.

"Detective Inspector," he responded, not looking up from the pad in his lap in which he was furiously scribbling notes. "And I want to pick his brain."

"But did it have to be here? And just him? Three is no number for a dinner party. Couldn't he have brought his wife?"

"Divorced."

"Girlfriend?"

"Not sure he has one."

Great! I thought, as my husband's responses were spat out

staccato fashion. Another man obsessed with self and career. It was going to be a wonderful evening.

Gloomily I returned to the kitchen, checked that all was well with the food, uncorked a bottle of wine to let it breathe and then decided that I needed a glass.

"Me too!" called Alan, hearing the pop of the cork.

"So soon?" I called back.

"If it's soon enough for you then it's soon enough for me."

"You're drinking too much," I said, pouring a second glass.

There was no response until I carried the drink through to him, when he said, "Pot. Kettle. Black."

So often these days his side of a conversation was truncated, as if words had become so precious to him that he was frugal with them, reserving them for his work, denying them to me. Frowning, I handed him his drink and then sat on the sofa facing him.

The pounds he had put on over the past months were becoming more noticeable, he had a visible paunch now where once he had been so slim, and his complexion was pasty, his eyes seemed to be weeping, red-rimmed, tired and lacking sparkle through working so many late nights.

Not only did I feel no love for him, nowadays I felt no attraction towards him either.

Sipping my drink, my mind searched for some way to cheer up the evening ahead.

"Well, I suppose your Detective Inspector might bring along his handcuffs," I said, and finally Alan raised his eyes from his notepad, looked hard at me.

"Do not, I repeat, do *not* inject any note of flippancy into this evening," he cautioned me. "I need Robert's input, I need his expertise as a policeman to make the work credible. If this one-off drama works then there could be a series to follow. Do not fuck the evening up with any crass comments or silly remarks."

"As if I would," I said, with a grin and a dismissive wave of the hand.

"Promise?" Alan insisted.

"Cross my heart and hope to wotsit," I said, my finger slowly marking a diagonal first one way and then the other, the manicured nail lightly scoring the skin where the neckline of my dress was cut low.

But already Alan's eyes were lowering, he was returning to his notes and failed to notice my nipples prick erect beneath the soft silk.

Detective Inspector Robert Gregg was a hunk, I had to concede: his lush blond hair was like the mane of a cartoon lion; his shoulders broad and square beneath the elegant suit; his manner easy and relaxed as if he could cope with any situation.

He smiled affably as I greeted him at the door, offered me a single rose and Alan a bottle of single malt.

But then Alan took over, I was chef and waitress and almost coincidental to the evening. Even before the entrée was set before them, he was quizzing the policeman, making notes in his pad right there at the table.

"What I'm interested in is the vice aspect and what temptation, what complications it might present," Alan was saying, as I came from the kitchen.

"I hope you're not asking if I'm a bent copper, Alan," Robert said, with a smile and the slightest of winks in my direction.

"Not at all! Not at all! You have the right to remain silent," Alan quipped. "But still –?"

"There are temptations that come one's way," Robert conceded. "And then there are aspects of vice that are cause for amusement, or sometimes revulsion."

"Amusement is good, it's always useful to inject some humour," said Alan eagerly, and I scowled, recalling that this was the very thing he had cautioned me against.

"Why just this week we brought in a professional domme –"

"Huh?" I said.

"Dominatrix," Robert explained, while Alan waved at me to be quiet. "Nothing terribly wrong about her practices, if you're into that sort of thing, except she was mixing in a spot of blackmail too."

For the next hour Robert kept Alan busy and me intrigued with his tales. The first bottle of wine was emptied, then a second. When I went through to the kitchen to open a third, and make coffee, I realized that I was perspiring heavily, my cheeks were burning and my whole body tingling as I thought of the depraved women and dominated men Robert had described.

I held the bottle of wine to my cheek, felt its surface smooth, cooler than my fevered flesh, then lowered it, held it between my thighs, pressed it against my knickers.

I was wet down there, incredibly wet, the fine silk was sopping, so I took off the knickers and tossed them into the laundry basket.

"Many men are weak, or want to be made to feel that way," Robert was saying, when I returned to the table. I topped up their glasses and then resumed my seat.

"Only some, surely not many?" said Alan, as if weakness was a concept that was alien to him.

"You'd be surprised, these women are skilled, they have their ways."

"And men too?" I slyly suggested.

"Sorry?" said Robert, turning to me.

"The roles can be reversed? There are men in whose presence a woman can be made to feel weak?"

"Oh yes, but of course," Robert agreed, and one anecdote flowed seamlessly into another.

We were sprawled around the table now, our chairs pushed back, the meal finished and our bellies full.

Finally Alan had stopped scribbling in that damned notepad, was slumped in his seat, his cheek propped against his fist and his eyes closed.

"He's cogitating; the artist deliberating?" Robert supposed, speaking in a whisper.

"He's sleeping; the piss artist dozing," I said derisively, my voice not as soft, knowing that it would take a sharp nudge in the ribs or a slap across the head to rouse my husband.

Robert smiled, reached out to touch his hand to my bare arm, as if someone should apologize for Alan.

"Oh fuck *him*!" I hissed, before grinning, and turned to Robert to gauge his reaction.

He was smiling still, no doubt used to much stronger language, and I got slowly to my feet, stepped around the table to stand in front of him.

I had kicked off my shoes earlier, so stood before him in my stockinged feet, reached down to take the hem of my dress and lifted it. Black silk legs were bared for his appreciation, dimpled knees, the soft swell of my thighs and then the milky flesh where the lace tops gripped. Drawing the dress higher, I bared my naked groin to him, the neatly trimmed bush of blond hair, the slight protuberance of my belly.

"Your presence has me weak already," I said, my fingers spreading between my thighs, opening like the petals of a flower responding to the warmth of the sun.

"And wet too, I see." Robert smiled up at me, reaching out to touch me.

Just the tip of a single finger touched the lips of my cunt but it delighted me more than any of Alan's barely remembered caresses, had the muscles in my thighs spasming with pleasure.

With no more than a cursory glance at my dozing husband, Robert rested his other hand on my hip, exerted a gentle pressure, and said, "Turn for me, Kathleen."

Making a slow pirouette, I presented my back to him, felt both his hands move to my groin, kneading my mound, stroking my labia, scratching through the soft fuzz of pubic hair.

One hand fell, the other pulled, I was drawn back a step towards him.

"You're sure about this, Kathleen?" he asked softly, and it was not for fear of waking my husband that my only response was to nod silently.

At that moment I couldn't give a fuck for my husband, had only one thing on my mind.

Inch by inch I was lowered into Robert's lap, he had his cock out ready for me and it was harder than I could remember a cock ever being, his fingers were splaying to part the lips of my cunt and let it nudge inside me.

"Oh my!" I gasped, as the first inch slipped inside me.

"Slowly, so you enjoy it, so you savour it," Robert told me, his hands on my waist to direct me, and gradually I felt him fill me, until my bare buttocks were settled on the soft wool of his trousers and he was buried deep inside me.

I wanted him to fuck me there and then, wildly and with passion, but he would not permit it, not yet.

Instead, his cock hard but motionless inside me, he crept his hands up my belly, beneath my dress, climbed up my ribcage to work inside my bra and cup my breasts. Fingertips caught my nipples between them, squeezed, making me squirm in his lap, my body stirring on his cock.

"Yes, that's it, Kathleen, slowly," he said, licking between my shoulder blades where the back of my dress left my skin bare, planting the gentlest of kisses which felt for all the world like moths beating their wings against me.

His body lifting a little in his chair, driving his cock just a little deeper inside me, he craned his head to lick at my neck, ran his tongue across my ear and then blew gently into it, making my arms break out in a series of goosebumps.

So long since that had happened, so long since Alan had been able to provoke that reaction in me, and I clamped my hands over Robert's, pressed them hard against my breasts until I thought I might scream with the pain.

"So long!" I sobbed. "So long!"

"You flatter me," Robert said, with a low chuckle.

My head rested back against Robert's shoulder, my eyes were closed as I savoured the sensation, as he had told me to; but now it was not the sensation of him growing ever harder inside me, then coming in a blistering orgasm at the same moment that I did, but of his cock wilting and shrinking from me like a shy meek creature.

And the wonderful thing was that it was as delightful as anything else I had experienced. There was none of the frustration I felt when Alan – on those rare occasions he could be bothered to try – came too quickly and shrank so alarmingly, as if out of shame. Now I felt a euphoric sense of power, a joy with the intensity of my orgasm and of Robert's too.

His hands still fondled my breasts, but gently now, with a tenderness I had forgotten could exist, and my body felt molten as it was cradled in his lap.

And still, through all this, my husband dozed, lost in a drunken stupor, perhaps creating dramas in his mind which would only ever be enacted on paper.

"Tell me, do you have your handcuffs?" I finally asked Robert, posing the question my husband had cautioned me against.

"Eh?" asked Robert.

"Your handcuffs," I repeated, turning awkwardly to kiss his cheek. "Do you have them with you?"

"Of course not!" he laughed. "Why on earth do you ask?"

"I've tried weak and enjoyed it, but now I want more. I want to experience the other side of the coin."

"Meaning?"

"It doesn't matter," I said, taking his arms from around me and rising from his lap.

I looked around the room for a moment, at the dining table littered with the last of the meal, the empty coffee cups, the dregs of wine in the glasses. Then I nodded, as if I had come to a decision, raised my hands and began to pull off my dress.

"Kathleen? What are you doing?" Robert asked.

"Ssh!" I told him, a finger to my lips as I bent to remove my stockings.

With a light step, like a villain on a pantomime stage, I crept up on my husband, gently lifted his head and rested it back. Then, laying his hands on the arms of the chair, I bound him to it, wrapping a stocking around each wrist.

"There, as good as any handcuffs." I smiled, returning to Robert's side and sitting on his knee.

"Effective enough," he agreed. "And now what?"

"Now we wake him," I said, to his great surprise. I picked up my glass of wine and dipped my fingers in, then flicked a few drops in Alan's face.

The first time he didn't stir; the second time he tossed his head slightly; on the third occasion his tongue came out and he lazily licked his lips.

"Come on, you fucker, wake up," I muttered, flicking more wine at him, and he gave a low murmur of appreciation as he lapped up the liquid from around his mouth.

"He's waking. Are you sure you know what you're doing?" said Robert, and in answer I set down the glass of wine, curled my fingers around his cock and began to stroke him.

More incoherent noises came from Alan, his head tossed, his mouth gaped, his eyes fluttered slowly open, blinking a time or two, then seemed to pop as he finally focused on me sitting naked on the policeman's knee.

"What –?" he began, then tried to rise, found himself tied and so thrashed about in the chair. "What the hell is going on?"

"Be quiet and be still, Alan," I calmly told him, not looking down at Robert's cock but feeling it growing ever larger in my hand, knowing that its state would be obvious to him.

"I demand –" Alan tried, but I cut him off sharply.

"No, Alan, you do *not* demand! Ever! That's the whole fucking point! You neither make demands nor satisfy them."

"What *are* you going on about, Kathleen?" he asked. "And you, get your fucking hands off my wife!" he snarled at Robert.

"I think you'll find it's she who has her hands on me," Robert answered back, smiling.

"You are the weak man Robert described, Alan," I continued. "That being the case, it is left to me to make the demands, which I shall do. I am going to show you what I will demand of you. Pay attention, Alan. Watch and learn."

Slipping from Robert's knee, I slid to the floor, resting my body against his chair. Regarding his swollen cock for a moment, bending it at a delightful angle, to bring a gasp from him and the better for my husband to see, I then raised my free hand to my face.

"Remember when I used to do this for you, Alan?" I said, and, looking directly into his eyes, I licked the palm of my hand, lapped the flat of my tongue slowly across it. "You used to love me doing this, didn't you?"

When I stroked my moist palm over the head of Robert's cock I heard a low groan. It could have been either man or it could have been both, but I didn't bother to check, simply lowered my mouth onto the erection, fastened my lips onto it, took it between my teeth.

One thing I *was* aware of, though, was that there were no longer any protests from my husband. Perhaps he was, indeed, watching and learning, and I revelled in the power I now had over both these men. I could make Robert come at any moment I chose, of that I was certain, and just as sure that afterwards I could do whatever I liked with my husband.

Slipping Robert's cock from my mouth, rising on my knees, I grinned as I folded my breasts around it, trapping it between them, then ground my body against him.

"Come for me, Robert, show Alan how it's done," I said, my eyes fixed on his, insisting, and he gave a loud sob as he spurted between my breasts.

I kept his cock trapped between my breasts for long seconds, a minute, more, holding it there until I was sure every last spasm of his orgasm had subsided, down to the very slightest twitch. Then I leaned back, turned slowly to face my husband, to let him see the spunk glistening between my breasts, then dipped a finger into it and wiped it across my mouth, moistening my lips.

On my knees I began to move towards Alan, my hands caressing my breasts as I inched closer, smearing them with Robert's milky emission.

"Now you're going to lick my breasts clean, Alan, and keep your eyes fixed on mine as you do it," I told him, and though he made no reply he was unable to look away from me.

I laughed softly, then got to my feet and stood before him, above him. I bent to plant a sticky kiss on his mouth and then offered my breasts to his lips.

"You have the right to remain silent," I told him, "but I must warn you that anything you say may be taken down and used against you."